Staircase to Writing and Reading

Staircase to Writing and Reading

a Rhetoric and Anthology

third edition

Alan Casty

Santa Monica College

Donald J. Tighe

Valencia Community College

PRENTICE-HALL, INC., Englewood Cliffs, New Jersey 07632

Library of Congress Cataloging in Publication Data

Casty, Alan, (date)
Staircase to writing and reading.

Includes index.
1. English language—Rhetoric. 2. College readers.
I. Tighe, Donald J., joint author. II. Title.
PE1408.C392 1979   808'.042   78-25595
ISBN 0-13-840579-4

third edition
Staircase to Writing and Reading:
a Rhetoric and Anthology
by Alan Casty and Donald Tighe

Printed in the United States of America

10 9 8 7 6 5 4 3 2

Editorial/production supervision and interior design by Charlotte Leonard
Cover design by Jorge Hernandez
Manufacturing buyer: Harry P. Baisley

"The Juggernaut of Time" was originally published under the title
"The Landscape of Our Lives," from *This Is Eric Sevareid,* by Eric Sevareid.
© 1964 by Eric Sevareid. Reprinted by permission of the Harold Matson Co., Inc.

"Laundromat," by Susan Sheehan, is reprinted by permission; © 1971,
The New Yorker Magazine, Inc.

The selection from "New Orleans, Mon Amour," by Walker Percy, originally
appeared in Harper's Magazine, September 1968. Copyright © 1968 by Walker Percy.
Reprinted by permission of McIntosh and Otis.

"Real Girls Ask for Mint Frappés," by Will Stanton, is copyright © 1967 by
The Curtis Publishing Co., Inc. Reprinted by permission of Paul Reynolds, Inc.,
599 Fifth Avenue, New York, N.Y. 10017.

PRENTICE-HALL INTERNATIONAL, INC., *London*
PRENTICE-HALL OF AUSTRALIA PTY. LIMITED, *Sydney*
PRENTICE-HALL OF CANADA, LTD., *Toronto*
PRENTICE-HALL OF INDIA PRIVATE LIMITED, *New Delhi*
PRENTICE-HALL OF JAPAN, INC., *Tokyo*
PRENTICE-HALL OF SOUTHEAST ASIA PTE. LTD., *Singapore*
WHITEHALL BOOKS LIMITED, *Wellington, New Zealand*

Contents

v

Contents

Preface

To help you see that good writing is a craft, a conscious art, *Staircase to Writing and Reading* stresses the rules of that craft, the principles of rhetoric: logic, order, and development. *Staircase* applies these rules to both writing and reading, for to read and write well you must apply the rules of rhetoric.

We have planned and written *Staircase* with one major point in mind: Good writing and reading rely on the writers' and readers' ability to think accurately, to apply the rules of sound logic. To write logically and to read with understanding, you need to know how to separate the general from the specific, the abstract from the concrete. You need to know where ideas and facts go on what we call the staircase of abstractions.

In Part I, the rhetoric, we start with the planning, sources, and strategies you use to carry out your purpose. We then study forming the main idea, the five basic types of thesis statements. Following this, we treat overall organization—introduction, body, and conclusion—and focus on the scratch, topic, and sentence outline. We then show how paragraphs, sentences and words help you develop your ideas.

In this third edition we have added a chapter on sentence combining techniques to better point up how you can make clearer the relationships between major and minor parts of your sentences. Because we know that most writers must touch up what they write before they give it to a reader, we show you how to spot and correct errors in logic, grammar, and mechanics.

Part II of *Staircase* contains essays arranged by topic. This sentence has three purposes. First, reading what great writers say gives you facts and ideas that stimulate your own thoughts. Second, seeing how well-known writers face and solve rhetorical problems as they write may help you solve your own.

We don't mean you should copy the style of Meg Greenfield, or George Orwell, or Margaret Mead. No, we don't expect you to try to write like someone else, especially like those who have been writing for a living for years. But students and professionals want the same results; they want to write so readers will understand them. And we know that the same writing tools are ready to help all writers who want to use them. If you see how professionals solve their writing problems, you may learn how to cope with yours.

You are more than a writer, however; you are also a reader. So the third purpose of Part II is to help you understand what you read—again by using the rules of rhetoric.

Both parts of *Staircase* introduce you to the most useful elements of rhetoric. We break each into small specific steps and examine and illustrate each step. We do not use elaborate definitions or complex patterns that will not be useful to you. Instead, we show you how to meet and solve your basic writing and reading problems, those problems that are likely to stump you in college or on the job.

In Part I, a student-teacher dialog allows you to review each important point after it is introduced. Following each explanation, a question is asked to call for an answer that drives home the point just discussed. The answer, and, where needed, an explanation of that answer, follows immediately. At the end of each chapter, detailed objective exercises allow you to apply the theory. It is unlikely that you will need to complete all of the exercises, but we believe that extensive application of the rules of rhetoric leads to writing skill. Each chapter also includes writing assignments that let you use your rhetorical tools in your own writing.

Following each reading selection in Part II, exercises stress the relation between Parts I and II. They concern the rhetoric and ideas of the essays, include a vocabulary study, and ask you to write—sometimes single paragraphs, sometimes entire essays. When you write, you can investigate topics related to what you read in *Staircase* and use the right rhetorical tools to make those topics interesting and informative.

The two major parts of *Staircase* are separate but related units. Part I provides the rules of rhetoric you need to write clearly. Knowing the rules, you can then read the essays in Part II with an awareness of how their structure contributes to their meaning.

ALAN CASTY
Santa Monica, California

DONALD TIGHE
Orlando, Florida

part one

Rhetoric
and
Writing

section one

Getting Ready

chapter 1

Preliminary Planning:
Evidence and Ideas

Writers have to be detectives. They have to find evidence, their clues, and draw conclusions from those clues. They then have to arrange both conclusions and clues to form their case.

We don't know how many clues writers need before they are ready to state their case. Neither can we say how many ideas the evidence will hold. We do know that writers must know the difference between facts and ideas. They have to be able to form ideas from clues, state those ideas clearly, and then arrange the clues under the right ideas. And that's what we want to talk about in this chapter—getting evidence and ideas and then putting them together in some kind of order.

Evidence or Ideas

It's hard to say which should come first in planning an essay—evidence or ideas. Some writers like to start with an idea and then collect evidence to support it. Evidence is supporting materials—statistics, examples, comparisons, contrasts, causes, effects, and expert opinion. Other writers like to start with facts on a topic and then form their ideas from those facts. Still others like to work with ideas and evidence at the same time. They shape their ideas as new facts turn up and collect new evidence as they find fresh ideas.

The writing task itself can help you decide whether you will first collect facts and then come to a conclusion about them or whether you will start with an idea and then gather facts to support it. If you are asked to write on the broad topic "Family Relationships," for instance, unless you have strong ideas about the subject to begin with, you'll probably work *inductively;* that is, you will collect evidence and then form ideas from that evidence. You may watch your family closely, draw conclusions from what you see or hear, put the facts and ideas in order, and then write your paper. You can see this inductive process on this staircase diagram:

CONCLUSION
My family doesn't get along very well.

EVIDENCE
Mother scolds children for misbehaving.

Father fusses at mother for scolding.

Sister sasses mother over evening dishes.

Brother teases sister until she cries.

I complain because I can't study.

CONCLUSION

EVIDENCE
The Gator Bowl is in Jacksonville, Florida.

The Orange Bowl is in Miami.

The Sugar Bowl is in New Orleans.

The Rose Bowl is in Los Angeles.

★   Which is the best conclusion you might form from the evidence on the staircase diagram above? _____

A. The major college bowl games are played January 1.
B. The bowl games are played by college teams.
C. The bowl games are played in the southern part of the United States.

☆   C. A is not supported by the evidence given here. The dates of the games are not part of the evidence. These games are, of course, played by college teams (B), but that information is not given in the evidence. All four cities listed are in the southern part of the United States. Therefore C is the best conclusion.

If the assignment asks you to defend or attack an idea, you will work *deductively*. You will start with an idea and then find evidence to support or destroy it. You may, for instance, be asked to support this idea:

College athletics is supported and controlled by the public, not by the schools.

To defend this idea, you have to get the facts. When you get the idea and evidence in order, your plan might take a staircase form:

CONCLUSION
College athletics is supported and controlled by the
public, not by the schools.

EVIDENCE
The public pays $150 million a year for tickets to college
athletic events.

Commercial TV brings college football to more than 100
million Americans weekly.

Commercial newspapers devote a great deal of space to college
athletics.

Public pressure forced the resignation or firing of three top
coaches last year.

Public pressure forced a major change in intercollegiate
basketball rules.

CONCLUSION
Critics praised the film "King Lear" highly.

EVIDENCE
Time called it a "motion picture event."

Newsweek referred to it as a "re-creation of original
Shakespeare."

The *Saturday Review* said it was a "truly artistic and tasteful
production."

Esquire . . .

★   Which of these comments best fills the *Esquire* step on the staircase
above?

A. *Esquire* called it a poor example of Shakespearean drama.

B. *Esquire* labeled it a fiasco, a tribute to poor direction.

C. *Esquire* nominated it for at least ten Academy Awards.

☆ C. If *Esquire* printed either A or B, then the Esquire critic did not praise the film. The writer intent on supporting the conclusion "Critics praised the film ..." should omit such negative evidence in his discussion. Or if he finds enough negative criticism, he must change his conclusion to sum up the evidence accurately.

Mid-steps: evidence into ideas, ideas into evidence

When you have a great deal of evidence, you may find you need to take mid-steps in your plan. In such a case, what you thought was a fact may also be doing the job of an idea and thus may be an idea and evidence at the same time. Here's how it would look on a staircase:

CONCLUSION (IDEA)
My parents enjoy taking their vacation in Florida.

EVIDENCE/IDEA
Dad enjoys both fresh and saltwater fishing there.

EVIDENCE
He fishes for bass in the lakes around Kissimmee.

EVIDENCE
He loves to fight the tarpon in Tampa Bay.

EVIDENCE/IDEA
Mother likes to visit the parks and play areas.

EVIDENCE
She thrills to the pageantry of Cypress Gardens.

EVIDENCE
She is delighted by the Magic Kingdom at Walt Disney World.

The important thing to remember is that these mid-steps, evidence/idea steps, are important levels under which you can put your facts in order in small units. If your plan is complex, these staircase landings help your readers by giving them logical resting places.

IDEA (CONCLUSION)

EVIDENCE/IDEA

EVIDENCE

EVIDENCE

EVIDENCE

EVIDENCE/IDEA

EVIDENCE

EVIDENCE

EVIDENCE

★ Put these items on the right step of the staircase above.

Chemistry   Religion
Natural Sciences   Biology
Philosophy   Literature
College Curriculum   Geology
Humanities

☆ Your diagram should look like this:

IDEA	*College Curriculum*
EVIDENCE/IDEA	*Humanities*
EVIDENCE	*Literature*
EVIDENCE	*Philosophy*
EVIDENCE	*Religion*
EVIDENCE/IDEA	*Natural Sciences*
EVIDENCE	*Biology*
EVIDENCE	*Chemistry*
EVIDENCE	*Geology*

It makes no difference if you put Natural Sciences before Humanities, and it doesn't matter if the three Natural Sciences and three Humanities courses are not in the same order (alphabetical) we used. What does matter is that you see that both Humanities and Natural Sciences are mid-points on the staircase and as such have the qualities of both ideas and evidence.

Using Available Sources

No matter how you combine evidence and ideas, you *do* need evidence. But where do you find this evidence? If you were planning a paper on how the newspaper cartoon strip ''Peanuts'' not only entertains but also teaches the public, you would get your evidence from three sources: Community Lore, Personal Experience, and Inference. At times these sources overlap.

Community lore

Most of us think that the dog is man's best friend, that all mothers love their children, that good will win out over evil. Though these glittering generalities are not borne out by the facts, we so want them to be true that we treat them almost as though they were. They are only a small part of a vast store of evidence and pseudoevidence that we may call Community Lore.

Community Lore is made up of the common beliefs and experiences of a given community—local, state, regional, national, international. As a college writer, you may assume, for example, that your readers' Community Lore includes the Bible, Shakespeare's tragedies (at least *Julius Caesar, Macbeth,* and parts of *Hamlet*), movies, television, and radio. You are fairly safe to assume that they have read the daily newspaper, *Playboy,* and, perhaps, *Reader's Digest, Time,* or *Newsweek.* You may be sure that most Americans have learned some of the sayings from Ben Franklin's *Poor Richard's Almanac* and thousands of old wives' tales.

Most of us think that comic strips entertain us, make us laugh; not too many take them very seriously. After all, we call them ''funnies.'' As you plan a paper whose thesis (''Peanuts'' instructs) is to disprove a common belief, you must consider as a source of evidence the common misconception that comic strips merely entertain. This evidence, used perhaps to introduce your paper, may get you and your readers on common ground, bring them into your paper by reminding them of the community's—and thus their—misconception.

Personal experience

We don't know enough about some subjects to write about them, for we have too little or no experience with them. Often, however, you make yourself think you know too little about a subject when really you know enough to write a good essay. On most topics you have evidence and ideas hidden away in your mind. Your job is to find them. With some effort you can recall what you have done that is relevant to the topic, and you can discover even more.

What You Read. You have probably read ''Peanuts,'' perhaps for years. When you chose to write about how this comic strip makes the reader think as well as laugh, it is likely that you had specific strips in mind. But memory is often sketchy, and you can read more, even reread. You may have a few favorites clipped and filed, or you can look for ''Peanuts'' strips in back copies of newspapers or in collections in books.

You may also have read *about* this popular comic strip or about its famous author. Interviews with Charles Schulz have been featured in many well-known magazines. You can read more. The resources of the library can help you find new evidence on the topic. The card catalog (the library's record of all its book holdings) will contain cards on books in your library about cartoons and even on books about or by Schulz himself. The *Reader's Guide to Periodical Literature* lists articles about ''Peanuts'' that have appeared in popular periodicals. The general reference section—encyclopedias, dictionaries, biographical sources, and so forth—may also give you some background useful to you as you plan your essay.

What You Hear. You have perhaps heard your family and your friends tell about ''Peanuts.'' Schulz's insight into human problems has made the strip a common topic of discussion. It has been referred to by newscasters commenting on world affairs. It has been used in ministers' sermons and in psychology and philosophy professors' lectures.

One of the most effective ways to hear new evidence is to interview people who know about the topic. An instructor in the Art Department, for instance, is likely to know about cartoonists' techniques in general or about Schulz's talent in particular. Your literature professor probably knows something about cartoons as vehicles for satire. ''Peanuts'' may be his favorite comic strip. Your fellow students will be quick to express their opinions.

What You Do. Though you may have drawn no cartoons, you have done those things cartoonists depict in their comic strips. Surely someone has asked you what you would do if you could live your life over again. And you have undoubtedly tried to answer the question.

©1960 United Feature Syndicate, Inc.

Inference

The most important source in planning your writing is your ability to make inferences from evidence, to take from the facts you collect an idea implicit in them, an idea they demonstrate. The *Standard College Dictionary* says *infer* means to ''derive by reasoning: to conclude ... from evidence of premises ...'' We make inferences in two ways: (1) inductively and (2) deductively. Two persons may make different inferences about the same evidence.

> ★ Does the strip above give the reader ''something to think about'' as well as something to laugh about?
>
> A. Yes   B. No

☆ A. At first we laugh at Charlie Brown's response to Lucy's question. But as we think about it, we, like Charlie, know her question has deep meaning. ''If I Had My Life to Live Over'' is not just a song title; it is a subject for serious thought. Frames one and three show Charlie Brown posed as a thinker who takes the question seriously. The implications become serious if the reader, like Charlie, really thinks about it. Under Schulz's surface humor lies a serious point. As a matter of fact, the success of ''Peanuts'' lies in a bit of Community Lore: that real truth often comes ''out of the mouths of babes.''

When we see Lucy threaten to slug Linus, her younger brother, we may infer that Lucy is a bully. Later, when we see her demand that poor Charlie Brown ''put 'em up,'' we feel sure our first inference was right. If more evidence reveals Lucy threatening those smaller than she, we may conclude that Lucy is a bully; there's no doubt about it. It's possible, of course, to make different inferences from the same evidence. We may infer, for instance, that Lucy is just trying to avoid being dominated by both Linus and Charlie Brown and that the best defense is a good offense.

When we infer from evidence, we are making an inference inductively. We can't be sure that the inference we make is the only one, but by careful analysis of the evidence, we can make sure that our inference is logical—that is, that it is a sensible interpretation of the facts—as we see them.

★ Which of these inferences is the safest one to make from the evidence in the ''Peanuts'' frames below? _____

A. Charlie Brown is a skillful kite flyer.
B. Charlie Brown will eventually fly his kite.
C. Charlie Brown knows nothing about building kites.
D. Charlie Brown is a failure at kite flying.

☆ D. If we can believe the evidence, Charlie Brown is not a skillful kite flyer (A). Since no frame even hints of success, a safer conclusion than B would be that he will never fly his kite successfully. There is no evidence to indicate that the kites are defective (C). The evidence seems overwhelmingly to support the conclusion that Charlie Brown is a failure at kite flying.

©1959 United Feature Syndicate, Inc.

©1959 United Feature Syndicate, Inc.

©1959 United Feature Syndicate, Inc.

©1958 United Feature Syndicate, Inc.

Reading more ''Peanuts'' strips will show that Charlie Brown is a failure not only at kite flying. We may make other inferences about Charlie's short-comings from the strips below. These inferences can become evidence from which a more general inference can be drawn.

©1958 United Feature Syndicate, Inc.

©1958 United Feature Syndicate, Inc.

IDEA (INFERENCE)
EVIDENCE (INFERENCES) Charlie Brown fails with a staff pen.
Charlie Brown can't get sick right.
Charlie Brown can't fly a kite.
Charlie Brown is gullible.

★   Which is the safest inference to make from the evidence inferred from the four comic strips above and shown on the staircase diagram?

————

A. Charlie Brown is a versatile fellow.
B. Charlie Brown will give up kite flying.
C. Charlie Brown is a born loser.

☆   C. When we say someone is versatile, we mean he is successful at performing various activities. Considering the evidence given above, Charlie Brown is not a versatile fellow (A). Charlie may give up trying to fly his kite (B), but the evidence does not bear out such an inference. Though C is an exaggerated inference, it best sums up the evidence.

Having made a sound inference, we may then use it as a *premise,* a starting point for evaluating new evidence, a point from which we can predict. Once we conclude, as we did in the preceding example, that Charlie Brown is a born loser, that conclusion becomes a premise from which we may infer more about Charlie's future. He will, most likely, lose in everything he attempts—baseball, kite flying, birdhouse building. When we use a premise as a starting point to infer about the future, we make an inference *deductively.* The following staircase diagram illustrates this:

IDEA (INFERENCE)
Charlie Brown is a born loser.

NEW EVIDENCE (INFERENCES)
Charlie Brown's aspirations for a winning baseball season are doomed.

Charlie Brown's enthusiasm for his new sister will end in disillusionment.

Charlie Brown's new plan for getting up his kite will end in failure.

Charlie Brown's attempt to build a new birdhouse will fail.

©*1958 United Feature Syndicate, Inc.*

©*1958 United Feature Syndicate, Inc.*

★   If we accept the premise ''Charlie Brown is a born loser,'' does the second strip provide the appropriate evidence to conclude the first strip above? _____

> ☆   If Charlie Brown is a born loser (and Charlie's failures seem to suggest that Schulz sees him as such), then Charlie's catching the ball would be inconsistent. Charlie is the eternal goat. He will have to bear up under his own sense of failure and the disappointment of his teammates, for he represents the little man whose endurance, certainly not his success, makes him admirable, or at least lovable. His missing the ball may not make us happy, but it strikes us as logical.

A thorough investigation of Community Lore and Personal Experience will turn up a great amount of evidence. Evidence itself, however, is meaningless. It takes on significance only as you make logical inferences about the patterns of meaning you see in that evidence.

WRITING ASSIGNMENTS

Use the method of preliminary planning described in Chapter 1 to plan and write a well-developed paragraph or essay on one of the following topics:

Student Rights	A Good Car	Professional Sports
Violence	Sororities	Fraternities
College Courses	Movie Morality	What Grades Mean
Inflation	Reading	Drugs

Exercises

1a

A. In the blank staircase diagrams below, arrange the jumble of ideas and evidence in logical order, the most general on the top step. Note that some of the sentences are both ideas and evidence.

1. Mohammad Ali is telling us some bug killer is "the greatest." O.J. Simpson keeps hurdling everything in sight on the way to pick up his Hertz Car. Television advertisers use professional athletes to hawk their wares. Even though he's retired, Joe Namath is still selling clothes, chairs, Brut, and cereal.

IDEA

    EVIDENCE

2. The first shelf was crammed with the latest issues of *Time, New Republic, Ramparts, National Review,* and *Playboy.* To the left of the magazines he had piled copies of the *New York Times, Denver Post,* and *San Francisco Chronicle.* On the middle shelf he had a set of the great books and a vast collection of science fiction novels and detective stories. On the top shelf he had numerous volumes on the art of cooking and gardening. His library testified to the breadth of his reading habits.

IDEA

    EVIDENCE

3. All dogs have to have expensive shots. Special breeds need costly surgery on both ears and tail. A dog is an expensive pet. Dog owners have to pay medical bills for their pooches. Most female dogs must be spayed by veterinarians who charge large fees.

IDEA

    EVIDENCE/IDEA

        EVIDENCE

4. Mathematics has never been very easy for me. Now that I'm in college, I am having trouble making passing grades even in business math. I never could solve the mysteries of X's and Y's, sines and cosines. In junior high I had serious trouble trying to learn even the simplest arithmetic. In high school I made D's in algebra and trigonometry. My eighth-grade math instructor threatened to fail me if I didn't learn to add correctly.

IDEA

    EVIDENCE/IDEA

        EVIDENCE

    EVIDENCE/IDEA

        EVIDENCE

    EVIDENCE

5. The business establishments are nothing more than three windowless cement block walls fronted by cheap imitations of colonial mansions, Spanish villas, Swiss chalets, and even Indian teepees. The apartment buildings look like turned-up egg cartons or French provincial prisons. The private homes seem to be merely cement block slabs with holes cut out for windows and doors. The architecture of Farnsworth City reveals lack of imagination. Point Paris, a plush, tall condominium city surrounded by high walls and well-guarded entrances, should be called The Bastille.

IDEA

    EVIDENCE

    EVIDENCE/IDEA

        EVIDENCE

    EVIDENCE

1b **A.** Select the most appropriate conclusion you might infer from the evidence below. Place the number of the conclusion you select in the blank below the evidence.

1. Evidence: My three-year-old Ford has 50,000 miles on it. It needs a new battery, the front wheel bearings are shot, the tires are thin, and the upholstery is frayed.

(1) ⎯⎯⎯⎯⎯

Conclusion: (1) American cars give good service for 50,000 miles, then fall apart. (2) Now is the time for me to trade for a new Ford. (3) My three-year-old Ford needs some minor repairs.

2. Evidence:

Saturday Morning TV Time

	NBC	ABC	CBS
9:00	Super	Space	Mighty
9:15	6	Station	Mouse
9:30	Atom	Porky	Underdog
9:45	Ant	Pig	Cartoon
10:00	The	King	Frankenstein Jr. &
10:15	Flintstones	Kong	The Impossible
10:30	Space	The	The Space
10:45	Kidettes	Beatles	Ghost
11:00	Secret	Casper the	Adventures of
11:15	Squirrel	Friendly Ghost	Superman
11:30	The	Milton the	The Lone
11:45	Jetsons	Monster	Ranger

(2) _____

Conclusion: (1) Saturday morning television is for a juvenile audience. (2) Saturday morning television is unfit to watch. (3) Television commercials are destroying television. (4) Television is strictly for kiddies, not for adults.

3. Evidence: The rainfall in Toongabura was 88.6 inches in 1960, 86.2 inches in 1961, 84.2 inches in 1962, 82.2 inches in 1963, 80.2 inches in 1964, and 78.2 inches in 1965.

(3) _____

Conclusion: (1) Toongabura rainfall declined steadily between 1960 and 1965. (2) Toongabura rainfall will eventually return to normal. (3) Toongabura rainfall will be 74.2 inches in 1967.

4. Evidence: Dave finished his research project instead of going to the party. He reads books on history when we go out to the movies. When he *does* go downtown, he goes to the library or the museum. He spent his Christmas money for an abstract painting instead of the tux he really needed.

(4) _____

Conclusion: (1) Dave prefers to improve his mind rather than to engage in social activities. (2) Dave is a bookworm. (3) Dave may make good grades, but he has no common sense. (4) Dave is not normal.

5. Evidence: ROTC students were caught cheating at Welbar Tech in 1970 and again in 1973. Seven ROTC men were expelled from Locke College in 1976 for selling tests they had stolen. Fourteen ROTC men were dismissed from Paltry University in 1978 for writing crib notes on their cuffs and fingernails.

(5) _____

Conclusion: (1) The academic standards at most institutions of higher learning are so stiff that to pass, even ROTC men are forced to cheat. (2) Even some reserve officer candidates have been caught cheating in college. (3) ROTC men, like other students, are dishonest.

B. Identify the evidence that does not support the conclusion. Place the number of the irrelevant evidence in the blank below the evidence. If all of the evidence is relevant, leave the blank empty.

1. Conclusion: The 1978 legislature favored education.
   Evidence: (1) It slashed $47 million from the junior college budget request. (2) It allocated $15 million for braille libraries for the blind. (3) It provided for a 25 percent increase in teachers' salaries at all levels. (4) It raised the tax on liquor to build a new state university at Bland.

(1) _____

2. Conclusion: Television drama features violence.
   Evidence: (1) CBS late movies feature gothic monster films at least twice a week. (2) At least three ABC shows specialize in clever ways to eliminate people by using modern sleuthing devices. (3) ''Kojak'' and ''Starsky and Hutch'' both feature city cops who take part virtually every week in shootings, knifings, stranglings, and robberies. (4) NBC evening news runs on-the-spot coverage of suicides, racial disturbances, fires, and other catastrophes.

(2) _____

3. Conclusion: Student complaints reveal the shortcomings of the present registration procedure.
   Evidence: (1) One student needed the signature of her adviser to complete registration; he was home in bed. (2) One student complained about having to stand in line for six hours to register. (3) One student blamed the complicated forms for her not being able to graduate on time. (4) Six students had to wait two hours to see a counselor who had resigned more than a year ago.

(3) _____

4. Conclusion: Charlie Brown is the eternal worrier.
   Evidence: (1) He worries that his newborn sister will be disillusioned by the unhappiness in the world. (2) He suspects that Lucy will pull the football away when she holds it for him to place-kick. (3) He doubts that he can catch the fly ball that means the third out and the championship. (4) He feels confident that this year his baseball team will win.

(4) _____

5. **Conclusion:** The trees in the back yard provided shade all day.
   Evidence: (1) Four jacaranda trees to the front of the south side protected the yard from the morning sun. (2) A row of towering punk trees on the west side protected the yard from the evening sun. (3) Two great water oaks farther back on the south side caught the noon and early afternoon rays. (4) Between the trees were low growing rose bushes, azaleas, and a sprinkling of periwinkles and African violets.

   (5) _____

1c

A. Form a conclusion that adequately sums up the evidence below. Write the conclusion on the lines provided.

1. **Evidence:** Former President Dwight Eisenhower played football for Army during his four years at West Point. Byron ''Whizzer'' White, now a justice of the United States Supreme Court, was an All-American football player and a Rhodes Scholar. Bill Bradley, who was forward for the New York Knicks, was a Rhodes Scholar before he joined the professional Knicks. Bill Russell, former center and coach of the Boston Celtics, has been a successful businessman and television commentator.

   Conclusion: _____

   _____

2. **Evidence:** In January Bill announced that he wanted to enlist in the Marines as soon as he finished high school. By February he had decided to enter Georgia State to major in engineering or chemistry. During March and April he told his parents that he had decided to become a plumber (early March), an electrician (late March), and an insurance salesman (April). By May he had taken the ACT tests and had decided to try for West Point. In June he applied for admission to Pleasant Community College so he'd have time to decide for sure what he wanted to do. When I talked to him in September, he was majoring in business administration.

   Conclusion: _____

   _____

3. **Evidence:** His history notes were disorganized and unreadable. His English notes were nothing but doodles. His psychology notes were composed of such comments as ''See page 74.'' He had nothing marked on page 74 in any of the four psychology texts used in the class.

   Conclusion: _____

   _____

4. **Evidence:** Kurt Henried played the part of the villainous Colonel Hindenburg in ''They Walked by Night.'' He was the monstrous General Fritz in ''The Rhine.'' He played a dictatorial Nazi SS officer in

"Hamburg to Berlin." He received acclaim for his portrayal of the brutal Hans Ichmann in "Journey to Paris." He was given the Academy Award for doing the hated Luftwaffe General Wagner in "They Flew by Night."

Conclusion: _____

_____

5. **Evidence:** On the front wall hung a stuffed rhino head and two enormous elephant tusks. Along the right wall stood a gigantic gun cabinet with every gun imaginable, from a blunderbuss to an elephant gun—fifty weapons in all. On the left wall was an assortment of stuffed birds —a pheasant, several eagles, an ostrich, and a vulture. On the back wall seventy-seven plaques and trophies signified that he shot straighter than other men with whom he had competed.

Conclusion: _____

_____

B. List at least three pieces of evidence that you could use to support the conclusions given below. List the evidence in the spaces provided.

1. **Conclusion:** The colors a person likes frequently match his temperament.

   Evidence: _____

   _____

   _____

   _____

   _____

2. **Conclusion:** Each college student has a different idea about how to study.

   Evidence: _____

   _____

   _____

   _____

   _____

3. **Conclusion:** Comic strips besides "Peanuts" make serious comments on life.

   Evidence: _____

   _____

   _____

_____

_____

4. **Conclusion:** College professors seem to agree about what constitutes effective writing.

   Evidence: _____

   _____

   _____

   _____

   _____

5. **Conclusion:** My reading of _____ made me aware of _____.

   Evidence: _____

   _____

   _____

   _____

   _____

chapter 2

Purpose and Strategy

After you have enough evidence and have found the ideas implicit in those facts, you can take the next step toward effective writing. You can decide your purpose and pick the strategy to achieve that purpose.

When you write, you may narrate, or describe, or explain, or argue. Or you may combine these types of writing. Your purpose will help you decide which type to pick. A letter to your parents, for instance, may include a paragraph or two about what you did on your trip to the lake last week (narration), a paragraph on the beauty of the rocks in one of the caves you saw (description), a diagram and discussion of the play your school used to win last Saturday's football game (exposition), and a paragraph that argues that your allowance is too small and ought to be larger (argument).

Narration

When you narrate, you put your thoughts in story form, in time order. Biographers, historians, fiction writers, and poets use narration. The paragraph below from Robert Daley's article "The Deadly Score of the Stakeout Squad" illustrates simple narration:

> A few weeks ago a Stakeout Unit was on duty at the Pitkin Avenue A&P in Brooklyn. It was three in the afternoon and the supermarket was full of shoppers, mostly housewives, when in sauntered a stickup man. Walking directly to the checkout counter, he said to the manager of the store: "You know what I want, give it to me." Indeed, the manager did know because this man had already

robbed that same store seven times, always armed with a gun. He was the reason
the stakeout team was there. This time he showed no gun, but when he patted
the bulge in his coat, the manager handed over the money. The robber thanked
him, nodded, and started out the door with the two stakeout men walking swiftly
behind him. In the street they grabbed him, disarmed him, took the stolen
money out of his pocket, and charged him with first-degree robbery. Later he
was charged with having committed two other robberies elsewhere in Brooklyn,
making a minimum of nine that could be documented. (*New York Magazine,* April
24, 1972. Copyright ©1972 by Robert Daley. Reprinted by permission of The
Sterling Lord Agency, Inc.)

★   Does the narrative above have a clear purpose? _____

A. Yes   B. No

☆   A. This tightly written, fast-moving account of the holdup of the
Pitkin Avenue A&P makes it possible for Daley to capture the surprise
and threat of the robber. In addition he captures the swiftness and skill
used by the police to stop, arrest, disarm, and charge the holdup man.

Description

When we describe, we paint a word picture. We tell what something looks like,
or tastes like, or smells like, or feels like, or sounds like. Good description
results from looking closely and presenting facts clearly.

There are two kinds of description: objective and subjective. As the label
makes clear, objective description does not reveal the writer's point of view; it
is impersonal. The writer presents facts.

This description from a newspaper want ad shows objective description:

House for Sale

3 BR's 2 Bath—Liv Rm—Fam Rm—Air Cond. Fenced Garden—Floodlights—
Fruit Trees. Close to High, Jr High, and Elementary Sch's. 5032 75th Avenue
South. SEE IT—Then call B. Z. Slepps at 397-5278.

★   What is the purpose of the description above? _____

A. To describe a house
B. To sell a house

☆   A and B. The purpose is twofold. (1) B. Z. Slepps wants to sell the
house (B). Selling is the purpose of most advertisements. (2) To sell it,
however, the company must first attract a buyer. He is attracted by the
objective description (A).

Subjective description, on the other hand, is imaginative. Though the writer still uses facts, he presents them to give his reaction to the material. Mark Twain's description of a part of his town on the west bank of the Mississippi shows subjective description:

> After all these years I can picture that old time to myself now, just as it was then: the white town drowsing in the sunshine of a summer's morning; the streets empty, or pretty nearly so; one or two clerks sitting in front of the Water Street stores, with their splint-bottomed chairs tilted back against the walls, chins on breasts, hats slouched over their faces, asleep—with shingle-shavings enough around to show what broke them down; a sow and a litter of pigs loafing along the sidewalk, doing a good business in watermelon rinds and seeds; two or three lonely little freight piles scattered about the "levee"; a pile of "skids" on the slope of the stone-paved wharf, and the fragrant town drunkard asleep in the shadow of them; two or three wood flats at the head of the wharf, but nobody to listen to the peaceful lapping of the wavelets against them; the great Mississippi, the majestic, the magnificent Mississippi, rolling its mile-wide tide along, shining in the sun; the dense forest away on the other side, the "point" above the town, and the "point" below, bounding the river-glimpse and turning it into a sort of sea, and withal a very still and brilliant and lonely one. (Mark Twain, *Life on the Mississippi.*)

★   What overall impression of the town does Twain give? _____

A. Activity and life
B. Drowsiness and inactivity
C. Confusion and violence
D. Sloppiness and vulgarity

☆   B. Twain recalls the "drowsiness and inactivity" of the scene. Closely following the colon, he uses three words that key this impression: "drowsing," "empty," and "sitting." The details that follow emphasize the sleepiness of a midwestern Mississippi River village. He then reaffirms the total effect with a final glimpse of the "point" that turned into "a sort of sea," "a very still and brilliant and lonely one."

Exposition

Exposition is a broader term than either *narration* or *description*. An expository theme may include both narration and description. Its purpose is to explain. If you tell someone how to read a book, for instance, you are using exposition. If someone asks you what you mean by a certain word and you define the word—that is, you explain what the word means—you are using exposition. You use exposition when you list examples to make clear a complex point, or when you compare or contrast two views of history, or when you explain how a dead battery in your car caused you to be late for class. It is important to understand exposition, for most college writing is expository.

The two paragraphs below show simple exposition:

The bandwagon is a device common enough to be well known, and you will be able to find examples easily. It is argument based on the great desire of most people to be on the winning side, or the popular side. In election propaganda it is clearly recognizable: "Vote for Yapp—he's sure to win anyway." In advertising, the usual method is to point out how many people favor a product, the conclusion being that you should favor it too. Since there is little space in advertising for arguments, the fact of popularity, granted that it is a fact, is frequently stressed more strongly than the reasons for popularity. Another example is the appeal, "Everybody plays the xylophone—why don't you?"

Any propaganda that urges an action or an opinion primarily because that act or opinion is popular is attempting to get you on the bandwagon. (William Hummel and Keith Huntress, *The Analysis of Propaganda.* Copyright 1949 by William Hummel and Keith Huntress. Reprinted with permission of Holt, Rinehart and Winston, Inc.)

★   Which is the author's purpose? _____

A. To explain what the propaganda device bandwagon is
B. To warn the reader not to be swayed by bandwagon
C. To illustrate that bandwagon is a propaganda device that is infrequently but effectively used

☆   A. The purpose, to define *bandwagon,* is stated clearly in sentence one and restated in paragraph two. B is perhaps implied, for when readers know what the term means, they can then be on guard against it. C is incorrect, for the first sentence suggests just the opposite; bandwagon is frequently, not infrequently, used.

Argument

Unlike exposition, which is generally objective, argument makes the writer take sides, take one side of an issue rather than another. When we argue, we have one of two purposes: (1) We try to get someone to accept our idea; (2) we try to get someone to do something, to take action.

Like exposition, argument may combine both narration and description, but it may also include some of the techniques of exposition. To convince your readers that communism will rob them of some of their vital freedoms, for instance, you will have to explain what communism is, to define it. To get someone to buy your car, you may have to describe it over the phone and later show him how it drives at high speed. Only after he knows the facts can you ask him to buy.

The following two paragraphs from Charlton Ogburn's "A Modest Proposal" show argument:

That the motorcar is imperiling our cities has become increasingly evident. The administrator of the Environmental Protection Agency declares that in many cities the present level of traffic is incompatible with safely breathable air. The noise of such traffic may well render all city dwellers stone deaf within thirty years. Going anywhere in the city without a car becomes ever more difficult and expensive; for, as private cars take away the passengers, public-transportation services have to be reduced and fares increased. And yet, going anywhere *with* a car also becomes more difficult and expensive as the streets become more congested and parking spaces more elusive. Above all, the cities are being rendered unfit for human habitation by the great mass of this army of motorized robots.

So people who can afford to get out of the city move to the suburbs and commute by car, exacerbating the very evil they are attempting to escape. Those who cannot afford to flee also cannot afford to support the city, which totters toward bankruptcy. (Reprinted from *Harper's Magazine,* October 1971, with the permission of the author.)

★   What is the purpose of Ogburn's two paragraphs? _____

A. To get the reader to accept a belief
B. To get the reader to act

☆   A. Ogburn's purpose is to get the reader to believe that the motorcar threatens to destroy the American city. He states his idea clearly in a topic sentence, the first sentence of the first paragraph. He supports his position with convincing evidence and drives home his idea in the last sentence of the first paragraph. He clinches his idea in the last sentence of the second paragraph.

Convinced that conditions need to improve, Ogburn's reader asks, "What can be done? How can we keep the cities from being killed by the motorcar?" To answer, Ogburn suggests using battery-driven Electricarts about a fourth the size of regular cars but able to haul four people in downtown areas. These carts, he explains, will be owned and operated by the city and will thus become a source of revenue. The small size of the carts will cut city motor traffic, unclutter city streets, and produce more parking space. Since the cars will be battery-driven, they will have no exhaust fumes and make little noise. Reduced traffic, he says, will make travel cheaper. When the city's streets and air are cleaned up, the exodus to the suburbs will stop and those who can afford to pay taxes will stay in the city. In short, he proves to his reader that his plan will improve things. Ogburn ends his argument with the following paragraph:

> Why not give Electricarts a trial? The central square mile or two or three of a middle-sized city could be selected—that is to say, be wired, equipped with Electricarts, and closed to motor traffic. We have nothing to lose by the experiment but money, and federal money at that; and if it works, our cities may again become places fit to live in.

★   What is the purpose of Ogburn's last paragraph? _____

A. To get the reader to accept a belief
B. To get the reader to act

> ☆   B. Having convinced his reader that a change is in order, that he
> has a plan for change, that his plan will work and be beneficial, and that
> his plan is superior to other plans, he makes a plea for action. After
> reading the closing paragraph, the reader is forced to ask, "Well, why
> not give Electricarts a trial?"

Whether you narrate, describe, explain, or argue, you must ask yourself
four questions to decide your strategy: (1) Who is the writer? (2) What is the
nature of the subject? (3) What is the nature of the audience? (4) What tone
best suits the purpose?

Who is the writer?

Since you are the writer, you must ask yourself a few questions: What subjects interest me? What subjects do I know enough to write about? What effect
will my personality have on my subject? Do I like to be humorous or do I
prefer to be serious? Knowing yourself will help you select a topic *right for you*.

> ★   Which of the following topics is likely to be best for an expository
> theme by a freshman writer? _____
>
> A. Philosophy
> B. The Need for Life Insurance
> C. Care of a Surfboard
> D. Newspaper Sections that Inform
>
> ☆   C or D. Only the rare freshman knows much about philosophy (A),
> a rather broad subject, too general for a short paper. B is better than A,
> but life insurance is a rather technical subject for most freshman writers.
> Many college freshmen are expert surfers, and most know something
> about the various informative sections of the local newspapers.

What is the nature of the subject?

Having looked at a few subjects in terms of your own knowledge and interests, think more about the subject itself. Since not many topics are basically
interesting, you must first find the special quality that makes it worth writing
about—its timeliness, novelty, usefulness. Second, since most freshman
writing assignments ask for a certain number of words (often 300-500), you
must choose a topic you can handle in that length. Third, you must decide
whether your purpose demands that you narrate, describe, explain, argue, or
combine these types of writing. Finally, you must know how many details you
need to develop your purpose.

★   Which of these topics is likely to be the wisest choice for a short expository paper for freshman English? _____

A. History
B. Religions of the World
C. College Education in the United States
D. Budgeting your Money in College

☆   D. A is too broad for a short paper. A simple list of the ''Religions of the World'' (B) is staggering. And although ''College Education in the United States'' (C) is a better choice than either A or B, it is still too general. What aspect of college education does the writer plan to discuss? D is interesting to college students, limited enough for a short paper, likely to be expository, and well within the experience of a freshman writer.

What is the nature of the audience?

Too many freshman writers ignore their audience. As a result, their readers often cannot follow the thought. It is important to be aware of your readers at all times, for they affect your word choice, sentence length and structure, paragraph development and arrangement, and other rhetorical qualities.

★   Which of these topics is most likely to appeal to an audience composed of a college instructor and twenty-five freshman English students? _____

A. Science
B. An Analysis of a Story
C. My Summer Vcation
D. Freshmen: Babies in College

☆   D. Both students and instructor are likely to respond to this timely and controversial topic. It involves both age groups: The students know it is about them; instructors know it is about persons they either are or should be interested in. A, ''Science,'' is too broad. ''My Summer Vacation'' (C) is trite, overused. B is too academic and rather broad.

What tone best suits the purpose?

Everyone has an attitude toward everything. Even if you don't care, you have an attitude—indifference. You show this attitude when you write. You sound angry or amused, serious or playful, thoughtful or whimsical. Your attitude toward both the subject and the audience affects your tone.

The subject itself often shapes your attitude. If you are asked to do a biology report, you must be neutral and objective. If your paper is about death, you should be serious. If your grandparents have recently been cheated by some phony house repair racket and you want to attack swindlers in the local newspaper, you will write an angry letter to the editor. Although you can write a biased biology report, a satirical essay on death, or a humorous attack on cheats, you mustn't confuse your reader with a tone unsuited to your purpose.

You are likely to be effective with a grade-school audience by being straightforward. Using irony—saying one thing and meaning another—will merely confuse most very young readers. An attack against patriotism will alienate the American Legion. Though you may be angry about the food in the cafeteria, you will not change conditions there if you write an abusive letter to the school authorities. On the other hand, an objective analysis of the situation and a sane suggestion for change might do the trick.

Most important, be consistent; a sudden shift in tone may confuse your reader. Humor can be effective, but nothing is less successful than an ill-timed joke.

WRITING ASSIGNMENTS

1. In a short narrative, prove or disprove one of the following:
   a. A stitch in time saves nine.
   b. A bird in the hand is worth two in the bush.
   c. True love never runs smooth.
   d. Still water runs deep.
   e. He who laughs last laughs best.
2. Write both an objective description and a subjective description on one of the following topics.
   a. Your own home or a room in it
   b. The college cafeteria or a restaurant
   c. An acquaintance of yours
   d. The scene of an accident
   e. A photograph or painting you admire or dislike
3. With your composition class and instructor as your audience, explain briefly but factually how your high-school work in English, history, physical education, chemistry, biology, mathematics, business, psychology, music, foreign language, or government did or did not prepare you for college. Remember, you are to write exposition, not argument.
4. In a brief letter to the editor of a newspaper or magazine you read, object to something that has recently appeared in that publication. Adopt a tone that suits your purpose but do not be unreasonable or illogical.

Exercises

2a   **A.** Label each passage appropriately: (A) Narrative, (B) Objective Description, (C) Subjective Description, (D) Exposition, (E) Argument (to get the reader to accept a belief), (F) Argument (to get the reader to act). Pick the label that best describes the type of writing. Put the correct letter in the space provided.

1. Make thee an ark of gopher wood; rooms shalt thou make in the ark, and shalt pitch it within and without with pitch. And this is the fashion which thou shalt make it of: The length of the ark shall be three hundred cubits, the breadth of it fifty cubits, and the height of it thirty cubits. A window shalt thou make to the ark, and in a cubit shalt thou finish it above; and the door of the ark shalt thou set in the side thereof; with lower, second, and third stories shalt thou make it. (Genesis 6.14–16.)

(1) _____

2. I suggest it would be more humane, and certainly more logical, to admit that our football team is a valuable thing, which is why we built the stadium. The money we will make from the team this year will be a substantial benefit to the university. Therefore, let's have our student play football untroubled by classes, and then go to classes untroubled by football. In short, don't require anything of him during the season, but keep him on campus in the summer. And if his eligibility should run out, continue his scholarship until he gets the degree of his choice. (Michael Shaara, "Colleges Short-Change Their Football Players.")

(2) _____

3. The method is this: Provide a small iron rod ... of such a length that one end being three or four feet in the moist ground, the other may be six or eight feet above the highest part of the building. To the upper end of the rod fasten about a foot of brass wire, the size of a common knitting-needle, sharpened to a fine point; the rod may be secured to the house by a few small staples. If the house or barn be long, there may be a rod and point at each end and a middling wire along the ridge from one to the other. A house thus furnished will not be damaged by lightning, it being attracted by the points and passing thro' the metal into the ground without hurting anyone. (Benjamin Franklin.)

(3) _____

4. I was so unplugged you wouldn't believe it. And in the one moment I looked over my shoulder at the humping-up sea and swung the board around shoreward I knew I was going to catch a 15-foot wave. The rest of it is engraved into my mind like electroplating: I came over the crest and started down. It was straight down, and it was dizzy. I'll never know quite how, but I got my feet under me and stood up on the board, arms up, flexed and full of fire. Behind me, the top of the wave sizzled, and for one quick second up there I could see all of Dana

Point, Capistrano Beach, the beige hills off inland, Omaha, Nebraska, and everything. (Phil Edwards, ''You Should Have Been Here an Hour Ago.'')

(4) _____

5. A certain man went down from Jerusalem to Jericho, and fell among thieves, which stripped him of his raiment, and wounded him, and departed, leaving him half dead. And by chance there came down a certain priest that way: and when he saw him, he passed by on the other side. And likewise a Levite, when he was at the place, came and looked on him and passed by on the other side. But a certain Samaritan, as he journeyed, came where he was: and when he saw him, he had compassion on him. And went to him, and bound up his wounds, pouring in oil and wine, and sat him on his own beast, and brought him to an inn, and took care of him. And on the morrow when he departed, he took out two pence, and gave them to the host, and said unto him, Take care of him; and whatsoever thou spendest more, when I come again, I will repay thee. Which now of these three, thinkest thou, was neighbor unto him that fell among the thieves? (Luke 10.29–37.)

(5) _____

6. If the veto of $150 million in school funds sticks, and the results are what virtually every state educator from the School Superintendent down predicts, the Republicans surely will find in September that at the captial in July they lighted a time bomb with a short fuse.

(6) _____

B. Identify the attitude of the author of each sentence below. Label each one appropriately: (A) Tactful, (B) Abusive, (C) Sarcastic, (D) Humorous, (E) Objective. Put the correct letter in the space to the right of the passage.

1. We could hardly expect an ''honest'' employee like you, Mr. Thomas, to know that taking company stationery is against the rules.

(1) _____

2. The blue coupe approached the corner from the west at forty-five miles per hour; the black sedan came from the east at sixty-five miles per hour.

(2) _____

3. Although I may be wrong about this, it seems to me that the parking problem may not be quite as bad as it at first appeared.

(3) _____

4. These stupid, narrow-minded liberal Democrats could have averted the impasse by doing something more than their usual lying.

(4) _____

5. The announcer roared with delight: "There's a lesson for ya, little leaguers, if ya want ta hit the batter, throw behint 'im."

(5) _____

2b   **A.** In the spaces state in your own words the writer's purpose in each of the passages in Exercise 2a-A above.

1. _____

_____

_____

2. _____

_____

_____

3. _____

_____

_____

4. _____

_____

_____

5. _____

_____

_____

6. _____

_____

_____

B. In the spaces, revise each passage in Exercise 2a-B above to produce a tone different from the one employed in the original.
Example:
1. If the dumbest voter in the county would swab the wax out of his ears, he could realize that the local fuzz are stealing him blind.

1. *If county residents believe the rumors they hear, they are likely to suspect the county law enforcement agencies of using public funds dishonestly.*

1. _____

_____

_____

2. _____

_____

_____

3. _____

_____

_____

4. _____

_____

_____

5. _____

_____

_____

section two

Organizing

chapter 3

Limiting the Subject:
The Process of Abstracting

What we are going to talk about now does not necessarily take place after your analysis and examination of your evidence. It might take place before, after, or at the same time. But it should take place. It is another way of thinking through your subject before you actually begin to develop it in a fully written paper. We call it limiting the subject.

The whole process of writing is like an inverted triangle: ▽ The job is to get from some broad and often vague idea down to the most specific, narrow way of explaining that idea. The idea of freedom can be used by anybody to mean almost anything. But talk about freedom is not meaningful until it is limited to a narrower, lower level of discussion. There is quite a difference between being free to complain about the mayor and being free to invade his private-office, or between being free to talk about owning firearms and being free to have a closet full of them. Getting down to that level, down to the facts— that is the job of writing. It is a job that goes on all through the process of writing a paper; but it has to start with thinking about the subject, and limiting it.

Do not leave your subject too broad, too general, too abstract and too vague for your knowledge, your audience, your purpose, your space, and your time. That will leave you too high up that inverted triangle. And you will never get down to that factual point at the bottom. Limiting your subject—lopping off the higher levels of that triangle ▽ —gives you a better start. It gives you a better chance at developing a meaningful, pointed discussion of your ideas.

★   Which would make the best limited subject? _____

A. American culture today
B. The revolution in American culture today
C. The revolution in the etiquette of dress in America today

☆   C. Why? B, it is true, has added the important qualification of the revolution, the extreme change in American culture. But C applies that qualification to the more graspable, workable area of dress. It is the combination of the two modifying points—revolution and dress—that gives you something to focus on and say something concrete about.

Limiting the subject, then, is cutting down the area you are going to deal with. It narrows your focus, as a movie camera does when it moves in for a close-up. This can be done in a number of ways, but all of them are part of the important process of *reducing the level of abstraction.* This process is important not only for improving the quality of your thinking generally; it will be the basis of the rest of this book about improving the quality of your writing. Since it is so important, we will examine this general logical process first, before going on with the more limited subject of limiting the subject.

Our thoughts and the language that gives them shape are a matter of *generalizing* and *particularizing.* After a child has touched something hot several times, he *generalizes:* Don't touch something hot or you'll hurt. Later, though, he also begins to *particularize:* You can touch something hot, like a match, on one end, if you are sure not to touch it on the other end. In great part, intelligence is a matter of generalizing and particularizing in effective combinations. What we are concerned with here are the degrees of generality, the levels of abstraction, in words and ideas. You need to be more aware of these degrees and levels, more aware of where you are on what we will call the *staircase of abstractions.*

Not all thoughts, or words, are equal. Some are broader, more general, than others: they include more variations, possibilities, aspects. These are at a higher level of abstraction, a greater degree of generality. They are higher on the staircase of abstractions.

★   Arrange the terms on the staircase in order of their degree of generality. Start with the broadest generality, the highest level on the staircase of abstraction.

A. motor vehicle
B. product
C. automobile
D. Ford

> ☆   B, A, C, D. *Product* is the most abstract term, the broadest category. It includes, refers to, all motor vehicles, but also all sorts of other things which are manufactured. *Motor vehicle* is next because it includes all automobiles, but also other items such as motorcycles. *Automobile* is next because it includes all Fords, but more than Fords. *Ford* reduces the abstraction to one particular type of automobile.

A statement is more general when it includes more possibilities, more possible subdivisions. One useful way of looking at this is in terms of quantity. The more general a term, the more items it refers to. But also, the more general a term, the more differences are included within it. There are more different things in the classification *product* than in *automobile*. On the other hand, the more concrete a term is, the less the differences and the greater the similarities among the things it refers to. There are more similarities among *automobiles* than among *products*. We'll put it another way. The more abstract your words, the less you can point to the specific things they refer to. The more concrete your words, the more likely you are to be able to point to them. *Creature* is more abstract, more general than *dog*. But *dog*, is, in turn, more general than *terrier*. *Terrier* is thus more concrete than *dog*. *School* is more general than *college*, but *college* is more general than *Harvard*. *Harvard* is thus more concrete than *college*.

> ★   Underline the more general term in each pair, the term that is higher on the staircase of abstractions.
>
> A. art, music
> B. rose, flower
> C. building, motel
>
> ☆   *Art, flower* and *building. Art* includes music, but also other forms of art. *Flower* includes roses, but also other forms of flowers. *Building* includes motels, but also other forms of buildings.

> ★   Arrange these terms in one sequence, placing the most general in the top stair of the staircase of abstractions: *Eastern U.S.; Kentucky; Southeastern U.S.; Louisville, Ky.; United States.*

☆   From top to bottom: *United States, Eastern U.S., Southeastern U.S., Kentucky, Louisville, Ky.* In establishing this sequence, we have analyzed the terms on the basis of one of the logical ways of determining the relationships among a series of terms. We have analyzed them on the basis of *place* and determined which is the most abstract reference to a place, which the most concrete and specific.

Analysis on the basis of time is a second basic way of setting up the relationships among a series of terms. Here is a sequence of references to time set up in a staircase of abstractions. Again, the terms at the top are more abstract.

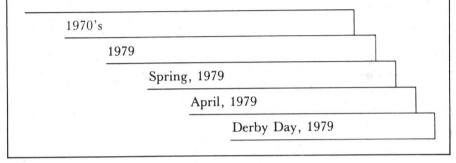

1970's

1979

Spring, 1979

April, 1979

Derby Day, 1979

A third method of analyzing the relationship of terms can get more complicated, since it does not refer to the tangible dimensions of space and time. It employs, rather, classification by logical category or topic and should be based on a consistent principle of analysis. The use of such a principle is illustrated in the following staircase. The term *creature* sets up our broadest category, highest on the staircase of abstractions. The term *animal* is a step lower, a subdivision. For an animal is one kind of a creature. The principle of analysis here, then, is *one kind.* A *horse* is one kind of animal, a *race horse* one kind of horse, Seattle Slew one specific race horse.

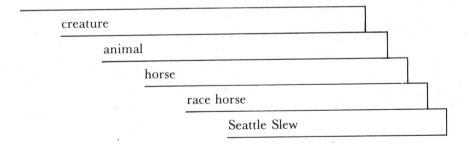

creature

animal

horse

race horse

Seattle Slew

★   Here is a harder group of terms; place them on the staircase of abstractions: *elected official, public servant, senator, member of Congress, junior senator from New York.*

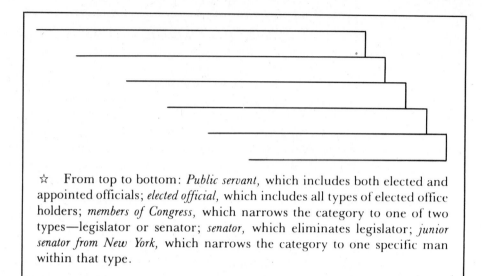

☆　　From top to bottom: *Public servant,* which includes both elected and appointed officials; *elected official,* which includes all types of elected office holders; *members of Congress,* which narrows the category to one of two types—legislator or senator; *senator,* which eliminates legislator; *junior senator from New York,* which narrows the category to one specific man within that type.

In addition to seeing these relationships between words and categories, it is also important to see when there is no relationship—that is, when one term is not a logical part of a sequence of abstraction. It is not a logical part if it is not based on the same principle of analysis as the rest of the sequence or does not take into account a modifying qualification added to a preceding term. For example, take this sentence: *public servant, elected official, policeman.* While a policeman is a public servant, he is not an elected official and so the sequence does not go in a straight line. The third term does not logically carry out the principle of analysis set by the second term.

★　　Is this a logical sequence of abstraction? _____

The American male, conformity of the American male, study habits of athletes.

☆　　No. The third term does not carry out the sequence determined by the qualification of *conformity* in the second term; it skips aside to a completely different way of qualifying the original term of American male. Here is another example of this same kind of skip or shift of logic: *Popular music, rock and roll programs on television, the problem of television rating systems.* Here the third term does pick up one element of the second (television) but it shifts completely away from the basic term *popular music.*

A third aspect of this logical process of reducing the level of abstraction is also important in writing. That is the recognition of terms that are equal, terms that are on the *same* level of the staircase of abstractions. Thus, in this group of terms—*mass media, television, radio*—the last two terms are equal subdivisions of the first. Neither is a subclassification of the other; both are subclassifications of the first term. Notice the contrast in this sequence: *mass media, television, rock and roll programs.* In this latter sequence there are no equal terms; the last is a subdivision, lower on the staircase of abstractions than the second.

★ Are any of the terms in this sequence equal, that is, on the same level of the staircase of abstractions? _____

Conformity in the American male, hair styles, musical tastes.

☆ Yes, the last two terms are equal subdivisions of the first; they represent two kinds of conformity in the American male.

These three aspects of reducing abstractions are central to the problem of writing effective papers: (1) You must recognize, use, and reduce the levels of abstraction. (2) You must be sure the sequence of terms you develop is, in fact, moving in a straight line, is a logical sequence. (3) You must recognize, use, and clearly indicate terms in the sequence that are equal subdivisions of some other term. These three aspects apply to all phases of the writing process, but they must first be applied to the process of limiting the subject of your paper.

Limiting Subjects

Limiting your subject is one application of this process of reducing abstraction. You should choose a subject within the broader subject assigned that is as limited, as concrete, as low on the staircase of abstractions as possible. It should avoid any illogical shift of thinking. It should clearly indicate any equal subdivisions of the initial subject. Don't be afraid that too limited a subject will not leave you enough to say. It works the other way. The more concrete and graspable your subject, the more you will be able to say about it, and the better you will be able to say it. You will be able to write a better essay on the limited subject of *a member of the Black Muslims speaking on campus* than on the broad, general subject of *dissent in a democracy*.

★ Which is the most limited subject? _____

A. Culture
B. American culture
C. American culture today
D. Changes in American culture today
E. Changes in American culture today that are produced by the mass media.

☆ E. Each item, in turn, reduces the level of abstraction of the subject. B narrows it in space, C narrows it in time. D further narrows and limits it to the category of *change*, E to *change produced by a specific means*. This narrowing and limiting process must be kept logical.

★ Which of the following is not a proper logical limiting of the general subject of pollution? _____

A. Smog

B. Three kinds of pollution

C. The dangers of scientific progress

☆   C. For it represents a skip of logic. This time it is a skip to an even broader generalization than the original subject. For pollution would actually be a limited subject derived from it; A and B do move in the proper limiting direction.

As it turns out, there are certain definable logical activities involved in properly limiting a subject. It will be helpful to describe several of these, even though you will not necessarily decide ahead of time to apply, say, method number three when you are thinking through your subject.

1. Modifying

One of the logical activities most frequently employed in reducing the level of abstraction of a subject is modifying. In the example above, when we added *today* to the subject *American culture* we used a single-word modifier to help reduce and limit the subject. A modifier adds a qualification, a restricting change. It eliminates the areas of the subject that lie outside that defined by the modifier: boy to fat boy, woman to tall woman, tall woman to tall, poised woman. In the same way, a group of words, a phrase, can restrict or further restrict the meaning: tall, fat boy to tall, fat boy in the window; conformity to conformity in the American male; students to students studying for finals. Thus, tall woman is lower on the staircase, refers to more limited, restricted category than woman.

★   Place the two terms on the proper steps of the staircase: *students studying for finals, students.*

☆

       students

         students studying for finals

The phrase *studying for finals* modifies the original term to produce the lower level of abstraction.

★ Underline the phrase that modifies the initial subject *progress:* the surprising progress in mental health.

☆ *In mental health.* This phrase restricts the discussion of progress to one specific subdivision. The word *surprising* is also an important modifier that will do a great deal to set the terms of the discussion, but it is not a phrase.

Full clauses also serve as modifiers of subjects. A clause is a group of words that includes a subject and verb. Thus, in E of the example above, the clause
s   v
that are produced by the mass media adds the last and most important modification to the original subject *American culture.*

★ Which statement about the subject *athletes* includes the most modification? _____

A. Athletes today
B. College athletes today

                                        s   v
C. College athletes today *who receive scholarships*

☆ C. Here a clause introduces the most important limited aspect of the subject. It is this clause that gives you something you can hang onto and write about.

Sometimes modifying involves a shift of emphasis, but this should not be confused with a faulty shift of logic. When you shift emphasis, your original subject becomes the grammatical modifier, but you are still focusing on that same subject. Thus, the change from *American culture* to changes <u>in American culture</u> does produce a new emphasis on changes, but it does not wander or leap from the original subject of American culture. We are still reducing that general subject to one of its aspects. The same is true for this shift: *conformity* to <u>the reasons for conformity</u>. But this is different from shifting from *American culture* to changes <u>in the culture of London</u> or from *safe driving* to the dangers <u>of riding in airplanes.</u>

2. Substituting or subdividing

Sometimes, however, the original term—such as *culture*—is dropped. Instead of modifying it, and thus still including it—as in *American culture* (with *American* as the modifier)—you substitute for it. That is, you replace it with a more concrete term that is one of its logical subdivisions: *television* replaces *American culture, smog* replaces *dangers of scientific progress.*

★   Place the two terms on the proper steps of the staircase: *smog, dangers of scientific progress*

_____

_____

☆   _____

dangers of scientific progress

smog

Substituting one type of danger reduces the level of discussion to a lower step on the staircase of abstraction, makes the discussion more concrete.

★   Which is a logical and limiting substitution for the general subject *college athletics?* _____

A. The proper role of football in college life
B. Mis-emphasis in college education today

☆   A. In A the logical subdivision *football* is substituted as a logical step in reducing the level of abstraction. Note also that modification and shift in emphasis also are logically applied. In B, however, a kind of free association has occurred in which we have moved from *college athletics* to an even broader subject.

★   Place these three versions of a subject in the proper levels on the staircase of abstractions: *the choice of a career, why I chose marine biology, a career.*

_____

_____

_____

☆   From top to bottom: *a career, the choice of a career, why I chose marine biology.* The last is the most limited subject. It substitutes a specific career for the more general term; it also modifies the original subject with the idea of a *choice.* It also adds an appropriate element: in this case *the writer, I.*

3. Adding

Adding an appropriate and logical element is another frequent method of limiting the subject; it can be applied at any stage of the process.

In the last example above, adding the further element of personal experience occurs at the same time that *marine biology* has been substituted for the general term *career*. Even though it is not a literal subdivision of the original term *career,* it is an appropriate addition because it supplies a valid and logical way of looking at and discussing the original subject.

Another kind of addition can be made after the level of abstraction is first reduced: an equal term can be added to the lower level. Take the general subject of *differences between the generations.* If this were first reduced to *the language gap between college freshmen and their parents,* a substitution would have taken place. At this lower level of abstraction, a parallel term can then be added to *parents,* changing the last part of the subject to *their parents and their teachers.*

Addition can also work another way—by introducing a comparison. If *American cars* were substituted for the general subject *automobiles,* the addition of *foreign cars* might be a further helpful step: American cars and foreign cars. This would suggest a *comparison* and lead to a further modification of the subject to the differences between American cars and foreign cars.

In a similar manner, a modifying element might be doubled by an addition. If *student jobs* were reduced to jobs after school, you might further add jobs before school as well. If *student tensions* were limited to the causes of student tensions, you might then change that to the causes and effects of student tensions.

★ Place these three terms in the proper steps on the staircase: *student jobs, jobs after school, jobs before school.*

☆

    student jobs
        jobs after school
        jobs before school

The last two terms, of course, could be reversed, since as the diagram indicates, they are both at the same level of abstraction. They would be two equal subdivisions for making more limited the discussion of the more abstract term *student jobs.*

★ In review, which of the following is not a logical limiting of the original subject of *student apathy?* _____

A. Student apathy in the classroom
B. The failure of the Young Democrats and Young Republicans
C. The administration's handling of the student political demonstration

☆ While C is a more limited subject, and lower on the staircase of abstractions, it is not a logical substitution for the term *student apathy.* It is a different subject, not a subdivision. B does not make a substitution of a logical subdivision and also doubles the subdivision into two equal components. A adds a modifier that appropriately limits the subject in a different direction than politics.

WRITING ASSIGNMENTS

1. Limit the following statements and general subjects by modifying, substituting, and/or adding.

Athletes are often criticized.	Heroism
Teenagers marry early.	Growing Up
Education is necessary.	Success
Laws should be changed.	The Place for Me
Roads cause accidents.	School Dances

2. Write an essay based on one of your limited subjects.
3. Limit the subject even further and write a single, well-developed paragraph.

Exercises

3a   **A.** On the line below place the letter of the item or the sequence of letters that best answers the question.

1. Which of the following is the most abstract? That is, which is at the highest step on the staircase of abstractions?

a. biologist   c. scholar
b. scientist   d. Dr. Kaplan

(1) _____

2. Which of the following is the most concrete—on the lowest step on the staircase of abstractions?

a. fuel   c. food
b. vegetable   d. carrot

(2) _____

3. Which of the following is the most abstract—on the highest step on the staircase of abstractions?

a. all-night grocery   c. Adolph's Foods
b. business   d. market

(3) _____

4. Arrange these items on a staircase of abstractions, starting with the most abstract.

a. 1964   c. twentieth century
b. 1960s   d. December 3, 1964

(4) _____

5. Arrange these items on a staircase of abstractions, starting with the most abstract.

a. Eastern Hemisphere   c. Japan
b. Hiroshima   d. Asia

(5) _____

6. Arrange these items on a staircase of abstractions, starting with the most abstract.

a. American novel   c. novel
b. literature   d. *The Great Gatsby*

(6) _____

7. If any of these items are equal—that is, on the same step on the staircase of abstractions—identify them; if none, state *none*.

a. living room   c. furniture
b. lamp   d. table

(7) _____

8. Which items are equal—on the same step on the staircase of abstractions?

a. painter   c. Van Gogh
b. artist   d. Cezanne

(8) _____

9. Which item is not a logical part of a sequence of abstraction?

a. art   c. painting
b. gallery management   d. German Expressionism

(9) _____

10. Which item is not a logical part of an equal set of items for the classification *college life?*

a. dances   c. elections
b. botany   d. sororities

(10) _____

B. On the line below place the letter of the item that best answers the question.
   1. Which is the most limited subject based on the general subject *drag racing?*
      a. Starting a drag racing club
      b. Drag racing in America
      c. Drag racing among American teenagers
      d. Dangers in drag racing

(1) _____

2. Which is the most limited subject based on the general subject *popular entertainment?*
   a. Trends in popular entertainment
   b. Popular entertainment and inflation
   c. Changes in popular entertainment
   d. Influences of rock music stars

(2) _____

3. Which item is not a logical limiting of the general subject *drag racing?*
   a. Starting a drag racing club
   b. The dangers of drag racing
   c. Increased gas prices
   d. Cooperation between drag racers and policemen.

(3) _____

4. Which item is not a logical limiting of the general subject *campus parking?*
   a. Unfair parking privileges
   b. Changes in parking areas
   c. Parking structures vs. parking lots

   d. Impolite campus policemen

   (4) _____

5. Which of the following limits the general subject *free speech in college* by modifying?
   a. Obscenity in campus productions
   b. Sale of *Playboy* in the bookstore
   c. Free speech in colleges with religious affiliations
   d. Free speech in America today

   (5) _____

6. Which of the following limits the general subject *highway safety* by substituting?
   a. The need for highway safety
   b. The highway patrol and highway safety
   c. Influences on highway safety
   d. The effects of the 55-MPH speed limit

   (6) _____

7. Which of the following limits the general subject *popular music* by adding?
   a. Imagination in popular lyrics
   b. The relation of Indian music and popular music
   c. The influence of Stevie Wonder
   d. Rhythm in popular music

   (7) _____

8. Which modifies the general subject *movies* with a phrase modifier?
   a. Movies that I have liked
   b. Why I liked *Star Wars*
   c. Art movies
   d. Movies with a message

   (8) _____

9. Which is not a logical substitution, or subdivision, for the general subject *new fashions?*
   a. The new look in men's shirts
   b. The trouble with sandals
   c. The artistry of fashion magazine advertisements
   d. The uses of Indian jewelry

   (9) _____

3b   Supply the material requested by each question. Place it in the spaces provided.

   1. Place the following terms in the appropriate steps on the staircase of abstractions: *weapons, atomic bombs, military supplies, modern weapons, atomic weapons.*

2. Complete the staircase by limiting the given terms with a sequence of three more terms that move down the steps of abstraction.

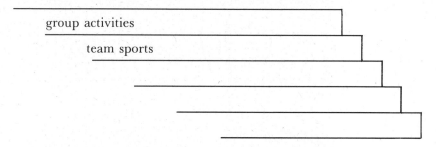

group activities

team sports

3. Complete this variation on the staircase by supplying three equal subdivisions for the given term.

exercise

4. Fill in this staircase by providing an abstract term and a logical sequence of four more terms that move down the steps of abstraction.

5. Limit the general subject *hiking* in two ways: (a) by adding a modifying phrase or clause, (b) by changing the emphasis and making *hiking* part of a modifier of another term.

a. _____

b. _____

6. Provide two limited subjects for the general subject *hobbies* by substituting logical subdivisions.

a. _____

b. _____

7. Provide three logical limited subjects for the general subject *pollution*, using any methods.

a. _____

b. _____

c. _____

chapter 4

The Thesis Statement

The revolution in clothing styles in America today is a limited subject, but it is not a thesis statement that can control and produce the development of a paper. A limited subject needs a comment about itself. A limited subject *and* the comment made *about* it produce a *thesis statement* that can set the exact terms for a paper.

We may call the comment about the limited subject an assertion, a claim, or a proposition. Whatever we call it, we have to first recognize the difference between a subject and a comment about a subject.

★ Which of the following include comments about a subject? _____

A. The trouble with summer in New York
B. Summer in New York can drain all of your energy.
C. The popular sport of baseball
D. Baseball deserves to be called our national pastime.

☆ B and D. They state a subject (which is also the grammatical subject of the sentence) and then go on to make some definite point about that subject. A comment about a subject also lowers the level of abstraction; it advances the discussion to a lower step on the staircase of abstractions.

The exact way in which the subject is made more concrete by the thesis comment determines and controls the direction the rest of the discussion will take.

Note these variations in the comment made about the subject *the revolution in clothing styles in America today*. Each will call for a different development and produce a different paper.

> The revolution in clothing styles in America today can be seen at all age levels.
>
> The revolution in clothing styles in America today has created a new kind of conformity.
>
> The impact of the mass media has produced the revolution in clothing styles in America today.

In the first, the emphasis is on the nature of the revolution—its characteristics in all aspects of our lives. The second emphasizes instead a harmful result of that revolution, and the third emphasizes the causes of that revolution.

Refining Thesis Statements

A limited subject improves the prospects for an effective paper; a sharply defined thesis statement further enhances those prospects. The more sharply defined and refined the thesis statement, the more clearly and logically developed the paper. The methods for achieving this sharp edge in the comment again involve the process of reducing abstraction. We'll first review that process.

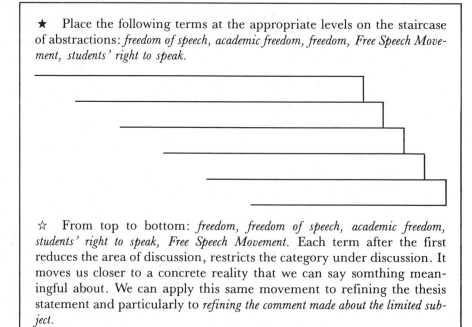

★ Place the following terms at the appropriate levels on the staircase of abstractions: *freedom of speech, academic freedom, freedom, Free Speech Movement, students' right to speak.*

☆ From top to bottom: *freedom, freedom of speech, academic freedom, students' right to speak, Free Speech Movement.* Each term after the first reduces the area of discussion, restricts the category under discussion. It moves us closer to a concrete reality that we can say somthing meaningful about. We can apply this same movement to refining the thesis statement and particularly to *refining the comment made about the limited subject.*

1. Modifying

One of the common methods of refining the comment made about the subject is to further qualify and modify the original terms. This is the same kind of modification used in limiting the subject.

★   Which thesis statement will best control the development and organization of a paper? _____

A. There are many reasons for choosing a career in marine biology.
B. I chose marine biology for reasons that are both personal and social, practical and idealistic.

☆   B. The clause after *reasons* is a modifier that sets more specific, concrete terms for the discussion of the subject than does the vague modifier *many*. Note how the same process works in these two examples:
A. Ministers in small towns must adjust to their communities.
B. Ministers in small towns must adjust *to the values of their provincial communities.*

★   Which of the above statements is at a lower step on the staircase of abstractions, A or B? _____

☆   B. The italicized words in B restrict more effectively the direction of the discussion, bring it to a lower level of abstraction. The two key terms in refining the comment—*values* and *provincial*—have been introduced through modifiers.

---

2. Substituting or subdividing

This method involves substituting more concrete terms for the original terms of the comment, providing subdivisions that are lower on the staircase of abstractions. The process is the same as limiting the subject by substituting a more concrete term: *college athletes* to *football players*.

★   Place these two items on the proper steps on the staircase: *psychological situation, hostility.*

☆ _____

| psychological situation |
| hostility |

Since *hostility* is one kind of psychological situation, it is a more concrete term and would be a substitution that refines a comment about a thesis to a lower level of abstraction, as in these two statements:

Charlie Chaplin's comedy *involves an interesting psychological situation.*
Charlie Chaplin's comedy *is often based on hostility.*

The second statement produces a more directive, controlling thesis statement.

★   Which comment on the subject *Early American literature* makes the more concrete substitution for the comment *had its roots in nonliterary areas of life?* _____

A. had its roots in religion and political science.
B. was a direct reflection of Calvinism and the theories of John Locke.

☆   B. In B the substitution specifically names the two subdivisions of the original terms that will form the basis of the discussion.

In the next examples the substitution is more subtle:

> Ministers in small towns must *adjust* to the values of the provincial community.
> Ministers in small towns must *appear to conform* to the values of the provincial community.

In the latter example, the substitution suggests that the ministers do not necessarily give up their views, but act strategically so that they can fulfill their functions and eventually influence the community. This sentence will produce a different, more interesting paper.

3. Adding

Adding an appropriate and equal logical element can be as helpful in refining the thesis statement as it was in limiting the subject.

> A shift to the quarter system produces academic problems for the student.
> A shift to the quarter system produces *personal, financial,* and academic problems for the student.

In the second example the two new terms are equal and appropriate additions. This next variation would also be logical, although based on a different analysis of the situation:

A shift to the quarter system produces academic problems for the student, organizational problems for the teacher, and administrative problems for the school officials.

★ Does item B produce a logical addition to the comment of A? _____

A. Protest marches illuminate the central issues of freedom of speech.
B. Protest marches illuminate the central issues of freedom of speech and *leave a great deal of debris for the sanitation department.*

☆ No. The additional term is not the same type of problem as the first term and will produce an irrelevant subdivision in the development of the paper.

---

4. Specifying or enumerating

It is sometimes helpful to state in your comment the exact subdivisions that the subject will be broken into. Thus, rather than

Scientific advancements have led to an increase in pollution.

you can specify the kinds of pollution:

Scientific advancements have led to an increase in the pollution of our air, our water, and our food.

★ Place the two terms on the proper steps of the staircase: *increase in pollution, increase in the pollution of our air, our water, and our food.*

☆

increase in pollution

increase in the pollution
of our air, our water, and our food.

The enumeration of the three kinds of pollution refines the thesis statement to a lower level of abstraction. It also helps by setting out the organization of the material that is to follow.

Similarly, the thesis sentence used above can be expanded to include the specifications *social* and *moral:*

Ministers in small towns must appear to conform to the *social* and *moral* values of the provincial community.

A comparison of this statement with the version we started with earlier (see p. 62) provides a good illustration of how a refinement of the thesis statement can produce a controlling direction for your paper.

The Key Terms of the Thesis Statement

However you arrive at the construction of your thesis statement, you must be aware of its key terms. You must recognize the important words that are going to shape and control your paper. You must understand the way in which those words determine the logical relationships between the parts of your paper.

For one thing, there is a matter of emphasis. The statement

Father's installing of the aquarium upset the entire family.

creates a different emphasis from

The new fish aquarium upset the entire family.

In the first, the stress is on the time and actions of the installation. In the second, the stress is on the aquarium itself.

Whatever the emphasis, the number of key terms is also important. This number sets the number of subdivisions you are committing yourself to deal with. In developing the second sentence above, you will have to be sure to explain three topics: the nature of the aquarium itself, the manner of the upsetting, and the effects produced on all the members of the family.

> ★   In this thesis statement, how many key terms will have to be dealt with? _____
> Television both limits and strengthens the imaginations of children.
>
> ☆   Five. The first is the subject *television*, which will have to be more specifically defined. The second and third are the two things it does: *limits, strengthens*. The fourth is the particular aspect, *imagination*, that is affected. The fifth is the *children*, the particular group to be discussed.

You should notice, further, that sometimes the most important words are not necessarily subjects and verbs. They may be modifiers, such as adjectives:

The new fish aquarium upset the *entire* family.

In this sentence the word *entire* commits you to discussing each of the members of the family in turn; you cannot focus on one or two members and leave out the rest.

The arrangement of the words of your thesis statement also determines the rest of your discussion, for the kind of sentence you write for your thesis statement determines the kind of organization you are committing yourself to follow. If your thesis sets up a three-part specification, you will have to hold to it. If your thesis sets up a comparison—*Foreign cars are more practical than American cars*—you will have to follow through with the comparison. If your it sets up a cause-and-effect relationship, cause and effect it will have to be.

★   Which of the following sets up a cause-and-effect relationship? ____

A. Many successful recording stars use dubbing, echo chambers, and filters.
B. Because of dubbing, echo chambers, and filtering, many recording stars have become very successful.

☆   **B.** Here the word *Because* sets up the cause and effect emphasis, but you should keep in mind that the same relationship can often be suggested without the actual use of this word.

Here are three variations on the same general idea; note how the construction of each sentence produces a different emphasis and sets up a different relationship between the parts of the essay.

Television programming lacks imagination and intellectual stimulus.

The rating systems have destroyed the possibilities of imagination and intellectual stimulus in television programming.

Because they promote an emphasis on a mass audience, the rating systems have destroyed the possibilities of imagination and intellectual stimulus in television programming.

To review the importance of the key terms of the thesis statement, we can analyze this example, written by H. L. Mencken:

The capital defect in the culture of These States is the lack of a civilized aristocracy—secure in its position, animated by an intelligent curiosity, skeptical of all facile generalizations, superior to the sentimentality of the mob, and delighting in the battle of ideas for its own sake.

★   Place these items on the proper steps of the staircase: *culture of These States, defect in the culture of These States.*

☆

culture of These States

defect in the culture of These States

The term *defect* lowers the level of abstraction. This key term not only lowers the level of abstraction, but sets up the basic critical position Mencken is going to take. The position, in turn, is to be based on the term *lack,* which he will go on to explain. Important in the exact definition of this lack is the modifier *civilized;* his definition of this term will be crucial in explaining the kind of aristocracy he is talking about. His sentence continues by specifying the subdivisions he is going to employ in his discussion.

> ★   How many subdivisions does Mencken commit himself to? _____
>
> ☆   Five. Each phrase after the dash emphasizes a different aspect of his subject.

Types of Thesis Statements and Types of Essays

We have pointed out that the form of your thesis statement helps determine the type of development you will follow in your essay. Here we will define five of the most common types of thesis statements and show the type of essay that each will produce.

1. Objective report

This kind of impersonal, generally agreed-upon thesis statement can be a description of a process:

> To start a sluggish power mower, three simple steps can be taken.

or a report of what someone else has said or written:

> Richard Nixon advocated a four-step approach to reducing Federal expenditures.

or a definition of a term or concept:

> Pornography is obscene or licentious writing or printing.

Whatever the exact purpose, this type of thesis statement will call for an objective tone and approach and produce an expository essay.

2. Personal "is" thesis statements

This type of thesis makes a more personal comment on a central quality or characteristic of a subject. But it is a comment that can vary from mild, generally agreed-upon terms to more subjective, judging, opinionated terms. Thus,

> Water-skiing is a strenuous activity that demands endurance and coordination.

'll produce a relatively objective expository essay, since *strenuous, endurance,* and *coordination* are not controversial or debatable terms. But

> Students for a Democratic Society is a threat to the security of the nation.

involves a more personal judgment and will lead to an essay of argument, for *threat to the security* is a controversial and debatable phrase.

★   Which of these makes a stronger personal judgment? _____

A. Current television does not demand a great deal of intellectual effort on the part of the audience.
B. Current television is a vicious threat to the intellectual growth of the nation.

☆   B. B takes an argumentative stance and will call for a more forceful, even emotional, approach and tone in the development of the essay. Notice also that in A the verb *is* does not actually appear, for a shortcut has been taken instead of saying *current television is a form of entertainment that does not demand . . .*

Certain forms of "is" statements can also lead to description or narration:

★   Which leads to narration? _____

A. The condition of his room is evidence of his rebellious state.
B. My first three weeks at State University made me aware that college students are not merely numbers on IBM cards.

☆   B. A calls for a description, while B calls for a summary of the events that produced the recognition of the "is" statement. B involves a double thesis statement. It has an "is" statement, but that statement is preceded by a cause-and-effect statement. This blending of types is a frequent occurrence.

---

3. Causal thesis statements

This type of thesis involves a linking of causes and their effects. It can stress both aspects equally or one more than the other. It can involve a varying number of causes or effects. It can include the words *cause* or *effect,* or some variation, like *because,* or it can merely imply their meaning with other words.

★   Do both of these thesis statements set up a cause-and-effect relationship? _____

A. The new student parking regulations have actually doubled the problems of commuting students.

B. Because they promote the emphasis on a mass audience, the rating systems
   have destroyed the possibilities of imagination and intellectual stimulus in
   television programming.

☆   Yes. The verb *have doubled* in A implies *have caused a doubling*. Incidentally, there are two cause-and-effect links in B. Besides the one
created by the word *because,* the verb *destroyed* implies *have caused the
destruction.*

Causal statements commit you to emphasizing the logical relationship of
causes and effects in your development. They can lead to exposition or argument, depending on how forceful or debatable your terms are.

4. "Should be" thesis statements

This type of statement usually calls for an argument, although it can vary in
tone and approach. Compare:

The student parking problem should be remedied by administrative action.
The President had better get one of his assistants to do something about the chaos of
   student parking or there will be an open rebellion.

Whatever the difference in tone, these statements advocate a future course of
action: what should be done or what should not be done. Your paper should
carry out this emphasis.

5. Comparison thesis statements

This type of statement sets up a similarity (comparison) or difference (contrast) between two terms of the subject. This basic comparison or contrast
should be stated in terms that are as specific and concrete as possible.

★   Which is the better contrast thesis statement? _____

A. The American pioneers and Americans today differ greatly.
B. The American pioneers and Americans today differ in their sense of personal
   worth and initiative.

☆   B. It sets up the pattern that item one differs from item two in terms
of subitems a and b. Specifying terms at a lower level of abstraction will
control the development of the essay more effectively and logically. The
following example makes the same kind of contrast—without the word
differ, but with the same specifying of the concrete terms of difference:
*TV good guys are handsomer, better groomed, and quicker on the draw than TV bad
guys.*

Comparisons and contrasts can be developed into essays of any of the four major types, as long as the emphasis on the logical relating of one item to another is maintained throughout.

WRITING ASSIGNMENTS

1. Here are five general subjects. Limit each and write a refined, concrete thesis statement that could serve as the controlling idea for a 300- to 500-word essay.

   politics
   advertising
   conformity
   civil rights
   recreation

2. Use one of the thesis statements to write an essay.

Exercises

4a   On the line below place the letter of the item or letters required that best answer the question.

A. 1. Arrange these items on a staircase of abstractions, starting with the most abstract.
     a. Freedom of speech
     b. Citizen's right to speak
     c. Freedom
     d. Student's right to speak

                                            (1) _____

2. Which of the following include both a subject and a comment about a subject?
     a. Superstar major league baseball players
     b. Superstar major league baseball players receive enormous salaries.
     c. The hitting strength of the Los Angeles Dodgers.
     d. The hitting strength of the Los Angeles Dodgers makes them pennant contenders.

                                            (2) _____

3. In which of the following does the comment about the subject include a modifying phrase?
     a. The manager of the team should be fired.
     b. The school grounds should be lighted at night.
     c. The tree in the yard is the most beautiful.
     d. The high cost of services is outrageous.

                                            (3) _____

4. Which comment employs the most concrete terms?
     a. My major reason for attending college is a good one.
     b. My reasons for attending college are both selfish and patriotic.
     c. My reasons for attending college are interesting.
     d. My reasons for attending college are clear.

                                            (4) _____

5. In which has the statement of *a* been refined by substitutions of more concrete subdivisions in both the subject and comment?
     a. Heroes want their rewards.
     b. Football stars want their rewards.
     c. Heroes want praise from their countrymen.
     d. Football stars want the admiration of coeds.

                                            (5) _____

6. In which has the statement of *a* been refined by adding to the comment?
     a. You can save money by being careful.
     b. You can save money be being careful and limiting your desires.

   c. You can save money by being careful while shopping.

   d. You can save money and time by being careful.

(6) _____

7. In which has the statement of *a* been refined by enumerating in the comment the subdivisions of the paper?

   a. Our system of electing a President should be improved..

   b. Our system of electing a President and congressmen should be improved.

   c. Our system of electing a President should be drastically revamped.

   d. Our system of electing a President should be improved by eliminating the electoral system and changing the voting day to Sunday.

(7) _____

8. Which is the most effective thesis statement?

   a. A poll of college students reveals criticisms of registration procedures.

   b. Student polls reveal their points of view.

   c. Student polls reveal their attitudes toward registration.

   d. A nationwide poll of college freshmen points out three weaknesses of present registration procedures.

(8) _____

B. **1.** Which thesis statement has the more active verb, one that will give a stronger thrust to a paper?

   a. TV ratings systems are unfair.

   b. TV rating systems produce repetitious programming.

(1) _____

2. Which thesis sentence has better emphasis?

   a. The new set has both good and bad features.

   b. The expensive maintenance of the new set far outweighs its good features.

(2) _____

3. Which thesis sentence has four key terms that must be dealt with?

   a. The spirit of the season is marred by the excesses of business.

   b. The spirit of the season is marred by the excesses of business and labor.

(3) _____

4. Which thesis statement is an objective report?

   a. Senator Blat advocates three methods for dissolving TVA.

   b. Senator Blat's three-point plan for dissolving TVA will bankrupt the farmers.

(4) _____

5. Which thesis is a causal statement?

   a. Current movies are an affront to morality.

b. Current movies have changed our attitudes.

(5) _____

6. Which thesis is a "should be" statement?
   a. The Dean's new policy had better not be applied to traditional student activities.
   b. The Dean's new policy will interfere with traditional student activities.

(6) _____

7. Which thesis is a comparison statement?
   a. Guitars allow for more inventiveness than trumpets.
   b. Guitars allow performers to use their inventiveness.

(7) _____

8. Which thesis has a sharper argumentative edge?
   a. A college education is the key to a good job.
   b. Go to college or get nowhere fast—that's the fact of life.

(8) _____

4b   Supply the material requested by each question. Place it in the spaces provided.

1. Sharpen this thesis statement by (a) adding a modifier to the comment and (b) adding a modifier to the subject.
   Pets can be a problem.

   a. _____

   b. _____

2. Sharpen this thesis statement by (a) substituting a more concrete subdivision in the comment and (b) substituting a more concrete subdivision in the subject.
   Exercise produces valuable results.

   a. _____

   b. _____

3. Sharpen the thesis statement by making both the subject and the comment more concrete.
   Public transportation needs improving.

   _____

   _____

4. Write a thesis that is an objective report.

   _____

   _____

5. Write a thesis that is a personal "is" statement (a) in mild, objective terms and (b) in stronger, argumentative terms.

a. _____

_____

b. _____

_____

6. Write a thesis that is a causal statement (a) in mild, objective terms and (b) in stronger, argumentative terms.

a. _____

_____

b. _____

_____

7. Write a thesis that is a comparison statement based on the contrast of differences.

_____

_____

chapter 5

Order: Basic Patterns

No matter what type of thesis statement you write or how much evidence you use to support it, you have to put all of it in order. As early as the fourth century *B.C.,* Aristotle, a Greek philosopher, said about plays, ''A whole is that which has a beginning, a middle, and an end.'' So too a ''whole'' essay must have a beginning, middle, and an end. These three parts we call the introduction, the body, and the conclusion.

The Three Parts

Introduction

The introductory paragraph(s) for the short paper—the type you are likely to write in this class—does three jobs: (1) It interests the reader. (2) It makes clear the thesis—both subject and comment. (3) It often states or implies the order of the paper.

An introduction generally has three or four sentences. The first makes clear the broad subject and tries to interest the reader. It puts the writer and the reader on common ground. The second is more specific. It narrows the broad topic and forms a bridge, a link, between the general topic and the thesis. The third sentence, often the last one, is the thesis. If it is a good one, the thesis makes clear the restricted subject and comment. Sometimes the introduction makes clear the order the paper will follow, often in a list of the main points. Sometimes this order will appear in the thesis statement itself; sometimes it will be in a fourth sentence written especially to make the order clear. The fourth sentence of paragraph one of this chapter is such a sentence. The thesis often appears in the introduction with its three parts clearly identified: the subject, the comment, and the order.

Body

The body of the short essay carries out the plan set up in the introduction. For one thing, it develops the thesis statement with such things as figures, facts, examples, illustrations, definitions, comparisons, contrasts, causes, or effects. Next, the evidence is arranged chronologically, spatially, or logically. When put in logical order, the evidence may be climactically arranged, the main point last, the next most important first, the other points grouped in the middle. In the second half of the chapter we will discuss organizing the body more fully.

Conclusion

The conclusion of the short essay does three things: (1) It reaffirms the thesis of the paper, either directly or indirectly. (2) It reaches a climax of interest. (3) It makes the paper sound finished. Like most introductions, conclusions are general. They return readers to the higher level on the staircase of abstractions that they started from in the introduction and thus round off the essay.

A note of warning is needed here. Writers should be sure to conclude what they have written in their paper. They should not tack on a moral or suggest a change when the purpose is not to moralize or to call for a change.

This student essay and diagrams make clear the overall organization of the short essay.

From Mendel to Frogs—Laboratory Reality

[1]   Biology lab bothers me. My lack of affinity for the laboratory does not extend to the subject itself, although I will admit that learning the postures of copulating earthworms and discovering that starfish are a lot like man when we're both eggs do not raise my blood pressure or start my hands tingling. When we studied hormonal behavior and human heredity, however, I enjoyed the lectures and subconsciously approved the objectives of the course. But the blunt realities of the laboratory sessions were almost more than I could stand.

[2]   Just as I found myself mildly entranced by Mendel and his peas, I had my perspective altered by my first biology lab—a three-hour study of fresh and salt water microscopic animals. Although I count myself fairly sophisticated, a knowledgeable young lady who deals easily with reality, my awareness of the paramecium and the amoeba was strictly textbook. Captured on the pages of Milne and Milne in cartoon squiggles that hardly depict the animal's true form, always stationary and unbending, they had not seemed living inhabitants of my environment. They are, after all, invisible. I had never seen an amoeba prance across the kitchen table, and few paramecia are big enough to pet. Fortunately, I had overlooked their existence. After watching them stiffen and collapse, pirouette by flagella and scuffle with paddling cilia across a microscope slide, I now dread aquatic outings for fear an army of these minute creatures will lodge

under my fingernails, travel up my nasal passages or secrete themselves in the intimate folds of my bathing suit.

[3]   Successive weeks and subsequent labs continued to shake my sophistication. I listened to the sizzling sound of a Coca-Cola dissolving metal, and my mind reeled from the memory of a similar bubbling sensation when my esophagus had eagerly lapped up a murky carbonated liquid. After bravely separating a sizeable portion of a wormlike planaria from itself one Thursday, I returned the following week to discover the beast had found another tail and abdomen somewhere and attached it at the exact point of severance.

[4]   But the lab on spinal frogs destroyed my conventional outlook, my admittedly unfounded faith in an orderly, predictable nature. Testing the hypothesis that responses to pain, temperature, and pressure involve the nerve pathways in the brain, we destroyed with a probe a frog's mind and stimulated actual nerve endings exposed by dissection. Reflex action apparently does not involve the brain, and muscles continue to be stimulated in a mindless animal. I shall never forget my black-speckled lily pad-sitter, surgical pins dangling from his appendages in defiance of our previous efforts to affix him to the dissecting pan, hopping spastically across the lab table, dragging his entrails. Lungs and liver hung beneath him, suspended by webs of soft tissue. His footing was impaired by the sheath of skin covering his right front paw, skin we had peeled back in order to apply the stimuli directly to the nerves of the forearm. Neither textbook print nor the embarrassed insistence of my lab instructor could convince me that the mangled frog had felt no pain from the minute his gray matter was scrambled.

[5]   If God above sends men back to earth in forms determined by their behavior in past lives, I hope He's reasonable about biology and doesn't return me as a laboratory frog. As for this life, next semester I am looking forward to geology and labs all about dead, dull, lifeless, inert, inanimate rocks. Meanwhile, I've given up swimming and Cokes.

Three comments about this essay may help you plan and write your own essays:

1. The title of an essay should stress the main idea. The title "From Mendel to Frogs—Laboratory Reality" does that: It points out the change in attitude of the writer from a mild interest in Mendel and his peas to shock at the maimed frog. This final shock gave the writer her opening sentence: "Biology lab bothers me."

2. The essay has a thesis statement which makes clear the subject, the comment, and the order. To give the paper unity and coherence, the topic sentence of each paragraph of the body either states or implies its relationship to the thesis statement on all three counts.

3. The writer has arranged the parts climactically as well as chronologically. In the fourth paragraph, the last paragraph of the body, she has put her best evidence, a long example of her most shocking experiment in the lab. In the second paragraph she includes the next most important evidence, her first mildly unnerving but memorable experience. In the third paragraph she includes two examples, neither as important as the two already mentioned but both giving her thesis support. She could, of course, have used more than two examples had she wanted to do so.

The Organization of an Essay

The diagram below shows the framework of the student essay above. It makes clear the three basic parts, the thesis statement and supporting ideas (topic sentences), and the evidence supporting each idea. The diagram should help you see the outline, the skeleton of the paper.

Basic patterns for the body

Good introductions and conclusions are like bookends: they hold up the ideas and keep the evidence in order. Take away either bookend and the whole structure may fall. But bookends alone do not make order. Putting books at random between two bookends may keep a room neat, but it will only seem to be in order. So between the bookends we use a system. We group by author or by subject or by type.

So it is with the body of an essay. It follows a pattern. And once you choose a pattern, you must stick to it, though you may combine the patterns in any one essay. There are three main patterns for organizing the body: (1) Chronological Order, (2) Spatial Order, (3) Logical Order, or Analysis. A fourth kind of order, a secondary kind, is Climactic Order. This last kind writers apply to material they have analyzed logically and wish to arrange for dramatic effect.

Chronological order

One of the patterns most often used to organize the body of an essay is chronological (time) order. This arrangement begins with what happens first and ends with what happens last. Straight narration—in fiction, for instance —relies mainly on chronological order. You use this order in autobiographical essays, process themes, history reports, and case studies for psychology.
This paragraph by Martin Tolchin follows chronological order:

> Most new words are absorbed gradually into the language, but there are exceptions. An awesome example is the phrase "atomic bomb." When it crossed the desk of a Merriam-Webster editor back in 1917 (it had been clipped from a sentence in The Yale Review, which read, "When you can drop just one atomic bomb and wipe out Paris or Berlin, war will have become monstrous and impossible"), it drew the penciled comment: "Fanciful." During the Thirties, the phrases "atomic energy" and "atomic ray" warranted dictionary listing, but "atomic bomb" remained in the realm of the improbable. It was not until 1945 that it exploded into print, when the bomb itself was dropped on Hiroshima. (Martin Tolchin, "About New Words." ©1957 by The New York Times Company. Reprinted by permission.)

INTRODUCTION	Interest	**Attention-Getter**	paragraph 1

Interest

Attention-Getter
Biology lab bothers me.

Thesis

SUBJECT ——→ *. . . the blunt realities*

ORDER ——→ OF EACH LABORATORY SESSION

COMMENT ——→ **almost turned me against biology**

paragraph 1

Topic Sentence

COMMENT ——→ **I had my perspective altered**
BY MY FIRST BIOLOGY LAB—
a three-hour study of fresh and salt
ORDER
water microscopic animals.

SUBJECT
    Textbook awareness
        Milne and Milne
        Invisibility
    Real awareness
        Actions of animals
        Result of labs

paragraph 2

Topic Sentence

ORDER ——→ SUCCESSIVE WEEKS AND SUBSEQUENT LABS
[subject key implied, not stated]
continued to shake my sophistication.
SUBJECT

    Coca-Cola
        Sizzling on metal
        Sizzling in esophagus
    Wormlike planaria
COMMENT
        Separating tail and abdomen
        Finding new tail and abdomen

paragraph 3

Topic Sentence

ORDER ——→ *. . .* THE LAB
on spinal frogs
destroyed my conventional outlook, my
SUBJECT
admittedly unfounded faith in an orderly,
predictable nature.

COMMENT
    Testing hypothesis
        Destroyed brain
        Stimulated nerve endings
    Watching frog
        Hopping spastically
        Trailing lungs and liver
        Impairing foot by skin

paragraph 4

CONCLUSION

Thesis

Reaffimed indirectly by showing that labs have caused change of attitude.

CLIMAX — Reference to God and plan for next semester.

NOTE OF FINALITY — Anticlimactic last sentence emphasizes through understatement.

paragraph 5

BODY

INTRODUCTION

BODY

CONCLUSION

★   List the words and phrases that demonstrate the chronological order of the paragraph above.

_____

_____

☆   You should have listed the following words and phrases: "absorbed gradually," "When," "back in 1917," "During the Thirties," "until 1945."

Spatial order

Like chronological order, spatial order seems natural. When using spatial order, writers arrange things as they are related in space. They may go from left to right or right to left, from front to back or back to front, from east to west or west to east.

This passage from Rachel Carson uses spatial order:

> All over the world the seas rose. They covered most of the British Isles, except for scattered outcroppings of ancient rocks. In southern Europe only the old, rocky highlands stood above the sea, which intruded in long bays and gulfs even into the central highlands of the continent. The ocean moved into Africa and laid down deposits of sandstones; later weathering of these rocks provided the desert sands of the Sahara. From a drowned Sweden, an inland sea flowed across Russia, covered the Caspian Sea, and extended to the Himalayas. Parts of India were submerged, and of Australia, Japan, and Siberia. On the South American continent, the area where later the Andes were to rise was covered by sea. (From *The Sea Around Us* by Rachel L. Carson. Copyright 1950, 1951 by Rachel L. Carson. Reprinted by permission of Oxford University Press, Inc.)

★   Which type of spatial order does Rachel Carson use in the paragraph above? _____

A. East to west   B. West to east

☆   B. Although there is some north-to-south and south-to north movement, Miss Carson makes a west-to-east (perhaps closer to northwest-to southeast) trip almost around the world. She leaves the British Isles and moves relentlessly—but not directly—east: Southern Europe, Africa, Sweden, Russia, the Caspian Sea, the Himalayas, India, Australia, Japan, Siberia, and finally South America.

Logical order

Sometimes it is wise to analyze your subject, to organize it by breaking it up into its parts. We call this logical order, or analysis. If you wanted to write about your favorite kinds of reading, for example, you might divide the kinds of reading you do into types: poetry, short story, novel, drama, and essay. If you are writing about types of college students, you could divide them into classes: freshmen, sophomores, juniors, and seniors. Once you have logically equal parts, you can use them as headings under which you may classify or list relevant supporting details.

Logical order needs a clear and consistent *principle of anaylsis.* The college registrar, for instance, uses credit hours as the principle by which he sets up class divisions. The dean of men and dean of women, depending on what they want to do, might choose sex as a principle of analysis and thus divide the student body into male and female, or they might pick marital status and thus separate the students into married and unmarried. Once you choose a principle of analysis, stick to it. Such subdivisions as freshman, married, and male, for instance, would not make sense, for no common principle of analysis links them.

This paragraph from Bergen Evans's ''Grammar for Today'' illustrates logical order:

> As a matter of fact, the educated man uses at least three languages. With his family and his close friends, on the ordinary, unimportant occasions of daily life, he speaks, much of the time, a monosyllabic sort of shorthand. On more important occasions and when dealing with strangers in his official or business relations, he has a more formal speech, more complete, less allusive, politely qualified, wisely reserved. In addition he has some acquaintance with the literary speech of his language. He understands this when he reads it, and often enjoys it, but he hesitates to use it. In times of emotional stress hot fragments of it may come out of him like lava, and in times of feigned emotion, as when giving a commencement address, cold, greasy gobbets of it will ooze forth. (Bergen Evans, ''Grammar for Today,'' *The Atlantic Monthly,* March, 1960.)

★ What principle of analysis does Evans use? _____

A. Chronological Order

B. Levels of Grammar

C. Types of Language

☆ C. He points out three clearly defined types of language the educated man uses under sharply defined circumstances: (1) ''a monosyllabic sort of shorthand,'' (2) ''a more formal speech,'' and (3) ''the literary speech.'' There is no time order (A) involved in the paragraph, and although grammar may be related to the subject, it is not mentioned in the passage.

WRITING ASSIGNMENTS

1. Write a four-or-five paragraph essay on one of these topics:

Trial Marriage	Films I Detest
Types of Teachers	The Well-Designed Home

Sports Personalities   Two Kinds of Jobs
The Pains of Maturity   The Effects of Advertising
An Exciting Experience   Politicians Today
Art I Enjoy   Women's Liberation

Make sure your paper has an introduction, body, and conclusion and that
it uses an appropriate pattern of organization for its body.

2. Write a 150-175-word paragraph on one of the ideas below. Label the type
of organization you use.

College (classes, students) are (different from, the same as) those of high school.

Not all athletes have strong backs and weak minds.

College students may be divided into three (academic, social) types.

College students must learn to budget their (time, money) wisely.

The college bookstore is laid out to (confuse, help) the student buyer.

Bad television programs have three distinct effects on me.

Exercises

5a   **A.** The four paragraphs of ''Canine Crisis'' are out of order. In the blanks below number each paragraph as it would appear if the paper were organized properly by introduction, body, and conclusion.

Canine Crisis

Providing for the dog's needs is so expensive that the animal should be an income tax deduction. There's the medical bill for shots to keep the mongrel healthy. Unless it's kept in the house, a female must be given ''preventive maintenance,'' a ten-to twenty-dollar investment. Otherwise, before you know it, you'll have more canine deductions in your family. And dogs have to eat. Don't think you can buy a case of Ken-L-Ration and be done with it. A dog can be as particular about food as a French connoisseur. To feed even a Chihuahua, you'll spend three to five bucks a week. If you own a big mutt, you need a doghouse. They're expensive. A carpenter will build a deluxe model for about seventy-five dollars. For about thirty dollars' worth of materials, a weekend's work, and a smashed thumb, you can build a leaky, 5' × 4' × 4' plywood box yourself. And these are only the major costs. Only those who can afford mink can really afford a dog.

_____

For ages the word has been going around that the dog is man's best friend. I agree. A dog can be handy as a night watchman around the house, as a pointer and retriever on a hunting trip, as a guardian and playmate for the children. But I contend that having a dog for a pet is so expensive and annoying that I can do without such a friend.

_____

A dog is such a nuisance that no one in his right mind would want to own one. Consider the dog owner blessed with a dog that fetches—slippers, rubber toys, newspapers. Have you eased your bare feet into slippers fetched by a slobbering basset hound, seen a living room demolished by a toy-retrieving boxer, tried to read a newspaper chewed to wet confetti by an obedient Boston bull? And dogs make noise. Some mutts howl all night. But you aren't the only one to endure sleepless nights; your neighbors let you know they didn't sleep either. Cops are frequent visitors to dog owners' homes. They inquire about holes reported dug in neighbors' flower beds, prize cats maimed and bleeding, and pet chickens and ducks sent to their eternal reward. Suspect: your pooch! You deny everything, of course. Rex, you assure the officers, was asleep by the hearth. But you secretly suspect him, because you don't really know where Rex was all week. And you remember wondering why feathers were floating in his water bowl yesterday. Dogs are pests. Neither a fire-breathing mother-in-law nor a nagging spouse will prove more annoying to man than a dog.

_____

Dog lovers will, of course, claim my argument one-sided, even exaggerated. They might consider me as cruel as the Russians, who—possibly attempting to solve their own canine crisis—shot Fido into orbit. But the fact remains, if our

best friends caused us the expense and annoyance our dog does, we'd soon encourage them to become astronauts.

B. Using the diagram for "From Mendel to Frogs—Laboratory Reality"
(p. 79) as a guide, make a diagram of the structure and content of
"Canine Crisis." Include in your diagram all of the characteristics called
for in the diagram guide. Remember, however, "Canine Crisis" has two
major divisions, not three.

5b   **A.** What kind of order is used by the writer in each of the passages below: (1)
Chronological Order, (2) Spatial Order, (3) Logical Order (Analysis)? Put
the right number in the blank below the passage.

[1]   The farmhouse stood in the middle of a very large yard, and the yard was fenced
on three sides with rails and on the rear side with high palings; against these
stood the smoke-house; beyond the pailings was the orchard; beyond the orchard
were the negro quarters and the tobacco fields. (Mark Twain, *The Autobiography
of Mark Twain.*)

(1) _____

[2]   Although every city-dweller is potentially a mugging victim, some are far more
predisposed to attack than others. Those who are on the sidewalks late at night
are, according to one recent study, three times as likely to be victimized as those
who stay indoors after dark. But at least people often have some control over this
factor; over their age they have none, though this too is a predisposing trait, the
elderly being too slow-moving to escape and too feeble to offer effective resistance
or counterattack, and hence being selected as victims more often than the young.
A related factor is the presence of impedimenta of one sort or another: the person
carrying a large grocery bag home is, other things being equal, slower-moving,
less able to look around, and less able to offer any defense than one carrying
nothing, and thus more likely to be selected as a victim.
        A fourth element is dress. Until recently, according to crime statistics, the
largest number of victims of robberies have been poor people, primarily because
they were the closest at hand to the robbers. Today, however, when urban decay
is causing slum areas to grow up within, or to intrude upon, solidly working-class
or middle-class neighborhods, the pattern is changing; along and just within the
borders of the healthy neighborhoods, the man or woman whose clothing indicates that he or she has at least a modest income, and is therefore likely to be
carrying a fair amount of cash, is particularly prone to attack. A fifth factor is
race, which is, obviously, somewhat correlated to that of dress. Although most
assaults and most homicides are committed by people of the same race as the victims—indeed, by relatives, friends, or acquaintances of the victims, in the course
of family or personal fights—robberies are another matter: almost half of them
are interracial, the victims being whites and the criminals Negroes (or, in some
cities, Puerto Ricans) who are total strangers to them. Non-white muggers most
often choose white strangers as their victims not only to avoid being recognized
and caught, but because such people, by and large, are more likely than non-
whites to have a fair amount of cash upon them—and also because many muggers undoubtedly derive special satisfaction from "making a hit" upon a
representative of the hated oppressors. (From *The Mugging* by Morton Hunt.

(2) _____

[3]   "At 1 A.M.," he says, "Broadway is filled with wise guys and with kids coming out of the Astor Hotel in white dinner jackets—kids who drive to dances in their fathers' cars. You also see cleaning ladies going home, always wearing kerchiefs. By 2 A.M. some of the drinkers are getting out of hand, and this is the hour for bar fights. At 3 A.M. the last show is over in the night clubs, and most of the tourists and out-of-town buyers are back in hotels. And small-time comedians are criticizing big-time comedians in Hanson's Drugstore. At 4 A.M. after the bars close, you see the drunks come out—and also the pimps and prostitutes who take advantage of drunks. At 5 A.M., though, it is mostly quiet. New York is an entirely different city at 5 A.M." (Gay Talese, "New York," © Gay Talese. Used by permission.)

(3) _____

[4]   My mother died and was buried right there at our permanent home. Following that my husband died during the time people were killed by some kind of disease and he also is buried there. After this happened, I moved to the cornfield which my husband had established. The cornfield is there now, and I still plant a little bit of corn every spring. (Asa Bazhonoodah, "They Are Taking the Holy Elements from Mother Earth.")

(4) _____

[5]   The extent to which our sense of humor can help us to maintain our sanity is the extent to which it moves beyond jokes, beyond wit, beyond laughter itself. It must constitute a frame of mind, a point of view, a deep-going, far-reaching attitude to life. A cluster of qualities characterizes this frame of mind: *flexibility,* in this case an individual's willingness to examine every side of every issue and every side of every side; *spontaneity,* his ability to leap from one mood or mode of thought to another; *unconventionality,* his freedom from the values of his time, his place, and his profession; *shrewdness,* his refusal to believe that anyone—least of all himself—is what he seems to be; *playfulness,* his grasp of life as a game, a tragicomic game that nobody wins but that does not have to be won to be enjoyed; and *humility,* that elusive quality exemplified by the man who can shrug off the insufficiency of his ultimate wisdom, the meaninglessness of his profoundest thoughts. (Adapted from Harvey Mindess's "The Sense in Humor." Copyright 1971 by Saturday Review Co. First appeared in *Saturday Review,* August 21, 1971. Used with permission of *Saturday Review* and the author.)

(5) _____

[6]   On a particularly forlorn corner of Columbus Avenue, John double-parked, dug a finger in my ribs, and pointed to what he described as a group of junkies "on the set." I turned to look and he said. "Don't just wheel around that way. If they see two of us staring, it's all over. Pretend you're talking to me and use the car mirror." Feeling very Gene Hackman, I did so and saw a group of stooped-over people not having very much to do with one another. "A junkie 'hanging' that way means either one, he's had his shot; two, he's steering people to a connection; or three, he's actually holding something. Watch, and you'll see some shit go down." After a moment or so, one of the men ambled over to another.

"Closer," said John, "closer, closer—" The two men exchanged a Harlem "take five" slap of hands and John said, "That was it." (Bruce Jay Friedman, "Lessons of the Street," *Harper's Magazine,* September, 1971. ©1971 by Bruce Jay Friedman. Reprinted by permission of Robert Lantz-Candida Donadio Literary Agency, Inc.)

(6) _____

[7]   Despite the confusion we're ready to go at the signal. Our books are packed. Our jackets are on. We pour through the door and out into the hall with a collective sigh. We rush for the stairs, dodging in and out among the slower boys. The noise is terrific. On the stairs we really let loose. Screams and yells float up from the lower floors. Fists bang against the metal side panels in continuous thunder. Down, down, down, rushing past the painted numbers, swinging round like crack the whip at the landings, leaping steps when there's room, pushing the boy in front, being pushed from behind, all of us mad with freedom. Down, down. So easily, so effortlessly. The stream carries us safely past the third, the second, the first, and out into the immense throng streaming through the banks of open doors to the streets. We flow over the sidewalk and between the parked cars onto the asphalt. In the darkness faces are indistinct. Matches flash for cigarettes. Around the corner the avenue gleams with neon. Most of us have already forgotten the five hours inside school because for most of us school is less than nothing. We spread like a liquid over the neighborhood and disappear into the subways. (From *Stop-Time* by Frank Conroy. Copyright ©1967 by Frank Conroy. Reprinted by permission of The Viking Press, Inc.)

(7) _____

[8]   The legal action results in part from NOW's monitoring of television programs during the course of a year and a half. At first, the monitoring seemed to show that all TV programs portray women equally—that is, in an equally bad light. But in the over-all studies conducted by more than 100 monitors, WABC-TV came out considerably worse than other stations. In news programs, women in the movement are made to seem ridiculous, snide remarks trailing after them like broken arrows. In sports coverage of the Olympics, when women won seven out of eight U.S. medals, reporter Doug Johnson led off this 40-second story with "Thank heaven for little girls." The "little girls" remained anonymous— although, rest assured, the women in Clifford Irving's life were covered in loving and lengthy detail. In public affairs programs women's needs and issues— divorce and alimony, The Equal Rights Amendment, child-care centers, the earnings gap, abortion—are for the most part ignored. (Judith Adler Hennessee and Joan Nicholson, "NOW Says: TV Commercials Insult Women," *New York Times Magazine,* May 28, 1972. ©1972 by The New York Times Company. Reprinted by permission.)

(8) _____

[9]   Until recently, a company furnishing its new offices would move most of its old furniture from the old quarters, and send the office manager out to buy new stuff as needed. The walls would be painted by the landlord in some color the office manager chose; what was hung on the wall would express exactly, for better or worse, the taste (or lack of interest) of the occupant (or his wife); lighting fixtures dropped down from painted plaster ceilings geometrically marked by structural beams; telephone cable and elecrical cord came out of wall sockets. Visitors could tell someone was a big shot by the number of windows in his office; and

only the really important people got carpeting underfoot. One of the most parodied magazine ads proclaimed that "a title on the door rates a Bigelow on the floor." (Martin Mayer, "The Suite Science," *Esquire,* March, 1973. First published in Esquire Magazine. Reprinted by permission of Curtis Brown, Ltd. © 1973 by Esquire, Inc.)

(9) _____

B. What kind of order is suggested by the thesis or topic sentences below: (1) Chronological Order, (2) Spatial Order, (3) Logical Order (Analysis). Put the right number in the space to the right.

   1. From the bed of the truck, you could see the entire design of the motocross track.

(1) _____

   2. She had planned her day so well that she know what she would be doing at every hour.

(2) _____

   3. An essay is composed of three parts: introduction, body, and conclusion.

(3) _____

   4. The President listed four reasons for putting a ceiling on the price of meat.

(4) _____

   5. For ten years he had been playing for the winning team he now coached.

(5) _____

   6. The community college undertakes three major functions.

(6) _____

   7. The library floor plan made all materials readily available to the scholars.

(7) _____

   8. The present definitions of a great number of English words have evolved slowly from their original meanings.

(8) _____

   9. Psychologists have identified three types of gamblers: social, sporadic, and compulsive.

(9) _____

   10. The poet's religious convictions seemed to change in stages during that ten-year period.

(10) _____

chapter 6

Order: Logical
Relationship and Outlining

Logical Relationships

Whatever your methods of organization, you must have logical relationships among the parts. Even after you have a rough idea about your introduction, body, and conclusion, you must be sure you've given your material the right emphasis. In short, you must know which parts are major, which minor; which are equal, which subordinate. You can have the clarity that goes hand in hand with logic if you see each part in the right place on the staircase of abstractions. But first let's review the logic behind the staircase.

In Chapter 5 we said that you could divide the kinds of reading you do into types: poetry, short story, novel, drama, and essay. These five parts are all equal, and, being types of reading, they have the same principle of analysis. All five, in addition, are subordinate to, more specific than, *types of reading*. To show the logical connections among these parts, let's see what they look like on the staircase:

| Types of Reading |
| Poetry |
| Short Story |
| Novel |
| Drama |
| Essay |

★   Which of the following is not on the right step on the staircase?_____

| A.   Vehicle |
| B.   Automobile |
| C.   Train |
| D.   Chevrolet |

☆   D. B, C, and D are all vehicles, but all three are not controlled by the same principle of analysis. Both *automobile* (B) and *train* (C) are types of vehicles, but *Chevrolet* (D) is a type of automobile. It is subordinate to *automobile,* not equal to it. It should, therefore, be indented and placed under *automobile.* The staircase should look like this:

| Vehicle |
| Automobile |
| Chevrolet |
| Train |

Because *poetry, short story, novel, drama,* and *essay* are equal parts of *types of reading,* they can be called major divisions of that topic. Thus, *types of reading,* is like a thesis statement, the main idea of an essay. The evidence—types of poems, short stories, novels, dramas, and essays, and titles of particular works —can then be grouped together and listed under the correct major divisions. It would look, in part, like this:

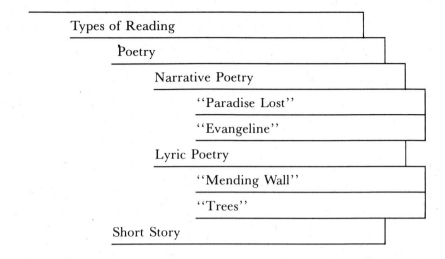

★ Which of these items is not on the right step on the staircase?_____

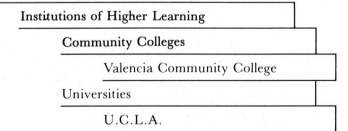

☆ E. *Universities* and *Community Colleges* are controlled by the same principle of analysis, for both are *Institutions of Higher Learning* (A). *Valencia Community College* (E) and *U.C.L.A.* (D) are logically equal, both specific types of *Institutions of Higher Learning.* But *Valencia Community College* is not a university, as the diagram suggests; it is not classified correctly under *Universities* (C). The staircase should look like this:

Institutions of Higher Learning	
	Community Colleges
	Valencia Community College
Universities	
	U.C.L.A.

The trick of organizing what you write, then, lies in your being able to imagine the ideas and evidence arranged logically to show which is major and which subordinate. To help you see these relationships—that is, to test whether all the parts are in order—you may wish to put them on a staircase of abstractions.

Look again at the second paragraph of "From Mendel to Frogs—Laboratory Reality."

> But the lab on spinal frogs destroyed my conventional outlook, my admittedly unfounded faith in an orderly, predictable nature. Testing the hypothesis that responses to pain, temperature, and pressure involve the nerve pathways in the brain, we destroyed with a probe a frog's mind and stimulated actual nerve endings exposed by dissection. Reflex action apparently does not involve the brain, and muscles continue to be stimulated in a mindless animal. I shall never forget my black-speckled lily pad sitter, surgical pins dangling from his appendages in defiance of our previous efforts to affix him to the dissecting pan, hopping spastically across the lab table, dragging his entrails. Lungs and liver hung beneath him, suspended by webs of soft tissue. His footing was impaired by the sheath of skin covering his right front paw, skin we had peeled back in order to apply these stimuli directly to the nerves of the forearm. Neither textbook print nor the embarrassed insistence of my lab instructor could convince me that the mangled frog had felt no pain from the minute his gray matter was scrambled.

To see more clearly the logical order of the ideas and evidence in the paragraph, now look at it in outline form on this staircase:

Topic Sentence: ... the lab on spinal frogs destroyed my conventional outlook, my ... faith in an orderly, predictable nature.

Testing the hypothesis

Destroyed brain

Stimulated nerve endings

Watching the frog

Hopping spastically

Trailing lungs and liver

Footing impaired by skin

★ What is the job of the last sentence of the paragraph? _____

A. To act as a topic sentence.
B. To act as a summarizing sentence.
C. To introduce a new idea.

> ☆   B. The last sentence sums up the evidence and ties in with the topic sentence; it re-emphasizes the central idea and points up the dismay of the writer. If the last sentence had been put in the diagram, it would have been on the same level of abstraction as the topic sentence.

The Outline

The staircase of abstractions makes clear the logical relationships among ideas. and facts in an essay. Often, however, you must show the plan of your essay in an outline. Three types of outlines are useful: (1) the scratch outline, (2) the topic outline, (3) the sentence outline.

The scratch outline

A scratch outline is informal; it may be no more than a random list of ideas and details on a subject jotted down as they occur to you. Such a list takes more definite shape as you develop and refine your plan. A scratch outline for a paper on the problems of being a bachelor might look like this:

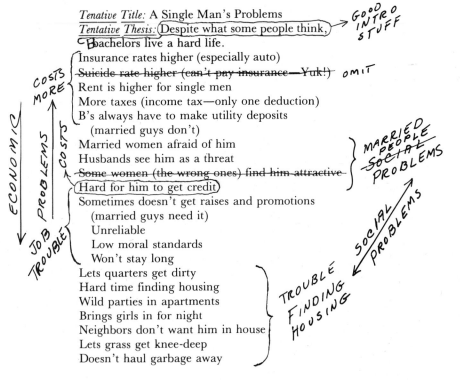

Although the scratch outline, as you can see, is not in final order, it lets you get your thoughts on paper so you can put them easily into either a topic or a sentence outline. Both topic and sentence outlines are formal. They include a title, a thesis statement, a logical arrangement of the parts on the staircase, and letters and numbers that label the divisions, subdivisions, and supporting evidence.

The topic outline

By adding a title, sharpening the thesis statement, arranging the ideas and facts on the right levels, and putting in number and letter symbols, you can make the scratch outline above into this topic outline:

The Plight of the Bachelor

Thesis Statement: The single man suffers both social and economic injustices.
- I. Social injustices
    - A. Suspected by married people
        - 1. Predator by women
        - 2. Competitor by men
    - B. Treated unfairly in housing
        - 1. Apartment owners
            - a. Parties
            - b. Girls
        - 2. House owners
            - a. House deteriorization
            - b. Grounds unkempt
- II. Economic injustices
    - A. Promotions scarce
        - 1. Unreliable
        - 2. Transient
        - 3. Immoral
    - B. Public services costly
        - 1. Automobile insurance rates
        - 2. Utility deposits
        - 3. Credit terms
        - 4. Income tax rates

Follow these rules for topic outlines:

1. Each item in the outline should be made up of a word, a phrase, or a dependent clause.

2. The first word in each topic heading on any level should be capitalized.

3. No punctuation should follow an item on any level

4. Items on the same level should be logically equal and, as closely as possible, grammatically equal. The following diagram illustrates topic outline parallelism.

- I. Noun

    - A. Prepositional phrase
        - 1. Participial phrase
        - 2. Participial phrase
    - B. Prepositional phrase
        - 1. Gerund phrase
        - 2. Gerund phrase
- II. Noun

5. Follow the principle of division. A division or subdivision should be composed of at least two parts: *I* should be followed by *II; A* should be followed by *B; 1* should be followed by *2;* and so forth. Remember, a whole cannot be broken into one part, but it may be divided into two, three, four, five or more parts.

6. Each item in a topic outline must support directly the superior (more general) heading that comes immediately before it. The Roman numeral divisions support the thesis; the capital letter subdivisions support the Roman numeral divisions under which they appear; the Arabic numeral subsubdivisions support the capital letter subdivisions under which they appear.

7. Outlines can reach lower than the three levels indicated in the sample topic outline above. They may be taken to the fourth, fifth, even sixth levels. The fourth level is labeled a., b., c., etc.; the fifth level (1), (2), (3), etc.; the sixth level (a), (b), (c), etc. Most outlines, however, are not taken below the third level.

8. Omit such headings as Introduction, Body, or Conclusion.

The sentence outline

The sentence outline is helpful when you write longer essays, for the sentences on each level remind you at all times of the close link between the subject and the comment of the thesis statement and the main divisions, and between the main divisions and subdivisions of the essay.

This sentence outline shows the correct form:

The Plight of the Bachelor

Thesis Statement: The single man suffers both social and economic injustices.
   I. The single man suffers social injustices.
      A. He is looked upon with suspicion by the married establishment.
         1. Married women avoid him as a predator.
         2. Married men distrust him as a competitor.
      B. He suffers unjust treatment when seeking housing.
         1. Apartment owners assume he'll throw wild parties and "bring girls in."
         2. House owners fear he will allow house and grounds to deteriorate.
  II. The single man suffers ecomonic injustices.
      A. He is often denied promotions to managerial positions.
         1. Many companies assume he is unreliable.
         2. Many companies assume he is a transient.
         3. Many companies assume he has low moral standards.
      B. He frequently pays more for public services than do married men.
         1. Automobile insurance companies charge him higher rates than they do married men.
         2. Utility companies often demand deposits from him they do not ask for from married men.
         3. Credit organizations have harsher terms for him than for married men.
         4. The government makes him pay a higher income tax than a married man pays.

Follow these rules for sentence outlines:

1. Rules 5, 6, 7, and 8 for topic outlines also apply for sentence outlines.

2. Each item in the sentence outline should be a complete sentence, beginning with a capital letter and ending with a period.

3. Items supporting the same idea on the same level should be grammatically parallel.

4. Each sentence should be clear and concise.

WRITING ASSIGNMENTS

1. Set up a thesis statement and scratch outline for an essay on one of these topics:

My Family's Talents	Dogs I Have Loved
Using a Summer Wisely	Games for Adults
Working for a Living	A Teacher's Qualities
Buying a Car	Types of Students
Women's Rights	Movies for Everyone
Helped by the Ad-man	Our Disappearing Natural Resources

2. Turn the scratch outline you made for *1* into a topic outline. Make sure you make the topic outline follow the rules.

3. Turn the topic outline you wrote for *2* into a sentence outline. Construct the sentence outline by the rules.

4. From the sentence outline you made for *3* write an essay.

Exercises

6a   **A.** To show their logical relationship, put these items on the staircase to the right.

1. Lipstick   1.
   Rouge
   Cosmetics
   Eye Shadow

2. *The Old Man and the Sea*   2.
   Periodical
   Newsweek
   Novel

3. Line Coach   3.
   Athletic Director
   Head Football Coach
   Backfield Coach
   Head Basketball Coach

4. Jane   4.
   Joe
   Men
   People
   Deedee
   Harold
   Women

B. Find the errors on the staircase below. Rearrange the items in the spaces to the right to show their logical relationships.

1.

automobile

vehicle

sports car

Jaguar XKE

1.

2.

Data Processing

Two-Year Program

Veterinarian's Assistant

Aviation Technology

Digital Computer Programmer

Licensed Pilot

Dental Technology

Animal Science Technology

Dental Hygienist

2.

C. In the blanks to the right of the staircase below put outline symbols—numbers and letters.

American writers and their works	_____
Novelists	_____
Ernest Hemingway	_____
For Whom the Bell Tolls	_____
The Old Man and The Sea	_____
William Faulkner	_____
The Sound and the Fury	_____
Sanctuary	_____
Dramatists	_____
Arthur Miller	_____
Death of a Salesman	_____
The Crucible	_____
Tennessee Williams	_____
The Glass Menagerie	_____
Cat on a Hot Tin Roof	_____
Poets	_____
Robert Frost	_____
''Mending Wall''	_____
''Death of the Hired Man''	_____
Carl Sandburg	_____
''Fog''	_____
''Chicago''	_____

D. Support the thesis statements by arranging the words or phrases in the spaces provided.

1. *Thesis:* Owning land makes one greedy, pseudo-creative, and selfish.

Wanting to improve it	I. _____
Wishing to keep others off it	II. _____
Adding to it	III. _____

2. *Thesis:* Children's fairy tales are often nothing more than stories to frighten children.

Mean stepmother	I. _____
Gullible little girl	A. _____
"Little Red Riding Hood"	B. _____
Cannibalistic witch	C. _____
Defenseless grandmother	II. _____
Desperate father	A. _____
"Hansel and Gretel"	B. _____
Vicious wolf	C. _____
Violent woodsman	D. _____

3. *Thesis:* Running a gas station involves both material and human expenses.

Upkeep	I. _____
Material expenses	A. _____
Maintaining property	1. _____
Expert mechanic or mechanics	2. _____
Supervising all employees	3. _____
Cost of land	B. _____
Repairing and replacing tools and equipment	1. _____
Original investment	2. _____
Employees	3. _____
Cost of building	II. _____
Repairing building	A. _____
Human expenses	1. _____
Being responsible for others' property	2. _____
Spending long hours	3. _____
Owner	B. _____
Cost of tools and equipment	1. _____

Qualified mechanics' helpers   2. _____

Service persons   3. _____

6b   **A.** Find the errors in both logic and form in the topic outline below. Rewrite the outline on a separate sheet of paper to correct the errors. Make the outline follow the rules.

Thesis: Teachers not interested in teaching prove harmful to their students.

   I. No interest in planning lectures
      1. Unprepared literature lecture.
         A. Undefined literary terms
         B. Professor Jones had not read a poem he assigned.
         C. Introduced irrelevant matter
      2. Disorganized art lecture
         A. He fails to learn the students' names.
            1. Reading names slowly and incorrectly
               a. Calls Nilson Nixon
            2. Calling students by wrong name
            3. Recording grades by wrong name
         B. Impatience with students' questions
            1. Frequently sarcastic
            2. Always condescending
            3. Rarely informative beyond notes
         C. Refuses to hold conferences
            1. Usually in library
            2. Always busy
            3. Frequently late
            4. Sometimes forgets
 III. Conclusion

B. Find the errors in the sentence outline below. Rewrite the outline correctly on a separate sheet of paper. Do the sentence outline by the rules.

Thesis: Every tourist should be aware of the perils of Florida beaches.

   I. Introduction
  II. The sand threatens all prospective bathers or sunbathers.
      A. It is always hot.
         1. Tourists get burnt feet walking in the sand to the water.
         2. Brown sand makes a blanket an absolute necessity.
         3. White sand is less hot but sears the tourists' eyes.
      B. It holds uncomfortable surprises for all.
         1. Sand fleas cause the tourist to scratch and swat.
         2. Sandspurs puncture the beach-goer's feet.
         3. Eyes, ears, and hair are filled with blowing sand.
 III. The sun and the unwary bather.
      A. It makes you dizzy and sometimes causes you to faint.
         1. Overexposure makes some bathers woozy.

B. It threatens every part of his body.
1. His unprotected back will break out in painful blisters after an hour's exposure.
2. His stomach skin will pain for days when he bends to tie his shoes or reaches up to stretch.
3. His shoulders will smart when even the lightest shirt fabric touches them.
4. His legs and arches will ache from walking in the sand.
IV. The surf contains a number of dangerous animals.
A. Small water creatures lie in wait for the swimmer.
1. The spiney sea urchin's protruding barbs threaten his feet.
2. Small crabs bite his toes.
3. Sharks lie buried in the sand, even in knee-deep water.
B. Large water creatures threaten his very life.
1. Sting rays leave painful, bleeding holes and have been known to cause heart attacks.
2. Transparent jellyfish itch and sting him.
3. Fast-moving barracuda threaten him with razor-sharp teeth.
4. Portuguese men-of-war have tentacles that have been known to entangle and kill swimmers.
V. He seems to be surrounded by mysterious menaces.
A. Others swimmers are not very trustworthy.
B. The red tide is likely to make bathing a noisome and thing.
C. The pollution count keeps rising even in open saltwater bathing areas.

section three

Paragraphing

chapter **7**

Paragraphs: Types
and Topic Sentences

The thesis statement of an essay leads to a movement down the staircase of abstractions—down from the general to the level of concrete, explanatory, clinching details. But this movement must be marked by clearcut in-between stages and stops—at the middle levels of abstraction. These in-between stages and stops are produced by paragraphs. Paragraphs collect, cluster, and group single statements and details so that they form distinct blocks of material— subdivisions of the thesis. In other words, they group details from the lowest level of abstraction, the most concrete, into middle-level stages of development. In this way they help to develop the thesis that is the essay's highest level on the staircase of abstractions. The most important kind of paragraph is called the development paragraph, but there are other types that also serve useful functions.

Types of Paragraph

The introductory paragraph

The chief function of the introductory paragraph is to present the thesis. But, as we saw in Chapter 5, if it is to present the thesis to best advantage, it must contain more than just the thesis sentence itself. Before it, or occasionally after it, comes the orientation material. This other material should interest the readers, attract their attention, whet their curiosity. It should introduce them to your attitude toward the subject and toward them; it should set your tone. Most of all, it should provide some further details of background, situation, or context in which the thesis is placed. What are some of the facts that make the thesis interesting and valid? What is the wider problem or situation of which it is a part? What are some of the reasons it should be discussed, or hasn't been discussed enough? What is it that makes you want to write about it and should make the reader want to read about it? Here are two examples. In the first, Huston Horn sets the tone and orientation by first humorously surveying a number of the usual insults to the Volkswagen. In the paragraph's last sentence, he reaches the specific claim that is to control the rest of his piece.

> On land or on the water the Volkswagen automobile is an inelegant, squatty, lumpy-looking piece of machinery that is not very big, does not go very fast, has very little chrome, makes too much noise and does not cost enough money. It has its engine in back, a pouty, hurt-feelings expression in front and a bottom so tight that the whole contraption is almost, but not quite, amphibious. In a country that has always bought cars on styling—not price or performance—Volkswagens in the U.S. have been laughed at, mocked, abused, and insulted, one baffled owner calling it "not really repulsive" and the rollicking *New York Times* calling it "breathtakingly ugly." Judging from appearances, it is easy to see that this base-born orphan of Nazi Germany is as out of place on Route 66 as a soapbox racer at Sebring. Still, pretty is as pretty does, and since the postwar emergence of the car and its square-shaped sister, a station wagon that inherited the family's plain looks, certain things have happened to suggest every car should be so homely. (From "The Beetle Does Float" by Huston Horn, *Sports Illustrated,* August, 19, 1963. ©1963, Time, Inc. Reprinted by permission.)

In the following example, J.B.S. Haldane also concludes his paragraph with his thesis about the subject.

> The most obvious differences between animals are differences of size, but for some reason the zoologists have paid singularly little attention to them. In a large textbook of zoology before me I find no indication that the eagle is larger than the sparrow, or the hippopotamus bigger than the hare, though some grudging admissions are made in the case of the mouse and the whale. But yet it is easy to show that a hare could not be as large as a hippopotamus, or a whale as small as a herring. For every type of animal there is a most convenient size, and a large change in size inevitably carries with it a change of form. (J.B.S. Haldane, "On Being the Right Size," *Possible Worlds.* Copyright 1928 by J.B.S. Haldane. Reprinted with permission of Harper & Row, Publishers, Inc.)

★   What has Haldane done in the first two sentences of his paragraph?

———————

A. Noted directly opposing theories to his own
B. Noted the value of the subject
C. Noted the absence of enough attention to the subject

☆   C. He first arouses interest by stressing that others have not taken the subject seriously enough and implying that they certainly should have.

The concluding paragraph

The concluding paragraph should not make your reader stop suddenly, with a detail, subpoint, or digression at a low, concrete level of your development. It should, rather, return him full circle to the broader level of your overall thesis. It should reassert, re-emphasize, possibly even redefine in some altered form your opening thesis. And it should do this with a flourish, with the best writing of which you are capable.

This reassertion of the thesis can be placed in a variety of final contexts: in a recapitulation of some of your subdivisions, in the setting of one last clinching example, in a glance at a broader problem or situation, even in the midst of a look at some related questions that you have not dealt with. Notice how H. L. Mencken redefines his thesis about ugliness in America in the first three sentences of this concluding paragraph.

> Here is something that the psychologists have so far neglected: the love of ugliness for its own sake, the lust to make the world intolerable. Its habitat is the United States. Out of the melting pot emerges a race which hates beauty as it hates truth. The etiology of this madness deserves a great deal more study than it has got. There must be causes behind it; it arises and flourishes in obedience to biological laws, and not as a mere act of God. What, precisely, are the terms of those laws? And why do they run stronger in America than elsewhere? Let some honest *Privat Dozent* in pathological sociology apply himself to the problem. (H. L. Mencken, "The Libido for the Ugly," *A Mencken Chrestomathy.* Copyright, 1927, 1949 by H. L. Mencken. Reprinted with permission of Alfred A. Knopf, Inc.)

★ What does he then do in the last part of the paragraph? _____

A. Cite a last significant example
B. Refer to a broader question
C. Recapitulate his subdivisions

☆ B. He places his thesis in the context of a broader question that he does not answer, but suggests needs answering.

The transition paragraph

While every essay must have introductory, concluding, and development paragraphs, it may or may not contain transition paragraphs. These paragraphs are usually quite short—often a single sentence, even an intentional fragment. They are used to emphasize a point of transition in a dramatic way, a movement from one section of material to another. They are probably more useful in longer essays, but can also be used with value in shorter pieces.

In this example from an essay on hummingbirds, Oliver Pearson clearly indicates that he is moving from one phase of his subject to another.

> In the face of two such unthinkable alternatives, any laboratory answer may seem foolish. But we can at least attempt a calculation, if only for the amusement of playing with the figures.

And in this one-sentence paragraph Erich Fromm marks the dividing line between two aspects of his subject. He has just explained that love is an art and he is now moving on to explain how it, like all arts, can be learned.

What are the necessary steps in learning any art?

The development paragraph

Development paragraphs are the main building blocks of an essay. They do two jobs at once. They clearly define a new stage or subdivision of the thesis, and they collect concrete details into a unified set that helps to explain that new stage or subdivision. In short essays, each development paragraph is often a separate subdivision of the broader thesis; but in longer essays (and possibly in short essays, too, on occasion) several paragraphs might be clustered together to develop a major subdivision. In either case, paragraphs are the means of blocking out the states, the parts of the essay. They are the means of organizing materials at the different levels on the staircase of abstractions.

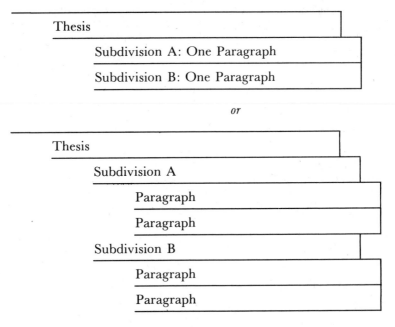

★ In the following example of a development paragraph, what one word defines the subdivision of a broader thesis that the whole paragraph will explain? _____

A dilemma is a situation, in logic or in life, from which there is literally no way out. If one turns one way, he is lost; if he turns another, the second horn of the dilemma catches him. The trial lawyer who demands that the witness "answer yes or no" when either answer will damage the witness's case is making use of the dilemma. Perhaps the best example of all is the ancient vaudeville wheeze: "Have you stopped beating your wife yet?" Either answer is an admission of guilt, and the form of the question allows no further possibilities. (William Hummel and Keith Huntress, *The Analysis of Propaganda*. Copyright 1949 by William Hummel and Keith Huntress. Reprinted with permission of Holt, Rinehard and Winston, Inc.)

☆ *Dilemma.* The first sentence defines the topic in terms that are at a middle level on the staircase of abstractions. The rest of the paragraph develops this definition in more concrete terms; but notice that all the development sentences are not on the same level of the staircase of abstractions:

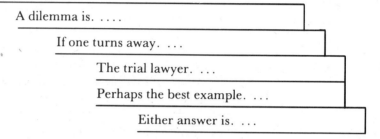

A dilemma is. . . . .

If one turns away. . . .

The trial lawyer. . . .

Perhaps the best example. . . .

Either answer is. . . .

Thus, the second sentence is a more concrete definition of the terms of the first. Both the third and fourth are equal, more concrete illustrations of that definition. Finally, the fifth sentence is a further, more specific development of the terms of sentence four.

The Topic Sentence

A topic sentence is the controlling sentence of a development paragraph. It does two jobs at once, and thus it becomes an important signal in showing the relationship of the parts of a paper. First, it shows the place of a development paragraph in the pattern of the whole essay; thus, it is a more concrete statement than the thesis of the essay and shows the intermediate level of abstraction, the subdivision that paragraph will develop. It is also the unifying, controlling center of the paragraph's concrete details; thus, it is a more abstract statement than the rest of the statements in the paragraph.

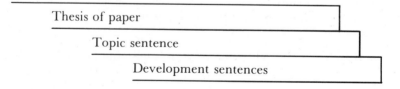

Thesis of paper

Topic sentence

Development sentences

★ The topic sentence of a paragraph is similar to what part of the introduction of the whole essay? _____

> ☆ *The thesis statement.* In the same way that a thesis statement makes a comment on a limited subject, the topic sentence makes a comment on an even more limited subject.
>
> ★ Underline the words which make a comment on the limited subject of this topic sentence.
> But varsity athletes today are really no different from other students.
>
> ☆ *Are really no different from other students. Varsity athletes today* is the limited subject.

The limited subject of the topic sentence *and* the comment made about it define the exact stage you are at in the development of the overall thesis. This topic sentence reduces logically the level of abstraction of that original thesis. If you had as the subject of your original thesis *varsity athletes in the twentieth century,* then *varsity athletes today* would be one of its logical subdivisions and an appropriate limited subject for a topic sentence. On the other hand, if you had *varsity athletes today* as an original thesis subject, it could still serve as the subject of a topic sentence if you then limited it with your comment. The comment in this case would indicate the stage of the original thesis. Note how the following examples are related on the staircase of abstractions:

Varsity athletes today are a new breed. (Thesis)
Varsity athletes today are better students. (Topic)
Varsity athletes today are no longer pure amateurs. (Topic)

1. Placing the topic sentence

Professional writers may occasionally omit the spelling-out of their topic sentence and merely imply it by the clear arrangement of their details. But this is a risky variation. We suggest that you regularly take advantage of the actual presence of the topic sentence. That way both you and your reader will know exactly where you are and where you are going. The topic sentence can turn up at any point of the paragraph, but it is most frequently found at the beginning or end—before or after the supporting details.

> ★ Which sentence in the following paragraph is the topic sentence?
> _____

In the four- to eight-year-old period I was very timid. I was worried about lions in the thicket in the large vacant lot next to our house on Cold Spring Street, in New Haven. A pal, Mansfield Horner, easily convinced me that there was a dinosaur at the bottom of his cellar stairs. I was afraid of the Italian women with huge bags dangling from their waists who came up the street in groups in spring, digging dandelions out of the lawns—afraid, I suspect, because someone had told me that they kidnapped children in those bags. I'd rush into the vestibule with palpitating heart when I saw them a block away, slam the door and peek at them through the little window in the door as they passed. (Benjamin Spock, ''Where I Stand—And Why.'' Published by permission of *Redbook* magazine, copyright ©1967 The McCall Publishing Company.)

☆   *The first.* The topic sentence provides the highest level of abstraction in a paragraph. In this one, Dr. Spock begins by announcing the controlling generality—*very timid.* In the rest of the paragraph he cites concrete examples that make clear how he was timid. He moves down the staircase.

In the next example, the topic sentence is also stated first, and is followed by concrete details that dramatize its key comment about its subject, *excitement.*

Supper was excitement. The heavy bowls of sugar and the pitchers of syrup shook with the vibration of the straining engines. There were heavy platters of thick-sliced country ham with red gravy, and of fried, tough round steak. There were bowls of stewed corn, string beans, boiled potatoes, and huge plates of soda biscuits and square-cut pieces of cornbread. There were always fresh round ''pounds'' of butter, soon gashed and reduced by the reaching knives. Strong coffee was poured from graniteware coffee pots into heavy, handleless cups. And always everything shook with the laboring of the wide paddle wheel as the heavy-loaded boat moved upstream. (From *The South and the Southerner* by Ralph McGill, copyright ©1959, 1963 by Ralph McGill, with permission of Atlantic-Little, Brown and Company.)

2. Refining the topic sentence

The topic sentence marks a midpoint between the overall thesis statement and the concrete supporting details. As such it should not be as broad or abstract as a thesis sentence, nor as limited or specific as a detail sentence. It should be written at the appropriate level on the staircase of abstractions.

★   Which statement is at a lower, more concrete step on the staircase, A or B? _____

> A. Among today's top television performers, Carroll O'Connor is one of the finest.
>
> B. Among today's top television performers, Carroll O'Connor is one of the most adept at subtle techniques that reveal character as well as get laughs.
>
> ☆ B. The more specific terms of B initiate a direction of discussion for the development sentences of the paragraph. The vague terms of A would leave you groping for something further to say. If, while writing, you can't seem to come up with any development sentences, that is a clear signal that your topic sentence has been at too high a level of abstraction and needs refining.

The logical processes for refining a topic sentence are the same that we discussed in talking about refining the thesis sentence.

Modifying the key terms of the subject or the comment about the subject (or both) is one of the most common methods of refining. Modifying reduces the level of abstraction by adding qualifications that limit the original terms.

> ★ In which of these sentences are the terms refined the most by modifying, A or B? _____
>
> A. Teaching a dog takes a great deal of patience.
> B. Teaching a dog to sit up and beg takes more patience than I possess.
>
> ☆ B. In B the modifier *to sit up and beg* refines the topic subject and the modifier *more than I possess* refines the comment. The additional qualifying terms not only give a sharper, more personal emphasis to the paragraph, but suggest more concrete ways in which the idea can be developed.

Substituting or *subdividing* involves replacing the original terms with more concrete terms, terms that are lower on the staircase of abstractions.

> ★ Which topic sentence has the more concrete terms? _____
>
> A. Lincoln was one of the greatest American presidents.
> B. Lincoln's compassion has endeared him to the American people.
>
> ☆ B. In B, *compassion* has been substituted for the general reference to Lincoln and *has endeared him* has been substituted for the vague *was one of the greatest*.

Adding an appropriate and equal term also works well in refining the topic sentence; but you should not commit yourself to more than you can handle in a single paragraph.

The closing scene of the novel is sentimental.

The closing scene of the novel is sentimental *and far-fetched.*

Finally, *specifying* or *enumerating* is helpful as well. In this refinement, you announce the exact subdivisions that the paragraph will take up.

Robert Frost's "Mending Wall" involves an interesting contrast of personalities.

Robert Frost's "Mending Wall" contrasts *two kinds* of personality—*the liberated and the trapped.*

3. Recognizing the key terms of the topic sentence

The key terms of the topic sentence should control the direction of the paragraph and the selection of its details. These key terms may be a part of the subject grouping—*The student before World War II.* Or they may be in the comment about the subject—*Students are always rebellious.* In the latter example it would not be enough to focus on the adjective *rebellious* alone; the significance of the adverb *always* would also have to be developed. The key terms may also be in both parts of the sentence—*The student before World War II was less rebellious.*

★   Underline the key term that determines the emphasis of the paragraph:

European automobiles differ according to the psychological motivations of the various national groups.

☆   *Psychological motivations.* The details of the paragraph will develop this idea.

WRITING ASSIGNMENTS

1. Write a full and effective introductory paragraph for two of the following subjects.

| Maturity | Required College Courses |
| Household Pets | Television Rating Systems |

2. Write topic sentences for three of the following paragraph subjects.

Installment Buying	Birth Control
Christmas Shopping	Vacation Spots
Cheating in Classrooms	Advertising

3. Develop full paragraphs for the topic sentences based on the list in (2).

Exercises

7a   **A.** On the line below place the number or letter that best answers the question.

1. How many major subdivisions are announced by the following introductory paragraph?

> Sky-rocketing costs have caused much debate over the value of continuing our programs of space exploration. The deaths of three astronauts have provided further reasons for doubt. Yet, despite the costs and dangers, the space program is valuable; for it improves our military preparedness, offers new frontiers of knowledge, and might even provide a source of vital raw materials.

(1) _____

2. Which sentence of this introductory paragraph announces the specific terms that will determine the development of the essay?

> I have done things and had things happen to me and nobody knows about it. So I am writing about it so that people will know. Although there are a lot of things I could tell about, I will just tell about the jumping because that is the most important. It gave me the biggest thrill. I mean high jumping, standing and running. You probably never heard of a standing high jumper, but that's what I was. I was the greatest standing high jumper ever was. (Michael Fessier, "That's What Happened to Me," *Story Magazine,* 1935. Copyright 1935, 1963 by *Story Magazine.* Reprinted by permission of Harold Matson Co., Inc.)

(2) _____

3. Which sentence of this concluding paragraph restates the four basic qualities of words that the essay had been concerned with?

> Anyone who listens carefully to common speech is bound to realize that though most people respond as if instinctively to the feeling and to the muscular quality of words, few pay attention to the histories and the root-pictures words can release. Those neglected qualities are there, however, and the poets have always found them a self-delighting source of excitement. The reader without some awareness of these qualities must inevitably remain insensitive to a substantial part of the life of a good poem.

(3) _____

4. Which sentence of the following paragraph is the topic sentence?

> At the other end of town, summer already offers us the contrast of its other wealth: I mean its silences and boredom. These silences do not always have the same quality, depending on whether they occur in shadow or sunlight. There is a noontime silence on the government square. In the shade of the trees that grow along each side, Arabs sell penny glasses of iced lemonade, perfumed with orange blossom. Their cry of "cool, cool" echoes across the empty square. When it fades away, silence falls again under the sun: ice moves in the merchant's pitcher, I can hear it tinkling. There is a siesta silence. On the streets around the docks, in front of the squalid barber shops, one can measure it in the melodious buzzing of the flies behind the hollow reed curtains. Elsewhere, in the Moorish cafes of the Casbah, it is bodies that are silent, that cannot drag themselves away, leave the glass of tea, and rediscover time in the beating of

their pulse. But, above all, there is the silence of the summer evenings. (Albert Camus, "Summer in Algiers," *Lyrical and Critical Essays,* ed. Philip Thody, trans. Ellen Conroy Kennedy, pub. Alfred A. Knopf, Inc. ©1968 by Alfred A. Knopf, Inc. ©1967 by Hamish Hamilton, Ltd. and Alfred A. Knopf, Inc.)

(4) _____

5. Which sentence of the following paragraph is the topic sentence?

And at the same time the forces of American commercialism are hugely dedicated to making us deliberately unhappy. Advertising is one of our major industries, and advertising exists not to satisfy desires but to create them—and to create them faster than any man's budget can satisfy them. For that matter, our whole economy is based on a dedicated insatiability. We are taught that to possess is to be happy, and then we are made to want. We even are told it is our duty to want. It was only a few years ago, to cite a single example, that car dealers across the country were flying banners that read "You Auto Buy Now." They were calling upon Americans, as an act approaching patriotism, to buy at once, with money they did not have, automobiles they did not really need, and which they would be required to grow tired of by the time the next year's models were released. (John Ciardi, "Is Everybody Happy?" From *Saturday Review,* March 14, 1964.)

(5) _____

6. Which sentence of the following paragraph is the topic sentence?

One of these friends was Rip, who was a sort of soft character. I guess he was a big liver-and white springer spaniel, but I don't believe he was much of a looker or a hunter either. Rip had droopy yellow eyes and a mighty mournful expression; he was known around our place as "Old Tear in Me Eye." However poor in the field or worthless he may have been, he did have one outstanding talent, which was catching flies. In summer he sat morosely out on a big rock in the sun and just snapped them up like a skunk eating bees. His precision was unerring, and I watched him with spellbound admiration. (From Elizabeth R. Choate, "Give Your Heart to a Dog," *The Atlantic Monthly* [December, 1954], p. 52. Copyright ©1964 by The Atlantic Monthly Company, Boston, Mass. Reprinted by permission of the author.)

(6) _____

B. On the line below place the material requested by each question.
   1. What one word in the topic sentence of the following paragraph sets the key term for the development of the paragraph?

A true education is a harrowing experience. A student who wants to be educated must be courageous indeed. He must expect all his comforts and illusions and complacencies to be ruthlessly ripped away. He must drink the cup of humility to its last lees and dregs. He must have the courage of a man about to sit in an electric chair; he must be prepared to watch his toenails curl and his flesh sizzle. In one sense, this is a lonely ordeal. Not that he can't communicate his experience, he can, of course—but he can't delegate it. He must feel it himself. The experience is intensely personal and individual, charged with pain and thrills, with glory and terror. (Wade Thompson, "My Crusade Against Fraternities," *The Nation,* September 26, 1959, p. 171.)

(1) _____

2. Which clause of the topic sentence—the first or second—sets the exact terms for the development of the paragraph?

But if the car owner can ignore the lack of public transport, he can hardly ignore the decay of services in general. His car needs mechanics, and mechanics grow more expensive and less efficient. The gadgets in the home are cheaper to replace than repair. The more efficiently self-contained the home, the primary fortress of independence, seems to be, the more dependent it is on the great impersonal corporations, as well as a diminishing army of servitors. Skills at the lowest level have to be wooed slavishly and exorbitantly rewarded. Plumbers will not come. Nor, at the higher level, will doctors. And doctors and dentists, in a nation committed to maiming itself with sugar and cholesterol, know their scarcity value and behave accordingly. (Anthony Burgess, "Is America Falling Apart?" ©1971 by *The New York Times Company.* Reprinted by permission.)

(2) _____

3. The details in the rest of the paragraph refer to which two words in the topic sentence in showing the differences being discussed?

With the content of animal protein in a diet perhaps the most significant index of its quality, the differences in various parts of the world are rather striking. In the U.S. the average daily intake is sixty-five grams. In Europe per capita intake is somewhat lower, but still quite a bit over the thirty grams accepted as the minimum requirement for adequate nutrition. In most other areas of the world, the figure is thirteen; in Ceylon, nine; and in India, six. In India, a daily diet of 1,000 calories is not uncommon; for most adults, this means virtual starvation. As someone once observed, "It is too much to let you die quickly, it is too little to let you live long." (Carl Bakal, "The Mathematics of Hunger," *Saturday Review,* April, 27, 1963, p. 17.)

(3) _____

4. Which is the most effective topic sentence?
   a. Of these, Paul Newman is the best actor.
   b. Of these, Paul Newman is the most convincing performer.
   c. Of these, Paul Newman is the most convincing portrayer of the man with a chip on his shoulder.
   d. Of these, Paul Newman is my favorite.

(4) _____

5. Which is the most effective topic sentence?
   a. The new Navy regulations have granted a surprising amount of freedom to sailors.
   b. The new Navy regulations are quite unusual.
   c. The new Navy regulations have caused many changes.
   d. The change in Navy regulations has surprised many people.

(5) _____

6. In which item is the topic sentence refined by modifying the terms of the comment?

A college education is becoming more essential.

a. A college education is like a union card.

b. A college education is becoming more essential in fields that did not used to require it.

c. A college education is a must.

d. A college education is demanded by the company I want to work for.

(6) _____

7. In which item is the topic sentence refined by substituting a more concrete subdivision?

I still remember many of my childhood toys.

a. I still have fond memories of my childhood toys.

b. I still think about my childhood toys.

c. I still remember the thrill of zooming down the driveway on my first bike.

d. I still remember how it felt to get toys and sports equipment.

(7) _____

7b

Supply the material requested by each question. Place it in the space provided.

1. Refine this topic sentence by modifying the terms of the comment: Home owners need help.

_____

_____

2. Refine this topic sentence by adding a comparison: The American people eat a great deal of meat.

_____

_____

3. Write a topic sentence to introduce and organize the rest of the paragraph printed.

(_____). He brought home some chicks, and I had to feed them. He forgot where he put his pet frog. He neglected to train a puppy, and we ended up with newspapers all over the floor. When he mentioned a monkey he had seen, mother drew the line.

_____

_____

4. Write a topic sentence to introduce and organize the rest of the paragraph printed.

(_____). At one time she was president of the PTA, the Bird Watcher's Association, and the Excelsior Bridge Club. She had us all addressing envelopes for the March of Dimes. She even had all the women on the block learning first aid for Civil Defense.

_____

_____

5. Write a topic sentence to introduce and organize the rest of the paragraph. (_____).
In the sink were three or four unwashed pots. The floor looked as if it had not been swept for weeks. Books were scattered all over the bed. Three of Harold's shoes were scattered about the room.

_____

_____

6. One of the ideas in the following group should serve as the basis of a topic sentence for a paragraph. Expand it into an effective topic sentence to introduce and organize the other ideas.
Always gazed out the window; made sarcastic remarks about other teachers; my worst teacher; wandered from the point; stressed memorizing petty details.

_____

_____

7. One of the ideas in the following group should serve as the basis of a topic sentence for a paragraph. Expand it into an effective topic sentence to introduce and organize the other details.
A help in learning your own language; a good form of discipline; practical for traveling in other countries; the value of learning a foreign language; useful in attending foreign movies.

_____

_____

chapter 8

Paragraphs:
Selection of Details

A sharply defined topic sentence not only demands further development but also sets up the direction of that development. It influences your selection of the details that you will use to complete the job of the paragraph. It helps you to keep these details unified, to place them at a concrete level on the staircase of abstractions, and to marshal them in sufficient numbers and appropriate types.

Unity

The unity of a paragraph is determined by the terms of the topic sentence. Interesting or concrete as a detail or phrase might be, it must be related to the key terms of the topic sentence. Otherwise, it must be omitted, sacrificed, at least for the moment—however painful that sometimes is.

> ★   Which sentence in the following list does not contribute a unified, related detail to the topic sentence below? _____
> Playing tennis keeps my father young.
>
> A. Running around the courts gives his muscles the tone and resilience of a teenager's.
> B. We still have the trophy he won for finishing first in the mile run in the state track meet when he was in high school.

C. Serving especially gives him a fine sense of coordination and balance.

D. Even just being out in the sun and air brightens his eyes after long hours in the law library.

☆   B. The details about his track days are not related, at least in the way they are presented. They might have been more effectively worked in as a contrasting background point, but that is unlikely. Even contrasts need to be in direct, if opposing, relationship to the terms of the topic sentence.

In the following paragraph all the details *are* unified.

Earline was a big, bouncy, uncomplicated girl who poked you in the ribs to make sure you got the point of her jokes. She had a passion for food, and a passion, very like in character, for what she called ideas. ''I can't get the McCarthy problem off my chest,'' she would declare, her carrying voice soaring above the sound of the juke box at the Owl. ''I can't bear to think he honestly represents the deep-down spiritual calibre of the average American.'' At a moonlight picnic, when the other couples had wandered off into the shade of the pine woods, she would remain sitting in full lunar glare beside Jim (somehow, he was usually paired off with Earline) and would say, less softly than the whippoorwills, ''Now take salvation through faith—here's my slant on it. ...'' Her strong white teeth would glisten just as they did when they were about to seize upon a king-sized hamburger, succulent with chopped pickle and mustard. Worse still, she called Jim—and would always call him—by the humiliating abbreviation of his middle name. She called him Mannie. (Francis Gray Patton, ''The Man Jones,'' *A Piece of Luck and Other Stories.* Copyright 1955 by Francis Gray Patton. Reprinted with permission of Dodd, Mead & Company, Inc.)

To be more specific, how do we determine that this is a unified paragraph? We note the specific terms of the subject of the topic and the specific terms of the comment about that subject. In this sample the first two sentences present these terms. *Earline* is the subject, but it is obvious that not just any further kind of statement about Earline would maintain unity. Only those that are more concrete explanations of the comment made about her will do the job. That comment centers on her being *big, bouncy, uncomplicated* and on her having a *passion for both food and ideas.* The third, fourth, and fifth sentences focus on her *passion for ideas* but also give an indication of her being *bouncy* and *uncomplicated.* The sixth sentence, while continuing the scene in which she discusses her *ideas,* also captures her *bigness* in the reference to the teeth and refers as well to her *passion for food.* The last sentence provides a climactic example of her being *bouncy* and *uncomplicated.*

In the Earline example, the subject of the topic was already at a concrete level on the staircase of abstractions; thus, the details of the paragraph were used to reduce the level of the *comment* only.

In this next example, note that in the topic sentence both the subject and the comment need to be made more concrete. And so throughout the paragraph details are used to reduce both terms.

The forces of morality rallied to the attack. Dr. Francis E. Clark, the founder and president of the Christian Endeavor Society, declared that the modern ''indecent dance'' was ''an offense against womanly purity, the very fountain-head of our family and civil life.'' The new style of dancing was denounced in religious journals as ''impure, polluting, corrupting, debasing, destroying spirituality, increasing carnality,'' and the mothers and sisters and church members of the land were called upon to admonish and instruct and raise the spiritual tone of these dreadful young people. President Murphree of the University of Florida cried out with true Southern warmth, ''The low-cut gowns, the rolled hose and short skirts are born of the Devil and his angels. and are carrying the present and future generations to chaos and destruction.'' A group of Episcopal church-women in New York, speaking with the authority of wealth and social position (for they included Mrs. J. Pierpont Morgan, Mrs. Borden Harriman, Mrs. Henry Phipps, Mrs. James Roosevelt, and Mrs. E. H. Harriman), proposed an organization to discourage fashions involving an ''excess of nudity'' and ''improper ways of dancing.'' The Y.W.C.A conducted a national campaign against the immodest dress among high-school girls, supplying newspapers with printed matter carrying headlines such as ''Working Girls Responsive to Modesty Appeal'' and ''High Heels Losing Ground Even in France.'' (Frederick Lewis Allen, ''The Revolution in Manners and Morals,'' *Only Yesterday*. Copyright 1931 by Frederick Lewis Allen. Reprinted with permission of Harper & Row, Publishers, Inc.)

★   In the staircase of abstractions, place the subject of the topic sentence of the above paragraph in the appropriate box. Then place the six subtopics from the body of the paragraph that reduce the level of this subject.

☆   *Forces of morality* is the subject of the topic sentence and should have been placed in the top box. The six more concrete references to the subject are these: *Dr. Francis E. Clark, religious journals, mothers and sisters and church members, President Murphree, group of Episcopal churchwomen,* and *The Y.W.C.A.* In a like manner, other elements in the paragraph make more concrete references to the comment about the topic, *rallied to the attack.* Charted, in abbreviated fashion, they look like this:

rallied to the attack
declared that. . .
The new style of dancing was denounced. .
were called upon. . .
cried out. . .
proposed an organization. . .
conducted a national campaign. . .

Appropriate Level of Abstraction

The details selected to develop the topic of a paragraph should not only be unified; they should be more limited, more specific, more concrete than the topic idea. Do not lengthen paragraphs by throwing in more generalities equal to the generality that you started with. You again have to recognize and use the degrees of generality, the levels of abstraction.

★   Which sentence in the following list is not concrete enough? _____
The American woman becomes a puppet when the lords of fashion speak.

A. She does everything they tell her to do.
B. She raises her hemlines on cue.
C. She lowers them when a new look is needed to pep up business.
D. She wears bright colors when colors are in, and will look as drab as a monk when colors are out.

☆   A. It is just another way of saying what the topic sentence said. You should not merely repeat the same statement in different but equally general words.

On the other hand, you have to be sure that your concrete details do have a more general topic to which they are related.

★   Does the following paragraph have an appropriately general topic sentence? _____

Small children can learn the rules of tennis and the basic strokes. Teenagers, who make up the largest group of devotees, often make the greatest strides in the shortest time. While the doubles played by married couples is not always of the highest quality, the couples do enjoy

> playing together. Even in their seventies, many men continue to play tennis, and play it well.
>
> ☆   No. It has a series of appropriately concrete details, but needs a more general statement to give the whole thing meaning and a more coherent movement from sentence to sentence.

In the examples used so far, all of the details have been equal to one another, equal subdivisions of a broader category. This is not always the case. The details of a paragraph may have other logical relationships to each other; there may be subdivisions of subdivisions. The characteristics of a good citizen, for example, may be classified into three subdivisions—awareness, knowledge, action. But then more concrete details, at a lower step on the staircase, may be provided for some or all of these, and not necessarily in the same quantity for each.

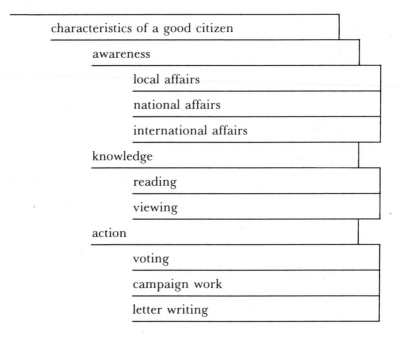

Quantity and type

A good paragraph should be long enough to clinch its point. Just what that takes will vary according to topic and even personality, or audience or general length of paper. Similarly, a stronger argumentative position might take more proof, a more general topic and comment more development. But generally speaking, you will do well to push yourself to one more sentence, one more detail, one more fact, one more step of the story. How? Why? What else? What then? So What? Have all the terms of the topic been discussed? Have they been reduced to concrete enough terms?

The way in which the terms are reduced to lower levels of abstraction will also vary. You can use anecdotes, examples, subtypes and classifications, physical descriptions, definitions, statistics. You can use words with strong emotional charge or neutral words. Again, your specific topic and purpose and your resources will influence the type of details you select.

WRITING ASSIGNMENTS

1. Write a fully developed paragraph for three of these topic sentences.

> Proverbs do not always contain sound advice.
> Slang can sometimes help make your point better than conventional language can.
> Americans are getting lazier.
> Practical jokes are not always funny.
> Women's fashions change more rapidly than men's.

2. Write a topic sentence for each of these subjects and then write a fully developed paragraph for one.

Student Newspapers   Television Personalities
A Successful Novel   The Typical American
A New Dance   The Jet Age

Exercises

8a   On the line below place the word, letter, or number that best answers the question.

1. Which detail would not be related to the key terms of this topic sentence?
   Folk songs are popular because of their greater realism.
   a. Political comments
   b. Honesty about love
   c. Interest in guitar playing
   d. Connection to the ecology movement

   (1) _____

2. Which detail would not be on the same level of abstraction as the others in developing this topic sentence?
   Cold as it seems in the daytime, at night Broadway is vibrant with warmth.
   a. Music coming out of bars
   b. People laughing in lines for movies
   c. People arguing politics in front of all-night restaurants
   d. Gaiety in the air

   (2) _____

3. Which detail would not be unified with regard to the key terms of this topic sentence?
   Inflation affected a varied cross section of the population.
   a. People on fixed incomes
   b. People on social security
   c. Hospital and medical fee increases
   d. Overcrowded conditions in hospitals

   (3) _____

4. Which detail would not be unified with regard to the key terms of this topic sentence?
   The pollution problem is too large for anything but direct government action to control.
   a. Refuse in streams
   b. Cars on streets and freeways
   c. Competition of imported cars
   d. Increased air travel

   (4) _____

5. In a paragraph on television westerns, which three details would be grouped under a major subdivision about the qualities of the hero?
   a. Hero wears light clothes.
   b. Monotonous plots
   c. The sheriff never drinks.
   d. Themes emphasize violence.
   e. A gun battle as climax
   f. Happy endings

g. Bad guys draw first.

h. Town has one main street.

(5) _____

6. Which detail is not on the same level of abstraction as the others as a subdivision in the development of a paragraph on historical novels?

a. Historical novels reduce war to manageable terms.

b. Such novels usually appeal to patriotic emotions.

c. Much historical fiction exploits violence and sex.

d. *Gone with the Wind* takes this approach to the Civil War.

(6) _____

7. Which of the following details reduces the level of abstraction of both the subject and the comment in this topic sentence?

The trends toward conformity have accelerated in recent years.

a. Restrictions on free speech have increased lately.

b. Conformist tendencies have spread even in elementary school children.

c. Conforming has become widespread.

d. A hardening of attitudes toward what is funny is plainly visible in this year's television programming.

(7) _____

8b   Supply the material requested by each question. Place it in the space provided.

1. Write three sentences that develop this topic sentence with three unified and concrete subdivisions:

Popular music reveals the qualities of youth today.

Use *It* as the subject in all and reduce the level of abstractions of the comment.

1. _____

_____

2. _____

_____

3. _____

_____

2. In this sentence of abstractions, place the comments from your three sentences in *1* in the appropriate steps under the comment of the topic sentence.

reveals the qualities of youth today.

_____

_____

_____

3. Write three sentences that develop this topic sentence:
Television provides many valuable services.
Use *It* as the subject of all and reduce the level of abstraction of the comment.

1. _____

_____

2. _____

_____

3. _____

_____

4. In this staircase of abstractions, place the comments from your three sentences in *3* on the appropriate steps under the comment of the topic sentence.

provides many valuable services.

5. Write three sentences that develop this topic sentence with three unified and concrete subdivisions:
Modern technology has aided the housewife.
In each one reduce the level of abstraction of both the subject and the comment.

1. _____

_____

2. _____

_____

3. _____

_____

6. Under the subject and comment of the topic sentence create your own staircase of abstractions for the key words of your three sentences in 5.

Modern technology

has aided the housewife.

chapter 9

Paragraphs: Patterns
of Development

Once you have refined your topic sentence and have a rough idea of the kind of details you have at your disposal, your next step is to consider the arrangement, the pattern of development in which you will place your details. And as you consider and work on your patterns, it may well be that you will have to reconsider either your topic sentence or the details you are going to use.

The conscious arrangement of a pattern for your paragraph may proceed in one of two basic ways. Your topic sentence itself may suggest or even demand a certain logical pattern: *This search for the largest audience possible produces some of the gravest problems in television.*

★　What pattern is suggested by this topic sentence? _____

A. A comparison
B. A cause-and-effect relationship
C. An enumeration of statistics
D. An illustrative anecdote

☆　B. The idea of one thing producing, or causing, others leads you to a pattern of cause-and-effect relationships.

Other types of topic sentences, however, may not call for any particular pattern of development, and so in these cases you can usually take your choice. In either situation, you need to be aware of the alternatives, the tools available for organizing the details that are the most concrete terms on the staircase of abstractions. Of the most frequently employed patterns, we will consider six in this chapter: enumeration, illustration, comparison and/or contrast, cause and effect, combined, and time or space.

Enumeration

The pattern of enumeration is usually a series of separate, parallel details, often building toward a climax with the most important fact last. This is a logical laundry list, a listing of relatively limited and brief concrete details, whether they are statistics, examples, or even authorities. They may all be examples of the same basic terms of the topic or some may be examples of one term, others examples of another. They may be definitions of several terms. They may be subdivisions, based on a consistent principle of analysis. As an example of the latter, when Samuel Taylor Coleridge wrote a paragraph explaining the four types of readers, he divided them into four classes, named them *Sponges, Sand-glasses, Strain-bags,* and *Mogul diamonds,* and then devoted a sentence to describing each.

In the following paragraph, notice that E. B. White enumerates many examples to develop his topic sentence.

> There is always the miracle of the by-products. Plane a board, the shavings accumulate around your toes ready to be chucked into the stove to kindle your fires (to warm your toes so you can plane a board). Draw some milk from a creature to relieve her fullness, the milk goes to the little pig to relieve his emptiness. Drain some oil from a crankcase, and you smear it on the roots to control the mites. The worm fattens on the apple, the young goose fattens on the wormy fruit, the man fattens on the young goose, the worm awaits the man. Clean up the barnyard, the pulverized dung from the sheep goes to improve the lawn (before a rain in autumn); mow the lawn next spring, the clippings go to the compost pile, with a few thrown to the baby chickens on the way; spread the compost on the garden and in the fall the original dung, after many vicissitudes, returns to the sheep in the form of an old squash. From the fireplace, at the end of a November afternoon, the ashes are carried to the feet of the lilac bush, guaranteeing the excellence of a June morning. (E. B. White, ''Cold Weather,'' *One Man's Meat.*)

★   How many separate examples does White use in this paragraph?

———

☆   *Twelve.* Some are in separate sentences, some are grouped in a single sentence. One, in the second sentence of the paragraph, is even in parentheses.

Here is another example.

> I began evaluating my fellow tramps as human material, and for the first time in my life I became face-conscious. There were some good faces, particularly among the young. Several of the middle-aged and the old looked healthy and well preserved. But the damaged and decayed faces were in the majority. I saw

faces that were wrinkled, or bloated, or raw as the surface of a peeled plum. Some of the noses were purple and swollen, some broken, some pitted with enlarged pores. There were many toothless mouths (I counted seventy-eight). I noticed eyes that were blurred, faded, opaque, or bloodshot. I was struck by the fact that the old men, even the very old, showed their age mainly in the face. Their bodies were still slender and erect. One little man over sixty years of age looked a mere boy when seen from behind. The shriveled face joined to a boyish body made a startling sight. (Eric Hoffer, *The Ordeal of Change.* Copyright 1952 by Harper & Row, Publishers, Inc. Reprinted with permission of the publishers.)

In this paragraph, Eric Hoffer has taken four sentences to complete his topic point, and then with the fifth sentence he begins an enumeration of the details that make clear the ways in which the faces were *damaged and decayed.*

Illustration

The pattern of illustration involves the use of an extended example (usually just one, but sometimes more) to develop the topic idea. This example may be a dramatized anecdote, a description of a single case, a single reference. It develops by going into one illustration in depth, rather than by providing a series of separate but parallel details.

In this sample Edgar Dale introduces his illustration with the word *Thus* and then tells a story.

Another frequent reason for failure in the communication of directions is that explanations are more technical than necessary. Thus a plumber once wrote to a research bureau pointing out that he had used hydrochloric acid to clean out sewer pipes and inquired, "Was there any possible harm?" The first reply was as follows: "The efficacy of hydrochloric acid is indisputable, but the corrosive residue is incompatible with metallic permanence." The plumber then thanked them for the information approving his procedure. The dismayed research bureau tried again, saying "We cannot assume responsibility for the production of toxic and noxious residue with hydrochloric acid and suggest you use an alternative procedure." Once more the plumber thanked them for their approval. Finally, the bureau, worried about the New York sewers, called in a third scientist who wrote: "Don't use hydrochloric acid. It eats hell out of the pipes." (Edgar Dale, "Clear Only If Known," *The News Letter,* Bureau of Educational Research, Ohio State University.)

★   In Dale's paragraph, which sentence is on a higher step on the staircase of abstractions? _____

☆   The first. It sets the topic, the generality, that is to be discussed. The story that follows is then at a more concrete, lower level of abstraction.

In this next paragraph the author sets up his central term—*suffocating*—first and then develops it with the expanded anecdote of his own personal experience.

Philadelphia is suffocating but in a different way. I speak from experience. Once I spent an hour in Philadelphia. I had got lost driving and instead of zipping by on the turnpikes, I found myself in the middle of town. I parked and got out and stood on a street corner near Independence Hall, holding my map and looking for a street sign and also sniffing the air to smell out what manner of place this was. Some young Negroes were moping around, no doubt sons of sons of the South. They looked at me sideways. I asked a fellow for directions but he hurried away. I hummed a tune and swung my arms to keep warm. Meanwhile all around us, ringing us 350 degrees around like a besieging army, were three or four million good white people sitting in their good homes reading *The Bulletin*. I got to thinking: I don't know a single soul in Philadelphia black or white. What is more, I never heard of anyone coming from Philadelphia except Benjamin Franklin and Connie Mack, or of anything ever happening in Philadelphia except the signing of the Declaration of Independence. What have all these people been doing here all these years? What are they doing now? They must be waiting. Waiting for what? For something to happen. Let me out of here! (Walker Percy, "New Orleans Mon Amour," *Harper's* Magazine, Sept., 1968. Copyright ©1968 by Walker Percy. Appeared originally in *Harper's* Magazine. Reprinted by permission of McIntosh and Otis, Inc.)

★   Which of the following two paragraphs is developed with the pattern of illustration? _____

A. For the primitive man the circle of solidarity is limited to those whom he can look upon as his blood relatives—that is to say, the members of his tribe, who are to him as family. I am speaking from experience. In my hospital I have primitives. When I happen to ask a hospitalized tribesman, who is not himself bedridden, to render little services to a bedridden patient, he will consent only if the latter belongs to his tribe. If not, he will answer me candidly: "This, no bother for me," and neither attempts to persuade him nor threats will make him do this favor for a stranger. (Albert Schweitzer, "The Evolution of Ethics.")

B. The undercurrent of admiration in hatred manifests itself in the inclination to imitate those we hate. Thus every mass movement shapes itself after its specific devil. Christianity at its height realized the image of the antichrist. The Jacobins practiced all the evils of the tyranny they had risen against. Soviet Russia is realizing the purest and most colossal example of monopolistic capitalism. Hitler took the Protocols of the Wise Men of Zion for his guide and textbook; he followed them "down to the veriest detail." (Eric Hoffer, *The True Believer*. Copyright 1951 by Harper & Row, Publishers, Inc. Reprinted with permission of the publishers.)

☆   A. In this paragraph Albert Schweitzer explains his topic point by reference to the single example of a tribesman in the hospital. In B Eric Hoffer develops his topic point (stated in the first two sentences) by reference to four separate but parallel examples: *Christianity, the Jacobins, Soviet Russia, Hitler.*

Comparison and/or Contrast

This pattern has two possibilities, but both are based on the same logical process. You explain one point by relating it to something that is similar or to something that is different. The relating of similar items is comparison; the relating of differing items is contrast. It is also possible to use both in a single paragraph of comparison *and* contrast.

In comparison and/or contrast patterns the two items being connected may both be equal parts of the topic: *The Colts' backfield is faster than the Rams'*. Or only one item may be the topic, with the second merely a means of describing or explaining the first: *The Colts' backfield reminds me of a well-tuned engine.*

Particularly in cases where the two items are equal parts of the topic, there are two basic ways in which the comparison/contrast may be made. First, all the details on one side may be separately presented, and then all the comparable details on the other: AAABBB. Second, a detail from each side may be alternated with a detail from the other: ABABAB.

★   In this paragraph of contrast are the details kept separate or alternated? _____

The most helpful phenomenon occurs on the university campuses. The scholar there is more than tolerated. He is actually the hero. When I remember the mores and patterns of my own college days and compare them to those of my children, I seem to have moved onto a different planet. Football games, raccoon coats, proms and a well-bred C average were our goals and our enthusiasms. We did not read, travel, discuss the arts, listen to Bach, or extend any sympathy to those who did. But the young now are so formidably intellectual, so on fire with the love of learning, that they fill me with an amused awe. They debate books, they rush to galleries, are knowing about art, religion, philosophy, history, even metaphysics, and all with the same zeal we used to reserve for tea-dancing at the Plaza. (Phyllis McGinley)

☆   *Kept separate.* Phyllis McGinley first refers to college students of the past, and then to college students of the present.

★   Is the following an example of a comparison or a contrast? _____

The space in question is not the ordinary living space of individuals and families but rather the interstices thereof. In New York millions of souls carve out living space on a grid like so many circles on graph paper. These lairs are more or less habitable. But the space between is a horrid thing, a howling vacuum. If you fall ill on the streets of New York, people grumble about having to step over you or around you. In New Orleans there is still a chance, diminishing perhaps, that somebody will drag you into the neighborhood bar and pay the innkeeper for a shot of

Early Times. (Walker Percy, op. cit. Copyright ©1968 by Walker Percy. Appeared originally in *Harper's Magazine*. Reprinted by permission of MacIntosh and Otis, Inc.)

☆   *Contrast.* Percy contrasts the differences between the experience of the streets in New York and New Orleans.

Here is one more example.

> With this type of person knocking about, and constantly crossing one's path if one has eyes to see or hands to feel, the experiment of earthly life cannot be dismissed as a failure. But it may well be hailed as a tragedy, the tragedy being that no device has been found by which these private decencies can be transferred to public affairs. As soon as people have power they go crooked and sometimes dotty, too, because the possession of power lifts them into a region where normal honesty never pays. For instance, the man who is selling newspapers outside the House of Parliament can safely leave his papers to go for a drink, and his cap beside them: anyone who takes a paper is sure to drop a copper into the cap. But the men who are inside the houses of Parliament—they can't trust one another like that; still less can the government they compose trust other governments. No caps upon the pavement here, but suspicion, treachery, and armaments. The more highly public life is organized the lower does its morality sink; the nations of today behave to each other worse than they ever did in the past; they cheat, rob, bully, and bluff, make war without notice, and kill as many women and children as possible; whereas primitive tribes were at all events restrained by taboos. (E. M. Forster, "What I Believe," *Two Cheers for Democracy*. Copyright 1939 by E. M. Forster. Reprinted with permission of Harcourt, Brace & World, Inc.)

In this paragraph, E. M. Forster states his topic point in the second sentence and then sets up a series of concrete contrasts between the major terms of the topic—*private decencies* and *public affairs.* He alternates from one side to the other, and then concludes with a more complicated set of contrasts in the last sentence.

Cause and Effect

This pattern is used to develop the cause-and-effect relationship established by a topic sentence. It organizes the details of a paragraph to show how one event, situation, or condition caused another, how one caused several others, how several caused several others, or several caused one. It can emphasize this basic causal relationship in several ways. For example, the several effects of a single cause can be emphasized: *A causes B, C, D.* Or the process can be reversed to show how several causes contributed to producing a central effect: *A is caused by B, C, D.* Or the relationship can involve a sequence of causes and effects: *A causes B, B causes C, C causes D.* Finally, this sequence in turn can be shown to have caused a final effect *E.*

In this paragraph, E. B. White intentionally exaggerates for humorous effect the cause-and-effect development of his topic sentence.

This tragedy, by itself, wouldn't have caused sport to decline, I suppose, but it set in motion a chain of other tragedies, the cumulative effect of which was terrific. Almost as soon as the shot was fired, the news flash was picked up by one of the sky writers directly above the field. He glanced down to see whether he could spot the trouble below, and in doing so failed to see another skywriter approaching. The two planes collided and fell, wings locked, leaving a confusing trail of smoke, which some observers tried to interpret as a late sports score. The planes struck in the middle of the nearby eastbound coast-to-coast Sunlight Parkway, and a motorist driving a convertible coupe stopped so short, to avoid hitting them, that he was bumped from behind. The pileup of cars that ensued involved 1,482 vehicles, a record for eastbound parkways. A total of more than three thousand persons lost their lives in the highway accident, including the two pilots, and when panic broke out in the stadium, it cost another 872 in dead and injured. News of the disaster spread quickly to other sports arenas, and started other panics among the crowds trying to get to the exits, where they could buy a paper and study a list of the dead. All in all, the afternoon of sport cost 20,003 lives, a record. And nobody had much to show for it except one small Midwestern boy who hung around the smoking wrecks of the planes, captured some aero newssmoke in a milk bottle, and took it home as a souvenir. (E. B. White, "The Decline of Sport (A Preposterous Parable)," *The Second Tree from the Corner.* Copyright 1935 by E. B. White. Reprinted with permission of Harper & Row, Publishers, Inc.)

★   Which pattern of emphasis does White employ? _____

A. A causes B, C, D.
B. A is caused by B, C, D.
C. A causes B, B causes C, C causes D.
D. E results because A causes B, B causes C, C causes D.

☆   D. Sport declined, he suggests, because the *firing of the shot* caused a *news flash* which in turn set off a whole chain reaction of events.

★   Which pattern of emphasis does the following paragraph employ?
_____

If the moon were suddenly struck out of existence, we should be immediately apprised of the fact by a wail from every seaport in the kingdom. From London and from Liverpool we should hear the same story—the rise and fall of the tide had almost ceased. The ships in dock could not get out; the ships outside could not get in; and the maritime commerce of the world would be thrown into dire confusion. (Robert Ball, *The Story of the Heavens.*)

A. A causes B, C, D.
B. A is caused by B, C, D.
C. A causes B, B causes C, C causes D.
D. E results because A causes B, B causes C, C causes D.

> ☆ A. Here the consequences are imaginary. *If* the *moon* were suddenly eliminated, the other details would then occur.

In the following paragraph by A. J. Liebling, a chain of cause-and-effect relationships is developed in this way: The use of television to sell beer and razor blades (causes) too many free fights (which cause) the disappearance of the small fight club (which causes) the inadequate training of young fighters (which causes) the crisis in boxing.

> The immediate crisis in the United States, forestalling the one high living standards might bring on, has been caused by the popularization of a ridiculous gadget called television. This is utilized in the sale of beer and razor blades. The clients of the television companies, by putting on a free boxing show almost every night of the week, have knocked out of business the hundreds of small-city and neighborhood boxing clubs where youngsters had a chance to learn their trade and journeymen to mature their skills. Consequently the number of good new prospects diminishes with every year, and the peddlers' public is already being asked to believe that a boy with perhaps ten or fifteen fights behind him is a top-notch performer. Neither advertising agencies nor brewers, and least of all the networks, give a hoot if they push the Sweet Science back into a period of genre painting. When it is in coma they will find some other way to peddle their peanuts. (A. J. Liebling, *The Sweet Science*. Reprinted with permission of The Viking Press, Inc.)

Combined Patterns

It is, of course, also possible to combine two or more of the basic patterns in a single paragraph. For example, you may enumerate several separate details and then provide an expanded illustration, or you may provide some details or an illustration and then have a comparison or contrast.

Time or Space

In the same way that contrasting, for example, is actually a way of ordering the details of a paragraph into a purposeful pattern, using time or space is an additional way of organizing the details or expanded illustration of a paragraph. When a narrative seems appropriate for developing your topic idea, then a chronological sequence of the events will give your separate sentences a meaningful pattern. When your support sentences are concerned with physical description, the order of space serves the same function. Guide the reader through the physical site by ordering the details in a pattern that he or she would encounter them in by following some logical course—around to the left, front to back, etc. Notice the way the novelist Raymond Chandler brings you through the site in the following sample:

> 1644 West 54th Place was a dried-out brown house with a dried-out brown lawn in front of it. There was a large bare patch around a tough-looking palm tree. On the porch stood one lonely wooden rocker, and the afternoon breeze made the

unpruned shoots of last year's poinsettias tap-tap against the cracked stucco wall. A line of stiff yellowish half-washed clothes jittered on a rusty wire in the side yard.

WRITING ASSIGNMENTS

1. Write a topic sentence, on any subject, that can lead to development by the pattern of enumeration or illustration. Then make whatever changes are necessary, if any, in the topic sentence so that it might be developed by each of these patterns: comparison of similarities, contrast of differences, cause and effect.
2. Write a fully developed paragraph for two of the topic sentences of *1.*
3. Broaden the scope of one of your topic sentences by raising its level of abstraction; use the revised form as a thesis sentence for a 300- to 500-word essay.

Exercises

9a   **A.** On the line below, place the letter that denotes the pattern of development illustrated by each sample paragraph.

a. Enumeration

b. Illustration

c. Comparison

d. Contrast of differences

e. Cause and effect

[1]   Dull and boring language is often spoken of as being full of platitude and cliché. Although the effect induced may be similar, the two terms are different in nature. A platitude is a flat idea, lacking any originality, but pronounced as if it were both novel and momentous. A platitude is an almost sure sign of pomposity. Men in public office are often guilty of platitudes, such as ''it is a great honor for me to be addressing this distinguished audience,'' or ''I pledge that I shall do my utmost to live up to the high honor you have accorded me.'' A cliché, on the other hand, is an expression which at one time did contain a fresh and forceful idea but which has become weak through repetition. A cliché is the result of linguistic inertia. Many clichés have become so embedded in our language that little or no thought is required to bring them to the surface. (From Charles Kaplan, *Guided Composition*. Copyright © 1968 by Holt, Rinehart and Winston, Inc.)

(1) _____

[2]   Inside the farmhouses in the mean winter months, life is a torpid wake for what was and what will be again when spring comes. If he is resourceful and lucky, the farmer can get occasional work and come home to the smell of meat frying on the kitchen stove. He will lie down on a pallet or on the bare floor behind the kitchen stove and let the healing warmth penetrate his arthritic joints, and for a while he can put out of his mind everything else in his world except the heat, the smell and the sound of grease crackling in the pan above him, and the beauty of his wife's hips as she moves about the kitchen. In another room, his children will huddle close to a space heater, staring at a television set turned up deafeningly loud because one of his children is partially deaf from too many colds that turned into too many untreated ear infections. The family will eat and sleep around the stoves. The pallet in the kitchen will become the bed for one of the middle boys. The parents and the babies will sleep in the two beds in the front room. The remaining one or two rooms are not heated, and the older children will sleep there, sometimes three or four to a bed. (Dwayne E. Walls, ''The Golden Token,'' in *The Chickenbone Special,* Harcourt Brace Jovanovich, 1971.)

(2) _____

[3]   Beyond technology is the larger question of attitude. Butchering on the farm when I was a boy had the quality of a ceremony. We would select, say, a steer, and pen it separately overnight. The next morning several of us boys—this was a boys' home as well as a farm—would walk the steer to a large compound and leave it standing, trusting as hell, near the concrete-floored area where we did the skinning and gutting. Then the farm manager, a man of great kindness and reserve, would take aim with a .22 rifle at the crosspoint of two imaginary lines drawn from the horns to the opposite eyes. And hold his bead until the steer was entirely calm, looking at him, a certain shot, because this man did not want to miss, did not want to hurt the animal he was about to kill. And we would stand in

a spread-out circle, at a respectful distance, tense with the drama of it, because we didn't want him to miss either. (Richard Rhodes, ''Watching the Animals,'' *Harper's* Magazine, March, 1970. Copyright ©1970 by Richard Rhodes. Originally appeared in *Harper's* Magazine. Permission granted by JCA Literary Agency, Inc.

(3) _____

[4]   School can help undo the damage. Actual personal experience with children of other groups can show a child directly, immediately and concretely that not all members of a group are blameworthy, stupid, dirty or dishonest. In addition, unprejudiced teachers can instruct children in the ways of clear thinking that underlie tolerance. There is a definite evidence that education reduces prejudices. It's been found, for example, that college graduates are less prejudiced on the whole than people with less education. Direct instruction about different groups and cultures, another study shows, reduced prejudice in those who were taught. (Ian Stevenson, ''People Aren't Born Prejudiced,'' *Parent's Magazine,* February, 1960.)

(4) _____

[5]   The family resemblance between football and war is, indeed, striking. Their languages are similar: ''field general,'' ''long bomb,'' ''blitz,'' ''take a shot,'' ''front line,'' ''pursuit,'' ''good hit,'' ''the draft,'' and so on. Their principles and practices are alike: mass hysteria, the art of intimidation, absolute command and total obedience, territorial aggression, censorship, inflated insignia and propaganda, blackboard maneuvers and stategies, drills, uniforms, formations, marching bands, and training camps. And the virtues they celebrate are almost identical: hyper-aggressiveness, coolness under fire, and suicidal bravery. (John McMurtry, ''Smash Thy Neighbor,'' *Macleans,* October, 1971.)

(5) _____

[6]   Nearly all the Southern writers I know were early, omnivorous, insatiable readers, and Miss Welty runs reassuringly true to this pattern. She had at arm's reach the typical collection of books which existed as a matter of course in a certain kind of Southern family, so that she had read the ancient Greek and Roman poetry, history and fable, Shakespeare, Milton, Dante, the eighteenth-century English and the nineteenth-century French novelists, with a dash of Tolstoy and Dostoievsky, before she realized what she was reading. When she first discovered contemporary literature, she was just the right age to find first W. B. Yeats and Virginia Woolf in the air around her; but always, from the beginning until now, she loved folk tales, fairy tales, old legends, and she likes to listen to the songs and stories of people who lived in old communities whose culture is recollected and bequeathed orally. (Katherine Anne Porter, Introduction to *A Curtain of Green* by Eudora Welty. Reprinted from *The Days Before* by Katherine Anne Porter by permission of Joan Daves)

(6) _____

[7]   A de-emphasis of privacy has affected in a very general way the conduct of our democracy. It is not only, as I have already suggested, that Congress deems itself privileged to pry into the lives of the people, but that the people feel entitled to pry into processes of government and into aspects of their elected officials that have traditionally been screened from immediate surveillance. Where no secrecy

is permitted, diplomacy becomes virtually extinct. As for negotiations between states, they can scarcely be carried on when each move and countermove of the bargaining process forms the substance of headlines within the hour. In such circumstances things must be said upon each side to captivate the crowd. The result is a lowering of the whole level of discourse between public men. I am tempted to mention, besides, the frantic kind of curiosity that allows the public to suppose that it is entitled to know the innermost biological details concerning the health of its representatives. That it should feel a responsibility for judging the fitness of a President to carry on his tasks is one thing; that it should, beyond that, consider it its privilege to subject his most initmate bodily functions to direct scrutiny could only happen where the foundations of privacy have been eroded. (August Heckscher, ''The Invasion of Privacy: The Reshaping of Privacy,'' Reprinted from *The American Scholar,* Volume 28, Number 1. Winter 1958/59. Copyright ©1958 by the United Chapters of Phi Beta Kappa. By permission of the publishers.)

(7) _____

B. On the line below place the word, letter, or number that best answers the question.

1. Which pattern of development from the list at the beginning of Exercise A is called for by this topic sentence?
   Living in fraternities radically changes the life of a college student—not always for the best.

(1) _____

2. Which patterns of development from the same list is called for by this topic sentence?
   Americans today differ from the old pioneers in their attitudes toward taking chances.

(2) _____

3. In the following paragraph, do the bulk of the details enumerate *causes* or *effects?*

The change of temper that came over American society with the loss of the Loyalists, was immense and far-reaching. For the first time the middle class was free to create a civilization after its own ideals. In rising to leadership it brought another spirit into every phase of life. Dignity and culture henceforth were to count for less and assertiveness for more. Ways became less leisurely, the social temper less urbane. The charm of the older aristocracy disappeared along with its indisputable evils. Although a few of the older wits like Mather Byles lingered on bitterly, and others like Gouverneur Morris accepted the situation philosophically, they belonged to the past. A franker evaluation of success in terms of money began to obscure the older personal and family distinction. New men brought new ways and a vulgar clamor of politics went hand in hand with business expansion. The demagogue and the speculator discovered a fruitful field for their activities. The new capitalism lay on the horizon of republican America, and the middle class was eager to hasten its development. (Vernon L. Parrington, *Main Currents in American Thought.* Reprinted with permission of Harcourt, Brace & World, Inc.)

(3) _____

4. In the following paragraph, are the details of the contrast *grouped* on one side and then the other or *alternated* between one side and then the other?

There are basic differences between the large and the small enterprise. In the small enterprise you operate primarily through personal contacts. In the large enterprise you have established "policies," "channels" of organization, and fairly rigid procedures. In the small enterprise you have, moreover, immediate effectiveness in a very small area. You can see the effect of your work and of your decisions right away, once you are a little above the ground floor. In the large enterprise even the man at the top is only a cog in a big machine. To be sure, his actions affect a much greater area than the actions and decisions of the man in the small organization, but his effectiveness is remote, indirect, and elusive. In a small and even in a middle-sized business, you are normally exposed to all kinds of experiences and expected to do a great many things without too much help or guidance. In the large organization you are normally taught one thing thoroughly. In the small one the danger is of becoming a jack-of-all trades and master of none. In the large it is of becoming the man who knows more and more about less and less. (Peter F. Drucker, "How to Be an Employee," *Fortune,* May, 1952, pp. 126-27.)

(4) _____

5. The following paragraph combines the patterns of cause and effect and comparison. Which sentences present the comparison?

The next ten years, I would guess, will *really* prove whether this nation or any nation so conceived and so dedicated can long endure and right now the prognosis is not good. We are losing ground nearly everywhere; we are not taking measures necessary to stop the loss; and hardly anybody seems to care. In our complacent, happy fashion, we assume that we can't lose—that if we stand firm, persevere and damn the Communists enough, Right will surely prevail in the end. Well, it didn't once before, when Athenian democracy was involved in a similar long, tiresome struggle with Spartan tyranny. On that occasion, an infinitely superior civilization went under, because it lacked the self-discipline to survive. One could cite other examples. Is it happening again, right here and right now? (Adlai Stevenson, from the Introduction to *Friends and Enemies.* Copyright 1959 by Adlai Stevenson. Reprinted with permission of Harper & Row, Publishers, Inc.)

(5) _____

9b Supply the material requested by each question. Place it in the space provided.

1. Write a topic sentence that calls for development by contrast of differences.

_____

_____

2. Write a topic sentence that calls for development by the pattern of cause and effect.

_____

_____

3. Write a paragraph that explains a striking character trait of a group or type of people by imitating the following use of an illustration.

Russians have an appealing aptitude for adding two and two and getting three or five. Hamilton Fish Armstrong, of the Council on Foreign Relations in New York, was astounded some years ago when a Russian acquaintance told him quietly that the distinguished quarterly he edits, *Foreign Affairs,* was subsidized by the House of Morgan. Mr. Armstrong, the most unsubsidized author imaginable, could not believe his ears. Blandly, triumphantly, the Russian pointed out that Russell C. Leffingwell, who is indeed a Morgan partner, was a member of the editorial board of the magazine, and had his name *printed*—ah!—on the masthead. It was impossible to convince the Russian that this did not prove, beyond peradventure of a doubt, that the Morgans ran Mr. Armstrong's magazine. (John Gunther, *Inside Russia Today.* Copyright 1958 by John Gunther. Reprinted with permission of Harper & Row, Publishers, Inc.)

_____

_____

_____

_____

_____

_____

_____

_____

_____

_____

_____

_____

4. Write a paragraph that develops this topic sentence with the pattern of enumeration: TV commercials provide some of the cleverest moments on the little screen.

_____

_____

_____

_____

_____

_____

_____

chapter 10

Coherence Between
and In Paragraphs

If the parts of your essay are unified and if they are logical subdivisions of a thesis, you still need to show the logic of your organization. You need to establish the *coherence* of your parts—the clear, logical, helpful relationships between the parts. You do this with the devices of rhetoric.

The preceding paragraph was just such a device. It established the coherence between this chapter and those that preceded it. How did it do this? It first referred to the materials of the preceding chapters and then pointed ahead to the materials of this chapter. Further, by its sentence strucure it showed the relationships between these materials: *If that is done, you still need to do this*.

These devices of rhetoric do two basic jobs. They show the coherence between major parts of an essay—in the case of your essays, mainly *between* paragraphs. And they show the coherence between the sentences *in* a single paragraph. We will call the first kind of coherence the marking of *transitions*. We will call the second kind the marking of *continuity*.

Effective Transitions

Your transitions are visual signals that mark the logical sequence of your thought. If that thought is hasty, confused, or digressive, no devices of writing are going to save it. But if that thought has created a logical pattern, that pattern can be given a greater emphasis and clarity by your use of the devices of transition. At each stage, these will show the reader where he is,

141

where he is going next, and what relationships between the parts he should keep in mind. One of the main jobs that the devices of transition perform is to keep the reader aware of the levels of the staircase of abstraction—whether a new block of material is at the same level as the previous block, whether it moves on to a more concrete level or returns to a higher level.

★   What words in this transition sentence show that the new block of material will be on the same step on the staircase as the previous block?

_____

An equally important result is overcrowding.

☆   *Equally important.* These words show that the new part is the equal of the previously covered part. The word *result* might also be serving as a transition signal here, especially if it is a term that has been used in a comparable position in the previous block of material.

In actual writing, these devices of transition are quite naturally used in various combinations; here we will artifically separate them for purposes of explanation.

1. The topic sentence

In addition to establishing the unity of a single paragraph, the topic sentence has another function. It also serves as a road sign. It shows the relationship between the one paragraph and the paragraph that came just before it, and it shows the relationship between the one paragraph and the controlling thesis of the whole essay. It provides new material; but it also provides a marker of transition.

> Unlike the Senate, who were narrow in their views, the President had a larger, idealistic vision of foreign policy.

Here, the last part of the sentence adds the new material, the topic to be developed in the paragraph—*the President's idealistic vision of foreign policy.* The first part of the sentence refers to the previous paragraph and establishes a basic contrast between the ideas of the President and the ideas of the Senate, which had been discussed previously.

★   In the following topic sentence, underline the word that starts the introduction of the new material:
Despite the Senate's primary responsibility, President Wilson was not without blame.

☆   *President.* Again, the last half of the sentence adds the new material and the first part refers to what was previously discussed. Further, the word *despite* shows the logical relationship between the materials, and the

> word *primary* shows that what is to be said about what the President did is not as important as what the Senate did. We should point out that the last half of the topic sentence need not always be the part that introduces the new material.

> Other factors have added to the growing powerlessness of the individual.

In this example, the last half of the sentence refers to the topic previously introduced—*the growing powerlessness of the individual.* The first part adds the new material—the *other factors* that produced this same result.

In all of the examples used so far, the transitional part of the topic sentence provided a résumé, or summary, of the ideas presented in the preceding sentence. This is not always the case:

> The third stage of the argument reaches deeper levels.

Here, only a general reference to the *argument,* rather than a specific summary, is used. And in addition, such key words as *third* and *deeper* set up the transitional relationships. We will examine the use of these other devices.

2. Key function words

One of the standard ways of showing the logical relationships of your parts is with a great variety of rhetorical function words. These are not tied to any particular subject or content, but can be used with any content to mark the logic of transitions.

One type of function word shows numerical relationship. These can be forms of numbers, such as *third* in the above example. Or they can be more generalized, such as *another, other, further, also, last, final.*

Another type shows emphasis and significance. These are usualy adjectives and adverbs, such as *deeper* in the above example, or *chief, main, primary, lesser, more important, most important, less important, opposite, contrasting, different, unique.*

A third type shows some form of grammatical and logical conjunction or connection. These include the many conjunctive adverbs, such as *however, moreover, thus, therefore, on the other hand, nevertheless, of course.* They include conjunctions, such as *despite, although, because, and, but, yet.* They include comparative words such as *like, as, than.*

> ★   Underline the three words that are the key function words in these transitional sentences.
>
> Another thinker of the later nineteenth century also helped to mould the climate of political opinion. Like Darwin, Freud was a scientist without pretensions to be a philosopher.

> ☆   *Another, also, like.* They set up the sense of addition and comparison that is the logical relationship between the new paragraph about Freud and the preceding one about Darwin.

3. Key content words

The insertion and repetition of key content words is also an important device. These words refer to key elements of the particular content of the essay and so establish the emphasis and definition of subdivisions. In the example *The third stage of the argument reaches deeper levels,* the word *argument* establishes the content repetition for the paragraph.

Sometimes these key content words are used to give the résumé of the preceding paragraph as well as the definition of the topic of the new paragraph.

> ★   Underline the two words that sum up the preceding topic.
> What holds true in the economic sphere is also true in the political sphere.
>
> ☆   *Economic sphere.* These content words sum up the previous point of emphasis, while the words *political sphere* sum up the new point of emphasis. The repetition of the word *sphere* with the two different modifiers make the transistion clear. The function word *also* and the comparative structure of the sentence complete the marking of the logical relationship between the paragraphs.

At other times these key content words do not establish a reference to the preceding paragraph, but rather emphasize the new stage only. In doing this they may still *repeat* the key words that had been used at the opening of the essay and also throughout the essay. Here is how Herbert J. Muller uses this device in an essay entitled "The Nature of Man." At the opening of his essay, Muller sets up four basic characteristics for man: "that man is a *social animal* (1), an animal with *unique powers of mind* (2), and therefore a *culture-building animal* (3). Through the development of culture, which long ago tended to obscure the individual, he eventually realized that he was also an animal with a distinctive *capacity for individuality or personality* (4)." (Italics and numbers added.)

As Muller reaches each of these subdivisions in the course of his essay, he begins the paragraph or group of paragraphs with sentences that repeat the key content words.

That man is a social animal should be as plain.

Here the first term *social animal* is repeated to set up the first major subdivision. There is also a comparison being made to a secondary transitional point that man is an animal.

> ★   Underline the three words that define the subject of the next stage, or subdivision, of the essay:
> Also beyond dispute, and a source of incessant dispute, are the powers of mind that most clearly distinguish man from all other animals.
>
> ☆   *Powers of mind.* This transitional sentence also sets up some other points (as are indicated by the *also,* the repetition of *dispute,* the *most clearly*);but its main function is to call attention to the movement to the second major subdivision.

Together with his sociality, it has made him a culture-building animal.

This sentence makes a reference to the second point and introduces the third, *culture-building.*

> ★   Underline the key content words that define the topic for the fourth subdivision:
> With this emerged the choicest and the most troublesome product of civilization—the self-conscious individual.
>
> ☆   *The self-conscious individual.* The phrase repeats, with a variation, the fourth term of the opening. The sentence also includes these key function terms: *choicest* and *the most troublesome.* These show the way in which the subdivision will be treated.

4. Pronouns

Pronouns, such as *this, that, it, he, they,* can also establish the logic of your transitions. Notice the use of *this* in the example just above. You should beware, however, of using a pronoun with too vague a reference. Your transitional pronouns should refer to nouns and ideas that were used in the immediately preceding sentences, not to nouns and ideas that have been obscured by other nouns and ideas that have come after them.

5. Synonyms

In this variation, you can use a substitute for a key word, rather than repeat the exact word itself. If in one paragraph you say someone was responsible, your transition may say that someone else was also *to blame.* If throughout an essay you are referring to the idea of *freedom,* you may use various synonyms, such as *liberty* or *the right to protest,* to announce your subdivisions.

Effective Continuity

The devices for achieving effective continuity between the sentences *in* a paragraph are, to a great degree, the same devices that are used for achieving effective transitions *between* the paragraphs of an essay. In both cases the same logical process is at work: the establishing of clear relationships between the parts. Within the paragraph, then, you want to make sure that the reader can move easily and smoothly from sentence to sentence and can understand how each new sentence is connected to the topic of the paragraph and to the sentence immediately before it, how each fits into the pattern established for the levels of abstraction.

1. The topic sentence

A sharply refined topic sentence is the first step in establishing a coherent paragraph. If its terms are concrete enough, pointed enough, and clearly enough related, they will lead you to establish logical relationships between the sentences. If, for example, your topic concretely sets up the terms of a description—such as *his room was like his face—cheerful*—you are not likely to wander incoherently in putting together details as you might be if the terms were vague—*his room had a certain personality to it.*

Besides its concreteness, a good topic sentence also has the value of suggesting the particular logical sequence or pattern for the following sentences: space, time, comparison and contrast, cause and effect, classification, etc.

But whatever the logical pattern established by the topic sentence, you must still use the specific devices that make that pattern visible to the reader. Notice how the italicized words in this passage by Alexander Petrunkevitch clarify the chronological pattern of the paragraph.

> *When* the grave is finished, the wasp returns to the tarantula to complete her ghastly enterprise. *First* she feels it all over once more with her antennae. *Then* her behavior becomes more aggressive. She bends her abdomen, protruding her sting, *and* searches for the soft membrane at the point *where* the spider's leg joins its body—the only spot *where* she can penetrate the horny skeleton. *From time to time,* as the exasperated spider slowly shifts ground, the wasp turns on her back *and* slides along with the aid of her wings, trying to get under the tarantula *for* a shot at the vital spot. *During* all this maneuvering, *which* can last for several minutes, the tarantula makes no move to save itself. *Finally* the wasp corners it against some obstruction *and* grasps one of its legs in her powerful jaws. *Now at last* the harassed spider tries a desperate but vain defense. The two contestants roll over and over on the ground. It is a terrifying sight *and* the outcome is always the same. The wasp *finally* manages to thrust her sting into the soft spot and holds it there for a few seconds *while* she pumps in the poison. *Almost immediately* the tarantula falls paralyzed on its back. Its legs stop twitching; its heart stops beating. *Yet* it is not dead, as is shown by the fact *that* if taken from the wasp it can be restored to some sensitivity *by* being kept in a moist chamber for several months. (From "The Spider and the Wasp," Alexander Petrunkevitch, Copyright ©1952 by Scientific American, Inc. August, 1952. All rights reserved.

2. Key function words

The same kind of rhetorical function words are used to show continuity between the sentences in paragraphs as are used in topic sentences to show transitions between paragraphs. You use words that show numerical relationships, words that show emphasis and significance, words that show grammatical and logical conjunction or connection.

★   *Nevertheless* is which type of function word? _____

A. A word that shows numerical relationships
B. A word that shows emphasis and significance
C. A word that shows grammatical and logical conjunction or connection.

☆   C.

3. Key content words

The key content words pick up the key terms of the topic sentence and use them—once more or with repetitions—to establish coherence through the sentences of a paragraph.

★   In this excerpt, what key term is repeated? _____

At this initial stage of the argument reason itself is not dethroned from its supreme role in the decision of political issues. The citizen is merely asked to surrender his right of decision to the superior reason of the expert. At the second stage of the argument reason itself is used to dethrone reason. The social psychologist, employing rational methods of investigation, discovers that men in the mass are often most effectively moved by nonrational emotions such as admiration, envy, hatred, and can be most effectively reached not by rational argument, but by emotional appeals. ... The appeal is no longer to the reason of the citizen, but to his gullibility.

☆   *Reason.* It is also used in the variation *rational* and, further, set off against its opposites.

4. Pronouns

The clear use of pronouns is a necessary part of paragraph continuity.

★   In this excerpt what is the chief pronoun used to establish continuity? _____

In general, men are passive under sense and the routine of habitual inferences. They are unable to free themselves from the importunities of the apparent facts and apparent relations which solicit their attention; and when they make room for unapparent facts, it is only for those which are unfamiliar to their minds. Hence, they can see little more than what they have been taught to see; they can only think what they have been taught to think. ...

☆   *They.* In addition to the six uses of *they,* there are also the variations of *themselves* and *their* used twice.

In the following example, note the uses of the pronouns *it* and *its*.

> For any number of reasons New Orleans should be less habitable than Albany or Atlanta. Many of its streets look like the alleys of Warsaw. In one subdivision, feces empty into open ditches. Its garbage collection is whimsical and sporadic. Its tax assessment system is absurd. It spends more money on professional football and less on its public library than any other major city. It has some of the cruelest slums in America and blood-sucking landlords right out of Dickens, and its lazy complacent city judges won't put them in jail. It plans the largest air-conditioned domed sports stadium in the world and has no urban renewal to speak of. Its Jefferson Parish is the newest sanctuary for Mafia hoods. Its Bourbon Street is as lewd and joyless a place as Dante's Second Circle of Hell, lewd with that special sad voyeur lewdness which marks the less felicitous encounters between Latin permissiveness and Anglo-Saxon sex morality. (Walker Percy, "New Orleans Mon Amour." Copyright ©1968 by Walker Percy. Originally appeared in *Harper's* Magazine. Reprinted with permission of McIntosh and Otis, Inc.)

5. Synonyms

The use of alternate words is of value within the paragraph in the same way that it is of value throughout the essay. Within the paragraph these synonyms often take the form of more *concrete* alternative terms. In this next example, the two key terms of *revolt* and *accepted American order* are repeated throughout the paragraph in the form of more concrete synonyms.

> A first-class revolt against the accepted American order was certainly taking place during those early years of the Post-war Decade, but it was one with which Nikolai Lenin had nothing whatever to do. The shock troops of the rebellion were not alien agitators, but the sons and daughters of well-to-do American families, who knew little about Bolshevism and cared distinctly less, and their defiance was expressed not in obscure radical publications or in soap-box speeches, but right across the family breakfast table into the horrified ears of conservative fathers and mothers. Men and women were still shivering at the Red Menace when they awoke to the no less alarming Problem of the Younger Generation, and realized that if the Constitution were not in danger, the moral code of the country certainly was. (Frederick Lewis Allen, "The Revolution in Manners and Morals," *Only Yesterday*. Copyright 1931 by Frederick Lewis Allen. Reprinted with permission of Harper & Row, Publishers, Inc.)

6. Maintenance of subject

Closely allied to the use of key content words, pronouns, and synonyms is the maintenance of subject. As much as possible, try to maintain the same grammatical subject throughout the paragraph, as in the use of *We* in the following example.

> We Americans have a strange—and to me disturbing—attitude toward the subject of power. We don't like the word. We don't like the concept. We are suspicious of people who talk about it. We like to feel that the adjustment of conflicting interests is something that can be taken care of by juridical norms and institutional devices, voluntarily accepted and not involving violence to the feelings or interests of anyone. We like to feel that this is the way our own life is arranged.

<u>We</u> <u>like</u> <u>to</u> <u>feel</u> that if this principle were to be understood and observed by others as it is by us, it would put an end to many of the misunderstandings and conflicts that have marked our time

7. Sentence patterns

A final useful device is the repetition of sentence pattern; this can also involve the repetition of key words.

★ In the paragraph cited just above, what four words introduce a sentence pattern that is repeated four times? _____

☆ *We like to feel.* And in addition, a *We don't like* pattern is used twice.

This repetition of sentence pattern does not always involve the repetition of key words. It may, instead, consist of the repetition of types of clauses or phrases: beginning a series of sentences with *-ing* terms such as *Walking down the street;* or beginning a series of sentences with subordinate clauses like *Because he had seen the light;* or using similar balanced or parallel forms, such as *not only this, but that.*

In this next example, Charles Kaplan uses the parallel pattern of "It's funny when ..." at the start of sentences.

Not everything that we call "funny" makes us laugh. Sometimes we call an event or a situation funny that is anything but humorous. It's funny when you search for your car keys in the pouring rain and you distinctly remember having had them in your hand just a few minutes earlier. It's funny when you clap a total stranger heartily on the back in the mistaken belief that he's an old friend. It's funny when you discover that your one-week-old fifty-dollar jacket has now been reduced to $29.95. It's funny when you discover, after you have finished typing your thirty-three-page term paper, that you have used the wrong footnote forms throughout. (Charles Kaplan, *Guide to Composition,* copyright © 1968 by Holt, Rinehart and Winston, Inc.)

WRITING ASSIGNMENTS

1. Write a topic sentence for each of the following subjects. Then develop each topic sentence into a paragraph of at least five sentences. Underline words in each sentence that establish the coherence of your paragraphs.
   College Grading
   Cheating
   The Personality of a Room
   Space Explorations
   School Cafeterias
2. Explain the kind of logidcal relationship established by each of the underlined coherence words in *1.*

3. Write a five-paragraph essay on one of the following subjects. Underline
the words that establish coherence between and in paragraphs.
A Type of Television Program
Popular Songs
Student Leaders
An Influential Teacher
Marriage Today

Exercises

10a **A.** In the topic sentences that follow identify each of the italicized transition words as one of the following types. Place the appropriate letter on the line below.

    a. Numerical relationship
    b. Modifier of emphasis or significance
    c. Logical conjunction or conjunctive adverb
    d. Repeated content word
    e. Pronoun
    f. Synonym

    1. *But* the unhappy truth is that scientists still know very little about smog's effects on human health.

(1) _____

    2. A *third* quality of English, therefore, is its relatively fixed word order.

(2) _____

    3. Not all the above *qualities* are in themselves necessarily good, nor have they all contributed to the general success of English.

(3) _____

    4. Yet *these* people are never content with what they have.

(4) _____

    5. All of this would seem extraordinary, but the *most* amazing truth of all is still to be defined.

(5) _____

B. In the paragraph that follows identify each of the italicized transition and continuity words as one of the types listed in Exercise A. Place the appropriate letter on the corresponding numbered line to the right.

The individual in today's world, *therefore,*[1] can no longer look to the nation as the main source of his security. *It*[2] is able no longer to protect *him*[3] against invasion or assault from other nations. *It*[4] is *able no longer*[5] to furnish the main conditions of *his*[6] growth or to safeguard his values or institutions or culture or property. No matter how wide the oceans that surround the *nation,*[7] no matter how bristling its defenses, *its*[8] people are totally vulnerable to shattering attack. The *nation*[9] possesses retaliatory power, true, but even in the exercise of that power, *it*[10] engages in a form of self-assault, for power in today's world is directed against the delicate and precarious conditions that make the existence possible, and indeed, against the mainstream of life itself. (Norman Cousins, " Triumph over the Bully," *Saturday Review,* May 14, 1960, p. 24. Copyright 1960 Saturday Review, Inc.)

(1) _____
(2) _____
(3) _____
(4) _____
(5) _____
(6) _____
(7) _____
(8) _____
(9) _____
(10) _____

C. On the line below write the key word or words that establish coherence in each of the following items. There may be more than one in each.

1. Nonetheless, apathetic pupils are the greatest problem of all.

(1) _____

2. For one thing, they spread an air of disconent.

(2) _____

3. But more importantly, they may have serious psychological problems.

(3) _____

4. These problems can warp their entire lives.

(4) _____

5. Consequently, teachers must concentrate on these pupils.

(5) _____

6. Another thinker of the nineteenth century helped to mould the climate of political opinion.

(6) _____

7. Freud, however, played a far different role.

(7) _____

8. Most of all, he showed us how to think about the unconscious.

(8) _____

9. On the other hand, he left many unsolved questions.

(9) _____

10. These questions still plague us.

(10) _____

10b   Supply the material requested by each question. Place it in the space provided.

1. Rewrite the second of these two sentences to establish better coherence by the use of a repeated sentence pattern:

As our population grows and our cities become more crowded, we will have to build better systems of mass transporation. It is also imperative to have more public recreation facilities.

_____

_____

2. Rewrite the second of these two sentences to establish better coherence by the use of a function word or phrase:

Businessmen have always praised Arthur Miller's play *Death of a Salesman*. The play is a savage indictment of business ethics.

_____

_____

3. Rewrite the second of these two sentences to establish better coherence by the use of the repetition of a key content word:

Teenage marriage creates many problems. It is difficult for young married couples to have the emotional maturity to adjust to each other's temperament.

_____

_____

4. Write a topic sentence on any subject. Imitate the transitional devices of comparison and repetition in this sentence:

What holds true in the economic sphere is also true in the political sphere.

_____

_____

5. Write a topic sentence on any subject. Imitate the comparative transitional device of this sentence:

And just as there is a best size for every animal, so the same is true for every human institution.

_____

_____

6. Write three sentences that explain a character trait of a type or group of people. Imitate the pattern of coherence established in this sample:

Americans are a slow people, but they seldom look back once they've changed. They do not give up an extreme position easily. But once they do give it up, they look upon it as an obstacle to be removed immediately.

_____

_____

_____

_____

_____

_____

7. Write a paragraph with three equal and related supporting details to develop this topic sentence:

The worst result of television is that it deadens the impulse to communicate with other people.

Underline your devices of coherence in the three sentences of development.

_____

_____

_____

_____

_____

_____

_____

section four

Shaping
Sentences

chapter 11

Sentence Patterns
and Sentence Combining

By themselves words are bloodless. Only as you put them together in
sentences do they develop a pulse, a heartbeat of meaning. Take the words
thoughts, language, and *shapes.* Alone each is anemic. Joined in a sentence,
Language shapes thoughts, they pulsate; they dare you to think, to talk, even to
argue. The sentence is essential to writers because it organizes their words into
living thoughts. It is the means of moving from the abstract to the concrete
and of showing the logical relationships between the abstract and concrete
elements of their thoughts and ideas.

The subject of a sentence is the word, phrase, or clause the sentence is
about. Your subject should capture your exact point of emphasis and should
be on the lowest level of the staircase possible that still keeps your point as
complete as you intend it to be. The verb is the word or group of words that
makes a comment about the subject. It is the basis of the part of the sentence
that makes a comment about the subject and thus makes it more concrete. The
subject and verb, plus at times an object or a noun or adjective complement,
make up the core, the basis of most sentences.

Before we take up basic patterns, however, we need to define a few key
terms. For our purposes, sentences are composed of nouns, verbs, adjectives,
and adverbs. These *parts of speech* can be single words or groups of
words—phrases and clauses.

Nouns are naming words: they answer the question *what.* They act as subjects or as objects. As objects they can receive the action of the verb, tell for
whom the action of the verb is performed, tell what a direct object is, or appear

156

as the key word in a prepositional phrase. They also act as complements after *to be* verbs and appositives that rename other nouns.

★   Underline the nouns in these two sentences.

1. The boys threw the ball.
2. Tom was the man.

☆   You should have underlined *boys, ball, Tom,* and *man. Boys* is the subject of the first sentence; *ball* is the object of the verb *threw; Tom* is the subject of the second sentence; and *man* is the noun complement.

Verbs are words that tell what subjects do or are. They can be transitive, intransitive, or linking. Transitive verbs take objects, words that receive the action of the verb. These verbs carry the action from the subject to the object. Intransitive verbs are complete in themselves; they do not depend upon an object to complete their meaning. A linking verb relates, or links, the subject to a noun or adjective complement. Linking verbs are usually parts of the verb *to be,* but they also include such verbs as *appear, become, feel, seem, smell,* and *taste.*

★   Underline the verbs in these sentences and mark them (T) transitive, (I) intransitive, (L) linking.

1. They drove the cars around the track.
2. In the morning we went to the store.
3. By December he was a man of distinction.

☆   You should have underlined *drove, went,* and *was. Drove* is a transitive verb; it carries the action from the subject, *They,* to the object, *cars. Went* is an intransitive verb; it is complete. *Was* is a linking verb, relating the subject, *he,* to the noun complement, *man.*

An adjective is a word that modifies a noun or words or groups of words used as nouns. By modifying, adjectives narrow the meaning of these other words and so help to make them more concrete. Adjectives answer the questions *which, what, what kind of,* or *how many,* as in the following sentence:

The *four-cylinder* car knocked over *three tall* trees on Central.

Adverbs modify verbs, adjectives, or other adverbs, and thus make them more concrete. They answer the questions *how, when, where, why, to what degree,* and *how often,* as is seen in these sentences:

He fought *courageously,* but the replacements arrived *too* late.
We visited there *regularly.*
He was a *very* big boy.

We don't always think of words by themselves; we often recognize them in groups. We call these word groups phrases and clauses. A phrase is a group of words (two or more) having no subject or verb but working as a unit. Phrases can do the work of nouns, verbs, adjectives, and adverbs. The phrases most frequently used begin with two kinds of signal words. One type begins with a preposition such as *of, in, on, by, to: to the house.* Another type begins with a verbal, either an *-ing* form of a verb or an infinitive form: *buying the car, to buy the car.* These phrases are particularly useful as modifiers that reduce the level of abstraction of the words that they are attached to.

★   Underline the phrases in these two sentences:

1. Humming the tune was his form of entertainment.
2. It had been seen in the sky.

☆   You should have underscored *Humming the tune,* which acts as a noun, the subject of the sentence; *of entertainment,* an adjective phrase telling what kind of form; and *in the sky,* an adverb phrase telling where.

A clause is a group of words having a subject and verb and working as a unit. Independent clauses are the main statements of sentences and begin with no particular signal word. Dependent clauses do the work of nouns, adjectives, and adverbs; they are a part of independent clauses or are attached to them. One type (which is used as an adverb) begins with a signal like *because, if, when, while, although,* etc. The other type (used as a noun or adjective) begins with *who, which, what,* or *that.* The noun clauses are used for complicated noun statements; the adjective and adverb clauses are modifiers that reduce the level of abstraction.

★   Underline the dependent clauses in these three sentences:

1. Who ruined the blanket was a mystery.
2. They were all pleased by his attitude, which made clear his eagerness.
3. While we were in Bermuda, our neighbors rebuilt our house.

☆   You should have underlined *Who ruined the blanket,* the subject of the first sentence; *which made clear his eagerness,* an adjective clause telling what kind of attitude; and *While we were in Bermuda,* an adverb clause telling when and modifying the verb *rebuilt.*

Normal Core Sentences

To write a sentence, you normally put the subject first, then follow it with the verb: You call this subject-verb arrangement normal word order. Sentences that follow this order are normal sentences. There are four basic normal core sentence patterns:

Normal Core Sentence Patterns

Pattern 1 (S–V)	*S subject* John	*V verb* farmed.	
Pattern 2 (S–V–DO)	*S subject* John	*V verb* planted	*DO direct object* trees
Pattern 3 (S–LV–NC)	*S subject* John	*LV linking verb* is (a)	*NC noun complement* farmer.
Pattern 4 (S–LV–AC)	*S subject* John	*LV linking verb* is	*AC adjective complement* skillful.

Pattern 1 is composed of a subject and an intransitive verb. Pattern 2 contains a subject, a transitive verb, and a direct object. The direct object receives the action expressed by the verb. Pattern 3 is composed of a subject, a linking verb, and a noun complement. Pattern 4 is composed of a subject, a linking verb, and an adjective complement. In Patterns 3 and 4, the verb is equivalent to an equal sign (John = farmer; John = skillful).

Most sentences you write will be more complicated than the four cores above; they will be more fully developed. But once the core is formed, you need only flesh it out with modifiers—single words, phrases, and clauses—that say exactly what you mean. Or transform it into one of its possible variations. The core words of a sentence are the words that give it its basic core pattern.

★   Underline the core words in this sentence:
Three tall men who ate with their gloves on flirted outrageously with the waitress.

☆   You should have underlined *men* and *flirted,* for they are the core words in this Pattern 1 normal sentence. *Men* is the subject; *flirted* is the verb. Every other word, phrase, or clause in the sentence in some way modifies the meaning of these core words and helps make the statement more concrete.

Most fully developed sentences are merely fleshed-out cores of one of the basic sentence patterns.

★   Match each of these sentences with the correct pattern. Put the correct letter in the blanks.

A. He was a soldier long before the   Pattern 1 _____
   war.
B. The enormous elm stood by the   Pattern 2 _____
   front porch

C. The sandy beach seemed beautiful   Pattern 3 _____
   in July.
D. John's mother gave his room to   Pattern 4 _____
   his sister.

☆   B, D, A, C. The core words in B are *elm*, the subject, and *stood*, the
verb (S–V). The core words in D are *mother*, the subject; *gave*, the verb;
and *room*, the direct object (S–V–DO). The core words in A are *He*, the
subject; *was*, the linking verb; and *soldier*, the noun complement
(S-LC-NC). The core words in C are *beach*, the subject; *seemed*, the linking verb; and *beautiful*, the adjective complement (S-LV-AC).

There are, of course, a number of variations on these basic cores. One example of a variation would be the reversed, or expletive, pattern: *There were fifteen people at the meeting.* In this variation, the subject comes after the verb, with
the word *there* in front of it. Another variation is the passive pattern; in this
pattern the subject is the person or thing acted upon: *Lovely green shoes were worn
by her.* These are useful patterns, but they are often misused; used carelessly,
they can blur emphasis or increase wordiness.

Sentence Combining

Often, beginning writers use too many sentences. Each idea, opinion, feeling,
or fact is kept in a separate sentence. This kind of writing has two chief flaws.
It blurs emphasis: minor points look like major points and vice versa. It blurs
logical relationships: it doesn't make clear exactly how one point is related to
another.

The cure is to combine those ideas in single sentences, giving proper weight
to the main points and establishing clear, logical relationships between parts.

★   Combine these two sentences: Sue met a young man. He was
charming.

_____

☆   You could have said *Sue met a charming young man* or possibly *Sue met a
young man who was charming.* The *charming* point does not need a whole
sentence by itself.

We can look at the same process in reverse. Here is a sentence that does
establish the right emphasis and relationship of parts: *The Sex Pistols, the most
popular punk band in England, gave an outrageous performance.*

That sentence is a combination of a series of points. You might think of
them in a sequence like the one that follows, but they hang together better when
they are reduced and combined: *The Sex Pistols are a punk band. They perform in
England. They are the most popular punk band there. They gave an outrageous performance.*

Some writers fail to make this necessary shift from thought to sentence pattern. They can end up with a whole paragraph of awkward, choppy sentences that lack emphasis and clarity. Here is an example of such a paragraph.

> They've come to Aspen. All of them have come. They've stormed in. The hot-doggers have come. The lounge lizards have come too. The ski bunnies have arrived. The Hollywood crowd is there. The snow has come too. It has come in abundance. Last year was different. It was a drought year. The drought was in the West. It was disastrous. This resort opened late. It is in Colorado. It was late by a month and a half. This year is different. The ski lift lines are long. The skiers have to wait in line. They wait as long as forty minutes. The time drags. The snow is deep. It is on the slopes. It is packed five feet there. It is fifteen feet high along the streets. The streets are in the city. The boutiques are on the curbs. Restaurants are busy. Tables must be booked in advance. At the Ute City Banque cafe they must be reserved four days in advance. That cafe is chic. Help-wanted ads have increased. They have tripled. They are carried in the *Aspen Times*. Restaurant owners are raiding each other. They are hiring each other's dishwashers.

★   On a separate sheet of paper, rewrite the choppy paragraph on Aspen. Combine the ideas and evidence to give them the emphasis they need and to show proper logical relationships.

☆   Your rewrite should look something like this paragraph from *Newsweek* (January, 23, 1978):

They've all stormed into Aspen; the hot-doggers and the lounge lizards, the ski bunnies and the Hollywood crowd. And so, in abundance, has the snow. Last year, during the West's disastrous drought, the big Colorado resort opened a month and a half late; now lift line waits can drag out to 40 minutes. The snow is packed 5 feet high along the city's boutique-lined curbs. Tables must be booked four days in advance at the chic Ute City Banque cafe. The Aspen Times's help-wanted ads have tripled, and restauranteurs are raiding each other's dishwashers. "If a guy gets $4.50 an hour," said one, "I'll offer him $5." Copyright 1978, by Newsweek, Inc. All rights reserved. Reprinted with permission.)

Main and secondary points

When you combine several points into a single sentence, you should keep track of which are the main points and which are the secondary points. Adding together two equal main points will need a different sentence pattern than combining a main point and a secondary one in a single sentence. Here are two equal ideas:

James liked water-skiing.
Sara enjoyed paddle tennis.

Rather than write these in two separate sentences, you'd need to combine them into one and set up the contrast with a word like *but: James liked water-skiing, but Sara enjoyed paddle tennis.* This pattern puts together two equal subject-and-verb statements to make clear that they are both main points. Coordinating conjunctions like *and, but, or* can also be used between single words and other grammatical elements to stress that you are combining two equal ideas.

> James liked water-skiing.
> He liked paddle tennis also.

Instead of two separate sentences, one combined sentence would read: *James liked water-skiing and paddle tennis.*

On the other hand, you frequently want to combine points that are not equal—one main and one or more secondary points. This combination will not use the pattern with the coordinating conjunctions.

> Joseph kept his Chevy in good shape.
> It was a 1968 model.

Here the second idea is clearly secondary and should not be added to the first with an *and*. Instead it can be reduced and placed inside the first statement as a secondary point.

> Joseph kept his 1968 Chevy in good shape.

Loose and periodic sentences

We'll be looking some more in the next chapter at sentences with two or more main points. Here we'll examine further the patterns for one main point and some secondary points. When you see that you have one main point, the next step is to decide to place the pattern for that main subject-and-verb statement first in the sentence or last. In what is called the *loose* sentence, the main, climactic pattern comes first; and then the secondary points are built up afterwards, accumulating additional elements as the sentence goes along. The following Pattern 1 normal sentence illustrates the loose pattern for combining a number of points into a single sentence:

> Joy's new car sputtered all the way to the garage at the other end of town.

The subject *car* and the verb *sputtered* both appear in the first four words.

Most sentences you write are loose. If you wrote all loose sentences, however, you would risk monotony. You try, therefore, to vary your sentence patterns. To do so, you sometimes use a periodic sentence, a sentence in which the main idea, the core, is at the end instead of at the beginning. This sentence is periodic:

> Posted at the door in his red and blue uniform that made him look almost like a figure out of a story book, the major-domo announced the guests.

The main idea of this sentence is *the major-domo announced the guests.* This core is held off until the very end. The twenty-three words in front of the main idea make up a long modifier that forces the reader to wait for the major idea, which is finally stated in a Pattern 2 normal sentence.

Because the periodic sentence holds back the main idea, you can call it a suspended-interest sentence. Rather than satisfy the reader's curiosity at the start, the periodic sentence gives him something to look forward to.

★ Underline the main subject, verb, and object of this periodic sentence:

If the legislature passes the new tax law over the senate's reservations and the governor's veto, the National Education Association will lift its sanctions.

☆ You should have underlined *National Education Association,* the subject; *will lift,* the verb; and *sanctions,* the object. The long *if* clause would follow rather than precede the subject and the verb if this were a loose sentence. The main idea, the core, is a Pattern 2 normal sentence.

★ Identify the loose and the periodic sentence below.

A. Braving the wind, the weather, and the water from Florida to Montreal and stopping only to sleep and to eat, the five-girl team water-skied to Canada.

_____

B. The five-girl team water-skied from Florida to Montreal along the inland waterways.

_____

☆ A is a periodic sentence. The subject, *team,* and the verb, *water-skied,* come at the end of the sentence. B is a loose sentence. The core—the subject, *team,* and the verb, *water-skied,* appears at the beginning of the sentence.

Emphasis

The emphatic spots in a sentence come at the beginning and at the end. You usually look for and find the subject and verb, the core, at the beginning; you generally remember the last word you read. When you combine several points in a single sentence, place the important material at the beginning and at the end of the sentence.

★ Which is the more effective sentence below?

A. John labeled each bottle of the deadly serum in the proper manner.
B. John labeled properly each bottle of the deadly serum.

☆ B. The two words *deadly serum* are much more important than the phrase *proper manner;* therefore, the writer gains emphasis by changing the phrase *in the proper manner* into a single word modifier, placing it in the middle of the sentence, and ending with *deadly serum.*

When you write sentences, put important words at the beginning and end of those sentences, the emphatic positions; put less important but functional elements in the middle, the unemphatic position.

Inversion

Another way to gain sentence variety is to use inverted word order. Remember, normal English sentences are arranged subject–verb–completers. You can gain both variety and emphasis by inverting, shifting, and reversing order. Assume that you wanted to combine these points in a single sentence:

> The rain fell all day.
> It was soft and tender.
> The earth had been parched.

You could order your combined version in one of the following ways. The first has the normal word order; the others move the parts around, producing some interesting examples of inversion. Notice the differences.

> The soft and tender rain fell all day on the parched earth.
> Soft and tender, the rain fell all day on the parched earth.
> On the parched earth all day the rain fell, soft and tender.
> All day the rain, soft and tender, fell on the parched earth.
> Soft and tender fell the rain all day on the parched earth.

Three rules should govern your use of inversion:

1. Use inversion sparingly.
2. Avoid stilted, artificial inversion.
3. Don't let inversion obscure meaning.

Whatever patterns you use, make sure you make the important shift from thought patterns to sentence patterns by using sentence combining. If you combine the ideas and evidence successfully, you will establish sharper emphasis and promote an understanding of the logial relationships of your points. As we proceed to the following two chapters, we will continue to talk about ways of achieving this emphasis, economy, and logic.

WRITING ASSIGNMENTS

Using a newspaper, magazine, or book as your source, find, copy, and bring to class at least one example of each of the following types of sentences:

1. Pattern 1	4. Pattern 4	7. Loose
2. Pattern 2	5. Passive	8. Periodic
3. Pattern 3	6. Reversed (Expletive)	9. Inverted

Exercises

11a   **A.** Underline the core words in these sentences. Mark them S, subject; V, verb, LV, linking verb, DO, direct object; NC, noun complement; or AC, adjective complement.

    S   LV   NC
Example: He was a fine *example* to the members of the board.

1. Seven weeks before school opened, Henry was the only member of the board still looking for a principal.

2. The team elected him their spokesman.

3. His feet were large for a boy his age.

4. Dropping the left wing and rolling over, the jet plummeted to earth.

5. At the end of the month, Dad sent the watch to Mary.

6. Before the long, hard winter set in, Clifford chopped the gigantic oak into two-foot pieces for burning.

7. The sparrows battered the tin sun shade for the better part of an hour.

8. During the long winter months she dreamed of knights and castles on the Rhine.

9. Surrounded by a border of plastic flowers and fluorescent tubes, the enormous jigsaw puzzle painting was hilariously funny.

10. The jury gave the verdict to the judge.

11. The exhausted troops pushed into the Everglades, where Seminoles lay ready to attack at all times.

12. He was the clerk of the County Court for seventeen years.

13. After the party, the County Commission fired the sheriff.

14. When she smiled, her broken plate was noticeable.

15. When she appeared in her gown, he fell in love.

B. Identify these sentences by putting the right letter in the blank: (A) Pattern 1, S–V; (B) Pattern 2, S–V–DO; (C) Pattern 3, S–LV–NC; (D) Pattern 4, S–LV–AC; (E) Passive; (F) Reversed (Expletive).

1. Several men deserted during the long daylight raid.

(1) ⎯⎯⎯⎯⎯

2. Trouble is a crutch that some persons enjoy leaning on.

(2) ⎯⎯⎯⎯⎯

3. Johnny threw the ball to Pete.

(3) ⎯⎯⎯⎯⎯

Despite the President's appeal, there were thousands of taxpayers who objected to the new tax bill.

(4) _____

5. She was a girl who knew no fear.

(5) _____

6. Terry's girlfriend wrote his research paper.

(6) _____

7. Regardless, the book was ordered for use by the students.

(7) _____

8. Harvey was a tall white rabbit who liked just about everybody.

(8) _____

9. The former President insulted the two journalists.

(9) _____

10. Marlon Brando was great when he played Stanley Kowalski in Tennessee William's *A Streetcar Named Desire*.

(10) _____

11. There was an uneasy calm settling over the ship as early as sunup.

(11) _____

12. They painted the porch last summer.

(12) _____

13. For his faithful service the department gave those black bookends to him.

(13) _____

14. Harry drove through the rain to the store.

(14) _____

15. The team won eight straight games.

(15) _____

C. Mark the L (loose) and P (periodic) sentences. Put the letter in the blank.

1. She took the bookcase with her to New York, where she eventually had to pawn it for six dollars.

(1) _____

2. If the children were to play their games behind the school instead of in the street in front, they would be safer.

(2) _____

3. In the beginning, when darkness was upon the face of the earth and the earth was without form and void, God said, Let there be light.

(3) _____

4. The clanking machinery dredged the sand and weeds out of Eagle Lake, leaving nothing but clear water.

(4) _____

5. The ideas of the leading American philosophers stirred him to read every book that he could lay his hands on.

(5) _____

11b   **A.** Use the words at the left to build the type of sentence indicated over the space to the right. Add any words needed to make the sentence readable. Mark the core words in each sentence.

Example:

balloon	enormous	*Pattern 1, S–V*
window	red	S V
sky	out	The enormous red *balloon floated* out
floated	into	the window and into the sky.
1. tree	more	*Pattern 1, S–V*
way	twenty	_____
progress	stood	_____
years	than	_____
tall		_____
2. general	his	*Pattern 2, S–V–DO*
troops	forced	_____
dead	to attack	_____
night		_____
3. season	New York	*Pattern 3, S–LV–NC*
Greyhound	tourist	_____
express	was	_____
Miami	during	_____

4. figures	grotesque	*Pattern 4, S–LV–AC*
Indians	were	_____
they	circled	_____
fire	as	_____
shadowy		_____

5. building	by	*Passive*
spot	was	_____
council	selected	_____

6. change	when	*Reversed (Expletive)*
morale	over	_____
team	was	_____
Blake	took	_____
miraculous	there	_____

B. In the spaces rewrite the passive patterns to make active patterns.

1. The city championship was won by the Carvel High football team.

_____

_____

2. George was forced into the trunk of the car by the four criminals.

_____

_____

3. After a grueling semester the grades were assigned to the students by the professor.

_____

_____

C. In the space below each of the Reversed (Expletive) patterns, revise the sentence to make a Pattern 1, 2, 3, 4 normal sentence.

1. There had been a party given to the men of the sixteenth unit.

_____

_____

2. There was silence in the town that had recently been the scene of violence.

_____

_____

3. In the morning there were long lines of angry shoppers waiting for the store to open.

_____

_____

D. Change these loose sentences into periodic sentences.
    1. Henry Fleming thought he had been cheated when the shooting had stopped and the victory had been won by the Blue, his own side.

_____

_____

_____

    2. We might decide to give up the ghost if we feel that the economic problems, the political upheavals, and the social unrest will follow us into the next decade.

_____

_____

_____

    3. CBS announced its fall ''Cartooniverse'' to climax the endless string of Saturday morning cartoon shows featuring the likes of Super Ghost, Malletman, Plastiwoman, Mighty Mouse, Atom Ant, and Frankenstein Junior.

_____

_____

_____

E. Change these periodic sentences into loose sentences.
    1. If the typewriter had worked when he needed it to type the script for the new play, he'd have the contract now.

_____

_____

_____

    2. When the priceless painting had been restored to its original owner by the police, the mystery was over.

_____

_____

_____

3. Surrounded by the craggy hills to the north, the roaring river to the
west, and the dense growth of the forest to the south and east, at last he
felt alone.

_____

_____

_____

F. Change these normal sentences into inverted patterns.
1. The rain beat down all day ferociously.

_____

_____

2. Birds filled the trees during the spring.

_____

_____

3. Henry Fleming clasped the flag in his moment of glory.

_____

_____

G. Revise these sentences to eliminate the poor sentence emphasis.
1. Late in the game Bill threw a touchdown pass and the offensive line
blocked well.

_____

_____

2. She felt that he had cheated her, therefore.

_____

_____

3. With his left hand the murderer pulled the knife out of his victim's
heart as he heard the men approaching.

_____

_____

H. Combine the choppy sentences into one, and write the one sentence in the spaces.

1. A movie was made.

It was entitled "The Blob."

It was made in the 1950s.

It was a science-fiction film.

It was one of the more disgusting such films.

It was a flimflam.

In it is a giant mass of jelly.

It is the Blob.

It goes berserk.

It threatens to gobble up civilization.

_____

_____

_____

2. Nothing can control the Blob.

It grows to huge proportions.

It has an appetite.

That appetite is voracious.

It eats humans.

It eats electricity.

Steve McQueen makes a discovery.

He does it accidentally.

He finds the Blob's weakness.

It can't stand cold temperatures.

_____

_____

_____

3. The Blob comes back.

It returns to haunt us.

It does this in Washington.

It comes in budget form.

It is the federal budget.

_____

_____

_____

4. Some people have understood the monster.
The monster is called the federal budget.
They are called technicians.
They work at the Office of Management and Budget.
They have understood it for a long time.

_____

_____

_____

5. The technicians may be inadequate.
They may not be able to handle the problem.
These are the problems of the 1978 federal budget.
There may be someone besides the technicians.
That person may be able to control the Blob, the budget monster.
Steve McQueen might have to be hired.

_____

_____

_____

I. Rewrite this paragraph by using sentence-combining techniques. In your revision, omit as many words as you don't need, add as many as you do need, and make the paragraph as interesting as you can.

Children don't see their parents read. Even preschool children don't see them read. The children don't see the need to read. The children don't visit libraries. They don't see their parents check out books. They don't see periodicals. There are none in the home. Periodicals don't arrive in the mail. The children don't see the need for magazines. They see no need for newspapers. They don't see books. They don't see magazines. They don't see newspapers. They don't see even comic books. In school reading is a problem. They don't have adequate instruction. This happens in the lower grades. It happens because teachers have to try to motivate too many children. It takes the teachers too much time. They sometimes have as many as forty students. These students have never seen the need to read. The teacher can't give special help. There is no opportunity. Reading becomes a chore. The students don't like to read. They don't like to read for schoolwork. They don't like to read for pleasure. They don't like school. That's because they can't read. At least they can't read well. They can't read well. That's because they don't like school. They can't read. As a result, they don't exercise their minds through reflection and imagination.

chapter 12

Using Coordination
and Subordination

Developing sentence patterns that clearly reflect the logic of your ideas is the bedrock of good writing. Like organizing materials and developing paragraphs, it, too, is a skill that can be refined by conscious application of the process we have called the staircase of abstractions. We have shown that from the very start, and at all stages of the job, writing a paper is based on reducing the level of generality—moving down the staircase of abstractions. In this way you move toward explaining your ideas in more concrete terms. At the same time you are showing which terms are equal—at the same level of abstraction—and which terms are more or less than others.

The two most important devices in writing sentences are used for these same two jobs. *Coordination* is used to maintain the same level on the staircase of abstractions and add new elements on that level. Thus, if you began with the word *boy* and added the word *girl*, you would be adding the same kind of word and maintaining the same level of abstraction. *Boy and girl*, then, is an example of coordination. Adding the two words to a staircase would place them on an equal step:

people	
	boy
	girl

In contrast, *subordination* is used to lower the level of abstraction by adding elements that reduce the original terms to a lower, more concrete level. If you added the word *tall* to the word *boy,* you would be adding a different type of word, producing a more concrete modification of the general word *boy.* This would reduce the word *boy* to a lower level of abstraction. *Tall boy,* then, is an example of subordination. Adding a modifier like *tall* limits the original term, creating a new step on the staircase:

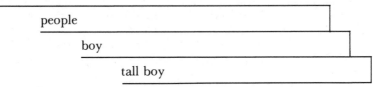

> ★   Which of the following involves coordination? _____
> A. The deer leaped and bounded.
> B. The agile deer leaped.
>
>
> ☆   A. It includes two of the same kind of words—in this case two verbs—joined by the *and,* and thus maintains the same level of abstraction. B. includes no two words that are of the same type. It does include a modifying adjective, *agile,* and so reduces the original term *deer* to a more concrete level. It reduces this level through subordination.

Thus, coordination means maintaining the same level of abstraction by adding and stressing further equal parts. Grammatically, this means adding nouns to nouns, verbs to verbs, word groups to word groups, even modifiers to modifiers.

Subordination means lowering the level of abstraction by adding the various kinds of modifiers to the original nouns and verbs.

Coordination

Coordination, the adding of elements that are equal logically, is achieved by adding elements that are equal grammatically. This adding of equals is effected by the use of parallel constructions. These parallel constructions develop your sentence horizontally; that is, they add further elements at the same level of abstraction.

Parallel sentences

To stress the logical parallels between the ideas of several different sentences, you can emphatically repeat the same sentence structure and thus create parallel sentences.

★   How many sentences in the following example repeat a parallel construction? _____

Style is an extraordinary thing. It is one of the subtlest secrets of all art. Through a sensitive appreciation of style, we can actually understand a creative artist more deeply than through weighing his subjects, dissecting his themes, or reading his biography. In painting, it is his composition, color-sense, and brushwork. In sculpture, it is the treatment of depths and surfaces and the choice of stones and metals. In music, it is surely the melodic line, the tone-color, and the shape of the phrase—who could fail to recognize the four hammer-blows in C minor as the very voice of Beethoven? In prose and poetry, it is the choice of words, their placing, and the rhythms and melodies of sentence and paragraph. (Gilbert Highet, "Style," Poets in a Landscape. Copyright 1957 by Gilbert Highet. Reprinted with permission of Alfred A. Knopf, Inc.)

☆   *Four.* Each of the four begins with the same construction: *In* _____, *it is* _____.

In the three sentences of the following example, similiar ideas are *not* presented in equal and parallel form. The first two do maintain a similar form, but the last does not follow it; and it is not a particularly emphatic form anyway.

Most athletes at Reedsville College did not come here to get professional contracts, though the President did make a joke about that. We didn't come to stay out of the draft either, at least not mainly, though the Dean hinted at that. And I suppose the profs think we just think we can flex our muscles and get good grades without working.

In the revised version, all three parallel ideas are presented in parallel construction, and the construction is made more emphatic and interesting: *What ever* _____, *the athletes (they)* _____.

Whatever the administration may imply, the athletes have not come here mainly to get professional contracts. Whatever the Dean may say, they have not come mainly to stay out of the draft. And whatever the faculty may think, they have not come mainly to get good grades by flexing their muscles at professors.

Parallel construction within sentences—types

Parallel constructions within single sentences are produced by adding a second grammatical element that is of the same type as the first, whether a clause, a phrase, or a single word. Thus, the second element maintains the

same level on the staircase of abstractions as the first, stressing to the reader
that these are two equal parts of your statement.

Developing *parallel clauses* means the addition of a complete statement (or
more than one) that includes a subject and verb. You may remember this as a
compound sentence. To *The boy ran,* you add *the girl laughed.* In *The boy ran, and
the girl laughed* you have two parallel clauses. Each has a subject and verb, and
the two are joined by a *comma* plus *and. And* is one of the basic coordinating
conjunctions that join together all kinds of parallel statements. The others are
but, or, nor, for, yet, and *so.* Parallel clauses can also be joined together by a
semicolon: The boy ran; the girl laughed.

★   Are there any parallel clauses in the following sentence? _____
He ground the powders, mixed the pills, rode with the doctor on his
rounds, held the basin when the patient was bled, and helped to adjust
plasters and to sew wounds.

☆   *No.* There are no complete subject-and-verb statements joined
in parallel constructions. What we have is one subject *He* with a number
of parallel single-word verbs: *grounds, mixed, rode, held, helped.* We also
have parallel phrases—*to adjust plasters and to sew wounds. but we have no
parallel clauses.* Clauses include complete subject-and-verb statements.

Phrases are groups of words that work together as a unit but do not have a
subject-and-verb combination. *To adjust plasters* and *to sew wounds* are examples
of these units. They happen to be infinitive phases. *-Ing* phrases are also very
common, such as *hitting the ball, flying the kite.* Prepositional phrases are the
most common of all—*to the house, by the book.* Using these phrases in intentional
parallel constructions adds clarity, emphasis, and interest to your sentences.

> *By hard work, by careful planning, and just by plain luck,* we managed to meet the
> deadline.
> He liked *walking in the woods* and *listening to the birds.*

Single words can also be used in parallel combinations. *The boy and the girl*
places two nouns in parallel form. *The boy ran and hopped* places two verbs in
parallel form.

All of the parallel constructions can be used either in the main elements of
sentences or in the modifying (and thus subordinate) elements. *The tall, thin
boy,* for example, includes two parallel modifying adjectives. This next
sentence includes two parallel but modifying (and thus subordinate) clauses:
Since we had run out of gas and since we had no money, we had to hitchhike.

★   Underline all the elements that are in parallel constructions.
John, who always looked for the easiest and fastest way, and Phil were
the candidates.

> ☆ *John and Phil; easiest and fastest.* There are two sets of parallels. *John and Phil* are parallel nouns, and the subject of the sentence. *Easiest and fastest* are two parallel modifying adjectives.

Parallel construction within sentences — methods

Parallel constructions can be achieved by *pairs*—whether of agreement or contrast. Adding a second similar element—*the boy and the girl*—or a second similar but contrasting element—*satisfaction, not fame*—produces a parallel pair. This can be done with clauses, phrases, or single words. In the following example, George Bernard Shaw uses a number of parallel sentences. But within these parallel sentences, he also uses many parallel pairs. And all of these pairs use the method of contrast, with a negative stated first. Shaw does this first with whole clauses, and then in the last sentence with pairs of single words.

> Your friends are all the dullest dogs I know. They are not clean: they are only shaved and starched. They are not dignified: they are only fashionably dressed. They are not educated: they are only college passmen. They are not religious: they are only pew-renters. They are not moral: they are only conventional. They are not virtuous: they are only cowardly. They are not even vicious: they are only "frail." They are not artistic: they are only lascivious. They are not prosperous: they are only rich. They are not loyal, they are only servile; not dutiful, only sheepish; not public spirited, only patriotic; not courageous, only quarrelsome; not determined, only obstinate; not masterful, only domineering; not self-controlled, only obtuse; not self-respecting, only vain; not kind, only sentimental; not social, only gregarious; not considerate, only polite; not intelligent, only opinionated; not progressive, only factious; not imaginative, only superstitious; not just, only vindictive; not generous, only propitiatory; not disciplined, only cowed; and not truthful at all: liars every one of them, to the very backbone of their souls. (George Bernard Shaw, *Man and Superman.* Reprinted with permission of The Public Trustee and The Society of Authors.)

> ★ How many contrasting pairs are included in Shaw's final sentence?
>
> ————
>
> ☆ *Eighteen.* The first is a pair of full clauses. The rest involve pairs of single words, though the very last is a slightly different variation: *not truthful at all: liars every one.*

Parallel construction can also be achieved by *series* of three or more items. Again, this can be done with clauses, phrases, or single words. The three-term series is probably the most famous rhetorical device in writing: *this government of the people, by the people, and for the people.*

> He was polite at all times, generous to a fault, and humble to the point of absurdity.

In this example, there is a series of three equal adjectives—*polite, generous,* and *humble.* Further, each has a prepositional phrase (or two in the last) attached for even greater emphasis of the parallelism.

★   Underline the words that are the basis of the parallel series.
She laid two fingers on my shoulder, cast another look into my face, turned the key in the lock, gently thrust me beyond the door, and left me to my own devices.

☆   *Laid, cast, turned, thrust, left.* The series is based on these five verbs. In addition, each is followed by a prepositional phrase—*on my shoulder, into my face, in the lock, beyond the door, to my own devices.*

Both parallel pairs and parallel series are most frequently established by the use of several kinds of *connectives.* These connectives can be coordinating conjunctions, such as *and, but, or, for, nor, yet, so.* They also can be prepositions. They can be the same—*in the house, in the yard, in the street.* They can be different—*of the people, by the people, for the people.*

★   Underline the connective that establishes the parallel construction.
He must be the most devious man alive or a fool.

☆   *Or.* The basis of the parallel construction is *devious man or fool.*

There is also a group of connectives that work in pairs: Both this, and that; either this, or that; not only this, but also that.

★   Underline the connectives that establish the parallel construction.
A person should not only take care of his physical self, but also make sure his emotions are healthy.

☆   *Not only, but also.* This pair of connectives sets up two parallel verb statements.

Subordination

Coordination stresses equality; subordination stresses inequality. Subordination is the adding of unequal elements that reduce the level of abstraction of the other parts of the sentence, that make them more concrete. It is achieved by the various types of modifiers, since it is a matter of presenting modifications and qualifications. These modifiers develop your sentence vertically; that is, they add further elements that bring the level of abstraction to a lower step on the staircase.

Subordinate modifiers are of three major types: single words, phrases, and clauses.

Subordination with single-word modifiers

Single-word modifiers (generally adjectives and adverbs) make other words more specific, more concrete; and so they reduce the level of abstraction. *Tall boy* is more concrete than *boy* because of the single-word modifier *tall*. *The tall boy ran quickly* is more concrete than *The tall boy ran* because of the additional single-word modifier *quickly*. These single-word modifiers can also be used in pairs and in a series: *The tall, thin boy; The tall, thin, gangling boy.*

★ Underline the single-word modifiers in the following sentence.
The brightly painted chair suddenly collapsed.

☆ *Brightly, painted, suddenly.* The sentence contains one surprise. *Painted* modifies a noun and *suddenly* modifies a verb. But *brightly* is also a modifier. It modifies another modifier, *painted*. *Very,* in *the very tall boy,* does the same thing.

Subordination with phrases

All of the standard types of phrases can be used as modifiers to make other words more concrete. When you use these phrases in pairs or in a series, you are also using parallel construction. But these are parallels at a subordinate level, a modifying level.

He ran *up the hill* and *through the woods.*

The prepositional phrases *up the hill* and *through the woods* are parallel. Both are subordinate to the word *ran* and thus reduce the level of abstraction of the statement. Thus, on a staircase, this statement would look like this:

He ran
up the hill
and through the woods.

The last two are on the same lower level of abstraction.

★ Underline the parallel construction that is the subordinate part of this sentence.
He saw me, and then he ran up the hill and through the woods.

☆   *Up the hill and through the woods.* This parallel pair of phrases is subordinate. It develops the sentence vertically, in the direction of greater concreteness. The other parallel pair—*He saw me, and then he ran*—is a pair of equal clauses. This second pair develops the sentence horizontally by adding an additional equal factor. On the staircase this last example would appear this way:

| He saw me |
| and then he ran |
| up the hill |
| and through the woods. |

Prepositional phrases are the most frequently used of all the modifying phrases.

★   In the center of the great city of London lies a small neighborhood, consisting of a cluster of narrow streets and courts, of very venerable and debilitated houses, which goes by the name of Little Britain.

How many prepositional phrases are included in the above sentence?

_____

☆   *Eight.* Notice that most are in sequence, one followed by another: *by the name of Little Britain.* In this way you reduce the level of abstraction by modifying a word in a modifier—*name*—by another modifier—*of Little Britain.*

Various kinds of phrases based on incomplete forms of verbs, called verbals, are also used for subordination and modification.

The boy *running the machine* cut his hand.

Here *running the machine* modifies *boy* in the same way that a prepositional phrase would.

The boy *with the red hair* cut his hand.
Running down the street, he tripped on a skate.

Here, *running down the street* specifies in more concrete terms the situation in which the tripping occurred.

> ★ Underline the verbal modifying phrases.
> Being unable to remove the chain, I jumped over it, and, running up the flagged causeway, knocked vainly on the door.
>
>
> ☆ *Being unable to remove the chain, running up the flagged causeway.* Actually, the first subordinate part has two verbal phrases in a sequence. *Being unable* specifies the background for *I jumped over it; to remove the chain* specifies further exactly what the writer was unable to do. The phrase *running up the flagged causeway* then specifies more concretely the situation in which the knocking occurred.

Subordination with clauses

Complete statements, with subjects and verbs, can be used in a subordinate way to modify parts of other clauses. These subordinate clauses are thus used as adjectives or adverbs.

The boy *who was short* could not see.
The*short* boy could not see.

In the first example the clause *who was short* modifies the noun *boy* in the same way that the single-word modifier *short* modifies *boy* in the second example.

Clauses which are used as adjectives to modify nouns usually begin with the words *who, which, that, what;* but sometimes these words are left out and just implied.

He had the book *that I wanted.*
He had the book *I wanted.*

In the second the *that* is not actually included, but by habit we can accept this shorthand version of *that I wanted.* For greater clarity these key words—which are called relative pronouns—should be included.

The preceding example would be set up this way on the staircase:

```
    ┌─────────────────────────────────┐
    │ He had the book                 │
    └──────┬──────────────────────────┤
           │ that I wanted.           │
           └──────────────────────────┘
```

The clause at the lower level—the modifier—makes more concrete the term *book* that is a part of the upper level.

★   Underline the adjective clause in the following.
Youth is a kind of delirium, which can only be cured by years of painful treatment.

☆   *Which can only be cured by painful treatment.* This subordinate part of the sentence reduces the level of abstraction by specifying a further characteristic of the *delirium.*

Clauses which are used as adverbs to modify verbs begin with words that are called subordinate conjunctions. These include such words as *because, when, if, although, since, after, before, until.* These clauses set up the reasons that things occur, the conditions under which they can occur, the time at which they occur.

> *Because he lost his way,* he sent up a flare.
> *When the dance ended,* a riot broke out.

In the first example the reason for sending up the flare is given; in the second example the time that the riot occurred is given. Both subordinate clauses make the statements more concrete.

★   Underline the adverbial clause that specifies the necessary condition for the occurrence of the major action of the sentence.
If you finish your chores, you can leave when your friends arrive.

☆   *If you finish your chores.* The other adverbial clause—*when your friends arrive*—specifies the time at which the action is to occur. The *If* clause sets up the condition that has to be fulfilled first if the action is going to occur at all. Again, both clauses are elements of subordination, leaving the *you can leave* as the major part of the sentence. The two subordinate clauses lower the level of abstraction of the general statement *you can leave* by modifying it in terms of a concrete condition and a concrete time.

In this example, notice how Ernest Hemingway makes his sentence more concrete by adding a whole series of subordinate terms that qualify and modify the first general statement—*It was very exciting.*

> It was very exciting, sitting out in front of a cafe your first day in Spain with a ticket in your pocket that meant that rain or shine you were going to see a bullfight in an hour and a half.

WRITING ASSIGNMENTS

1. Select one of the following subjects:

Required Courses vs. Electives
Basketball vs. Football
Television vs. Movies
American Cars vs. Foreign Cars
Rock Groups vs. Big Dance Bands or Jazz groups

For the subject you have selected, write four alternate thesis sentences that could serve as the basis of an essay. The four thesis sentences should be based on the following sentence patterns, one for each sentence.

a. A sentence with two parallel main clauses.
b. A sentence with a main clause and a subordinate modifying clause.
c. A sentence with a contrasted parallel pair.
d. A sentence with at least two modifying phrases.

2. Select one of your sentences from *1* and develop it in an essay of 300 to 500 words.

Exercises

12a **A.** On the line below place the letter of the device of sentence structure that best describes the key feature of the sentence pattern illustrated by each example.
  a. Parallel clauses
  b. Parallel phrases
  c. Parallel single words
  d. Single-word modifier
  e. Phrase modifier
  f. Clause modifier

  1. We found people who had lost all their holdings; we found people who had not eaten a full meal for a week; we found people who had given up all hope.

  (1) _____

  2. The new model is longer, sturdier, and heavier.

  (2) _____

  3. It was the oldest of the buildings in this part of town.

  (3) _____

  4. Grabbing his coat, scooping up his books, and throwing his change in his pockets, he was on his way.

  (4) _____

  5. If you see him there, you will know what I mean.

  (5) _____

  6. The cat that had the babies has left our house.

  (6) _____

  7. I love watching birds; they soar, they float, they glide.

  (7) _____

  8. He started to sing when he heard the good news.

  (8) _____

B. On the line below place the word or words that best answer the question.
  1. What is the first word of the modifying subordinate clause?
  We did not see the fireman who rescued the child.

  (1) _____

  2. What are the first words of the parallel phrases?
  He ran through the door, across the yard, and down the alley.

  (2) _____

3. Which three single words are in a parallel series?
   The last, best, and fullest meal was at your house.

   (3) _____

4. What is the first word of the phrase modifiers?
   The car turning the corner is my old one.

   (4) _____

5. Which words are in the parallel contrast?
   Greed, not honor, rules the world today.

   (5) _____

6. Which two words are parallel?
   I met Lucy at the dance and asked her over to dinner.

   (6) _____

7. What are the two single-word modifiers?
   The careless workman was suddenly surprised by the boss.

   (7) _____

8. What is the first word of the modifying subordinate clause?
   Because it was almost spring, we began planning our trip.

   (8) _____

9. What is the first word of the phrase modifier?
   We found him in an old, noisy barroom.

   (9) _____

10. What three single words are in a parallel series?
    I found the record, paid by check, and went to the bank on the way
    home.

   (10) _____

12b   A. Each of the following includes a central statement plus a modifier or
          modifiers. For each sentence, place the group of words or single words on
          the appropriate steps on the staircase of abstractions so that you show the
          way the modifiers reduce the level of abstraction. Note the sample: He ran
          to the bank.

   He ran
        to the bank

1. The driver stepped into the cab.

2. He saw the fireman who was climbing through the window of the house.

3. I want the book in the red cover.

4. I laughed when I saw the players in their new socks.

B. Write sentences as indicated.
1. The following list contains three items which are parallel. Write a sentence that uses the three parallel items in a series.
   a. watching soap operas
   b. playing games
   c. various contests
   d. reading books

   _____

   _____

2. The following list contains three items which are parallel. Write a sentence that uses the three parallel items in a series.
   a. educational
   b. entertains
   c. inspiring
   d. profitable

   _____

   _____

3. The following list contains two items which are parallel. Use the two parallel items to make a sentence with two parallel clauses.
   a. left
   b. courageous
   c. honor
   d. waited

   _____

   _____

4. Convert the first sentence into a modifying phrase that will be an effective part of the second sentence.
   He admitted his mistake. He showed real courage.

   _____

   _____

5. Convert the first sentence into a modifying phrase that will be an effective part of the second sentence.
   The hikers walked through high grass. They managed to avoid getting poison ivy.

   _____

   _____

6. Convert the second sentence into a modifying clause that will be an effective part of the first sentence.
   I liked the book. I got it for Christmas.

   _____

   _____

7. Expand the sentence by adding a parallel modifying phrase.
   We walked through the valley.

   _____

   _____

C. Write a sentence as indicated. Underline the element called for in each.
   1. A sentence that includes a modifying clause.

   _____

   _____

   2. A sentence that includes a series of three equal nouns.

   _____

   _____

3. A sentence that includes a contrasting parallel pair.

_____

_____

4. A sentence that includes a modifying prepositional phrase.

_____

_____

5. A sentence that includes two prepositional phrases that are not parallel.

_____

_____

6. A sentence that includes two parallel main clauses.

_____

_____

7. A sentence that includes two single-word modifiers.

_____

_____

chapter 13

Refining Sentence Patterns

When you write a sentence, you normally use both coordination and subordination. (We did in the previous sentences; can you pinpoint the use of each?) And so in this chapter we will consider their interaction as you choose the patterns of sentences and revise the patterns of sentences.

Choosing Sentence Patterns

One of the main considerations in using coordination and subordination effectively is achieving the right emphasis in your sentences. This emphasis of thought is achieved by choosing the right level of emphasis for the words of your sentences. You place words in major or subordinate parts of the sentence depending on what things you want to stress. Match the form to the thought. Place major thoughts in major positions in the sentence patterns; place minor thoughts in subordinate positions. For example, if a word is a lesser part of the thought, don't make it a part of the basic subject–verb–object pattern; get it in as a modifier. If it does not deserve equal weight, don't join it to a major part with an *and;* get it in as a modifier.

> ★   Do the following sentences achieve the right level of emphasis?
> ———

> The causes of World War I were many. They were mainly social, economic, and political. They were the result of years of aggressive foreign policy.
>
> ☆ *No*. Too much emphasis is placed on *many* and on *social, political, and economic,* since these words are used as one of the major parts of the sentence patterns. This misemphasis not only produces the wordiness of the passage, but also tends to blur the proper emphasis, which should be on *years of aggressive foreign policy.*

One step toward achieving better emphasis would be this placement:

> Among the *many* causes of World War I, the *social, economic,* and *political* were the most important. They were the results of years of aggressive foreign policy.

This places *many* in a subordinate position, but leaves *economic, social,* and *political* in a major position. A more complete remolding of the pattern would be this:

> The many *social, economic,* and *political causes* of World War I were, in turn, the results of years of aggressive foreign policy.

This pattern is a better reflection of the logical emphasis and relationships of the ideas.

1. The right subject

In choosing the appropriate sentence pattern, you first need to choose the right subject. Make sure that the word you are using in the subject position is really your main point of emphasis and not just some vague filler.

> ★ Which sentence has the best subject? _____
>
> A. The subject of stone carvings has always interested me.
> B. Stone carvings have always interested me.
>
> ☆ B. Words like *subject* are of no interest or help. Get what you are really talking about into the subject position.

One frequent slip is to let the proper subject get lost in some modifying position; thus, you end up with a wrong or vague point as the subject:

> My feeling toward foreign films is one of disinterest.

Notice that the core pattern comes out: *feeling is one*. Not very interesting. To say it with better emphasis you could get the *I* out of the modifying *my* form: *I have no interest in foreign films.* Or you could stress the films: Or you could stress the films: *Foreign films bore me.*

2. A concrete subject

Another way of looking at your choice of subject is to consider its level on the staircase. Is it concrete enough? Does it capture your main point of emphasis as specifically as possible?

★   Which sentence has the most concrete subject? _____

A. The effects of the new factory were disturbing.
B. The dangers produced by the new factory were disturbing.

☆   B. The subject *dangers* certainly sets the direction of meaning more clearly, though it might need more definition in further sentences.

It is not just empty words like *effects* that can get you off in a vague direction. In the sentence *The mystery still bothered me, mystery* is a fairly meaningful word. But a more concrete naming of what the mystery was would give a more helpful subjet: *The disappearance of my notebook still bothered me.*

3. Parallels and subordinates

In choosing the appropriate sentence pattern, you also need to keep in mind the different types of parallel constructions available. Keep in mind the ways of building pairs and series, the kinds of connectives you can use. Apply these to give form to and sharpen the logic of your thinking.

In the same way, you should consciously apply the methods of producing subordination. Here you not only decide which words and ideas need subordination constructions, but also choose among the subordinate constructions the most suitable for your job. Should you use a single word, a phrase, or a clause?

★   Is the modifying clause the most suitable subordinate construction?
_____
The boy who was tall and thin read the poem.

☆   *No.* In relation to the major point of reading the poem, the fact that he was tall and thin is not important enough to warrant a modifying clause. *The tall, thin boy* would be sufficient.

Revising Sentence Patterns

Your first choice of a sentence pattern may not be your best choice. Often, as a matter of fact, your choice of one pattern can give you a greater insight into what you actually did mean to say and so allow you to go on to revise your sentence into a more effective pattern. In revising the coordination and subordination of your sentences, you will generally follow two methods: reducing and shifting.

1. Reducing

The goal is, in part, to reduce the number of words and sentences that you use. But that is not all. By reducing the number of words and sentences, you are also strengthening the logic of your statements. You are achieving better emphasis, showing clearer relationships of ideas.

Reducing predication is one method. You reduce the number of subject-and-verb combinations in your sentences, eliminating either separate sentences or clauses within sentences. To eliminate these excessive subject-and-verb combinations you may sometimes just omit trivial or irrelevant material; but in the main you will be restating the material in other forms, leaving out the subject-and-verb constructions.

★   Which sentence shows the results of reducing predication? _____

A. Betty was smiling sweetly. She asked for an increase in her allowance.
B. Smiling sweetly, Betty asked for an increase in her allowance.

☆   B. It reduces the number of subject-and-verb combinations to one and restates the remaining material—*Smiling sweetly*—in the form of a subordinate modifier.

This example also suggests another point to consider in reducing predication: You need to determine which is the major material and which is the material to be reduced in form and made subordinate. In other words, exactly what do you want to emphasize? A reversed emphasis in the revision about Betty might have been *Asking for an increase in her allowance, Betty smiled sweetly.*

★   In reducing the predication of the following sentences (and making them one sentence) what verb should receive the major emphasis? _____

The old woman lived alone. She bequeathed her bathtub to a plumber. He had done her plumbing for twenty-five years. He did it free.

☆   *Bequeathed.* Not all of the other subject-and-verb combinations can be eliminated completely, but two can be omitted and the other turned into a subordinate statement. The revision might read like this: *The lonely old woman bequeathed her bathtub to a plumber who had done her plumbing free for twenty-five years.* The second sentence has become the main statement; the third is retained as a subordinate clause. The material of the first and fourth sentences is restated in the form of single-word modifiers.

Reducing forms sometimes involves reducing predication, but it has other possibilities as well. You reduce major clauses to subordinate; you reduce subordinate clauses to phrases or single-word modifiers; you reduce phrases to single words. Again, the goal is appropriate emphasis and clear depiction of relationships.

★   Which sentence has the most appropriate emphasis? _____

A. He didn't take the advice given to him by his doctor.
B. He didn't take his doctor's advice.

☆   B. In A the extra words devoted to the obvious fact that the doctor gave him the advice distract attention from the main subject-and-verb combination and its object, *advice*.

★   In reducing forms in the following sentence, which verb should be retained? _____
The targets that are supplied in skeet shooting are discs made of clay.

☆   *Are*. The clause *that are supplied in skeet shooting* can be reduced to a single-word modifier *skeet*. The phrase *made of clay* can be reduced to a single word modifier *clay*. The result of the two reductions is *Skeet targets are clay discs*.

Reducing means, first of all, checking to see whether you need all the subject-and-verb combinations that you have. Often the same information can be conveyed by using single-word modifiers or phrases instead of whole subject-and-verb patterns. Using the briefest form possible not only cuts down on excess words; it gets the right emphasis established. In turn, reducing means even getting your subordinate elements down to the most basic form possible—phrases instead of clauses, words instead of phrases.

2. Shifting

In shifting, you establish more appropriate and effective relationships between the parts of a sentence. You shift materials which should be subordinate from coordinate forms to subordinate forms. You shift materials which should be coordinate from subordinate forms to coordinate forms. In other words, you make a better match between your ideas and your sentence patterns. Those things which are coordinate come out coordinate. Those things which are subordinate come out subordinate.

On a staircase, this statement—*The boy had red hair and he won*—would look like this:

> The boy had hair
>
> red
>
> and he won.

★ Does the pattern on the staircase indicate that the two subject-and-verb combinations (the two clauses) are parallel? _____

☆ *Yes.* They are both at the same level of abstraction.

★ Is the parallel construction an appropriate pattern for the material of the sentence? _____
The boy had red hair and he won.

☆ *No.* The two coordinate subject-and-verb combinations are not a logical pair. That he has red hair is not a parallel point to his winning. You would thus need to shift the form to show the actual relationship between the two points.

★ Which shift achieves the better, more logical emphasis? _____

A. The boy who won had red hair.
B. The boy with red hair won.

☆ B. The major point of emphasis is his winning and the pattern should make that emphasis clear. The identifying mark of his having red hair is more appropriate as a subordinate modifier. In shifting, too, you need to determine which is the major material and which is the minor.

We have looked at an example of shifting from coordination to subordination. The following example illustrates the reverse of the process. On the staircase, this sentence—*The movie, which frightened him, also pleased him.*—would look like this.

> The movie also pleased him
>
> which frightened him

★   Underline the subordinate clause in that same sentence:
The movie, which frightened him, also pleased him.

☆   *Which frightened him.* This material, however, is not actually subordinate to the material of the other clause.

★   Which provides the better revision? _____

A. The movie, which pleased him, also frightened him.
B. The movie both pleased and frightened him.

☆   B. A merely reverses the subordination and thus also creates a misemphasis. For the two statements are equal in logic and should be stated in the parallel construction of B.

A more complicated example of confusion of emphasis is provided in this sentence about golf:

★   Underline the subordinate modifying clause in the sentence.
Golf is a means of support for professional golfers, who play in tournaments throughout the world to support themselves by earning prize money.

☆   *Who play in tournaments throughout the world to support themselves by earning prize money.* With this as a subordinate statement, *Golf is a means* comes out as the major statement. And it is an empty one at that. It causes the confusion of emphasis and the repetitions of the rest of the sentence. The job of revision here is to get the right statement as the major subject-and-verb statement.

★   Which is the *least* effective alternative for the major subject-and-verb statement? _____

A. Golf supports professional golfers . . .
B. Professional golfers support themselves . . .
C. Professional golfers play in tournaments . . .

☆   A. Both B and C act as the beginning of a reasonable revision, although the emphasis is different in each:

> B. Professional golfers support themselves by playing in tournaments through-
> out the world.
>
> C. Professional golfers play in tournaments throughout the world to support
> themselves.

In these two examples the difference of emphasis is achieved by the difference in subordination. In *B support* is made major and *playing* is used as part of
a subordinate modifier. In *C play* is made major and *support* is used as a part of
a subordinate modifier. In the original sentence *play* had been subordinate,
but was subordinate to the wrong major element: *Golf is a means.* Thus, revision *B* keeps *playing* subordinate but attaches it to a more appropriate and
meaningful major element: *Professional golfers support themselves.* Revision *C*
shifts *play* to the major element and adds a meaningful subordinate element: *to
support themselves.*

> ★   In review, consider the revision from A to B. Did this revision in-
> volve *reducing* or *shifting?* _____
>
> A. She dresses in a beautiful manner.
> B. She dresses beautifully.
>
> ☆   *Reducing.* A subordinate modifying phrase—*in a beautiful manner*—
> is reduced to a single-word modifier *beautifully.* But there is no shift in the
> logical relationships between the parts of the sentence: *She dresses* is still
> the major element; *beautifully* is still a subordinate element. The effec-
> tiveness of the reduction is not only a matter of cutting out three words;
> it achieves a better emphasis on the modifying word *beautifully,* rather
> than burying that point in a modifying phrase that actually emphasizes
> the meaningless word *manner.* Both reducing and shifting can help you to
> achieve this more accurate kind of emphasis.

WRITING ASSIGNMENTS

1. Select one of the following subjects:

> The Change in Parent-Children Relationships
> The Change in Boy-Girl Relationships
> The Trends in Fashions
> The Trend in Popular Entertainment
> The Change in Student Goals

Limit the subject you have selected, and then write four thesis sentences
that could serve as the basis for an essay. The four thesis sentences should
be based on the following sentence patterns, one for each sentence:

    a. A sentence with two parallel main clauses

    b. A sentence with a main clause and a subordinate modifying clause

    c. A sentence with a contrasted parallel pair

    d. A sentence with at least two modifying phrases

2. Select one of your sentences from *1* and develop it in an essay of 300 to 500 words.

Exercises

13a   On the line below place the letter of the item that best answers the question.

1. In which sentence is there a greater emphasis on the word *riderless?*
   a. The riderless horse leaped over the fence.
   b. The horse leaping over the fence was riderless.

   (1) _____

2. In which sentence are *gentle* and *witty* given equal emphasis?
   a. He was gentle but witty.
   b. The witty man was gentle.

   (2) _____

3. In which sentence is there a greater emphasis on the word *useful?*
   a. The book is very repetitious, although it is quite useful.
   b. Although the book is very repetitious, it is quite useful.

   (3) _____

4. Which sentence has the more effective pattern?
   a. Listening to the radio when you are in the car is fun.
   b. Listening to the radio in the car is fun.

   (4) _____

5. Which sentence has the more effective pattern?
   a. I went to school at Taft High, at which I found the work too difficult.
   b. When I went to Taft High, I found the work too difficult.

   (5) _____

6. Which sentence has the more effective pattern?
   a. The water was cold, and Harry was shocked when he walked into it.
   b. When he walked into the cold water, Harry was shocked.

   (6) _____

7. In which sentence has the revision been achieved by both reducing predication and shifting?
   She was only a beginner, but Sue won first place in the long jump.
   a. Only a beginner, Sue won first place in the long jump.
   b. Although she was only a beginner, Sue won first place in the long jump.

   (7) _____

8. In which sentence has the revision been achieved by shifting?
   We were blinded by the snowstorm. We lost our way.

a. We were blinded by the snowstorm and lost our way.

b. When we were blinded by the snowstorm, we lost our way.

(8) _____

9. In which sentence has the revision been achieved by reducing forms?
Although they were worn, the shoes were serviceable.
a. The shoes were worn but serviceable.
b. Although worn, the shoes were serviceable.

(9) _____

10. In which sentence has the revision been achieved by reducing predication?
The sweater, which was bright red, could be seen from afar.
a. The bright red sweater could be seen from afar.
b. The sweater was bright red and could be seen from afar.

(10) _____

13b   **A.** Rewrite each of the following sentences to get better emphasis and more concreteness in the subject.

1. The analyzing of the new evidence turned up by the investigation was handled by our ace investigator, Sam Columbus.

_____

_____

2. Many things in backgammon take a long time to understand.

_____

_____

3. It is amazing every time I hear the way she sings.

_____

_____

4. My response to a movie like that is one of utter amazement.

_____

_____

5. The kind of thing that bothers me about people is when they talk during movies.

_____

_____

B. Supply the material requested by each question in the space provided.

1. Reduce the following to a single sentence:

Flowers can be sent by Western Union. Money can also be sent. This is something many people do not know.

_____

_____

_____

2. Reduce the following to a single sentence:
   Every week a vote is taken for the top college team. Sports writers vote. Coaches also vote. Radio announcers vote, too.

_____

_____

_____

3. Reduce the following to a single sentence by emphasizing one of the statements as a main clause and subordinating all other material. Camille Pissaro was a painter. He was French. He flourished in the late nineteenth century. He was an impressionist.

_____

_____

_____

4. Reduce the following to a single sentence by emphasizing one of the statements as a main clause and subordinating all other material: There are floods on the Mississippi River. The floods come in the spring. Sometimes they cut new channels for the river.

_____

_____

_____

5. Improve the following by making one of the main clauses a subordinate modifier (not necessarily a clause) of the other:
   Grace called him early in the afternoon, and the reason she called was she told him she was marrying Sam.

_____

_____

_____

6. Improve the following by making one of the clauses a subordinate modifier (not necessarily a clause) of the other:
   Dancing requires coordination, and in this respect it is like most sports.

_____

_____

_____

7. Improve the following by making one of the clauses a subordinate modifier (not necessarily a clause) of the other:
   We had been told about the dangerous tide; this was on the day we arrived.

_____

_____

_____

8. Convert the first sentence of the following to a modifying phrase for the second:
   The policeman was taken by surprise. He had no excuse.

_____

_____

_____

9. Convert the first sentence of the following to a modifying phrase for the second:
   The bus driver drove through the snow on Christmas. He counted more than twenty stalled cars.

_____

_____

_____

10. Combine the following into a single sentence by emphasizing one of the sentences as a main clause and changing the other into a subordinate modifier:
    John lacked confidence. He did not do well in public speaking.

_____

_____

_____

section five

Refining Diction

chapter 14

Diction: Denotation, Context, Connotation

When Richard Brinsley Sheridan's Mrs. Malaprop said in *The Rivals,* "Illiterate him ... from your memory." the eighteenth-century theater audience laughed. They knew, of course, that she meant *obliterate,* not *illiterate.* With that play the word *malapropism* was born. It means a confusion of words with similar sounds.

We often find malapropisms in writing (usually a result of spelling errors). One writer, for instance, said she wanted to spell in a more effective *manor,* instead of *manner;* another wrote that a lifeguard can save a drowning woman by *raping* her, not *wrapping* her, in a blanket. The wrong word can make readers laugh, but it can also confuse them.

A word must mean the same to both the writer and readers. If you have a private meaning for a word you use and your readers don't know that private meaning, they can't know what you mean. Neither can readers force their own private meanings on words and expect to understand what you mean. That's why you need to check the meaning of your words with the dictionary.

Denotation

When scholars put together a dictionary, they list the meanings words have to people in certain communities. These meanings we call *denotations.* A word, of course, may have more than one meaning. The word *set,* for instance, has several meanings. Look at these four sentences:

She had a large *set* in her ring.

The player *set* the book on the table.

The sun *set* late that evening.

He followed a *set* pattern to his goal.

Webster's New World Dictionary has almost a full page of meanings for *set.* Those definitions are what we agree it means; they are its *denotations.*

To make sure you know the denotations of the words you hear and speak and read and write, own and use a standard college desk dictionary. Ask your instructor to suggest one to you.

Context

As you have seen, the word *set* has more than one meaning. To know which meaning the writer was using you had to study the *context,* the words around *set.* The position of the word, for instance, told you whether it was being used as a noun or a verb or an adjective. The rest of the sentence helped you decide whether the word *set* meant a group of games in tennis, radio receiving equipment, false teeth, or something else.

We usually define the context of a word as its verbal setting—the sentence, paragraph, chapter, book in which the word appears. Look at this sentence from the article "Ride the High Waves" in *Surfer Magazine:*

When you can hang ten, you are ready for the big time.

The title of the article and the magazine itself tell you that here *hang ten* refers to a surfing skill—putting all ten toes over the front edge of the surfboard on a ride. The same phrase in an argument against capital punishment would mean something else.

Most words have more than one meaning. Through the verbal setting, the context, writers control the meaning of the words they use so that the readers know which of those possible meanings is right in this instance.

★   Does this sentence make clear what the writer means by *booked?*

———

They booked him yesterday.

A. Yes   B. No

☆   B. You should have said no, for the *him* of the sentence may be in trouble with the police or may be engaged to speak or act at some time in the future. Because the context does not control the meaning of the word, however, the reader cannot know which meaning is appropriate.

The context of a word includes more than its verbal setting. The person using the word, for instance, is part of its context. You don't expect puns in reports of scientists, for you know that they want to keep the meanings of their words to one scientific denotation, the one that says exactly what they mean. You have to look for double or triple meaning, however, when you read fiction or drama. When you read poetry, you can expect the words to have several meanings at the same time, as you can see in this poem by Siegfried Sassoon:

Base Details

If I were fierce and bald and short of breath,
    I'd live with scarlet Majors at the Base,
And speed glum heroes up the line to death.
    You'd see me with my puffy petulant face,
Guzzling and gulping in the best hotel,
    Reading the Roll of Honor, "Poor young chap,"
I'd say—"I used to know his father well.
    Yes, we've lost heavily in this last scrap."
And when the war is done and youth stone dead,
I'd toddle safely home and die—in bed.*

★   Which of these meanings does the title, "Base Details," have?

_____

A. Military Assignments   B. Dishonorable Facts

☆   A and B. It has both meanings. B is more important than A. The officers, *scarlet Majors,* have been assigned to the military base to send the young recruits into battle. A military assignment is called a *detail;* a military installation is called a *base.* (Look up both *base* and *detail* in your college-level desk dictionary.) The facts in the poem do reveal dishonorable and shameful details about war and imply clearly the dishonor of those who run the machinery of war. Thus, the poet has used a purposeful double meaning by having his words convey two ideas at once. Knowing that the poet wrote realistic war poems that showed the horrors of war, sympathy for its victims, and bitterness toward its makers helps us to see the double meaning in the title.

★   How many meanings does *base* have in the sentence below? _____
Because she scratched her gold ring, the base metal was exposed.

A. one   C. three
B. two   D. more

> ☆ A. The context, the sentence, points directly at one meaning only; "the metal under a plating." Apparently the ring is gold plated, not solid gold.

The time in which the word is used will determine what a writer means by it, and thus time becomes an important part of the context of a word. As you know from reading his plays or poems, some of the words used by Shakespeare in the sixteenth century have reversed meaning since then. Similarly, forty years ago, a *tough* girl was a disgrace to the Christian community; today a *tough* girl is likely to be elected Miss Christian League of Decency.

Connotation

Words have *connotations* as well as denotations. The dictionary gives denotations, but it does not list the many emotional shades of meaning a word might have. These emotional meanings are called connotations. Connotative words stir emotional responses—fear, hate, love, religious fervor, patriotism—in those who use them and in those who read or hear them.

The word *mother,* for instance, makes most red-blooded Americans feel warmth and love and security. The writer who uses the word *mother,* then, must be aware that these good vibrations are likely to affect the person who reads it. Unless these subjective radiations are controlled by the context in which the word appears, its meaning will, no doubt, be distorted.

> ★ In these pairs of words underline the ones that have the stronger connotative values.
>
> A. car, Cadillac
> B. swimsuit, bikini
> C. ship, the Titanic
>
> ☆ *Cadillac, bikini, the Titanic.* A *car* to most of us is "any vehicle on wheels"; a *Cadillac* is a car, but most of us associate with it feelings of comfort, luxury, ease, even financial success and security. A *swimsuit* is a garment worn for swimming; a *bikini,* a type of swimsuit, suggests, in addition to swimming, warm summer days, sandy beaches, and the shapes of lovely suntanned girls. A *ship* is a vessel that moves on the water; the *Titanic,* the ship that couldn't, yet did, sink, suggests man's struggle against the forces of nature. It suggests cold and the agony of men drowning.

Words may have positive or negative connotations. To a child who still believes in Santa Claus, *reindeer* means more than "any of the several species of large deer with branching antlers." Rather, it means Christmas—presents, stories, candy, bright decorations, the Christ child, and joy. The word *communist,* on the other hand, suggests such things as Stalin's mass murders and Red China's threats to world peace. As a result, it is hard—even impossible— to be objective about the teaching of a college professor who has been called a communist or the talent of a musician or poet who has been labeled a Red.

★ In these sentences underline the word in parentheses that has the most positive connotation.

A. The fiery senator from New York (guided, directed, dictated) the country's future.
B. Enraged, the fierce grizzly attacked the defenseless (rodent, rabbit, bunny).

☆ For A you should have underlined *guided,* for it has a positive connotation implying that the senator set an example the people chose to follow, or, at most, he made suggestions. *Directed* suggests that the senator took a stronger hand in affairs but that the country was still not told what to do; it was merely led firmly. *Dictated* has a negative connotation connected with strong-arm government; it might even suggest the kind of totalitarian rule of dictators like Hitler and Mussolini. In B you should have underlined *bunny,* an affectionate term for rabbit, a child's term. One might even think of the Easter Bunny. *Rodent* has negative connotations as a result of its regular association with mice and rats— vermin. *Rabbit* is, of course, associated with hunting.

When you use words, you should know their denotations—all of the meanings the dictionary lists. If you use the words with which you are familiar, you generally know whether they have positive or negative connotations beyond their dictionary meanings. No matter how many denotative and connotative meanings a word has, you must shape the context to make clear which meaning you have in mind.

Tone

Your word choice affects the tone of what you write. As we said in Chapter 2, tone is a product of the writer's attitude toward both his subject and his audience. Happy, sad, gay, melancholy, serious, angry, indignant, satirical, playful—you shape your tone as you write.

The words you use show your attitude. When you wish to appear objective, neutral, unemotional, you choose words with low connotative values. And you put the words you do choose in a context that points up their denotations. When you wish to be subjective, biased, emotional, you select words for their connotative values.

★ Identify the tone in this paragraph from H. L. Mencken:

Let the farmer, so far as I am concerned, be damned forevermore. To Hell with him, and bad luck to him. He is a tedious fraud and ignoramus, a cheap rogue and hypocrite, the eternal Jack of the human pack. He deserves all that he ever suffers under our economic system, and more. Any city man, not insane, who sheds tears for him is shedding tears of the crocodile. (H. L. Mencken, ''The Husbandman,'' *Prejudices: Fourth Series.* Copyright 1924, 1943 by H. L. Mencken. Reprinted with permission of Alfred A. Knopf, Inc.)

A. happy   C. indignant
B. playful   D. angry _____

☆ Here Mencken is angry, combining exaggeration (*be damned forevermore, all that he ever suffers*) with strong connotative words (*damned, Hell, tedious fraud and ignoramus, cheap rogue and hypocrite, Jack of the human pack*).

WRITING ASSIGNMENTS

1. Read the movie reviews in an issue or two of *Time, Playboy, Newsweek, New Republic,* or *New Yorker* and write a brief report on the writers' use of connotative language.
2. Read a news article on a controversial subject and then write a report on the diction employed in that article. As you read and write, consider what this chapter says about denotation, context, and connotation.
3. Compare or contrast two or three articles from different newspapers or magazines on the same news item. Write a report on how these publications differ in word selection. Account for the difference.
4. Write an essay on one of the following topics:
   The Language of Politics
   Language That Really Works
   Students and Instructors Speak Different Languages
   When to Use Emotional Language
   The Tone My Father Uses
   A Minister's Language
   Words That Sell
   How Car Advertisers Use Words
   Man Speaks to Woman

Exercises

14a   **A.** On the line to the right write the letter of the correct meaning (denotation) for the italicized word in each sentence.

1. Did you see him *draw* the whole Coke up the straw in one mouthful?
2. After going through the entire file of fingerprints, he was ready to *draw* his conclusions.
3. When Joe Summers called Bill Hutchinson, Tessie pushed him out to *draw* the slip of paper.
4. The Christmas crowd was quiet as they watched him *draw* the sketches in white on the black paper.
5. We do plenty of fishing on the grass flats so we need a boat that will *draw* no more than two feet of water.
6. The trouble with cheap underwear is that hot water will cause the material to *draw* up.

a. "(of a vessel) to need a specific depth of water to float in"
b. "to inhale or suck in"
c. "to wrinkle or shrink by contraction"
d. "to deduce; infer"
e. "to sketch someone or something in lines or words"
f. "to choose or to have assigned to one at random, by or as by picking an unseen number"

(1) _____

(2) _____

(3) _____

(4) _____

(5) _____

(6) _____

B. On the line write the word in the parentheses which best expresses what the writer means. Consider the denotation, context, and connotation of the word.

1. I could see the (strident, confident, diffident) look in my opponent's eye; I knew that I would win again.

   (1) _____

2. For ten years he had (inflicted, conflicted, afflicted) a kind of economic punishment which had held up the economic growth of the entire town.

   (2) _____

3. I hid in the bushes near the sidewalk in my yard, (staring, peering, gazing, looking) out two or three times to watch their progress and to make sure the street was clear.

   (3) _____

4. Just as the little boy got in front of me, (lurking, cowering, browsing, trembling) there in the bushes, I jumped out, pounced upon him, and sent him sprawling on the sidewalk.

(4) _____

5. After a while I ran into my deserted house and sat there alone, frightened and listening to every rustle and noise I heard outside, as if I expected some (intuition, execution, refraction, retribution).

(5) _____

6. My alternating affections and cruelties were (indelible, indicative, inexplicable, inevitable), for I had been brought up to love my fellow man.

(6) _____

7. Henry Aaron trotted over and gingerly tossed the ball underhanded across the wire fence to the boys, and that (usual, casual, flamboyant, flippant), gesture was performed with such fine aristocracy that it was a pleasure to watch.

(7) _____

8. As a child, I never wanted to be a fireman or a policeman; in fact, I never had any of the other standard juvenile (inspirations, aspirations, invocations, avocations).

(8) _____

9. The (consistence, resistance, resilience, persistence) of the notion that everyone in America has the opportunity to succeed is difficult to account for when we see the number of failures we have produced since the beginning of the republic.

(9) _____

10. So resilient was the coyote's foothold on existence that it began to seem as if the settlers sought to (illuminate, exterminate, invigorate, illustrate) a phantom.

(10) _____

14b   A. In each sentence below, underline the incorrect word. In the blank below write the word that should have been used.

1. Since age twelve, I have been able to remember the immortal chill of the gas that they gave me when I had my tonsils out.

(1) _____

2. He was the victim of an ailment so common that most people would consider it important.

(2) _____

3. The two blondes, who were in their middle thirties, were preened and polished, their immature bodies softly molded within tight dark suits.

(3) _____

4. A good deal of the younger generation's behavior is admirable and promising, much of it is at least reprehensible, and most of it is preferable to the torpor of the Eisenhower years.

(4) _____

5. If a wife, a home, children, and permanence are merely allusions, then the American home is doomed.

(5) _____

6. The popularity of *Peanuts* is due not to its inherited humor, but to the manner in which it is interpreted by its readers.

(6) _____

7. The numerous articles in the popular magazines that deal with psychology contest to the extreme the American reader's interest in that subject.

(7) _____

8. Since the beginning of the comic strip medium, there have been many entries based on the attics of children.

(8) _____

9. *Dennis the Menace* is funny for what Dennis does, not why he does it; the humor in *Dennis* is implicit, and needs not even the tinge of psychology for its success.

(9) _____

10. Charlie Brown works hard at being a failure; he is, in fact, an apathetic figure.

(10) _____

B. To change the highly emotional tones to a more neutral tone, rewrite each of these sentences in the space provided.

1. Having endured two boring hours of the nonsense of NBC, CBS, and ABC nightly TV programming, he was ready to quit the boob-tube watching and begin reading comic books.

_____

_____

_____

_____

2. The Rotarians, the Kiwanians, the Ku Kluxers, and other reactionary organizations are nothing more than political acid peddlers, liars, and petty thieves.

_____

_____

_____

_____

3. The smooth-shifting purr of the Torko-drive transmission makes the dynamic Buick, the automobile abounding with standard extras, the most imminently appealing buy of all the medium-priced sports-luxury cars: To own a Buick is to buy the good life.

_____

_____

_____

_____

4. Every *thinking* college student has the right to come and go as he pleases, without government agents, businessmen, religious fanatics, uptight parents, cops, and college administrators and faculty hacks imposing their wills.

_____

_____

_____

_____

5. Dear Crook:
   Having been ripped off by virtually every incompetent repairman in this seedy burg—from bungling garage mechanics to mindless television "fixers"—I want you to know that *your* "service" is without a doubt the worst, for you not only overcharged me for your pseudolabor (thirty dollars to fix a door handle!), but you billed me twice for replacing three expensive parts that weren't even broken.

   Insincerely yours,
   John (Blackhand) Bates

_____

_____

_____

_____

chapter 15

Diction: Using Words Correctly and Effectively

Sometimes writers say they have trouble making their ideas clear because of their small vocabulary. They feel they don't have enough words at their command. Writers often do have limited vocabularies. But most beginning writers suffer not from knowing too few words, but from not using the words they do know.

In this chapter we will show you how to use the vocabulary you already have and how you can avoid common errors that many beginning writers make as they use their vocabularies.

Using the Vocabulary You Have

Writing means finding the right word to say what you mean. Beginning writers, unfortunately, often think they have to impress their readers by using fancy language, words with a dictionary flavor. The fact is, most of your ideas can be made clear with the words you know. Your job as a writer is to find not the big word, the abstract word, but the precise word, the one that says exactly what you mean.

General to Specific

Too many writers settle for less than the precise word. We often choose the general word rather than the specific, the vague and colorless in place of the concrete and colorful. Too often, for instance, we use *things* when we mean *problems, aspects* when we mean *advantages*. In short, because we are often in a hurry, we settle for the nearly correct word and hope that the reader will know what we mean. We figure that even though we write *doohickey* or *thingamajig*, we will really convey *toggle bolt* or *mustard plaster*. As a result, our writing becomes a mixed bag of vague words that force each reader to guess at what we mean.

★   Which of these sentences is more effective? _____

A. The experience was one of the most exciting things of my life.
B. As the roller coaster shot down the steep hill and clacked around the first bend, my heart pounded, my ears rang, and I shrieked with fright and delight.

☆   B. Instead of the vague word *experience*, the subject of A, the writer of B specifies the quality of the experience, a ride on a roller coaster. For the actionless verb *was*, in A, the writer uses the more muscular *shot, clacked, pounded, rang,* and *shrieked*. The writer of B needs no flimsy evaluation (''the most exciting thing''), for he takes the reader on the ride with him through precise and objective language. The writer of A has stayed too high on the staircase of abstractions.

Down the Staircase of Abstractions

To find the right word, take a trip down the staircase of abstractions. On the lower steps you are likely to find the word which limits the meaning so that your idea is conveyed specifically. Read this sentence, for instance:

> We did things today.

What does the writer mean by *things,* a vague word, almost meaningless, certainly colorless? Did he play basketball? Read novels? Plan an essay? All three? Or did he form a thesis statement and make a sentence outline?

> We did things today.
>   We planned an essay today.
>   We formed a thesis statement and constructed a sentence outline today.

The word *things* and its kin—*aspects, areas, fields*—are too often easy substitutes for ''real'' words. But we will say more about such ''jargon'' later in this chapter.

★　Arrange these words on the staircase to the right.

A. canine

B. Rex

C. quadruped

D. boxer

E. dog

F. animal

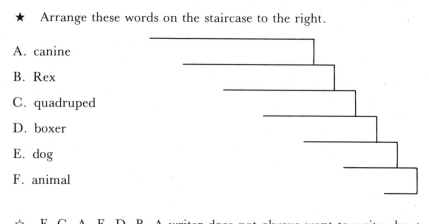

☆　F, C, A, E, D, B. A writer does not always want to write about Rex. He may wish to write about animals in general. But he is more likely to engage his reader with the specific "snarling boxer" than with the general "angry animal."

Your purpose in writing is to make your ideas accurate, specific, and concrete; to paint "in living color," as the television phrase has it, the idea you have in mind. You must paint your picture, however, with words instead of oils and lenses, tubes, and transistors. At least part of a writer's success, then, depends upon finding the word on the right step on the staircase of abstractions, the step that best suits the purpose.

★　Underline the word in the parentheses that most effectively conveys the writer's ideas.

My Florida-bred (car, Mercury) (moved, slid) gingerly from the (highway, Turnpike) into the (Beckley, city) turnoff, followed the (road, cloverleaf) around and began the gradual descent of the insidiously curving road. Rain and snow (clung to, was on) the (window, windshield), dimming my view; I felt the tires (slither, fail to hold) on the (pavement, hidden patches of ice); my numb hands (held, gripped) the (icy, cold) steering wheel; my foot (was near, hovered over) the break pedal. A (movement, swipe) of the windshield wipers brought a (shape, sign) on the right into view: DRIVE CAREFULLY—WE CAN WAIT! The sponsors? An undertaking firm. "They won't have long to wait," I thought, (steering, pulling) the (vehicle, car) sharply against a (slipping motion, skid). So this is (it, West Virginia)?

☆　Each time you should have underlined the more specific word, the word on the lower level of the staircase of abstractions. The success of the paragraph lies in the writer's using the specific word, the concrete word. Here they are in order:

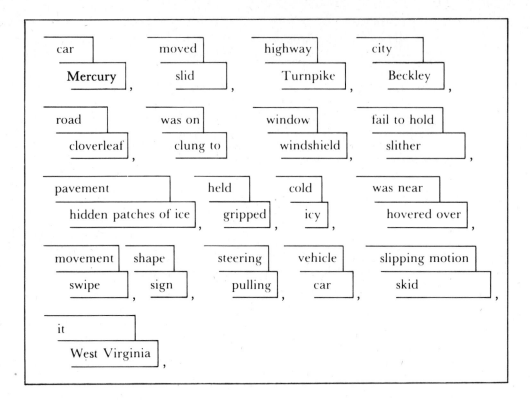

Formal and Informal

Good writing, however, is a result of more than finding the right level on the staircase of abstractions. You may, for example, be on the right level on the staircase but have more than one choice to make from words on that level. Your choice must then depend upon whether your style and tone are formal or informal. As the diagram below shows, the fourth level on the staircase offers the writer a number of choices.

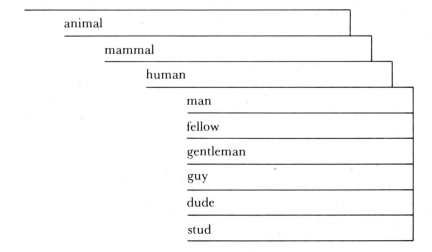

Since all six of the words on step four are equally specific, the writer must choose the word that best fits the style and tone. The dictionary lists discriminated synonyms for the first three words on level four; the last three are slang terms.

Words, like clothes, must suit the occasion. The writer must decide whether the essay is formal or informal and use language suited to the style chosen.

★ Underline the word in both sentences that is either too formal or too informal.

A. Ramming his shoulder into the charging fullback, Fat Jack Fisher, our all-state guard, apprehended the ball carrier, heaved with all his might, and threw him for a six-yard loss.

B. The delicately carved arms of the statue extended outward and upward framing the goddess' noodle and giving the impression of universal beauty.

☆ You should have underscored *apprehended* in sentence A. More appropriate in this context would have been *caught, trapped, smeared,* or *tackled.* In B, *noodle,* a slang term for head, is out of place in the sentence. *Skull* is more formal that *noodle,* but unless the writer is being ironic or trying to frighten the reader, it too is out of place.

Idiom

An important part of our vocabulary is composed of phrases peculiar to our language. We call these language customs *idioms.* In the United States, persons who are ill go "to the hospital"; in England such persons go "to hospital." American idiom puts the word *the* before *hospital*; British idiom leaves out *the*. Both are right. It depends on where you are. But both follow unwritten but strict rules. Here are a few of the many idiomatic expressions used by native speakers of American English:

be taken in	have a mind to	pick off
feel up to	jump on	run down
get in trim	keep to oneself	sick and tired of
hard and fast	out of tune	short of

★ Underline the phrase in this sentence from George Orwell's essay "Shooting an Elephant" that does not reflect appropriate American idiom.

Early one morning the subinspector at a police station the other end of the town rang me up on the 'phone and said that an elephant was ravaging the bazaar. (George Orwell, "Shooting an Elephant," *Shooting an Elephant and Other Essays.* Reprinted with permission of Harcourt Brace Jovanovich)

> ☆ You should have underlined *the other end of the town;* American idiom
> calls for *at the other end of the town.* You might also have underlined *rang me
> up.*

Figurative language

Figurative language makes your writing vivid through comparison—not
literal comparison but metaphorical comparison To describe the running
power of an all-American fullback, you might say, "He lowered his head and
charged like an angry bull." The figure of speech, the comparison (*like an
angry bull*), is not meant literally, for a bull has four legs, a man only two. They
cannot be compared literally. But the comparison adds color and shape to the
sentence by making vivid the quality, the brute force, of the fullback's running
style. We will mention only four types of figurative language here—metaphor,
simile, personification, and allusion—for these are the types you are likely to
use.

Metaphor. A metaphor compares by saying that one thing *is* something
else. When Edgar Allen Poe, for instance, says that science is a vulture whose
wings are dull reality, he is using a metaphor. This bird of prey, science, says
Poe, destroys a poet's heart and imagination with cold, hard facts. By saying
science is a vulture, Poe brings a negative emotional response from his reader.
When Robert Frost writes, "The sun's a wizard/By all I tell; but so's the
moon a witch," he is using a metaphor.

> ★ Underline the metaphor in this sentence.
>
> His mind was a calculating machine that put the figures in order.
>
> ☆ You should have underlined *his mind was a calculating machine,* for it is
> an indirect comparison in which the writer says that one thing is
> something else. Through the comparison you get a visual picture of the
> accuracy with which the subject's mind works with figures.

Simile. A simile is a figurative comparison announced by the words *like, as,*
or *than.* Because of the signal words, a simile is easier to spot than a metaphor.
When you say that the fire that burned down your town's only school was like
the fires of hell, you have used a simile. When the coach moans that his team's
infield is as leaky as a sieve, he is using a simile. Both simile and metaphor use
comparison to make the object or idea under consideration clearer than it
otherwise would be. They make the new or strange clear by comparing it with
something familiar. The success of the metaphors and similes above depends
on the reader's familiarity with a vulture, a witch, a wizard, a calculating
machine, the fires of hell, and the leakiness of a sieve.

★ Underline the similes in this passage from George Orwell's ''A Hanging.''

A sickly light, like yellow tinfoil, was slanting over the high walls into the jail yard. We were waiting outside the condemned cells, a row of sheds fronted with double bars, like small animal cages.

☆ You should have underlined *like yellow tinfoil* and *like small animal cages*. With both similes Orwell captures the feeling of depression and confinement that pervades the prison yard as preparations are made for the execution of one of the prisoners. Similes and metaphors can be positive or negative. The examples above seem to be the latter.

Personification. Personification occurs when a writer gives human qualities to an animal, inanimate object, or idea. We use personification when we say, ''Shakespeare's plays have ruled the English theater with a monarch's power.''

★ Which of these three sentences includes an example of personification? _____

A. Jason is a pig.
B. He played the back nine like a pro.
C. Hitler's crippled thought grew rapidly into a limping giant.

☆ C. A includes a metaphor, an outright statement that something is something else. B includes a simile, a comparison introduced by the signal word *like*. C gives an idea (*Hilter's thought*) human characteristics (*crippled, limping giant*); therefore it employs personification.

Allusion. An allusion is a type of comparison. It is an indirect reference to a work of art, a famous person, a piece of literature. When Emily Dickinson refers to herself as the *''Queen of Calvary,''* she is alluding to Christ's place of crucifixion; Christ was the *''King of Calvary.''* When you ask a person who is sitting, meditating, elbow on knee, chin in hand, whether he is posing for Rodin, you are alluding to a famous sculpture, Rodin's *Thinker*. When you tell a friend who is always looking at his watch that he is going to be *''late for a very important date,''* you are alluding to the movie version of *Alice in Wonderland*, which pictured a white rabbit constantly rushing to a meeting for which he was late.

★ Underline the allusion in this sentence from Herbert Gold's essay ''A Dog in Brooklyn'':

> The encounter with classroom reality has caused many teachers, like Abelard meeting the relatives of Eloise, to lose their bearings.
>
> ☆   You should have underlined *like Abelard meeting the relatives of Eloise,* for Gold alludes to the romantic and violent love story of teacher and pupil to suggest how some teachers react to the classroom situation. (A good encyclopedia will give you more background for the allusion.) An allusion develops through suggestion. The reader who understands the allusion recalls, perhaps, an entire novel, play, painting, sculpture, historical period.

Avoiding Common Errors

Wordiness

Faced with writing a short essay and encouraged to develop their ideas fully, writers often confuse development with padding; that is, they conclude that a great many words are needed to make an idea clear.

Wordy: There are fifteen soldiers who are waiting to be transferred. (10 words)
Better: Fifteen soldiers are waiting to be transferred. (7 words)
Concise: Fifteen soldiers await transfer. (4 words)

> ★   Take out the words not needed in the following sentence. Rewrite it in the space provided.
>
> It is my opinion that if there had been more men in the uniform of the United States Cavalry at the famous Battle of the Little Big Horn there would have been an outcome different from the one that occurred; i.e., General Custer would have remained alive. (47 words)
>
> _____
>
> _____
>
> ☆   You might have revised it something like this: *General Custer would have lived if he had had more troops with him at the Battle of the Little Big Horn.* (21 words)

Clichés

Successful writers use fresh diction. As soon as they fall into the trap of using stale and hackneyed language, they begin to sound like a broken record, their pens playing in the same grooves over and over. Ready-made phrases, clichés, stifle originality. The cliché addict is likely to write the following sentence (the clichés italicized):

In this day and age in which we live, we the people of the free world must *toe the line* and *keep our shoulders to the wheel* if we are to *stem the tide* of *the ever-growing cancer of communism.*

★　In the blanks below, revise this sentence to eliminate the trite language.

The tried and true woodsman raised his trusty rifle to his sturdy shoulder, aimed with deadly accuracy, and squeezed off the single messenger of death, which, like a bolt from the blue, quenched the flame of life in the defenseless little bunny.

_____

_____

☆　You might have revised it as follows: *The hunter killed the rabbit with one shot.*

Jargon

Jargon, another word trap, is a specialized vocabulary understood by persons of a specific profession or interest group but not clear to those outside the special circle. Most of us have been in school long enough to have learned quite a bit of educational jargon that too often gets into our writing. This empty language includes such words as *aspects, case, concept, condition, factor, field, nature, tendency, type,* and many more utility words.

★　In the space below revise this sentence to take out the jargon.

In the area of spelling, Harry had a tendency to have trouble with the types of words that are composed of two syllables.

_____

_____

☆　You might have revised it to read: *Harry had trouble spelling two-syllable words.*

A special kind of jargon appears in the sports pages of newspapers and in radio and television sportscasts. It includes such words as *quintet* for *basketball team, pigskin* for *football,* and *timber swinger* or *lumberman* for *batter.*

★　In the space below revise the sentence to eliminate the journalese, sports jargon.

The fast-breaking Mountain Lion hoopsters are slated for their premier tiff at the local dribble emporium.

_____

_____

☆   You might have rewritten the sentence like this: *The Concord College basketball team will play their first game in the college fieldhouse.*

Slang

Amusing when fresh, slang stales quickly. Once stale, it becomes trite at best and confusing at worst. In the past few years, for example, the word *groovy* became popular slang and then quickly disappeared. It is doubtful that readers fifty years from now will understand what *groovy* meant in the late 1960s and early Seventies. Though "Ain't she the cat's pajamas?" was *heavy* when Grandma wore her version of the miniskirt, it is outdated today.

★   To omit the slang, rewrite this sentence in the space below.

Like dig it, man, when the cops pick you up for dragging, they take your hog and throw you in the slammer.

_____

_____

☆   You might have revised it to read like this: *Listen, when the police arrest you for racing, they take your motorcycle and put you in jail.*

Pretentious Diction

Writers sometimes feel that a dull subject can be made interesting if they use big words. When they use such language, they use pretentious diction. Big words will never hide an empty idea, but they will often cloud a good idea. Those who like pretentious diction would never say *The cat killed the rat;* they prefer *The feline administered the coup de grâce to the rodent.*

★   To take out the pretentious diction, rewrite this sentence in the space below.

Firmly putting my feet down alternately—first one, then the other—I removed from my overshoes the frozen white crystalline droplets of water that had fallen softly during the night and now covered the ground outside.

☆   You might have revised it like this: *I stomped the snow off my boots.*

WRITING ASSIGNMENTS

1. For a week record the words you hear people use incorrectly. Write them in a notebook and be ready to make an organized oral report on your findings. Make a scratch outline for your report.

2. Choose an article from the readings section of this text, and plan an oral report on the outstanding characteristics of the writer's word choice. The categories established in this chapter may give you a basis for your analysis.

3. Select a piece by a writer you admire—novelist, short story writer, poet, dramatist, essayist—and write an essay about that writer's use of words. Make sure you select specific details to support your ideas.

4. Write an essay on one of the following:

   My Vocabulary: Suitable for Most Occasions

   A Time for Slang

   A Case for Figurative Language

   Language Varies According to Time, Place, and People

   Leave My Language Alone

Exercises

15a   **A.** Arrange these words from general to specific on the staircases on the right (most general on the top step).

1. shotgun
   firearm
   handgun
   weapon
   gun
   rifle

2. *Time*
   pamphlet
   propaganda
   Esquire
   Chicago Tribune
   printed matter
   magazine
   newspaper
   Newsweek
   New York Times
   San Francisco Chronicle

3. Chevrolet
   Pinto
   transportation
   Ford
   automobile
   Maverick
   vehicle
   Plymouth
   Mustang

4. pork

   peas

   flank

   nourishment

   sausage

   vegetables

   round

   hamburger

   meats

   corn

   food

   beef

   potatoes

   bacon

   steak

   beans

   ham

   porterhouse

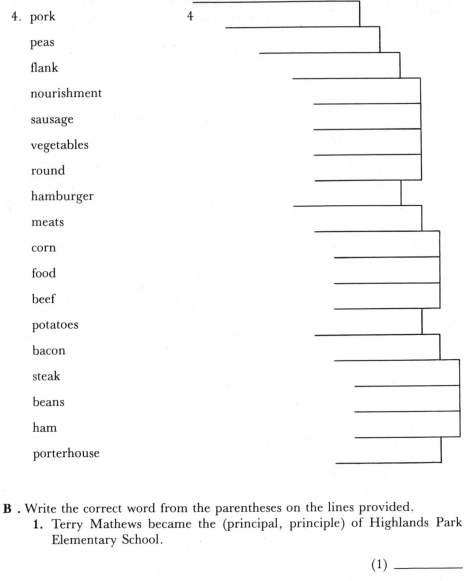

B . Write the correct word from the parentheses on the lines provided.

   1. Terry Mathews became the (principal, principle) of Highlands Park
   Elementary School.

   (1) ——————

   2. (Their, There, They're) the only family on the block that has a car for
   every child.

   (2) ——————

   3. Following his trip to Puerto Rico, Harry looked as (healthy, healthful) as
   ever.

   (3) ——————

   4. Of course you can't do much of a job on the harder wood unless you use
   a (coarse, course) grade of sandpaper.

   (4) ——————

5. When she found out that the sorority had scheduled the party at Disney World, she decided she would go (to, too, two).

(5) _____

6. When he drove the ball into the rough, he had to make a very close shot between two tall pines so that he could get (threw, through) to the fairway.

(6) _____

7. Although he received very little national recognition for the years he struggled in the small college, he was able to (affect, effect) numerous changes in his school's policies.

(7) _____

8. In the middle of the third act, (to, too, two) of the members of the audience danced in the aisles.

(8) _____

9. The enormous center of the football team seemed to be the player with the most (timidity, temerity), for he was constantly allowing smaller men to push him around.

(9) _____

10. T.S. Eliot's many (allusions, illusions) to the classics make his poetry difficult reading for readers who want merely to be entertained by what they read.

(10) _____

11. Following a race (to, too, two) the top of the Washington Monument, the children sat panting at the top, unable to talk for ten minutes.

(11) _____

12. When Kareem Abdul Jabbar wears a pin stripe suit, he gives the (affect, effect) of being even taller than he is.

(12) _____

13. He paid the month's rent in advance, and the family stayed (there, their, they're) until March 1.

(13) _____

14. Because he had not finished his work by noon, they were unable to (except, accept) his application for the early flight.

(14) _____

15. As he told about the attack of the enormous shark, the lawyer gave him an (incredible, incredulous) look and bluntly told him that he was under oath.

(15) _____

15b A. Underline the figurative language in these sentences and indicate in the blanks below whether it is M (metaphor), S (simile), P (personification), or A (allusion).

 1. The press box on the top of the stadium made the whole thing look like a fat woman with a black eye.

(1) _____

 2. He shot out of the barn like a surfboard on the crest of a tidal wave.

(2) _____

 3. When Matilda cooked, the kitchen came alive; the mustard, ketchup, nutmeg, and all the condiments lined up to present themselves for her inspection.

(3) _____

 4. Although the captain had no wooden leg, he stood like an Ahab on the bridge of the ship; when he moved he limped.

(4) _____

 5. She was an octopus when it came to basketball; she seemed to have one more arm than it was possible to have.

(5) _____

 6. In the middle of the storm he walked six miles to carry the total stranger to the doctor, and like the Good Samaritan of old, he paid the bill.

(6) _____

 7. He was so efficient at his job that to watch him you'd have thought he was a machine programmed to do the office work perfectly.

(7) _____

 8. Science knows the price of everything but the value of nothing.

(8) _____

 9. I cannot, my dear, live without you; you are indeed the cream in my coffee.

(9) _____

 10. Autumn is nothing more than an enormous harvester who brings plenty to a hungry world.

(10) _____

B. In each of these sentences underline the words(s) that is either too formal or too informal. Write the correct word in the blank.

 1. I never really dug the purpose of this elaborate opening ceremony.

(1) _____

2. Between classes we ambled quickly to the bookstore to pick up our texts for the semester.

    (2) —————

3. Sitting through high school graduation, I began to apply my gray matter in relation to the ceremony.

    (3) —————

4. Graduation ceremonies either should be altered and updated or should be scratched.

    (4) —————

5. Tim had punched Bill Jackson so hard that his ring had made a two-inch cut just below the right eye. Their altercation got them both in trouble.

    (5) —————

6. As they went down the church aisle, her father snatched a mimeographed Sunday bulletin and perused it hastily.

    (6) —————

7. His experience with opera had taken him to four continents in twenty years. He had, in fact, organized the national opera of Brazil. He was, in short, an opera buff.

    (7) —————

8. Frank Shorter is a skinny marvel of a guy who thinks running constantly. His grueling daily workout forces him to run in rain, snow, sleet, and mud. In twenty years of running he has never been thwarted by the weather.

    (8) —————

9. Her mother had given her a bottle of expensive perfume for Christmas. It had a smell about it that I cannot quite describe—a delicate smell.

    (9) —————

10. After he was hit head on by the rugged center, the quarterback hopped up and tripped back to the huddle.

    (10) —————

C. To omit the wordiness, cliches, jargon, slang, or pretentious diction, rewrite the following sentences on a separate piece of paper.

1. As her nimble fingers caressed the keys of her Royal standard, her ever-present employer hovered over her delicate shoulders waiting with baited breath for the skillfully typed messages he had pronounced into his dictaphone that very morning.

2. In the area of reading alone, the outstanding athlete and scholar had

burned the midnight oil night after night attempting to assuage his burning thirst for knowledge.

3. The local five from Bishop Barry secured the trophy for the hard-fought Sunshine City Tourney by outlasting the Northeast quintet, dribblers par excellence, in a 60-59 nail-biter.

4. The plumber secured the copy of the evening news and hungrily devoured each tidbit while he languidly ate his cheese and salami sandwiches and grabbed some shut-eye before the afternoon shift.

5. That's right, folks. Now's the time to boogie on down to Mark's big store for your groovy teentogs, those classy rags for the in-crowd only.

6. The person who shared his college domicile, a cubicle of small proportions, ever and anon was interrogating him about how he could acquire the wherewithal to pursue his education at his revered alma mater.

7. Joe Colleges who are taking advantage of the situation in the library are reading the usual run of modern novels and are ending up with something to write home about.

8. The two attractions that are located in Orlando have been given permission to erect small signals of a directional type on major streets in the city of Orlando.

9. Having perused my copy of *Batman Comics,* the diminutive custodian of the natatorium threw that periodical in the waste container.

10. The squares all hang around Sam's Diner and pretend they dig that groovy combo that plays those jazzed-up versions of Bach.

section six

Checking Up

chapter 16

Checking Your Thinking:
Logic

The logic of your writing—your rhetoric—is, finally, the captive of the logic of your thinking. Now, thinking is hard enough. Thinking about thinking can get even more troublesome; but in this chapter we will try to do just that. We will describe the kinds of generalizations that you write about in your papers and the ways in which you arrive at them and try to prove them. We hope to make you more aware of what goes on when you—and the people you read and listen to—think and argue.

Induction—From Fact to Generalization

We do not, as it turns out, always begin at the beginning when we think. But when we do, we begin with some facts, some evidence. This kind of beginning is called *induction:* we begin with some evidence and then try to draw some generalizations from what we think the evidence shows. This process of induction is what is usually called the scientific method; evidence is studied, and various tentative laws or generalizations are drawn. In this way we are all scientists. If we picked a half dozen apples off a tree—three green and three red—and found that all the green were sour and all the red were sweet, we could then build two generalizations: *green apples are sour, red apples are sweet.*

Put another way, building generalizations from evidence is moving up the staircase of abstractions. On the basis of material at a lower level of abstraction, we make a statement that is more abstract, at a higher step on the staircase. Logic, then, is based on the careful use of these two kinds of statements. Induction starts with statements at lower, concrete levels; this is the evidence.

It then tries to define the higher-level abstraction, the generalization that this evidence can be a logical part of, can lead to. The logic of the generalization depends upon the kind of connection that can be made between the lower-level evidence and the higher-level generalization.

1. Evidence and generalizations

One of the first problems we encounter in inductive thinking is keeping in mind the difference between evidence and generalizations. There are three main stages: the raw data itself, statements of evidence that put the data into words, and generalizations that build larger abstractions on the evidence. For example, *There are 5,280 feet in a mile* is a statement of fact or evidence. Statements of evidence can be verified, checked, proved by referring to the data of experience—in this case going to measure something. On the other hand, generalizations are based on other statements, on the statements of evidence which are the factual reports of experiences. Thus, *Comic books encourage juvenile deliquency* is a generalization. It can be defended only by referring to some other, more concrete statements about juveniles who read comic books; even then, it would be an interpretation of that data, not a statement of evidence.

Here is a typical sequence: The FBI's *Uniform Crime Report* of 1970 summarizes police data. It lists, for example, numbers of violent crimes reported per 100,000 population for all 50 states. North Dakota has 34.2, New York has 676.0; others are in between. Using those statistics, we could make a generalization: *More violent crimes per 100,000 population were reported in New York in 1970 than in any other state.* This is a rather low-level, concrete generalization. It still stays statistical and stays very close to the evidence. It does not make any judgments beyond the summary word *more*.

In turn, we could say *New York is the most violent state in the nation.* This is a higher level generalization that gets us more into the realm of interpretation and judgment. We have moved from evidence to a summary of statistics and then to an interpretation of statistics.

★   Which is a statement of evidence?

A. The six convicted boys read comic books in the courtroom.

B. Comic books encourage juvenile delinquency.

☆   A. A is a specific, concrete report that can be checked against experience: they either did or didn't read the books in the courtroom. If you were to draw any further conclusion from the statement, you would be going beyond the mere citation of facts. B is a generalization, much higher on the staircase of abstractions. To be proved, it would need to be supported by a number of more factual statements. Even then it would be debatable, for generalizations are interpretations of facts, and so are subject to debate. If, for example, 80 percent of the boys in a reform school read comic books, this evidence would not necessarily prove that the comic books had a direct effect on their being in reform school.

Other things, such as home life and environment, might well be part of the cause. But with evidence we are on different ground; either 80 percent did or didn't read comic books, whatever we then want to make of it.

★   Which is a generalization that will need to be supported by statements of evidence?

A. From 1970 to 1972, violent crime in the suburbs increased 27%; in the cities it increased 21%.
B. Suburbs are now more violent than cities.

☆   B. B is an interpretation of some evidence. It would not, incidentally, be an acceptable interpretation of the evidence cited in A, for even though the increase in the suburbs is higher, that does not necessarily mean the suburbs are "more violent" than the cities.

2. Types of evidence

The kinds of experience that you can refer to in supporting your statements vary a great deal. You can, first of all, refer to experience that you have personally observed. To observe this data you can either create a situation—an experiment—or use experiences you have already had. You can create an experiment to test when water freezes or you can use your memories of your summer vacations to support the statement; *Palm Springs is always hot in the summer.*

You can also refer to the testimony of witnesses of certain experiences. But you need to take into account the degree of reliability of these witnesses, the possible personal biases they may bring to bear on reporting their experiences.

One of the most important types of witness is the authority, one who not only has observed certain data but has, by training and experience, a certain competence in the field. Authorities are a most useful form of evidence, but they can also be misused. The main problem is using them in fields outside of their direct competence and expertise. A physicist may know all about the characteristics of an atomic explosion, but he may not be as valid an authority on the effects of atomic radiation on humans as would a chemist or biologist. Even when kept within their fields of competence, authorities can be misused. You may actually misunderstand them or inaccurately misrepresent them by taking one remark or case out of context. Or you may be using an authority who is outdated.

Another form of evidence beyond your own experience is the document, whether this be an original text or a statistical summary. Statistical documentation is particularly persuasive, but not necessarily foolproof. Averages and percentages are especially devilish when not approached with care and common sense. To say that violent crime in the suburbs increased at a rate 6 percent higher than crime in the city does not, for example, make any statement about the total amount of crime, nor the relationship of that total amount in both places. Thus, there is no contradiction between the statement about the 6 percent difference and the statement that the city rate is 1047.5 per 100,000 inhabitants and the suburban rate 205.7. They are statements about two different kinds of evidence, two different ways of approaching the same level of abstraction.

3. Validity of evidence

Whatever the type of evidence, or combination of types, you want to be sure that it is valid evidence, a firm foundation for your generalization. For one thing, it needs to be *thorough* enough. Any evidence is, of course, a selection from the whole of experience; but, still, different kinds of generalizations will require a different degree of completeness in this selection. The sampling of evidence should be based on enough cases, should have enough quantity. But the sampling should also be *representative* enough. Twenty people, for example, may be enough quantity on which to base a generalization about a certain group; but it is also important to see that the twenty represent a good cross-section of the various types of people within the group.

Even when thorough and representative enough, evidence also needs to be *appropriate*. It needs to be relevant to the type of generalization involved. A generalization about the comparative literary abilities of T. S. Eliot and Mickey Spillane is not appropriately proved by reference to royalty statistics. A more appropriate type of evidence would be reference to authorities— literary critics. In other words, does the evidence really prove the generalization?

4. Types of generalizations

It is useful to see that the generalizations based on your evidence can be of three general types.

First of all, there is what we might call the *descriptive generality*. It is a restatement at a higher level of abstraction of the terms of the concrete data. Thus, it can state that something is true of all the members of a classification: *Green apples are sour.* In this form, it is based on evidence that is a repetition of the same item over and over again. One green apple after another is tested. A descriptive generality can also be a summary in words of statistical data: *Since 1967, the number of homicides in Detroit has doubled.* Though a generalization, it is still rather close to the data, the kind of low-level statistical summary we mentioned above. In turn, the descriptive generality can move higher on the staircase, involving more interpretation and judgment: *Detroit is the most violent city in the nation.*

Evidence and summary statements can also lead to the second type of generalization: the *causal generality,* or *hypothesis.* This type of generalization is based on one particular type of interpretation: cause and effect. The causal generality, or hypothesis, states that something causes something else. It is built by using a number of different items of evidence and claiming some relationship between them, when all are considered together. Thus, the hypothesis claims that something caused them all to occur, or one caused another to occur, or they caused something else to occur. For example, if we add another summary of statistics about Detroit, we could have these two statements: *Since 1967, the number of homicides in Detroit has doubled; since 1967, the number of pistols in Detroit has doubled.* Both of these are still descriptive generalities. But you may have begun to think of some further connection between the two, a cause-and-effect connection. As a casual hypothesis, that connection would be stated like this: *The doubling of the number of pistols in Detroit since 1967 has led to the doubling of the number of homicides.* This would be a rather shaky hypothesis, for it takes into account only one possible kind of evidence for the conclusion. There may be other factors that could also cause the increase in homicides.

Many hypotheses put together different pieces of evidence to find an interpretation that can account for the combination of all. This is what a detective does in finding the common denominator that can account for all the clues. A doctor's diagnosis is a similar hypothesis. The combination of the various symptoms is said to be caused by the fact of a particular disease.

★ Of the following items about Chicago's schools, which could be seen as the result of the others in combination? _____

A. Only door near principal's office is left open.
B. School violence decreased 11%.
C. Students carry ID cards.
D. Armed guards patrol half of schools.

☆ B. Thus, the hypothesis would be that the decrease in violence has occurred because of the combination of the other items.

★ Which of the following is a causal generality, a hypothesis? _____

A. Athletes are indifferent students.
B. The rigors of football season harm the grades of the players.

☆ B. A merely makes a description of something that is said to hold true for all members of the class: *athletes.* It is a descriptive generality and would be based on a repetition of the same kind of evidence: The grades of athlete A, the grades of athlete B, etc., possibly in comparison to the grades of student A, the grades of student B, etc. On the other hand, B makes a statement of cause and effect: the rigors cause the bad grades. It would be based on a combination of different kinds of evidence. Not only would grades be taken into account, but also the various things that take up the time of the player. And then a further relationship would be drawn between these different types of evidence, to show that one set caused the other.

In addition to making descriptions of what *is* or of what *caused* something to be what it is, generalizations can also make *prescriptions*. That is, they can be statements of what *ought to be*. These are usually based on the other types of generalization: Because A is so, or A is caused by something, B should be or should not be done: *Since athletes are indifferent students, they should have close supervision.* The second half of the sentence is the prescription; the first half is the descriptive generalization.

★   Which statement includes a prescription? _____

A. Everything is more expensive that it used to be.
B. Fraternities foster snobbishness.
C. Something should be done about all that misleading advertising.

☆   C. A is a descriptive generality, and B is a hypothesis. C is a prescription about what should be done, based on a descriptive generality that is not actually stated in its full terms: *much advertising is misleading.* Like all prescriptions, then, it is interpretation of another interpretation of the evidence; and it is thus that much further removed from the world of fact into the world of opinion.

---

5. Validity of generalizations

The three traditional tests of generalizations are *completeness, simplicity, inevitability*. First, does your generalization take into account all of the available evidence? You cannot conveniently leave out relevant information that would contradict your generalization. For example, a detective cannot ignore the troublesome clues of a case. Secondly, your generalization should be the simplest that is nonetheless complete enough. Do not over-elaborate. Do not add complications and extra assumptions that are not necessary to explain the facts. If a piece of paper blows off the table every time the door opens, the breeze that comes in the door is enough of an explanation. You need not conjure up evil spirits who come in the door and move the paper. And finally, your generalization should be as inevitable as possible. That is, it should follow from the evidence in as direct a way as possible, particularly when cause and effect are involved. If you went swimming and then got a stomachache, is there actually evidence from the swimming experience that would allow you to conclude that the swimming caused the stomachache? If you had eaten three green apples and then got a stomachache, a more likely cause-and-effect relationship could be established. Coincidence is the danger in many causal hypotheses. Things may happen at the same time or one after the other, without there being any necessary causal connection between them.

Deduction—From Generalization to Generalization

Inductive thinking and arguing moves from evidence to generalization—up the staircase of abstractions. But you do not always begin your thinking and arguing with evidence. You often begin with generalizations you already assume to be true, without going back to prove these generalizations. You then apply these assumed truths—which are generally at an upper step on the staircase—to a new specific case that has come up which is at a lower step. Thus you are moving down the staircase, finding a relationship between one generality and another. The result is a conclusion that tells you something about the new specific case. Each time you see a green apple, you don't start experimenting. You carry with you the assumed truth that green apples are sour; you apply it to the new case of this green apple and come up with the conclusion that this apple is going to be sour.

Here is another example:

1. Students who study will pass their tests. (Assumed generalization)
2. Joe is a student who studies. (New specific case)

Applying *#1* to *#2,* we get:

3. Joe will pass his tests. (New generalization)

This three-part sequence of thought is called *deduction*. What you are doing is showing the logical relationship between two statements; evidence has nothing to do with it. In its basic form, the logical relationship works this way:

The first statement—the assumed truth— is a broad generality, higher on the staircase of abstractions. It usually is a statement about *all* the members of a classification, even if the word *all* is not used, as in *#1. Students who study will pass their tests.* The statement places this group—*students who study*—in an even broader classification—*people who pass tests.* Thus, this first statement in deduction says one set or classification of items is a logical member of another set or classification.

The second statement—the new specific case—says somethig about a third, more limited set or classification—Joe, for example, in *#2. Joe is a student who studies.* This second statement thus places the new item—Joe—in one of the groups of the first statement; in this case, he is placed in the group of students who study.

The third statement or conclusion results from this combination of classifications. If Joe is a member of one class and all the members of that class are members of a broader class, then he is going to be a member of that broader class also: *#3. Joe will pass his tests.*

This sequence of three statements is called a *syllogism,* but we'll not worry about the term.

1. Consistency, not truth

The first thing to note about this kind of thinking is that you skip over truth. You assume things are true; you assume that your two basic statements are true. You are concerned, then, with being consistent in your argument, with following out the logical relationships of the parts, with following the rules of the game.

★   Is the following argument consistent? _____

1. All communists are dangerous.
2. Joe is a communist.
3. Joe is dangerous.

☆   *Yes.* It is not necessarily true; either of the first two statements might be questioned. But once these two statements are *assumed* to be true, the argument does follow consistently. The first generality is applied to the specific case of the second to arrive at the conclusion. We can say the argument is valid—although not necessarily true.

---

2. Validity

We cannot prove the truth of a deductive argument; only induction based on evidence can prove truth. Rather, we are concerned with the logical consistency of the argument, its validity in relating levels of abstraction. Testing this validity can get very complicated. We will focus only on the basic form of the process and its key testing points.

First of all, the form relates one broader generality to a more limited generality.

★   Which of these two statements is the broader, more abstract generality? _____

A. All college students are intelligent.
B. Sandra is a college student.

☆   A. It places one broad abstract class—*college students*—in an even broader class—*people who are intelligent.* B then places a more specific item, *Sandra,* in what we might call the middle-level classification—*college students.*

One of the best ways of seeing how these relationships work is to use circles to represent the classifications. Two circles are used to show the relationship of the parts of the first statement: *All college students are intelligent.* The outer circle is the broadest generality and in this case will represent *those who are intelligent.* The inner circle is *college students.* Since all college students are said to be intelligent they go completely within the outer circle.

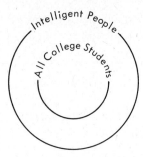

Next, *Sandra* (the third classification) is lower on the staircase of abstractions; items that are lower, less abstract are placed inside the more abstract items. Since Sandra is a college student, she is placed inside that circle.

As it turns out, Sandra also ends up within the large circle. Since she is in one circle, and it is in another, she too is in the other. Thus, the circles show it is valid to say: *If all college students are intelligent, and Sandra is a college student, she is therefore intelligent.*

Our third basic statement, our conclusion, then, is *Sandra is intelligent.*

★   Does this three-part sequence lead to a valid conclusion? _____

1. All psychiatrists are well educated.
2. Mrs. Gable is a psychiatrist.
3. Mrs. Gable is a compassionate woman.

☆   *No.* The conclusion must place the specific case within one of the two classifications set up by the first statement, or no conclusion can be drawn. The only conclusion possible here is that she is *well educated.*

But even if the specific case is placed within one of the two classes set up by the original statement, the logic of the relationships may be violated and an invalid conclusion reached. One of the most frequent causes of logical trouble is placing the third and most specific classification in the largest classification and then concluding that it is therefore also in the middle-level classification.

1. All college students are intelligent.
2. Sandra is intelligent.
3. Sandra is a college student.

By placing *Sandra,* in statement *#2,* in the broadest classification *(those who are intelligent),* we do not logically guarantee that she is a member of the middle-level class *(college students).* In the circles she could be placed in either of two places and thus no conclusion about her being a college student is logically possible.

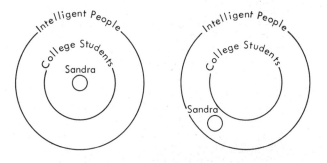

★   Is the following a valid sequence? _____

1. Only college students are intelligent.
2. Sandra is intelligent.
3. Sandra is a college student.

☆   *Yes.* For in this case nobody but college students is said to be intelligent, and so the first two circles would be the same and Sandra would have to be placed in both:

The difference between *all* and *only* in the previous two examples is one of the main problems in this kind of thinking, as is the difference between *all* and *some.* If just *some* college students are intelligent, placing Sandra in the class *college students* will not validly prove she is *intelligent.*

★   Is the following a valid sequence? _____

1. All communists are against the Senator.
2. Jones is against the Senator.
3. Jones is a communist.

☆   *No.* Because *Jones* is part of the largest class (*those against the Senator*), it does not logically follow that he must be a member of the middle-size class (*communists*). In the circles he could appear in one of two positions:

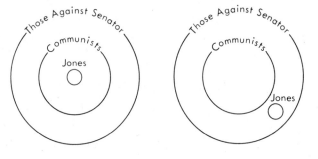

Common Fallacies

Here is a checklist of some of the common fallacies of thinking that pop up frequently in writing—yours and everyone else's. Watch out for them.

1. Faulty assumptions

Too often we take for granted the very assumptions that need to be proved as true before an argument can even begin. These vague assumptions are then applied to a series of further statements, so that what results may be consistent, but distorted. A speaker, for example, says, *"Inasmuch as educational institutions are the most important base from which Anti-Americanism thinking springs, they should receive primary consideration."* Then he goes on to talk about what needs to be done. But he is assuming, without proof, that educational institutions *are* this base. Whatever he says is irrelevant until the assumption is proved to some degree.

2. Hasty generalizations

This type of generalization is based on too little evidence, usually some limited personal experience: *"I spent a day in Atlanta; I know what those Southerners are like."*

3. Faulty dilemma

This is an oversimplification of issues into only two values, two sides. It is often called *black-and-white* thinking. It sets up *either-or* situations— *"You are either against the communists or against me and my program"*—and does not allow the range of alternatives that are available. One might well be against both the communists *and* the speaker, or be against some communists and against some of the speaker's program, etc.

4. After this, therefore because of this

This sets up a faulty cause-and-effect relationship by assuming that B was the result of A merely because it occurred after A did. Time sequence is not enough to guarantee cause and effect.

5. Evading the issue

We often argue around an issue, rather than speaking directly to the point. In this, we may praise the audience—argue to the people—to get them to agree with us on a point we don't really explain. We may use name-calling—arguments against the man—to attack the other side or our opponent on a personal basis, again not directly discussing the arguments. We may also malign the patriotism or loyalty of those who disagree with us. Or we may use such esteemed values as *patriotism, loyalty, belief in God, motherhood* to defend our side. In this we attempt to transfer the feelings associated with certain basic ideals to our own issues by allying our side with these ideals.

WRITING ASSIGNMENTS

1. Write an essay that defends an argumentative generalization about one of the following subjects. Be sure to use evidence properly, provide valid sequences of argument, and avoid logical fallacies.

    Required Courses   Abortions
    The Grading System   The Death Penalty
    Freeways   Restrictions on Smoking
    Family Celebrations   Student Government
    Gun Laws   Athletic Scholarships

2. Write an analysis of the argument of a newspaper or a magazine editorial or column.

Exercises

16a   **A.** On the line provided, place the letter or letters that best answer the question.

1. Which statement is a summary of factual evidence, whether accurate or not?
   a. California is the most heavily populated state in the U.S.A.
   b. Love is the dominant emotion in every living person.

   (1) _____

2. Which statement is in the form of factual evidence, whether accurate or not?
   a. Abraham Lincoln was President of the United States for three successive four-year periods.
   b. American tourists make a poor impression abroad.

   (2) _____

3. Which statement is in the form of factual evidence, whether accurate or not?
   a. Three red-headed people complained to the sales manager.
   b. Red-headed people have quick tempers.

   (3) _____

4. Which statement is a hypothesis?
   a. The professors in this department show favoritism.
   b. With so many mothers working, it's a wonder juvenile delinquency hasn't increased more.

   (4) _____

5. Which statement is a hypothesis?
   a. Capital punishment ought to be abolished.
   b. The rise in incidence of lung cancer is a result of the increase in the consumption of alcohol.

   (5) _____

6. Which statement is a prescription?
   a. Chess is a more intellectual pastime than bridge.
   b. Recent events illustrate the need to make a college education mandatory.

   (6) _____

7. For which generalization would valid evidence be more available?
   a. Advertising writers are neurotic.
   b. The winters in Florida are mild and sunny.

   (7) _____

8. For which generalization would valid evidence be more available?
   a. College teachers are more impersonal than high-school teachers.
   b. Television has had a bad effect on the morals of children.
   c. Grade schools used to be more effective in teaching reading.

   (8) _____

B. On the line provided, write V (Valid) or I (Invalid) or the letter that best answers the question. Use circles in testing your answers.

    1. Is the following deductive sequence of argument valid or invalid?

        a. All angels are butterflies.

        b. Al Capone is an angel.

        c. Al Capone is a butterfly.

(1) _____

    2. Is the following deductive sequence of argument valid or invalid?

        a. All rats like cheese.

        b. Robert likes cheese.

        c. Robert is a rat.

(2) _____

    3. Is the following deductive sequence of argument valid or invalid?

        a. Only Frenchmen are great lovers.

        b. Jacques is a great lover.

        c. Jacques is a Frenchman.

(3) _____

    4. Is the following deductive sequence of argument valid or invalid?

        a. Some Democrats are not liberal.

        b. Jim is a liberal.

        c. Jim is not a Democrat.

(4) _____

    5. Is the following deductive sequence of argument valid or invalid?

        a. All good citizens vote.

        b. Clyde Barrow voted.

        c. Clyde Barrow was a good citizen.

(5) _____

    6. Which statement provides a valid conclusion to these two parts of a deductive argument: Only nuts are nourishing. Pecans are nourishing.

        a. Only pecans are nuts.

        b. Pecans are nuts.

        c. Only pecans are nourishing.

(6) _____

C. On the line provided, place the letter of the item from the following list that best describes the content of each argument:

        a. Logical argument

        b. Faulty assumption

        c. Hasty generalization

        d. Faulty dilemma

        e. After this, therefore because of this

        f. Evading the issue

1. Tuesday I argued with my instructor about my chemistry grade. Wednesday we had an examination. It's easy to see why I failed.

(1) _____

2. My opponent in this campaign has elected to take the low road of personal vilification. I shall take the high road. But if he and his henchmen will come up out of the political mud long enough to think about what true, honest democracy is, they will stop their disgraceful tactics.

(2) _____

3. Paralleling the Communist Party line in so many instances forces liberals to face up to the alternatives: Either they have been duped, or they have consciously and deliberately supported communist goals. Come on, liberals, what's your choice?

(3) _____

4. All the girls from Winnetka are snobs. Why, I knew one of them, Janet Lee or Lane or something like that, and every time I called her for a date she made some silly excuse and would never see me.

(4) _____

5. Before we can vote intelligently on the new bill, gentlemen, we have to first examine what forces got us to ever agree in the first place to adopt a foreign aid program that has been such an obvious failure.

(5) _____

16b   Supply the material requested by each question. Place it in the space provided.
   1. Briefly describe three kinds of evidence you could use to support the following generalization:
   Young men are the worst automobile drivers on the road.

   _____

   _____

   _____

   2. Briefly describe three kinds of evidence you could use to support the following generalization:
   American movies have improved in the last few years.

   _____

   _____

   _____

   3. Write a descriptive generality based on the following statistics:

Causes of Death

	1927	1947
Respiratory diseases	21.4%	6.9%
Cancer	8.3%	15.1%
Heart	33.9%	57.7%
Accident	12.7%	7.0%
Suicide	4.3%	2.3%
All other	19.4%	11.0%

_____

_____

4. Write a hypothesis based on the statistics given in 3.

_____

_____

5. Rewrite the following in the form of a three-step sequence of deductive argument (note that one statement must be supplied).
That must be a valuable book because it is more than one hundred years old.

1. _____

2. _____

3. _____

6. Write a valid conclusion to these two parts of a deductive argument:
Sorority girls are sophisticated and well bred. Marilyn is a sorority girl.

_____

_____

7. On a separate sheet, analyze the fallacies in the following inductive argument.

Since Russia abandoned its athletic isolation in the 1952 Olympics, its athletes and teams have been stacking up an impressive series of victories. In 1954 alone the speed skater Shiloh won the world championship in Japan, their skiers took the biggest events in Sweden, their distance runners, men and women, took home firsts from France, their hockey team beat the Canadians for the title, and they won three out of five events at the Henley Regatta in England. Many more examples could be cited. But it is clear that the Western nations, lulled into laziness by their mechanical gadgets, cars, and television sets, have become soft from lack of exercise, and are in a physical decline.

chapter 17

Checking Your Writing: Revision

As you have seen, writing means choosing a topic, restricting it, forming a thesis, gathering enough relevant evidence to support the thesis, organizing it logically, building paragraphs, composing sentences, and picking the right words to convey your ideas.

When you have finished this rough work, you are ready to revise. You are ready to polish your work, to turn out a finished paper that is both informative and interesting. This second major step, revising, is the key to a good paper. In fact, some well-known writers claim, *"Writing is really revising."*

This original and revised version of a student theme points out some of the hard work and close reading it takes to revise the rough draft of an essay.

Original—Paragraph 1

Advertising

D-G

/1/ Consumers often <u>are fooled</u>

CAN YOU BE MORE

by advertising. /2/ Often they

SPECIFIC? THE PAPER

sp
don't know what some of the words

IS ABOUT HOW THEY

that advertisers <u>use mean.</u> /3/

ARE FOOLED.

Television advertisers <u>deduce</u>

CLUMSY PHRASE
AWK

D-WW

customers because (they) convince

REF -CONFUSING

253

them) to buy (almost anything.) /4/   REF-CONFUSING

Television viewers do not realize   TRY SPECIFICS: "FROM
                                            ____ TO ____ "
they are being cheated. /5/ They

don't recognize that the ads use   D-G

tricky means to impress customers.   BE MORE SPECIFIC.
                                            THIS PAPER IS ABOUT
/6/ Congress should pass a law   PERVERTED LOGIC

against such methods.

A. The title is too general. It does not make clear the thesis (subject and comment) of
   the paper. What aspect of *advertising* are you writing about? What do you want to
   say about the subject?
B. To interest your reader in sentence 1, use an example of a customer fooled by the
   faulty logic of an ad.
C. Sentences 3, 4, and 5 are choppy. Combine them.
D. Does sentence 5 state the thesis clearly?
E. Sentence 6 is not needed. Leave it out.

Revision—Paragraph 1

Advertisers: Masters of Illogic

/1/ When John and Susy Q.
Public dash to K-Mart or Zayres
to plop down twenty or more bucks
for a Double Mac hamburger cooker,
they are probably succumbing to
the illogic of Hamilton Beach's
television advertising. /2/ They
ought to know there is no relation
between the skill of Joe Namath
and the performance of a hamburger
cooker. /3/ Television has become
a tool that the twentieth-century
advertiser uses to deceive
potential customers. /4/ By using

```
perverted logic, modern admen

convince the public to buy

everything from Hefty garbage bags

to Buicks.
```

A. The title now focuses the reader's attention on the thesis.

B. In sentences 1 and 2, the Double Mac ad illustrated the result of television illogic. This opener interests the reader and restricts the topic. In place of the general "are fooled by advertising," the writer has substituted the specific "is succumbing to the illogic of Hamilton Beach's television advertising."

C. The coherence of paragraph 1 is improved. One of the striking improvements is in sentence length. Whereas the sentences in the original were short and choppy (6, 13, 12, 9, 12, 8 words), the revision offers more variety (36, 21, 15, 17 words).

D. Sentence 4 now states the thesis clearly. Put last, it makes a good link between introduction and body.

Original—Paragraph 2

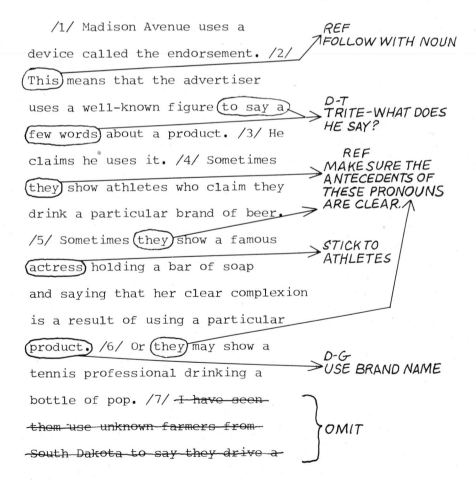

```
/1/ Madison Avenue uses a            REF
device called the endorsement. /2/   FOLLOW WITH NOUN
This means that the advertiser
uses a well-known figure to say a    D-T
                                     TRITE—WHAT DOES
few words about a product. /3/ He    HE SAY?
claims he uses it. /4/ Sometimes     REF
                                     MAKE SURE THE
they show athletes who claim they    ANTECEDENTS OF
                                     THESE PRONOUNS
drink a particular brand of beer.    ARE CLEAR.
/5/ Sometimes they show a famous     STICK TO
                                     ATHLETES
actress holding a bar of soap
and saying that her clear complexion
is a result of using a particular
product. /6/ Or they may show a      D-G
tennis professional drinking a       USE BRAND NAME
bottle of pop. /7/ I have seen
them use unknown farmers from        OMIT
South Dakota to say they drive a
```

~~particular make of car.~~ /8/ Beer,   } OMIT

soap, and underarm deodorant, use   } AWK
                                           } REWRITE
famous people in their (ads.) /9/   } SENTENCE

The viewer of the endorsement

commercial assumes that if a

famous person recommends a

product it must be good.

A. The topic sentence (1) of paragraph 2 is too general. Though "the endorsement" is
   a subdivision of "tricky means," you should emphasize that illogical advertising
   techniques motivate the consumer to buy.
B. Eliminate wordiness by combining sentences 2 and 3.
C. Sentences 4-6 develop examples that need no development. Combine these
   sentences into one with a three-part parallel structure: "pitching prowess and shaving cream, broken field running and rental cars . . ."
D. Sentence 7 is not related. "Unknown farmers" are not "well-known figures."
E. The three-part subject of sentence 8 ("Beer, soap, and underarm deodorant")
   merely restates what has been made clear in sentences 4-6. Specific sports
   figures—perhaps some women—can be used as examples to emphasize that endorsement ads work.
F. The clinching, summarizing sentence (9) is good.

Revision—Paragraph 2

/1/ One of Madison Avenue's

most successful but illogical

advertising techniques is the

endorsement. /2/ Often featuring

sports celebrities clutching

some product and claiming they

were teethed on it, the endorse-

ment convinces many uncritical

consumers to buy. /3/ The success

of the ad depends upon the

viewer's seeing a relationship

between pitching prowess and

shaving cream, broken field
running and rental cars, tennis
skills and Pepsi. /4/ That there
is no relationship does not
destroy the effectiveness of the
ad. /5/ When Bubba Smith, Billy
Martin, and K.C. Jones claim the
beer they drink is best because
it tastes good and has "less
calories," thousands of Americans
rush out to buy Miller's Light.
/6/ After watching O.J. Simpson
zip through the airport to his
ever-ready rental car, millions
of Americans want nothing but
Hertz. /7/ When a manufacturer
persuades Chris Evert to endorse
fish eggs, we can expect a run on
caviar. /8/ The victim of the
endorsement commercial is supposed
to assume that if a famous athlete
recommends Dudley Dentures, they
must be good.

A. Sentence 1, the first part of the topic sentence, now ties in closely with the thesis statement (sentence 4, paragraph 1): "illogical technique" with "perverted logic." Sentence 2, the second part of the two-sentence topic sentence, emphasizes the thesis comment by making clear that "the endorsement convinces many uncritical consumers to buy."

B. Sentence 3 compresses three sentences into one to produce a more concise yet fully developed sentence.

C. Sentence 4 emphasizes the endorsement technique's illogic and introduces the three parallel examples in sentences 5, 6, and 7. The climactic example (sentence 7) completes an arrangement that moves from what we have seen to what we may see.

D. Sentence 8, a good clincher to begin with, is improved by the substitution of "Dudley Dentures" for "a product." The more specific label enhances the immediacy and thus the effectiveness of the example.

E. Specific details have improved the entire paragraph.

Original — Paragraph 3

/1/ The bandwagon technique is used in ads. /2/ (This) relies on the assumption that the opinion of the mass is a surefire way to be confident of what you buy. /3/ The everybody's-doing-it commercial is an example. /4/ A particular soft drink company asks the consumer to get on the bandwagon and buy (Coca Cola,) it is hard to resist this technique. /5/ After all this soft drink is used all over the world, the real thing. /6/ Our getting on the bandwagon with pill buyers is another example of the (affect) of this advertising device. ~~/7/ LSD is one of the biggest threats to American youth and the government must do something about it.~~

REF
FOLLOW WITH NOUN, OR COMBINE SENTENCES 1 AND 2 AND ELIMINATE "THIS"

CAPITALIZE TRADE NAME

CS

C
ADD COMMA TO PREVENT MISREADING

D-WW

A. The topic sentence of paragraph 3 does introduce a subdivision of "perverted logic" (sentence 4, paragraph 1) but the comment "is used in ads" lacks emphasis, for it does not tie in with the thesis comment "convince the public to buy." Combine sentences 1 and 2 to play up the effect of the bandwagon technique.

B. In sentence 3 do not devote an entire sentence to tell the reader what is clearly implied. Introduce Coca Cola quickly and omit "a particular soft drink company." Should the extremely popular slogan "the real thing" appear in quotes as part of the development? Eliminate the comma splice in sentence 4 by combining the second main clause with sentence 5. Make the revised sentence a question.

C. No evidence in sentence 6 supports the assertion that we do get on the bandwagon with pill buyers. Perhaps a list of patent medicines most Americans use would be convincing—Alka-Seltzer, aspirin, laxatives.

D. Although LSD is in the news, it is not relevant here, for it is not advertised commercially on television. Omit sentence 7 and supply another clincher.

E. Paragraph 3 is slow because of heavy reliance on ''to be'' verbs.

Revision—Paragraph 3

/1/ The bandwagon, another advertising technique, motivates the consumer by exploiting his illogical conclusion that mass opinion is a qualified guide to purchasing. /2/ The everybody's-doing-it television commercial, as typified by the Coca Cola people, illustrates this propaganda device. /3/ Who can turn down the invitation to drink with his neighbors? /4/ Who can resist the whole world? /5/ That millions of Americans got on the Fidel Castro bandwagon in the fifties does not dampen the consumer's desire to be like everybody else. /6/ That Americans are fast becoming a race of hypochondriacs does not deter thousands from joining the throng who stuff their medicine cabinets with Alka-

```
Seltzer, Bayer Aspirin, Carter's

Pills, Pepto-Bismol, and other

patent medicines. /7/ Good heavens,

millions of people can't be wrong!
```

A. The revised topic sentence includes two ingredients that link it to the thesis: (1) "the bandwagon technique," a subpoint of "perverted logic," and (2) "motivates the consumer by exploiting his illogical conclusion," a phrase that re-emphasizes the thesis comment, "convince the public to buy."

B. The Coca Cola example is no longer words. The weak assertions in sentences 4 and 5 of the original are now effective parallel rhetorical questions.

C. Expanding sentence 6 of the original by specifying brand names of patent medicines calls attention to the gullibility of the American consumer.

D. The exclamation (sentence 7) brings the paragraph to a close with an illogical comment that emphasizes the shaky reasoning employed by the consumer and capitalized on by the advertisers.

Original — Paragraph 4

```
/1/ Advertising men use a

device called post hoc ergo

propter hoc (after this, therefore
                                        → REF
because of this). /2/ (This) asks        FOLLOW WITH NOUN

the (childish) consumer to believe
                                        → TOO
that if one event follows ahother,        OPINIONATED

surely the first caused the

second. /3/ This device appears

in shampoo, mouthwash, and coffee

ads. /4/ The unwary consumer

rarely asks whether this is
                                        → REF
logical. /5/ They assume that            FOLLOW WITH NOUN

dandruff is a threat to happiness.      → AGR-P
                                          THE ANTECEDENT OF
/6/ And that people stay away from        "THEY" IS "CONSUMER"

you even if you have clean-                 FRAG
                                          SENTENCE 6 IS
smelling breath. /7/ They also          → A FRAGMENT.

forget to remember that good            → AWK, D-W
```

coffee is the result of coffee-
making ability. /8/ It doesn't
have anything to do with the brand
of coffee you use.

LOGIC
SENTENCES 7 AND 8 ARE
NOT TRUE. SOME COFFEE
IS BETTER THAN OTHERS,
AND WILL BREW A
BETTER POT.

A. The topic sentence (1) should stress not only that the admen use the technique but also that the technique motivates the consumer to buy.
B. In sentence 3, demonstrate the faulty logic by expanding the examples briefly: "This device implies that dandruff, not bad temper, causes unpopularity; that, etc."
C. Since the real backbone of this advertising technique is oversimplification, develop in sentence 4 the admen's oversimplified method of solving the problem: Use Certs and "she'll kiss you again."
D. Following sentence 4, show in one or two sentences the real reasons for promotion: skill and hard work.

Revision—Paragraph 4

/1/ Many consumers buy because
they become convinced by TV
advertising logic that if one
event follows another in time,
surely the first caused the
second. /2/ They are victims of
a propaganda device called post
hoc ergo propter hoc (after this,
therefore because of this)
reasoning. /3/ Persons who accept
the television commercial's causal
analysis of life's problems are
convinced that unpopularity is a
result of dandruff, not bad
temper; that demotion is a result
of bad breath, not incompetence;
that marital problems are a result

of bad coffee, not selfishness.

/4/ The adman's solution to these

problems is simple: Shampoo with

Head 'n' Shoulders and you'll

have dates; eat Certs and "she'll

kiss you again"; use Folger's

coffee and your husband will love

you. /5/ That Sally Dandruff is

popular and Mary Shiny-Scalp is

not does not shake our faith in

this television logic. /6/ We

ignore the fact that the new vice-

president of the firm has the

worst breath in town (a result of

hard work and the ulcer that goes

with it). /7/ Sad to say, we still

swallow the post hoc fallacy even

after we discover that using the

right product has no effect on

our problems.

A. The topic sentence (1) supports the subject and the comment of the thesis statement.
B. Sentence 3 develops the three items that appeared in the original to point out not
merely the general kind of ad that employs *post hoc* logic but also its illogic.
C. Sentence 4 now includes specific ads that employ *post hoc* reasoning. In sentences 3
and 4 you employ a three-part parallel structure to emphasize the illogic of the *post
hoc* technique.
D. The clinching sentence (6) emphasizes the central point of paragraph 4: that despite
the illogic of the *post hoc* fallacy, the consumer believes that because ''one event
follows another in time, surely the first caused the second.''

Original—Paragraph 5

In conclusion, the advertisers

who use faulty logic to fool

```
customers should be prevented from

doing so by the government.
```

A. Only on rare occasions (perhaps to promote humor) should you open a concluding paragraph with "In conclusion."
B. This one-sentence jolt does not sum up what has been discussed in the paper. The body of the essay makes clear that customers are motivated to buy through the perverted logic used in television commercials.
C. Though this brief conclusion adds a note of finality, it is in no way climactic.

Revision—Paragraph 5

```
/1/ Any student of logic knows

that faulty premises lead to false

conclusions, even though the

syllogism is valid. /2/ But the

success of television commercials

proves that even the student of

logic is being fooled, for

sensible as he is, when he buys a

product, he picks the brand the

advertisement claims "gives him

more for his money." /3/ He

doesn't even think to ask, "More

than what?"
```

A. Sentence 1 points up the meaning of the paper; it shows the result of the illogic of television commercials—corruption of the logician, the man who should be able to combat the adman's trickery.
B. Sentence 2 dramatizes the problem in the same manner that the Double Mac ad did in paragraph 1, and thus it serves as an envelope in which to enclose the essay.
C. Also important, the conclusion reaffirms the purpose and effects a climax of sorts.

A Checklist For Essay Revision

You may find the following list of questions a helpful guide to revision.

Title

1. Is the title interesting and short (no more than five words)?
2. Does it point up both the subject and comment of the thesis?

Introduction

1. Does the introduction interest the readers; establish common ground with them; state the purpose clearly?
2. Is the thesis restricted sufficiently for the essay you wish to write?
3. Are the key terms of the thesis clear?
4. Does the introduction imply or state the organization of the essay?
5. Is the introduction coherent?

Body

1. Will the body hold the reader's attention?
2. Does the body develop the thesis convincingly? Have you investigated your sources of material thoroughly—Community Lore, Personal Experience, Inference?
3. Does the body include any irrelevant material?
4. Are the major subdivisions all on the same level of the staircase of abstractions, all logically equal? Is the most important subdivision last? The second most important first?
5. Is all of the evidence arranged logically on the correct step of the staircase of abstractions?
6. Does each paragraph of the body have a clear purpose?
7. Is the body coherent?
    (a) Do the topic sentences of the main divisions relate directly to the thesis?
    (b) Do the opening sentences of each paragraph of the body supply adequate transition with the immediately preceding paragraph?
    (c) Does the topic sentence of each paragraph introduce the central idea of that paragraph?
    (d) Does the clinching sentence of each paragraph of the body emphasize the central point of that paragraph?
    (e) Do the sentences of each paragraph move smoothly from one to another to promote easy reading?

Conclusion

1. Does the conclusion reaffirm the thesis?
2. Does the conclusion climax the reader's interest?
3. Does the conclusion give the paper a note of finality?

Sentences

1. Are the parts of the sentences (single words, phrases, and clauses) coordinated and subordinated logically?
2. Are the sentences sufficiently varied in structure and length?
3. Does the arrangement of the parts of the sentence give your ideas proper emphasis?

Diction

1. Does the diction contribute to the meaning and tone?
2. Have you avoided the pitfalls of diction: wordiness, jargon, clichés, pretentiousness?
3. Does the figurative language add color and clarity to your ideas?

Grammar and mechanics

1. Does the essay contain any major grammatical flaws?
    Disagreement of subject and verb
    Disagreement of pronoun and antecedent
    Sentence fragments
    Comma splices
    Run-together sentences
    Vague pronoun references
2. Does the essay contain any serious punctuation errors?
    End punctuation—periods, question marks, exclamation points; Internal punctuation—commas, semicolons, colons, dashes, apostrophes, brackets, parentheses, quotation marks
3. Does the essay contain any serious spelling errors?
4. Does the essay contain any serious capitalization errors?

chapter 18

Glossary to Common
Writing Problems

This chapter is a guide to instructors' marking symbols and an aid to revision. Even though the scope of *Staircase to Writing and Reading* forces us to limit the size of this handbook/glossary, in it we have identified the common problem areas that keep student writing from being acceptable. If the instructor uses the symbols in marking student themes and if the students take advantage of the instructors' comments and consult the glossary, many of these grammatical and mechanical problems will be corrected. For a more thorough treatment of such writing problems, we suggest you consult the *Prentice-Hall Handbook for Writers* or any other college-level handbook that works for you. If your college or university has a writing lab, we suggest you take advantage of its resources.

Abbreviations ABR

Keep abbreviations to a minimum in your writing. Consult your college-level dictionary for correct forms. Some dictionaries have special sections for abbreviations.
Abbreviate the following:

   —academic degrees: B.S., M.A., Ph.D.
   —names of agencies: FBI, SPCA, TVA, UNESCO, WAC
   —technical terms: AM, LSD, mph, VHF
   —time: 1973 A.D., 1300 B.C., 8:15 *a.m.* (A.M.)
   —titles preceding proper names: Dr., Mr., Ms. (for Miss or Mrs.)

When titles are used alone, write them out.

> CORRECT: The doctor is on his way.

Adjectives and Adverbs   ADJ-ADV

Adjectives modify nouns and pronouns.

> CORRECT: The red balloon sailed over the trees. (*Red* is an adjective modifying the noun *balloon*.)
> CORRECT: She was beautiful. (*Beautiful* is an adjective modifying the pronoun *she*.)

Adverbs modify verbs, adjectives, and other adverbs.

> CORRECT: He walked briskly to the store. (*Briskly* is an adverb modifying the verb *walked*.)
> CORRECT: She was a very tall woman. (*Very* is an adverb modifying the adjective *tall*.)
> CORRECT: They ran too quickly and tripped. (*Too* is an adverb modifying the adverb *quickly*.)

Do not confuse adverbs and adjectives. Use them correctly.

> INCORRECT: She sings good (*Good* is an adjective; it cannot modify the verb *sings*.)
> CORRECT: She sings well. (*Well* is an adverb modifying the verb *sings*.)

Agreement: Pronoun and Antecedent   AGR-P

Pronouns agree with their antecedents in person, number, and gender.

> INCORRECT: When one eats with the servants, you are a servant. (*One* is third person; *you* is second.)
> CORRECT: When one eats with the servants, he (or one) is a servant. (*He* and *one* are both third person.)
> ALSO CORRECT: When you eat with the servants, you are a servant.
> INCORRECT: The company put their advertising in *Time*. (*Company* is singular; *their* is plural.)
> CORRECT: The company put its advertising in *Time*. (*Company* and *its* agree in number.)
> INCORRECT: Everybody put their books down. (*Everybody* is singular; *their* is plural.)
> CORRECT: Everybody put his books down. (*Everybody* and *his* agree in number; both are singular.)

Anybody, each, every, everyone, somebody, someone are considered singular. Pronouns that take their places are singular.

> CORRECT: Elizabeth Taylor now lives in her husband's home state. (*Elizabeth Taylor* is feminine gender; so is *her*.)

Agreement: Subject and Verb   AGR-S

Verbs agree with their subjects in number and person.

> CORRECT: We were watching a movie. (*We,* the subject, and *were,* the verb, agree; both are first person and plural.)
>
> CORRECT: He was a member for two years. (*He,* the subject, and *was,* the verb, agree; both are third person and singular.)
>
> CORRECT: They were going to be on stage. (*They* and *were* agree; both are third person and plural.

With a compound singular subject connected by *and,* use the plural form of the verb.

> INCORRECT: Harry and his wife was the real killers.
>
> CORRECT: Harry and his wife were the real killers.

With a compound subject connected by *or,* make the verb agree in number with the part of the subject closest to it.

> INCORRECT: The birds or the dog were afraid.
>
> CORRECT: The birds or the dog was afraid.
>
> CORRECT: The dog or the birds were afraid.

When a singular subject is followed by *as well as, in addition to, together with,* use a singular form of the verb.

> INCORRECT: Mary as well as John visit Seattle yearly.
>
> CORRECT: Mary as well as John visits Seattle yearly.

When words, phrases, or clauses come between subject and verb, be careful to make the verb agree with the subject, not some other word.

> INCORRECT: The boy with the two women throw a mean curve.
>
> CORRECT: The boy with the two women throws a mean curve. (*Boy,* not *women,* is the subject of the verb *throws.*)
>
> INCORRECT: The men led by the major was found alive.
>
> CORRECT: The men led by the major were found alive. (*Men,* not *major,* is the subject of the verb *were.*)

Apostrophe   APOS

Use an apostrophe (')

> —to signal the possessive case of nouns and some pronouns
>
> > CORRECT: The book's cover is torn. (Form the possessive case of most nouns by adding the apostrophe and *s.*)

CORRECT: The girls' hats were thrown on the lawn. (Form the possessive case of plural nouns by adding the apostrophe after the *s*.)

CORRECT: We saw someone's hat on the bed. (*Someone* is an indefinite pronoun.)

—to signal contractions: it's (it is), wasn't (was not), can't (cannot).

—to make plurals of letters or numbers.

CORRECT: He confuses his *b*'s and *d*'s his *3*'s and *8*'s. (Some writers omit the apostrophes in such cases.)

Do not use apostrophes to signal possessive pronouns: hers, his, its, ours, theirs, yours.

Awkward   AWK

When sentences reveal no particular grammatical error but are still not acceptable English, they are often marked simply *awkward*.

AWKWARD: In the evening he arrived at the party before the arrival of the rest of the guests and guessed that they would arrive later.

IMPROVED: Although no other guests were at the party when he arrived that evening, he assumed they would come later.

Body   BY

See pages 72, 103–4.

Capital Letters   CAPS

Capitalize

—the first word in a sentence and the first word in a line of poetry. (Some contemporary poets do not use conventional capitalization.)

—all proper names

—titles of articles, books, stories, etc.

CORRECT: The title of the article was "A Flag of Many Colors." (Some writers capitalize the first letter of every word in a title—"A Flag Of Many Colors.")

—the pronoun *I*.

—*mother, father, uncle,* etc. when used as names.

CORRECT: We went to town to meet Father.

CORRECT: David left school to see his father.

—president when referring to the President of the United States.

CORRECT: John F. Kennedy was President for more than three years.

CORRECT: He had been the president of the firm.

—references to the Deity.

CORRECT: Jesus is the Savior; there is no doubt of His divinity.

—place names: Hershey Park, Oleander Avenue, Ohio River, Hilton Hotel.

Case: Nominative, Possessive, Objective   CSE

Most problems with case are caused by pronouns, not nouns, for except for the possessive case, nouns in different cases have the same form. The following sentences illustrate (in italics) the correct case forms for the representative noun *boat* and the third-person plural pronoun.

> *Nominative*
>> The *boat* sailed to China. (Subject of sentence)
>> *They* sailed away. (Subject of sentence)
>> The vessel was a *boat* with four sails. (Noun complement)
>> It was *they* who called. (Pronoun complement)
>
> *Possessive*
>> The *boat's* (one boat) sails fell. (Modifier)
>> The *boats'* (more than one boat) sails fell. (Modifier)
>> *Their* mainmast toppled in the gale. (Modifier)
>
> *Objective*
>> The wind blew the *boat*. (Direct object)
>> The wind blew *them* off course. (Direct object)
>> The wind howled around the *boat*. (Object of preposition)
>> He got away from *them* in the story. (Object of preposition)
>> He gave the *boat* a paint job. (Indirect object)
>> He gave *them* the boat. (Indirect object)

Coherence   COH

See pages 141–49.

Colon   COL

Use the colon (:)

—after the salutation of a formal letter: Dear Sir:

—to introduce a formal series or list: He brought the following items to the lecture: a quill pen, some foolscap ...

—to separate clauses in which the second amplifies the first: When she came in frowning, we knew what would happen: she would return the papers and berate us again.

—to satisfy convention: (1) between hours and minutes in figures (4:37 a.m.), (2) between chapter and verse in reference to the Bible (Judges XVII:7–9), (3) between place of publication and publisher (Englewood Cliffs, N.J.: Prentice-Hall), (4) between volume and page number of a book or periodical (*The American Scholar,* 36:533)

Comma   C

Use a comma (,)

—to satisfy convention: (1) addresses (St. Petersburg, Florida; Princeton, New Jersey; Mercer County, West Virginia; London, England), (2) dates (September 15, 1969), (3) degrees and titles (Harold Miller, Jr.; David Miller, Ph.D.; Gerhardt Prescot, president of IBM), (4) direct address (You know, Tim, that John has left.), (5) figures (commas after hundreds, thousands, millions, billions, etc.—18,642,321), (6) salutation of friendly letter (Dear Skip,), (7) weak exclamation (Well, we shall see), (8) quotations (He answered, "Find me an honest man." "Find me," he answered, "an honest man." "Find me an honest man," he answered.)

—to separate independent clauses joined by a coordinating conjunction (*and, but, for, nor, or, yet, so*).

CORRECT: He gave the book to Tom, and Mary put it on her desk.

—to separate items that contrast sharply.

CORRECT: Her figure, not her face, brought her success.

—to separate coordinate items in a series.

CORRECT: We were offered coffee, tea, or milk for lunch. (Coordinate items in a series—the comma before the conjunction is optional unless its absence would cause misreading.)

CORRECT: The red, white, blue, orange, and green (orange and green) Buick appeared garish. (Coordinate adjectives)

CORRECT: The team kicked, passed, ran, and tackled (ran and tackled) with equal skill. (Coordinate verbs)

—to set off introductory words, phrases, or clauses.

CORRECT: Therefore, I can see no reason to try. (Transitional word)

CORRECT: In the meantime, he fixed both the washer and the dryer. (Prepositional phrase—a good many writers prefer to omit the comma after introductory prepositional phrases and short adverb clauses unless doing so might confuse the reader.)

CORRECT: Having him in the boat, we were forced to sneak by the law. (Verbal phrase)

CORRECT: Because his head was bleeding, the doctor took him ahead of the rest. (Adverb clause)

—to separate nonrestrictive words, phrases, and clauses from the rest of the sentence.

CORRECT: His oldest sister, Jane, cooked dinner. (One-word appositive)

CORRECT: We shall, however, find another way to do it. (One-word transition)

CORRECT: The troop's favorite activity, camping in the valley, had to be put off because of the rain. (Verbal phrase)

CORRECT: This ship, for example, was on the seas for fifty years. (Transitional phrase)

CORRECT: His three bicycles, which were parked next to the tree yesterday, had been taken. (Adjective clause)

CORRECT: His explanation, that he had punctured a lung, was an adequate excuse for his absence. (Noun clause)

CORRECT: He wrote and mailed the letter Thursday, though he knew his cousin had moved to a new address. (Adverb clause)

—to prevent misreading.

CORRECT: Two hundred years before the war was in its infant stages.

IMPROVED: Two hundred years before, the war was in its infant stages.

Comma Splice   CS

A comma splice occurs when a comma is used to separate two independent clauses not closely related, when no coordinating conjunction is used.

> INCORRECT: His large German shepherd barked at the children, his garden hose caused the postman to fall and hurt himself.

Correct a comma splice by one of four methods, the one best suited to the meaning you wish to convey: (1) Use a period instead of a comma; (2) use a semicolon instead of a comma; (3) retain the comma and add a coordinating conjunction; (4) subordinate one of the independent clauses.

> IMPROVED: His large ... children. His garden ... hurt himself.
> IMPROVED: His large ... children; his garden ... hurt himself.
> IMPROVED: His large ... children, and his garden ... hurt himself.
> IMPROVED: As the large German shepherd barked at the children, his garden hose caused the postman to fall and hurt himself.

Conclusion   CON

See pages 72, 102.

Coordination   COOR

See pages 173–78, 191–98.

Dangling Modifier   DM

Modifiers must have words to modify. When they don't, they are called dangling modifiers. Often such modifiers merely create humor, but they can be confusing. To correct a dangling modifier, place the word being modified and the modifier as close together as possible or make the modifying phrase a clause by supplying a subject and verb.

> DANGLING: Coming out of the building, the temperature had dropped twenty degrees. (Is the temperature coming out of the building?)
> CORRECT: Coming out of the building, we noticed that the temperature had dropped twenty degrees.
> CORRECT: By the time we came out of the building, the temperature had dropped twenty degrees.
> DANGLING: To buy on time, they will charge a high interest rate. (You, not they, are buying.)
> CORRECT: To buy on time, you must pay a high interest rate.
> DANGLING: While carrying heavy packs, the mountains came into view. (People, not mountains, carry heavy packs.)
> CORRECT: While carrying heavy packs, we approached the mountains.

CORRECT: While we were carrying heavy packs, the mountains came into view.
DANGLING: When three, my liberal father told me the facts of life.
CORRECT: When three, I learned the facts of life from Father.
CORRECT: When I was three, my liberal father told me the facts of life.

Dash   DH

Use a dash (—)

—to indicate a sharp turn in thought.
  CORRECT: His grandmother—assuming he had one—must have been a bit prudish.
—to indicate a broken thought.
  CORRECT: He answered slowly, "It was my impression that—"
—to separate appositives from the rest of the sentence.
  CORRECT: The enticing food—turkey, chicken, mashed potatoes, cranberry sauce,
    hot rolls, peas—made our mouths water.
—to emphasize a summarizing comment.
  CORRECT: Courage, honesty, loyalty, courtesy, obedience—all of these traits were
    necessary to the knight during the Middle Ages.

Diction: General to Specific   D-G

See pages 217–20.

Diction: Idiom   D-ID

See pages 221–22.

Diction: Jargon   D-J

See pages 225–26.

Diction: Pretentious   D-P

See pages 226–27.

Diction: Trite   D-T

See pages 224–25.

Diction: Wordy   D-W

See page 224.

Diction: Wrong Word   WW

Avoid inaccurate word choice.

Exclamation Mark   EM

Use the exclamation mark (!) at the end of a sentence to show heightened emotion. Use it infrequently. Under no circumstances should you use more than one exclamation mark at the end of a sentence.

Fragment   FRAG

Do not punctuate a phrase as a sentence.

INCORRECT: The dog ran down the alley as fast as he could. With his tail between his legs. (The second group of words punctuated as a sentence is a prepositional phrase.

CORRECT: The dog ran down the alley as fast as he could with his tail between his legs.

INCORRECT: We spent the entire Saturday morning. Listening to Hal Holbrook imitate Mark Twain. (The second group of words punctuated as a sentence is a participial phrase.)

CORRECT: We spent the entire Saturday morning listening to Hal Holbrook imitate Mark Twain.

INCORRECT: To buy the boat at the lowest possible price. He borrowed the money after the Christmas rush. (The first group of words punctuated as a sentence is an infinitive phrase.)

CORRECT: To buy the boat at the lowest possible price, he borrowed the money after the Christmas rush.

Do not punctuate a subordinate clause as a sentence.

INCORRECT: He called the judge's attention to the beauty contestant's fatal flaw. That her ankles were fat. (The last group of words punctuated as a sentence is really a noun clause in apposition with *flaw*.)

CORRECT: He called the judge's attention to the beauty contestant's fatal flaw, that her ankles were fat.

CORRECT: He called the judge's attention to the beauty contestant's fatal flaw—fat ankles.

INCORRECT: He opened to the chapter on women. Who wore rings on their necks. (The last group of words punctuated as a sentence is really an adjective clause that should modify *women*.)

CORRECT: He opened to the chapter on women who wore rings on their necks.

INCORRECT: Because he had left his keys in his blue suit. He was unable to open the desk drawer. (The first group of words punctuated as a sentence is an adverb clause that should modify the verb *was*.)

CORRECT: Because he had left his keys in his blue suit, he was unable to open the desk drawer.

Introduction   INTRO

See pages 71–72.

Italics   IT

Use italics (represented in typed and handwritten copy by underlining)

—to indicate titles of separate publications—books (Hemingway's *Farewell to Arms*, Capote's *In Cold Blood*), magazines *(Commentary, Time)*, newspapers *(San Francisco Chronicle)*, pamphlets *(Memorandum: A Call for Action)*, musical compositions (Lennon and McCartney's *Michelle*), plays (Ibsen's *Ghosts*), movies (McCullers's *Reflections in a Golden Eye*).

—to indicate names of ships *(Queen Mary II)*, trains *(Rock Island Silver Streak)*, airplanes *(Sacred Cow)*.

—to mark foreign words and phrases *(femme, idée fixe, memento mori)*. Check your college-level desk dictionary to determine whether the foreign word or phrase should be italicized.

—to emphasize words, letters, and figures spoken of as such.

CORRECT: The word *angel* often appears in print misspelled.

—to give a word special emphasis.

CORRECT: That calendar *was* there this morning.

Logic   LOGIC

See pages 236–47.

Manuscript Form   MS

Please follow the form required for submission of written matter.

Misplaced Modifier   MM

To avoid confusion, place modifiers as near as possible to the word or words they modify.

CONFUSING: He drove the second-hand hulk into the garage and almost polished it until it looked new. (Because the adverb *almost* immediately precedes the verb *polished,* there seems to be some doubt about whether the car was polished or not).

CLEAR: He drove the second-hand hulk into the garage and polished it until it looked almost new.

CONFUSING: The roast lay in the center of the table in front of the guests on the serving tray. (Most guests do not congregate on serving trays, though the word order of this sentence suggests they do. Put the prepositional phrase *on the serving tray* closer to *lay,* the word it modifies.)

CLEAR: The roast lay on the serving tray in the center of the table in front of the guests.

CONFUSING: The Chevy roared over the finish line which had reached 110 miles per hour. (Do finish lines go 110 miles per hour? To modify accurately, place the adjective clause next to *Chevy.*)

CLEAR: The Chevy, which had reached 110 miles per hour, roared over the finish line.

CONFUSING: They wanted after a while to walk to the movie. (Does the writer want the phrases *after a while* to modify *wanted* or *to walk?* The misplaced prepositional phrase is called a squinting modifier.)

CLEAR: After a while they wanted to walk to the movies.

CLEAR: They wanted to walk to the movies after a while.

Numbers   NOS

In general, write out numbers that can be expressed in one or two words.

CORRECT: He will be twenty-one in July.
CORRECT: His company was made up of fifty-six men.
CORRECT: There were 191 tires in the barn.

Use figures for

—sentences containing more than two numbers.
—sums of money, except for round numbers.
  CORRECT: He owed me 38¢ for the bread.
  CORRECT: We made a hundred dollars on the deal.
—page and chapter numbers.
—street and apartment numbers.
—dates.
—hours (with a.m. p.m.).

Avoid starting sentences with numbers, but if you do, write the number out.

CORRECT: Four hundred and eighteen mice scampered around the barn.
BETTER: There were 418 mice scampering around in the barn.

Outline   OUT

See pages 89-92.

Paragraph ¶

See pages 100-104.

Parallel Sructure //

Give equal logic elements parallel grammatical form.

INCORRECT: His possessions covered the desk, the dresser, and on the floor.
CORRECT: His possessions covered the desk, the dresser, and the floor.
INCORRECT: The new motor was both a pleasure and it was a nuisance.
CORRECT: The new motor was both a pleasure and a nuisance.

Parentheses   PAR

Use parentheses ( )

—to enclose a cross reference.
  CORRECT: Coleridge brought his whole life to bear on his poetry (See John Livingston Lowes' *The Road to Xanadu.*)
—to enclose an explanation.
  CORRECT: After his illness (he had infectious hepatitis) he went back to school.
—to set off numbers or letters in a formal list.
  CORRECT: The essay was broken into its three parts: (1) introduction, (2) body, and (3) conclusion.
—to repeat a sum previously written in words (used chiefly in business correspondence).
  CORRECT: We paid him seventy-five dollars ($75.00) to paint the rear wall.

Passive Pattern   PASS

Use the passive pattern only when you wish to emphasize the receiver of the action rather than the doer. In the passive pattern, the subject is the receiver of the action.

PASSIVE: The ball was thrown by John.
ACTIVE: John threw the ball.

Do not overuse the passive pattern, for it lacks liveliness. It can rob a sentence of vitality and contribute to wordiness.

PASSIVE: The car was taken by him. (Six words)
ACTIVE: He took the car. (Four words)

The verb in the passive pattern is always a verb phrase consisting of a part of the verb *to be* plus the past participle: *was taken, is spoken,* will *be used.*

Period   PD

Use the period (.)

—to end-punctuate a declarative sentence.
  CORRECT: Follow a declarative sentence with a period.
—with abbreviations that call for periods (etc., Mr., LL.D., Esq.) Consult your college-level desk dictionary for proper punctuation of abbreviations.

—to indicate ellipsis, omission of words in a quoted passage.
CORRECT: "... we went to the tavern on the mall."
CORRECT: "The poets ... traveled all over Europe and Asia."
CORRECT: "American literature reached its height in 1960. ..."
—between dollars and cents and before a decimal ($5.75, .078 grade-point average).

Question Mark   QM

Use the question mark (?)

—to end-punctuate an interrogative sentence, a sentence that asks a question.
CORRECT: Did he go to the hospital today?

Do not use a question mark

—to end a question that is really a polite request.
INCORRECT: Will you meet me in my office at noon?
—to end an indirect question.
INCORRECT: He asked whether we would come?
CORRECT: He asked whether we would come.

Quotation Marks   QUOTE

Use double quotation marks (" ")

—to enclose a direct quotation of a word, a phrase, a clause, a sentence, a paragraph either spoken or written.
CORRECT: She called him the "toast" of elementary school.
CORRECT: He made his bid, he insisted, "in lieu of" a donation.
CORRECT: "Because of your extracurricular activities," he dismissed you.
CORRECT: "I shall now therefore humbly propose my thoughts, which I hope will not be liable to the least objection." (Jonathan Swift)
—to enclose the titles of parts of publications—chapter, essay, poem, short story—and titles of songs.
CORRECT: His best chapter is entitled "The Mysterious Box."
CORRECT: We enjoyed reading John Collier's short story "Witch's Money."
CORRECT: Edgar Allan Poe's "The Raven" is one of the most popular lyrics of our time.
CORRECT: She had bought a guitar version of "I Want to Hold Your Hand."

Use single quotation marks (' ')

—to enclose a quotation within a quotation.
CORRECT: Robert laughed and said, "When he asked you, 'Why does the chicken cross the road?' you could have answered, 'To get to the other side.'"

When using other marks of punctuation with quotation marks

—Always put commas and periods inside quotation marks.
   CORRECT: "Had you won," he laughed, "I'd have said, 'Good for you.'"
—If only the quotation is a question, put the question mark inside the quotation marks; if the whole sentence is a question, put the question mark outside.
   CORRECT: He said, "Do you have a dog?"
   CORRECT: Did he say, "Find your book and study"?
—If only the quotation is an exclamation, put the exclamation mark inside the quotation marks; if the whole sentence is an exclamation, put the exclamation mark outside.
   CORRECT: His final comment was "Sit!"
   CORRECT: For heaven's sake, don't "justify God's ways to man"!
—Place the semicolon and the colon outside the quotation marks, unless, of course, they are a part of the quotation.
   CORRECT: She looked at me and said, "Try to see it my way"; but no matter how I tried, I saw it my own way.
   CORRECT: We took his advice and "followed the instructions to the letter": We fasted Thursday and Friday and ate all fifty eggs on Saturday.
—Place the dash that signals an interrupted quotation inside the quotation marks.
   CORRECT: She was flabbergasted: "You must be the one who—"
—See under *Period* above for using periods with quotation marks to indicate ellipsis.

Reference of Pronoun   REF

Make sure the antecedent of the pronoun is clear to the reader.

   CONFUSING: He finally accepted the job, which made me feel better. (Does *which* refer to *job* or to the whole main clause?)
   CORRECT: He finally accepted the job, a fact which made me feel better.
   CORRECT: His accepting the job made me feel better.
   CONFUSING: We had to change the sheets for Bill and Fred because they were dirty. (Were the sheets dirty or Bill and Fred?)
   CORRECT: We had to change the sheets for Bill and Fred because the linen was dirty.
   CONFUSING: For three days and nights he had been lost in the great forest. During this time he had had no food or water. At night he was attacked by the cold and the marauding wolves; during the day he was bitten by the bugs. This destroyed his sanity. (How much of the problem does the writer sum up with *this* in the last sentence?)
   BETTER: This predicament destroyed his sanity.
   BETTER: These problems destroyed his sanity.

Run-together   RT

A fused sentence occurs when two independent clauses run together with no punctuation to separate them.

   RUN-TOGETHER: He was lost because he did not know the way he almost never got home.

Correct the run-together sentence by supplying appropriate punctuation. (A comma after *lost* or after *way* in the example above will not correct the problem; it will produce a comma splice.)

> IMPROVED: He was lost because he did not know the way. He almost never got home.
> IMPROVED: He was lost. Because he did not know the way, he almost never got home.

Semicolon   SEMI

Use the semicolon (;)

—between closely related independent clauses in a compound sentence if they are not connected by a conjunction.

> CORRECT: Her brother had done the best work; he had, as a result, been appointed leader.

—before a coordinating conjunction connecting two independent clauses containing other internal punctuation.

> CORRECT: Having written several letters, he decided to see her in person; but instead of going to the right address, he ended up in the wrong section of town.

—before a conjunctive adverb *(however, nevertheless, therefore)* connecting two independent clauses.

> CORRECT: He bought her the largest dress in the store; however, it was not large enough.

—with elements in a series containing other internal punctuation.

> CORRECT: The following officers were elected: June Smith, president; Harry Taylor, vice president; Ellen Parker, secretary; Tim Leslie, treasurer.

Do not use the semicolon

—after the salutation of either a business or friendly letter.

> INCORRECT: Dear Sir; and Dear Skip;
> CORRECT: Dear Sir: and Dear Skip:

—to introduce a series.

> INCORRECT: They had a delicious breakfast; bacon, eggs, buttered toast, jelly, and coffee.
> CORRECT: They had a delicious breakfast: bacon, eggs, buttered toast, jelly, and coffee.
> CORRECT: They had a delicious breakfast—bacon, eggs, buttered toast, jelly, and coffee.

Shift in Person   SHIFT-P

An unnecessary shift from third to second person destroys coherence.

> CONFUSING: All students should have their assignments proofread carefully, and you must turn them in on time. (The shift from third person—*students and their*—to second person—*you*—causes the problem.)
> CONSISTENT: All students should have their assignments proofread carefully, and they must turn their papers in on time.

Shift in Subject   SHIFT-S

An unnecessary shift in subject destroys coherence.

> CONFUSING: After they found the dead twigs on the tree, the pruning was begun in earnest. (Avoid shifting from *they,* the subject of the subordinate clause, to *pruning,* the subject of the main clause. Note that the shift of subject brings a shift from the active verb *found* to the passive construction *was begun,* a second confusing mistake.
>
> CORRECT: After they found the dead twigs on the tree, they began pruning in earnest.

Shift in Tense   SHIFT-T

An awkward shift in verb tense damages coherence.

> CONFUSING: She said she planned to go and then turns around and insists she wants to stay. (The shift from past tense—*said* and *planned*—to present tense—*turns, insists,* and *wants*—confuses the reader.)
>
> CORRECT: She said she planned to go and then turned around and insisted she wanted to stay. (All verbs—*said, planned, turned, insisted, wanted*—are now in past tense.)

Thesis Statement   TS

See pages 55–65.

Topic Sentence   TOP

See pages 104–8.

part two

Rhetoric and Reading

Introduction: Suggestions
for Successful Readers

Your recognition and understanding of the principles and methods of rhetoric—the logic of writing—can help you improve your reading. Your reading speed may well increase, but that is not our main concern. Our concern is with your comprehension—your understanding of why a piece was written; what it says, both in overall statement and major subpoints; how it makes those statements and how each part fits in. A successful author has refined the answers to those three questions—*Why?*, *What?*, and *How?*—by applying the principles of rhetoric. You, as a successful reader, can best understand his writing on the same basis. And so we will here briefly examine those elements of the rhetoric of writing that can provide you with a valuable rhetoric of reading. Like the rhetoric of writing, this rhetoric of reading will apply the concept of the staircase of abstractions.

At the broadest, highest level of abstraction we encounter the question *Why?*—the author's purpose and his overall strategy in carrying out that purpose. What is his intention in writing the piece— what does he want to do with the subject? We can gain an inkling of the answers to these questions early in our reading of the material and can thus be on firm ground in approaching the piece from the most helpful perspective. One helpful approach to determining the author's intention—and thus responding to the materials lower on the staircase of abstraction within the broader pattern most appropriate for them—is to apply the four categories of rhetorical purpose discussed in Chapter 2. Within these, the writer may, first of all, be concerned with objectively explaining something about his subject: informing us, analyzing for us, classifying, defining. This objective explanatory approach is *exposition*. Or he may wish to persuade us of something that is more debatable. This statement of opinion, his attempt to sway us, is *argument*. Or, thirdly, he may have chosen to describe something the senses can perceive, that is, write a *description*. Or he may have chosen to trace a sequence of actions, that is, write a *narration*.

Not all writing falls neatly into just one of these basic categories. Authors and their works are more complex than that. Description and narration are often used to help develop a further purpose— either exposition or argument. Or exposition may be used to help develop an argument. Thus, combinations of purpose may be involved in what you read; but you can still seek the common denominator. If you recognize a narration, is the story itself the whole purpose? Or is there a deeper purpose? What, possibly, is the story being used to show or prove? The same approach can apply to humor and entertainment generally. Is a laugh or your entertainment allied with another purpose? What is the underlying purpose and intention of the author and what is merely the strategy he employs to carry it out?

Closely related to these questions of purpose is the matter of *attitude*. What is the author's attitude toward his purpose and toward his subject, or toward you, his audience? Even if he is arguing, he can be arguing coolly and logically, or angrily and heatedly. He can see something funny in the situation or something frightening. He can even see something so frightening that he has to be funny. Similarly, he can approach the audience as equals, as friends, as enemies, as insiders or outsiders. His attitude, then, is in his own posture, his own stance toward the materials and the situation in which he is writing. It results in his particular approach to the subject and the writing situation.

One of the best clues to attitude and to the author's approach to this subject is his *tone*. This is the tone of voice in which he is speaking to you—a result of the language he chooses, the combinations of diction he creates. Through an author's tone we sense his wit, his indignation, his sadness, his awe, his nostalgia, his objectivity, his friendliness, his superiority.

Sometimes tone is evident from the first line, from the first paragraph. Sometimes it (and the other clues to purpose and attitude as well) will not be clear to you until much if not all of the piece is read. At least this might happen until you are practiced in this sort of reading. So it will be necessary to reread, just as it is necessary to revise your writing once you have the whole before you in a first draft. You cannot always rely on your first reading to bring you the comprehensive, analytical understanding of the material that you are after. But the clues and the general shaping that that first reading supplies will then be valuable in your rereading.

Moving down the staircase, we reach the level of the next major question— and in many cases the most important question— *What?* This question leads us to the level on the staircase of the author's basic statement—his thesis statement about his subject—and to those intermediate levels that are his major subpoints, or subdivisions, of that thesis.

As we have seen in Chapter 4, this thesis includes a limited subject, which lowers the level of abstraction of the background subject, and a comment about that limited subject, which makes even more concrete what the piece is saying about this subject. Thus, for the reader, the thesis also indicates what the piece is *not* saying. It shows you the limitations the author has set for himself, how much of the general subject he is going to deal with. Be sure that you read him within the boundaries of those limitations. In the same way, within the area he has chosen he has also marked out subdivisions: time sequences, or narrative sections and explanatory sections; causes and effects; comparative sections; sections of equal classifications. These subdivisions complete the pattern of his basic statement, his thesis. They work out his ideas at the intermediate level on the staircase.

Your recognition and understanding of these subdivisions are a part of answering the question *How?* For the questions overlap. *How* an author makes his statements, *how* he uses his parts—these are inseparable from *what* he is saying. And your understanding of what he is saying depends finally on *how* you can read the clues of his details and organization, the ways in which he makes his statements.

Recognition of the main subdivisions, for example, is recognition of the techniques and devices of *organization*. Often the overall pattern of organization is clearly suggested by the opening of the piece. The writer may indicate he is going to make comparisons, or show cause and effect; he may actually enumerate the equal subclassificatons he is going to take up. On the other hand, he may begin his narrative or description, or his joking or name-calling from the start. In other cases, though, the roles that the individual sections or parts are going to play may not be so directly defined; and other clues will have to help provide those definitions.

Whether or not the opening provides a clear idea of the overall pattern of organization, *paragraphs* and particularly the *topic sentences* of paragraphs are important clues. The topics of the individual paragraphs are the core statements in explaining the thesis; each paragraph will make some kind of core statement and then develop it with some concrete details. These core statements are frequently contained in a topic sentence, although it is also possible that the topic sentence may be only implied by the details of the paragraph. When it is present, the topic sentence is most frequently found at the start of the paragraph, but it may appear in other positions (the second most frequent placement is at the end of the paragraph). In any case it is the most general statement to be found in the paragraph. It sets the subpoint of the thesis the paragraph will develop, and it also sets the relationship between that subpoint and what has come before.

In short pieces of writing, each paragraph may be a separate subdivision; in longer pieces, a number of paragraphs may form a subdivision, each contributing material at a lower level of abstraction to fill out the intermediate level of the subdivision.

These relationships between the parts—and between the levels of abstraction they are on—are conveyed throughout a piece by the coherence terms of its *transitions*. An improvement in your recognition of transitions—the logical movement from one part, one subpoint or subdivision to another—will lead to a general improvement of your reading.

More specifically, recognizing transitions (as well as determining purpose, thesis, and paragraph topics) is noticing important *words* and *phrases*. These may be *function words* or *content words*.

Function words are an important part of the rhetoric of writing and reading and are used no matter what the subject or content of a piece of writing. They are various kinds of conjunctions, prepositions, modifiers, or even numbers that establish emphasis and relationships between the parts. They usually appear toward the beginning or end of paragraphs. They include such words of emphasis as *first, second, third,* or *most, chief, last.* They include such words of relationship as *and, but, for; on the other hand, furthermore, therefore, nevertheless, however; similar, other, another, finally, next; because, after, despite.* They are the chief clues to the organization of a piece of writing.

Content words are those that are central to the development of the particular subject at hand. They are often the words that are most fully defined, although it is also possible that the author assumes you know their definition. In either case, you have to be sure you understand them. Skipping over words that you do not know is often skipping over the important core of what you are reading. These words are given strong emphasis. They are placed conspicuously at the beginning and end of pieces, at the beginning and end of paragraphs and sections. They are usually repeated at key points of emphasis and transition throughout. If, for example, an author emphasizes the word *aristocracy* in his opening, each further use of the word will be significant. You need to notice particularly how the key content word may be differently modified at different parts of the material. Thus, the author may be contrasting a *fake aristocracy* with a *genuine aristocracy;* his use of the different modifiers when he repeats the key word will be your clue to the stages of his argument. He may also use synonyms—other ways of referring to the same important point—or he may use significant antonyms—words that set sharp contrasts to the key words: *aristocracy vs. proletariat; teenage world vs. adult world.*

The subdivisions of the piece set its intermediate terms on the staircase of abstractions. Within these subdivisions are the details, the examples, illustrations, the definitions—the concrete materials that reduce the level of abstraction to the lowest, most specific steps on the staircase. One of the chief tasks of the successful reader is seeing the point of the details: just what topic is being illustrated by the details; how are they related to other data cited?

Finally, both the language selected by the author and the details selected produce an overall effect that carries the tone, the style of the piece. In the same way that tone and style can help you to determine the purpose and attitude of an author, they can help you to follow more accurately his organization and to respond more precisely to the function of individual parts and details. Sharpen your ear so that you can tell when an author is being humorous, or sarcastic, or ironic, or is exaggerating intentionally, or is angry, or nostalgic, or bitter. For the more readily you can recognize his tone, the more readily you will be able to see its use. You will be able to see why he is applying stylistic devices, what role they play in his statement, how they help to develop his purpose and thesis.

section one

Of Time and Place

Susan Sheehan

Laundromat

[1] It is one-forty-five on a cold, winter-gray Friday afternoon. There are about a
dozen people inside the Apthorp Self-Service Laundromat, between Seventy-
seventh and Seventy-eighth Streets on the west side of Broadway. The laundromat is a long, narrow room with seventeen Wascomat washing machines—
twelve of them the size that takes two quarters, five of them the size that takes
three—line up on one side of the room, and nine dryers on the other. At the
back of the alleylike room, four vending machines dispense an assortment of
laundry supplies, which cost ten cents an item, to the younger customers; the
older customers (more cost-conscious? more farsighted?) bring their own soap
powders or liquids from home in small boxes or plastic bottles. On the laundromat's drab painted walls are a clock and a few signs: "No Tintex
Allowed," "Last Wash: 10 P.M.," "Not Responsible for Personal
Property." "Pack As Full As You Want." On the drab linoleum floor are two
trash cans (filled to the brim), a wooden bench, three shabby chairs (occupied)
and a table, on which a pretty young black girl is folding clothes, and at which
a dour, heavyset black woman in her sixties is eating lunch out of a grease-
stained brown paper bag. The heavyset woman has brought no clothes with
her to the laundromat. The regular patrons believe she has nowhere else to go
that is warm, and accept her presence. On a previous visit, she had tossed a
chicken bone at someone, wordlessly, and the gesture had been accepted, too,
as a reasonable protest against the miserableness of her life.

[2]   Half the people in the laundromat have two washing machines going at once. The machines keep them busy inserting coins, stuffing in clothes, and adding detergents, bleaches, and fabric softeners at various stages of the cycle (twenty-five minutes). The newly washed clothes are retrieved from the washing machines and transferred, in a swooping motion, across the narrow corridor to the dryers. No one dares leave the laundromat to attend to other errands while his clothes are drying (at the rate of ten cents for ten minutes, with most requiring twenty or thirty minutes), because it is known that clothes that have been left to their own devices in the dryers have disappeared in a matter of five minutes.

[3]   A middle-aged man whose clothes are in a small washing machine is standing in front of it reading a sports column in the *News,* but most of the other patrons who are between putting-in and taking-out chores seem to be mesmerized by the kaleidoscopic activity inside the machines. In one washing machine, a few striped sheets and pillowcases are spinning, creating a dizzying optical effect. In another, a lively clothes dance is taking place— three or four white shirts jitterbugging with six or eight pairs of gray socks. In a third, the clothes, temporarily obscured by a flurry of soapsuds, still cast a spell over their owner, who doesn't take her eyes off the round glass window in the front of the machine. The clothes in the dryers—here a few towels, there some men's work pants—seem to be free-falling, like sky divers drifting down to earth. The laundromat smells of a sweet mixture of soap and heat, and is noisy with the hum and whir of the machines. There is little conversation, but a woman suddenly tells her teen-age daughter (why isn't she in school at this hour?) that she takes the family's clothes to the self-service laundromat, rather than to the service laundromat right next door to it, where clothes can be dropped off in the morning and fetched in the evening, because everything at the service laundromat is washed in very hot water, which shrinks clothes that have a tendency to shrink. ''Here you're supposed to be able to regulate the temperature of the water, but sometimes I punch the warm button and the water comes out ice-cold,'' she says. ''Oh, well, you sort of have to expect things like that. The owner is very nice. He does the best he can.''

[4]   A middle-aged man wearing a trenchcoat takes a load of children's clothes out of a large washing machine, folds them neatly, and runs out of the laundromat with the damp pile of girls' school dresses and boys' polo shirts and bluejeans over one arm. (What is his hurry? Will the children's clothes be hung up to dry on a rack at home?) A young Japanese boy, who is holding a book covered with a glossy Columbia University jacket, takes a few clothes out of a dryer. They include a lacy slip and a ruffled pale-pink nightgown with deep-pink rosebuds on it. (His girl's? His bride's? Or only his sister's? Is the nightgown's owner at work, putting him through school, or has she become a Liberated Woman and declined to go to the laundromat?) Two little children run down the narrow center aisle playing tag, chanting in Spanish, tripping over laundry carts, and meeting with scowls from the grownups. A washing machine goes on the blink. Someone goes next door to the service laundromat to summon the proprietor, who comes over immediately, climbs on top of the broken machine, reaches behind it, and restores it to working order in no

time. He apologizes, in a Polish accent, to one of his regular customers for the scruffiness of the three chairs on the premises. "Six months ago, I brought in here three first-class chairs," he says. "Fifty-dollar chairs. The next day, they were gone."

[5]   People come and go, but the population inside the laundromat remains constant at about a dozen. The majority of the customers are blacks and Puerto Ricans who live in nearby tenements and welfare hotels. Most of the whites in the neighborhood live in apartment houses, and have washing machines and dryers in their apartments or in the basements of their buildings, or send their clothes out to local Chinese laundries. One white woman, a blonde in her fifties, says, to no one in particular, that she comes to the laundromat because the laundry room in the basement of her apartment building is not safe. "There have been incidents there," she says meaningfully. "I would love to have my own washing machine, but the landlord says he has to pay for the water, so he won't allow it. I hate coming here and wasting an hour in this depressing place. I wash everything I can by hand at home; that way, I only have to come here with the big things every two weeks, instead of every week. I dream of having my own washing machine and dryer. If I had my own machines, I could fix myself a cup of coffee, and a bun, turn on the TV, and sit down in my easy chair; meanwhile, the clothes would all be getting done. It would be heaven."

VOCABULARY

Use the context of the essay and your dictionary to define the words listed below.

1. dispense (par. 1)	6. optical (par. 3)
2. dour (par. 1)	7. obscured (par. 3)
3. retrieved (par. 2)	8. proprietor (par. 4)
4. mesmerized (par. 3)	9. scruffiness (par. 4)
5. kaleidoscopic (par. 3)	10. premises (par. 4)

RHETORIC AND IDEA

1. Does Susan Sheehan state her opinion of the laundromat in paragraph 1? In paragraph 5? How is that fact related to her purpose in this description? In other words, what is that purpose—for example, a vague judgment, an impression, a complaint, what?

2. Her main emphasis in each of the five paragraphs is on what? What is she mainly describing in the piece?

3. What is the use made of the example of the lady with no laundry in paragraph 1? That is, how is she related to the other people? Does she show anything about all of them?

4. One constant aspect of these people's lives is repeated at the end of paragraph 2 and paragraph 4. Why does the author repeat this point, and what does it show about the lives of the people in the laundromat? What other statement by a woman is related to this point?

5. Summarize the explanation of the woman to her daughter (in paragraph 3) and discuss the logic of her argument, her reason for coming to this laundromat.

6. Notice the unanswered questions in paragraph 4. What effect on the reader do you think the author is after here? Why does she ask the questions and not answer them?

7. What does the white lady in paragraph 5 mean by "incidents"? What is your interpretation of the motives, the reasons behind her speech?

8. Explain the parallel sentence structure of sentence two of paragraph 2. In the same paragraph, does the last sentence stress parallelism or subordination? Explain.

WRITING ASSIGNMENTS

1. Organize a description of a specific place (whether a city, a resort, a natural area, a place of business or entertainment, your own room or backyard) around a definite controlling characteristic. That is, what is its personality, its particular feel? Select details and illustrations to get that impression across to your reader.

2. Without stating a direct opinion, write a description of a store or restaurant that does try to sway the reader to either like it or not like it. Do this by your selection of details, choice of words—not by any direct summation of your point.

3. Focus on the people that one would typically see at a particular place or event. Give the setting and then briefly describe several people, their personalities, their actions.

Lorraine Hansberry

On Summer

[1]   It has taken me a good number of years to come to any measure of respect for summer. I was, being May-born, literally an "infant of the spring" and, during the later childhood years, tended, for some reason or other, to rather worship the cold aloofness of winter. The adolescence, admittedly lingering still, brought the traditional passionate commitment to melancholy autumn—and all that. For the longest kind of time I simply thought that *summer* was a mistake.

[2]   In fact, my earliest memory of anything at all is of waking up in a darkened room where I had been put to bed for a nap on a summer's afternoon, and feeling very, very hot. I acutely disliked the feeling then and retained the bias for years. It had originally been a matter of the heat but, over the years, I came actively to associate displeasure with most of the usually celebrated natural features and social by-products of the season: the too-grainy texture of sand; the too-cold coldness of the various waters we constantly try to escape into, and the icky-perspiry feeling of bathing caps.

[3]   It also seemed to me, esthetically speaking, that nature had got inexcusably carried away on the summer question and let the whole thing get to be rather much. By duration alone, for instance, a summer's day seemed maddeningly excessive; an utter overstatement. Except for those few hours at either end of it, objects always appeared in too sharp a relief against backgrounds; shadows too pronounced and light too blinding. It always gave me the feeling of walk-

ing around in a motion picture which had been too artsily-craftsily exposed. Sound also had a way of coming to the ear without that muting influence, marvelously common to winter, across patios or beaches or through the woods. I suppose I found it too stark and yet too intimate a season.

[4]   My childhood Southside summers were the ordinary city kind, full of the street games which other rememberers have turned into fine ballets these days and rhymes that anticipated what some people insist on calling modern poetry:

> Oh, Mary Mack, Mack, Mack
> With the silver buttons, buttons, buttons
> All down her back, back, back
> She asked her mother, mother, mother
> For fifteen cents, cents, cents
> To see the elephant, elephant, elephant
> Jump the fence, fence, fence
> Well, he jumped so high, high, high
> 'Til he touched the sky, sky, sky
> And he didn't come back, back, back
> 'Til the fourth of Ju-ly, ly, ly!

[5]   Evenings were spent mainly on the back porches where screen doors slammed in the darkness with those really very special summertime sounds. And, sometimes, when Chicago nights got too steamy, the whole family got into the car and went to the park and slept out in the open on blankets. Those were, of course, the best times of all because the grownups were invariably reminded of having been children in rural parts of the country and told the best stories then. And it was also cool and sweet to be on the grass and there was usually the scent of freshly cut lemons or melons in the air. And Daddy would lie on his back, as fathers must, and explain about how men thought the stars above us came to be and how far away they were. I never did learn to believe that anything could be as far away as *that*. Especially the stars.

[6]   My mother first took us south to visit her Tennessee birthplace one summer when I was seven or eight, I think. I woke up on the back seat of the car while we were still driving through some place called Kentucky and my mother was pointing out to the beautiful hills on both sides of the highway and telling my brothers and my sister about how her father had run away and hidden from his master in those very hills when he was a little boy. She said that his mother had wandered among the wooded slopes in the moonlight and left food for him in secret places. They were very beautiful hills and I looked out at them for miles and miles after that wondering who and what a *master* might be.

[7]   I remember being startled when I first saw my grandmother rocking away on her porch. All my life I had heard that she was a great beauty and no one had ever remarked that they meant a half century before. The woman I met was as wrinkled as a prune and could hardly hear and barely see and always seemed to be thinking of other times. But she could still rock and talk and even make wonderful cupcakes which were like cornbread, only sweet. She was captivated by automobiles and, even though it was well into the thirties, I

don't think she had ever been in one before we came down and took her driving. She was a little afraid of them and could not seem to negotiate the windows, but she loved driving. She died the next summer and that is all that I remember about her, except that she was born in slavery and had memories of it and they didn't sound anything like *Gone with the Wind*.

[8]   Like everyone else, I have spent whole or bits of summers in many different kinds of places since then: camps and resorts in the Middle West and New York State; on an island; in a tiny Mexican village; Cape Cod, perched atop the Truro bluffs at Longnook Beach that Millay wrote about; or simply strolling the streets of Provincetown before the hours when the cocktail parties begin.

[9]   And, lastly, I do not think that I will forget days spent, a few summers ago, at a beautiful lodge built right into the rocky cliffs of a bay on the Maine coast. We met a woman there who had lived a purposeful and courageous life and who was then dying of cancer. She had, characteristically, just written a book and taken up painting. She had also been of radical viewpoint all her life; one of those people who energetically believe that the world *can* be changed for the better and spend their lives trying to do just that. And that was the way she thought of cancer; she absolutely refused to award it the stature of tragedy, a devastating instance of the brooding doom and inexplicability of the absurdity of human destiny, etc., etc. The kind of characterization given, lately, as we all know, to far less formidable foes in life than cancer.

[10]   But for this remarkable woman it was a matter of nature in imperfection, implying, as always, work for man to do. It was an *enemy*, but a palpable one with shape and effect and source; and if it existed, it could be destroyed. She saluted it accordingly, without despondency, but with a lively, beautiful and delightfully ribald anger. There was one thing, she felt, which would prove equal to its relentless ravages and that was the genius of man. Not his mysticism, but man with tubes and slides and the stubborn human notion that the stars are very much within our reach.

[11]   The last time I saw her she was sitting surrounded by her paintings with her manuscript laid out for me to read, because, she said, she wanted to know what a *young person* would think of her thinking; one must always keep up with what *young people* thought about things because, after all, they were in *charge*.

[12]   Every now and then her jaw set in anger as we spoke of things people should be angry about. And then, for relief, she would look out at the lovely bay at a mellow sunset settling on the water. Her face softened with love of all that beauty and, watching her, I wished with all my power what I knew that she was wishing: that she might live to see at least one more *summer*. Through her eyes I finally gained the sense of what it might mean; more than the coming autumn with its pretentious melancholy; more than an austere and silent winter which must shut dying people in for precious months; more even than the frivolous spring, too full of too many false promises, would be the gift of another summer with its stark and intimate assertion of neither birth nor death but life at the apex; with the gentlest nights and, above all, the longest days.

[13]   I heard later that she did live to see another summer. And I have retained my respect for the noblest of the seasons.

VOCABULARY

Use the context of the essay and your dictionary to define the following words:

1. aloofness (par. 1)   6. ribald (par. 10)
2. melancholy (par. 1)   7. pretentious (par. 12)
3. bias (par. 2)   8. austere (par. 12)
4. stature (par. 9)   9. frivolous (par. 12)
5. palpable (par. 10)   10. apex (par. 12)

RHETORIC AND IDEA

1. Write in your own words a thesis statement for Hansberry's essay. Begin the statement with *although*.

2. Hansberry's essay is organized into six units that include these paragraphs: (1) paragraphs 1 through 3, (2) paragraphs 4 through 5, (3) paragraphs 6 through 7, (4) paragraph 8, (5) paragraphs 9 through 12, and (6) paragraph 13. Explain briefly what goes on in each of the units.

3. To gain proper emphasis for her examples, Hansberry uses chronological order, but she also uses climactic arrangement. Explain how both kinds of order work to make her essay seem both logical and emotionally satisfying.

4. In the last sentence of paragraph 7, Hansberry relies on common knowledge when she alludes to Margaret Mitchell's novel (or the film) *Gone with the Wind*. She assumes that the reader knows what slavery was like in the novel or the film. She also says that her grandmother's memories of slavery "didn't sound anything like" the book or the film. What was slavery like in *Gone with the Wind?* What was slavery really like as Grandmother remembered it?

5. In paragraph 1, Hansberry uses the four seasons as one half of a rhetorical framing device. In which paragraph does she complete the frame? Explain.

6. In sentence 1 of paragraph 3, Hansberry uses the phrases "carried away" and "rather much" as the comment of her topic sentence. Read the rest of the paragraph carefully, and underline or make a list of the words or phrases in the paragraph that repeat the concept of hyperbole (overstatement) and thus give the paragraph emphasis.

7. In the last sentence of paragraph 2, Hansberry uses parallel structure to emphasize her "displeasure" at summer:

> by-products of the season:
> the too-grainy texture of sand;
> the too-cold-ness of the various waters we try to escape into,
>   and
> the icky-perspiry feeling of bathing caps.

Explain how the repetition of the pattern helps her emphasize the point she wants to make. Find in the essay at least two other examples of the same device, and explain what makes them effective.

WRITING ASSIGNMENTS

1. Using notebook paper and your own evidence, fill in the blanks of the two sentence patterns below. Have at least five words in each of the three parallel items, and make sure the items are concrete, as are the three parallel items in Rhetoric and Idea question 7 above.

   a. At one time I (liked, disliked) _____,
      but as time passed, I began to (like, dislike) what

      (it, he, they, etc.) offered: _____:

      _____; _____; and _____

      _____.

   b. At one time I (trusted, distrusted) _____,
      but as time passed, I began to (trust, distrust) what

      he/she said: that _____; that _____

      _____; and that _____.

2. Describe in a single, well-developed paragraph a summer, autumn, winter, or spring scene so that your reader will know why you like or dislike that season. Make clear what you are describing by being specific about the time and place and by using concrete details to help your reader see what you see, hear what you hear, feel what you feel, smell what you smell, taste what you taste. Have a topic sentence either stated or implied. Gain coherence and emphasis by repeating key comment words or ideas.

3. Write an essay in which you trace by examples what caused you to change your mind about something: seasons, a person, a neighborhood, a school, the military service, a television program, a politician. Before you organize your ideas and evidence, review your answers to Rhetoric and Idea questions 2 and 3 above. Feel free to follow the same organizational pattern that Hansberry uses.

Jon Carroll

Summery Probation:

A Remembrance

of Tents Past

[1]   The bus would always be late, and we would huddle on the early morning
street corner like refugees, surrounded by battered suitcases and ragged
bedrolls, nervously eyeing the strange kids around us. The other boys
seemed to be either psychopathic loners being sent to camp as a condition of
parole, or shy, tearstained lads being sent away in the hopes that the Great
Outdoors would prove to be a bracing cure for suspected latent homosexu-
ality. Already the lines were drawn: the tormentors and the victims. They
were united only by the fervent hope that the bus would not arrive at all. But it
always did.

[2]   In Pasadena in the mid- 1950s, where I gained my personal experience with
the American custom of deporting children between June and September, the
most common terminus of the terrifying journey was Catalina Island. This involved not only an endless, largely silent bus ride down Figueroa to San
Pedro, but also a choppy, fume-filled trip by water taxi out to the island itself.
The combination of the small, noisy boat and the hot, damp tuna fish sandwiches combined to create conditions noticeably inferior to those enjoyed by
inmates of Algerian prisons. By the time the island itself hove into view, the
tuna fish had been returned to the ocean in an altered form, and the pale,
putative fun-seekers were prepared for any sort of random psychological
violence. In other words, a completely apt introduction to the summer camp
experience.

[3]   As it happens, I know too much about summer camp. I served time at Camp Orizaba on Catalina and Camp Bluff Lake near Big Bear, both run by the YMCA; Camp Cherry Valley on Catalina, operated by the Boy Scouts; Boys' Camp near Lake Arrowhead, owned by the Boys' Clubs of America; Camp Pacific in Carlsbad, run by a military academy whose name blessedly escapes me; and Mar Casa on Balboa Island, franchised by the Pasadena Presbyterian Church. I hated them all.

[4]   Time has served, for most adults, to gather a rosy mist around the experience of camping, so that today's parents may be seen to grin sincerely as the fruits of their loins are led trembling with fear to encounter nature in the company of older men who have been unable to find useful year-round employment. But summer camps back then—and I am not persuaded that the situation has changed significantly—were, in essence and in function, concentration camps for young boys. It is an institution not without social utility—the savages of today are the civil servants of tomorrow, and someone has to effect the transformation. But let us at least forget the idealized visions of wholesome young people learning to paddle canoes and tool leather and sing "Swing Low, Sweet Chariot" as they grow in wisdom and in stature. Let us not kid our kids.

[5]   Summer camps were reasonably blatant about their true nature. Military terminology and procedures were everywhere employed. The dining facilities were called mess halls. The day started with a recorded version of reveille played over the camp loudspeaker. Bunks were inspected by martinets carrying thin batons. Rank was signified by various emblems and badges.

[6]   Even the crafts programs, which might be considered immune from the general authoritarian Gestalt, were operated along military lines. Each camper was compelled to make something, usually a lanyard or a wallet. These artifacts were considered by camp administrators to be useful in proving to parents that the time away from home had been well spent. I am regrettably hopeless when it comes to any skill requiring manual dexterity, and several times I was given lanyards by counselors and told to claim them as my own. A crafts instuctor at Mar Casa refused to allow me to make a blue and green lanyard—that color combination was considered unmanly.

[7]   Once a week, the whole camp turned out for some variety of mega-game, generally an invasion fantasy worked out by the senior staff. At Orizaba it was called Pirates and Castlemen. All the Pirates would leave camp for a remote gathering area, then attempt to filter back, by land and by sea, take the Castlemen flag down from the flagpole and substitute the Jolly Roger. Since the only approved method of "killing" a member of the opposing team was to lift him off his feet, campers were encouraged to strip to their underwear and grease their bodies, thus making them slippery and hard to lift. This day-long orgy of greased youth hugging each other in the name of mock combat carries implications too obvious to explore further.

[8]   After military discipline came religion. Each camp featured some secret chapel area, hallowed ground to which campers would journey on Sundays, there to sing "Onward Christian Soldiers" and "Holy, Holy, Holy" and listen to the chaplain warn of the perils posed by nubile young women in the

pay of Soviet Russia. At Mar Casa we would go to bed each night carrying candles and singing "We are climbing Jacob's Ladder, soldiers of the cross."

[9]   But, someone is sure to remark at this point, what about the good parts, the skits around the campfire, the exposure to the world of nature, even the camaraderie of boys caught in the same trap? I can truthfully reply that the only really good times I had came at Mar Casa, which is located on Balboa's main drag, a block from the Jolly Roger, a well-known hangout for heedless youth. On occasion, a few of us were able to sneak up the street, order a burger and chat up a few girls. We were always punished for these transgressions, but we always repeated them. That's one thing summer camp taught me: escape.

VOCABULARY

Use the context of the essay and your dictionary to define the words listed below.

1. latent (par. 1)
2. putative (par. 2)
3. apt (par. 2)
4. terminology (par. 5)
5. reveille (par. 5)
6. martinets (par. 5)
7. batons (par. 5)
8. authoritarian (par. 6)
9. Gestalt (par. 6)
10. nubile (par. 8)

RHETORIC AND IDEA

1. Write a thesis statement for Carroll's essay.
2. Carroll's nine paragraphs make up three distinct parts: (1) paragraphs 1 through 3, (2) paragraphs 4 through 8 (4,5 through 7,8), and (3) paragraph 9. Explain briefly what each of the sections does. Consider the subpoints in section 2.
3. Using the notes you prepared for 2, write a rough topic outline for Carroll's essay.
4. Sentence 1 of paragraph 2 is a topic sentence for that paragraph. What word or words in that first sentence make clear the writer's attitude? List or underline the words in the paragraph that emphasize his attitude.
5. The first sentence of paragraph 5 is the topic sentence for that paragraph. Rewrite the sentence so that it more bluntly states "the true nature" of summer camps and thus sets up a clearer key term to emphasize the comment.
6. What makes the last sentence of paragraph 3 especially effective? Consider in particular its position and its length.
7. The first sentence of paragraph 8 is a transitional hook. It sums up what went before ("After military discipline") and introduces what is to follow ("came religion."), thus connecting the parts of the essay. Test the first sentence of other paragraphs in the essay to see if they too hook paragraphs together. Explain how they do or do not work to supply coherence between paragraphs.

8. Discuss the connotation of the phrase "served time" as it is used in sentence 2 of paragraph 3. Why is (or isn't) this phrase especially appropriate?

WRITING ASSIGNMENTS

1. Using the following two sentences as topic sentence and concluding sentence and filling in the blanks, write a paragraph that you develop with evidence from personal experience.

   topic sentence: As it happens, I know too much about _____.

   concluding sentence: I _____ them all.

   Before you write your paragraph, review paragraph 3 of Carroll's essay.

2. Write an essay on one of the following topics:

   Jobs I Have (Loved, Hated)
   All Summer Camps Aren't Bad

   The Trip to _____ Was Pure (Hell, Heaven)
   Working in Summer Camps
   Military Discipline Is (Necessary, Unnecessary) for Kids

E. B. White

Once More to the Lake (August 1941)

[1]   One summer, along about 1904, my father rented a camp on a lake in Maine and took us all there for the month of August. We all got ringworm from some kittens and had to rub Pond's Extract on our arms and legs night and morning, and my father rolled over in a canoe with all his clothes on; but outside of that the vacation was a success and from then on none of us ever thought there was any place in the world like that lake in Maine. We returned summer after summer—always on August 1st for one month. I have since become a salt-water man, but sometimes in summer there are days when the restlessness of the tides and the fearful cold of the sea water and the incessant wind which blows across the afternoon and into the evening make me wish for the placidity of a lake in the woods. A few weeks ago this feeling got so strong I bought myself a couple of bass hooks and a spinner and returned to the lake where we used to go, for a week's fishing and to revisit old haunts.

[2]   I took along my son, who had never had any fresh water up his nose and who had seen lily pads only from train windows. On the journey over to the lake I began to wonder what it would be like. I wondered how time would have marred this unique, this holy spot—the coves and streams, the hills that the sun set behind, the camps and the paths behind the camps. I was sure the tarred road would have found it out and I wondered in what other ways it would be desolated. It is strange how much you can remember about places like that once you allow your mind to return into the grooves which lead back. You

remember one thing, and that suddenly reminds you of another thing. I guess I remembered clearest of all the early mornings, when the lake was cool and motionless, remembered how the bedroom smelled of the lumber it was made of and of the wet woods whose scent entered through the screen. The partitions in the camp were thin and did not extend clear to the top of the rooms, and as I was always the first up I would dress softly so as not to wake the others, and sneak out into the sweet outdoors and start out in the canoe, keeping close along the shore in the long shadows of the pines. I remembered being very careful never to rub my paddle against the gunwale for fear of disturbing the stillness of the cathedral.

[3]   The lake had never been what you would call a wild lake. There were cottages sprinkled around the shores, and it was in farming country although the shores of the lake were quite heavily wooded. Some of the cottages were owned by nearby farmers, and you would live at the shore and eat your meals at the farmhouse. That's what our family did. But although it wasn't wild, it was a fairly large and undisturbed lake and there were places in it which, to a child at least, seemed infinitely remote and primeval.

[4]   I was right about the tar: it led to within half a mile of the shore. But when I got back there, with my boy, and we settled into a camp near a farmhouse and into the kind of summertime I had known, I could tell that it was going to be pretty much the same as it had been before—I knew it, lying in bed the first morning, smelling the bedroom, and hearing the boy sneak quietly out and go off along the shore in a boat. I began to sustain the illusion that he was I, and therefore by simple transposition, that I was my father. This sensation persisted, kept cropping up all the time we were there. It was not an entirely new feeling, but in this setting it grew much stronger. I seemed to be living a dual existence. I would be in the middle of some simple act, I would be picking up a bait box or laying down a table fork, or I would be saying something, and suddenly it would not be I but my father who was saying the words or making the gesture. It gave me a creepy sensation.

[5]   We went fishing the first morning. I felt the same damp moss covering the worms in the bait can, and saw the dragonfly alight on the tip of my rod as it hovered a few inches from the surface of the water. It was the arrival of this fly that convinced me beyond any doubt that everything was as it always had been, that the years were a mirage and there had been no years. The small waves were the same, chucking the rowboat under the chin as we fished at anchor, and the boat was the same boat, the same color green and the ribs broken in the same places, and under the floor-boards the same fresh-water leavings and debris—the dead hellgrammite,[1] the wisps of moss, the rusty discarded fishhook, the dried blood from yesterday's catch. We stared silently at the tips of our rods, at the dragonflies that came and went. I lowered the tip of mine into the water, tentatively, pensively dislodging the fly, which darted two feet away, poised, darted two feet back, and came to rest again a little farther up the rod. There had been no years between the ducking of this dragonfly and the other one—the one that was part of memory. I looked at the boy, who was silently watching his fly, and it was my hands that held his rod, my eyes watching. I felt dizzy and didn't know which rod I was at the end of.

[1]Insect used for bait.

[6]   We caught two bass, hauling them in briskly as though they were mackerel, pulling them over the side of the boat in a businesslike manner without any landing net, and stunning them with a blow on the back of the head. When we got back for a swim before lunch, the lake was exactly where we had left it, the same number of inches from the dock, and there was only the merest suggestion of a breeze. This seemed an utterly enchanted sea, this lake you could leave to its own devices for a few hours and come back to, and find that it had not stirred, this constant and trustworthy body of water. In the shallows, the dark, water-soaked sticks and twigs, smooth and old, were undulating in clusters on the bottom against the clean ribbed sand, and the track of the mussel was plain. A school of minnows swam by, each minnow with its small individual shadow, doubling the attendance, so clear and sharp in the sunlight. Some of the other campers were in swimming, along the shore, one of them with a cake of soap, and the water felt thin and clear and unsubstantial. Over the years there had been this person with the cake of soap, this cultist, and here he was. There had been no years.

[7]   Up to the farmhouse to dinner through the teeming, dusty field, the road under our sneakers was only a two-track road. The middle track was missing, the one with the marks of the hooves and the splotches of dried, flaky manure. There had always been three tracks to choose from in choosing which track to walk in; now the choice was narrowed down to two. For a moment I missed terribly the middle alternative. But the way led past the tennis court, and something about the way it lay there in the sun reassured me; the tape had loosened along the backline, the alleys were green with plantains and other weeds, and the net (installed in June and removed in September) sagged in the dry noon, and the whole place steamed with midday heat and hunger and emptiness. There was a choice of pie for dessert, and one was blueberry and one was apple, and the waitresses were the same country girls, there having been no passage of time, only the illusion of it as in a dropped curtain—the waitresses were still fifteen; their hair had been washed, that was the only difference—they had been to the movies and seen the pretty girls with the clean hair.

[8]   Summertime, oh summertime, pattern of life indelible, the fade-proof lake, the woods unshatterable, the pasture with the sweetfern and the juniper forever and ever, summer without end; this was the background, and the life along the shore was the design, the cottages with their innocent and tranquil design, their tiny docks with the flagpole and the American flag floating against the white clouds in the blue sky, the little paths over the roots of the trees leading from camp to camp and the paths leading back to the outhouses and the can of lime for sprinkling, and at the souvenir counters at the store the miniature birch-bark canoes and the post cards that showed things looking a little better than they looked. This was the American family at play, escaping the city heat, wondering whether the newcomers in the camp at the head of the cove were "common" or "nice," wondering whether it was true that the people who drove up for Sunday dinner at the farmhouse were turned away because there wasn't enough chicken.

[9]   It seemed to me, as I kept remembering all this, that those times and those summers had been infinitely precious and worth saving. There had been jollity and peace and goodness. The arriving (at the beginning of August) had

been so big a business in itself, at the railway station the farm wagon drawn up, the first smell of the pine-laden air, the first glimpse of the smiling farmer, and the great importance of the trunks and your father's enormous authority in such matters, and the feel of the wagon under you for the long ten-mile haul, and at the top of the last long hill catchng the first view of the lake after eleven months of not seeing this cherished body of water. The shouts and cries of the other campers when they saw you, and the trunks to be unpacked, to give up their rich burden. (Arriving was less exciting nowadays, when you sneaked up in your car and parked it under a tree near the camp and took out the bags and in five minutes it was all over, no fuss, no loud wonderful fuss about trunks.)

[10]   Peace and goodness and jollity. The only thing that was wrong now, really, was the sound of the place, an unfamiliar nervous sound of the outboard motors. This was the note that jarred, the one thing that would sometimes break the illusion and set the years moving. In those other summertimes all motors were inboard; and when they were at a little distance, the noise they made was a sedative, an ingredient of summer sleep. They were one-cylinder and two-cylinder engines, and some were make-and-break and some were jump-spark, but they all made a sleepy sound across the lake. The one-lungers throbbed and fluttered, and the twin-cylinder ones purred and purred, and that was a quiet sound too. But now the campers all had outboards. In the daytime, in the hot mornings, these motors made a petulant, irritable sound; at night, in the still evening when the afterglow lit the water, they whined about one's ears like mosquitoes. My boy loved our rented outboard, and his great desire was to achieve singlehanded mastery over it, and authority, and he soon learned the trick of choking it a little (but not too much), and the adjustment of the needle valve. Watching him I would remember the things you could do with the old one-cylinder engine with the heavy flywheel, how you could have it eating out of your hand if you got really close to it spiritually. Motor boats in those days didn't have clutches, and you would make a landing by shutting off the motor at the proper time and coasting in with a dead rudder. But there was a way of reversing them, if you learned the trick, by cutting the switch and putting it on again exactly on the final dying revolution of the flywheel, so that it would kick back against compression and begin reversing. Approaching a dock in a strong following breeze, it was difficult to slow up sufficiently by the ordinary coasting method, and if a boy felt he had complete mastery over his motor, he was tempted to keep it running beyond its time and then reverse it a few feet from the dock. It took a cool nerve, because if you threw the switch a twentieth of a second too soon you would catch the flywheel when it still had speed enough to go up past center, and the boat would leap ahead, charging bull-fashion at the dock.

[11]   We had a good week at the camp. The bass were biting well and the sun shone endlessly, day after day. We would be tired at night and lie down in the accumulated heat of the little bedrooms after the long hot day and the breeze would stir almost imperceptibly outside and the smell of the swamp drift in through the rusty screens. Sleep would come easily and in the morning the red squirrel would be on the roof, tapping out his gay routine. I kept remembering everything, lying in bed in the mornings—the small steamboat that had a long

rounded stern like the lip of a Ubangi, and how quietly she ran on the moonlight sails, when the older boys played their mandolins and the girls sang and we ate doughnuts dipped in sugar, and how sweet the music was on the water in the shining night, and what it had felt like to think about girls then. After breakfast we would go up to the store and the things were in the same place—the minnows in a bottle, the plugs and spinners disarranged and pawed over by the youngsters from the boys' camp, the fig newtons and the Beeman's gum. Outside, the road was tarred and the cars stood in front of the store. Inside, all was just as it had always been, except there was more Coca-Cola and not so much Moxie and root beer and birch beer and sarsaparilla. We would walk out with a bottle of pop apiece and sometimes the pop would backfire up our noses and hurt. We explored the streams, quietly, where the turtles slid off the sunny logs and dug their way into the soft bottom; and we lay on the town wharf and fed worms to the tame bass. Everywhere we went I had trouble making out which was I, the one walking at my side, the one walking in my pants.

[12]   One afternoon while we were there at that lake a thunderstorm came up. It was like the revival of an old melodrama that I had seen long ago with childish awe. The second-act climax of the drama of the electrical disturbance over a lake in America had not changed in any important respect. This was the big scene, still the big scene. The whole thing was so familiar, the first feeling of oppression and heat and a general air around camp of not wanting to go very far away. In midafternoon (it was all the same) a curious darkening of the sky, and a lull in everything that had made life tick; and then the way the boats suddenly swung the other way at their moorings with the coming of a breeze out of the new quarter, and the premonitory rumble. Then the kettle drum, then the snare, then the bass drum and cymbals, then crackling light against the dark, and the gods grinning and licking their chops in the hills. Afterward the calm, the rain steadily rustling in the calm lake, the return of light and hope and spirits, and the campers running out of joy and relief to go swimming in the rain, their bright cries perpetuating the deathless joke about how they were getting simply drenched, and the children screaming with the delight at the new sensation of bathing in the rain, and the joke about getting drenched linking the generations in a strong indestructible chain. And the comedian who waded in carrying an umbrella.

[13]   When the others went swimming my son said he was going in too. He pulled his dripping trunks from the line where they had hung all through the shower, and wrung them out. Languidly, and with no thought of going in, I watched him, his hard little body, skinny and bare, saw him wince slightly as he pulled up around his vitals the small, soggy, icy garment. As he buckled the swollen belt, my groin felt the chill of death.

VOCABULARY

Use the context of the essay and your dictionary to define the words listed below.

1. incessant (par. 1)	6. undulating (par. 6)
2. placidity (par. 1)	7. indelible (par. 8)
3. primeval (par. 3)	8. petulant (par. 10)
4. transposition (par. 4)	9. imperceptibly (par. 11)
5. mirage (par. 5)	10. premonitory (par. 12)

RHETORIC AND IDEA

1. Which of the sources of evidence does White use most fully to develop his thesis? Explain.
2. On the surface, "Once More to the Lake" is a personal reminiscence about a family vacation spot; beneath the surface, however, it comments on man's identity and mortality. Explain. Take into consideration the last sentence of the essay.
3. Is "Once More to the Lake" description, narration, exposition, or argument? Explain.
4. Explain how the descriptive passages promote the central idea of White's essay. Consider especially paragraphs 4 through 12.
5. White puts heavy emphasis on sensory details. Find examples of his use of details that do appeal to the senses—taste, sound, smell, touch, and sight.
6. Does White use enough evidence to prepare the readers for the concluding sentences of paragraphs 5 and 6? Explain.
7. Illusion plays an important part in "Once More to the Lake." How often does White use the word *illusion?* How many of the writer's experiences at the lake were illusory?

WRITING ASSIGNMENTS

1. Using your five senses to help you gather evidence, describe in a paragraph or an essay one of your favorite places: your room, your favorite nightspot, the gymnasium, a restaurant, an amusement park, the beach, your car, your boat, a lake.
2. Using only one of your five senses, write a paragraph or essay describing a person you know well, a spot you like to relax in, a sport you enjoy, a neighbor you see frequently.
3. Write an essay in which you describe how some person, place, or thing has changed over the years. Use your five senses as a source of evidence.
4. Write an essay on one of the following topics:

    Fathers and Sons

    Fathers and Daughters

    My Room Reflects My Personality

    When Time Stood Still

    My Favorite City

    Mothers and Sons

    Mothers and Daughters

    I Am My Mother's (Father's) Child

A. Alvarez

Shiprock

[1]   I suppose the first sight of a mountain is always the best. Later, when you are waiting to start, you may grow to hate the brute, because you are afraid. And when, finally, you are climbing, you are never aware of the mountain as a mountain: it is merely so many little areas of rock to be worked out in terms of hand-holds, foot-holds and effort, like so many chess problems. But when you first see it in the distance, remote and beautiful and unknown, then there seems some reason for climbing. That, perhaps, is what Mallory meant by his "Because it's there."

[2]   I first saw Shiprock on a midsummer day. I was exhausted, having driven the two-and-a-half-thousand miles from New Jersey to New Mexico in relatively few days. Moreover, I was unfit; I had not climbed for several weeks and I looked forward without much pleasure to what would probably be thirty-six hours on a vertical face. Finally, I had that morning left my wife and baby son in Taos; and going off for a big climb is always a wretched business; it leaves you tense and sick at heart. I think now that serious climbs are for bachelors; they become so much more difficult when you leave anything behind.

[3]   I was feeling, in short, just a bit sorry for myself as I drove across the rolling Apache country and into the wastes of the Navajo reservation. The area set aside by the U.S. Government for the Navajo Indians is the most desolate land in the world, flat, dried-up, harsh, stony. But, recently, oil and uranium

have been found and a little wealth is beginning to creep in. In places the desolation seems almost busy—though no less desolate. It was a few miles south of one of these little centres, a new boom town called Farmington, that I first saw Shiprock. I had come out, imperceptibly, on top of a huge flat hill. To the north and west the desert dropped away to a lower level. A long way north rose the blue tiers of the Mesa Verde, where the prehistoric cave cities are. Sweeping round to the south, the desert was ringed with smaller mesas, the queer, flat-topped hills, looking like bits of plain set up on vertical cliffs. But in the west, about fifty miles away, below the sinking sun, where the desert seemed blank and endless, was Shiprock. Its bluish, hazy mass swam sheer out of the desert, rising eighteen hundred feet to the huge twin east and south towers. Between them peered the north tower, farther away and seeming smaller: then the bulk of the mountain bending a little towards the western desert.

[4]   I had never even seen a photograph of it before. Perhaps that is why I had agreed to join the climbing party. But in the later afternoon sun it looked very beautiful. No wonder it is the sacred mountain of the Navajos. It dominates the whole landscape continuously and effortlessly. As I drove towards it, it was hidden at times by corners and edges of sandstone, but it controlled, always, my whole sense of direction. According to the picture post-cards, Shiprock got its name because at sunset it looks like a great ship floating forward across the desert. Perhaps it does. But in Navajo myth it stretches towards heaven and the souls of men descend to earth from it. It dominates their cosmology as it dominates the landscape.

[5]   There is a tiny Indian town of Shiprock, about twenty miles from the mountain. I had arranged to meet my Princeton climbing companions there. "O, we'll meet at the main restaurant," we had said. "If we're not there, we'll be camping under the climb." It was vague, of course, but then none of us knew what the town—or the mountain, for that matter—would be like. Mercifully, there were only a couple of restaurants, a couple of gas stations, a school and a couple of trading posts. There were mule carts in the street, which made it look more like Mexico than I had ever seen before in the States, and Indians were cramming into the usual pick-up trucks to return to their villages for the night. The men, small, thickish and rather saturnine, wore the regulation denims, except for a few wrapped in their blankets like dark, heavy Della Robbia[1] infants. But the women were splendid, skirted to their feet and shawled in vivid reds, purples and oranges. In the huge golden sunset they looked oddly unreal—or at least, unexpected—as if I'd walked into the middle of some vast play, and didn't know the plot.

[6]   There is a big motel and restaurant run by the Navajos. One of the Princeton cars was outside it, but there was no sign of my friends in the cafe. They had left half an hour before, the proprietress told me. They would be under the mountain. It was almost dark now, so, with nothing to lose, I ordered a meal. If we were to climb the next day, heaven knew when I'd next eat properly.

[7]   Then I set about finding my way out to the rock. The directions were simple enough: go south on the main road until the gravelled turn-off to Lukachukai.

---

[1]Andrea Della Robbia: (1435-1525), Florentine worker in bas-relief, known especially for his bambini medallions.

Follow that for eight miles over the desert. When you come to the ridge, go right on a track straight towards the mountain. It was quite dark by the time I started, but the full moon was up, my headlights were good and the others would probably have lit a fire. I wasn't worried.

[8]   At first, the driving was easy enough. But it was darker than I thought and the eight miles bumping along the gravel road across the desert seemed long and slow. Finally, a great black wall of rock loomed up on either side of the road: the ridge. My headlights made strange, impertinent shadows on it. There was a track off to the right just before the ridge, but it seemed improbably vague. So I went past the thing and saw another. There seemed nothing to do but take it. As I swung the car off the road, it was like walking unexpectedly into the deep-end of a swimming pool. The car jerked and heaved and wallowed. The track was hardish sand, full of pot-holes and strewn with rocks. Sometimes it would go round the litte dunes, sometimes it went over them. Then I usually had to back the car and take a run at the rise, careering over the top, headlights flailing in the air, not knowing if the track went straight on over or turned on the top.

[9]   It took me about an hour to drive two miles. Finally, of course, I went wrong. I found myself with the car stuck in the sand on the top of a dune, the track entirely vanished and what appeared to be a vertical drop on three sides. The only way off was to back down the steep slope I had just come up. Without a reversing light, it seemed impossible. The great black ridge rose sheer above me, its darkness jagged and menacing against the sky. I could just make out the peak of Shiprock heaving up darkly behind it. There was no sign of the others' fire, only that great black, menacing ridge looming up in front, and the desert, eerie and shimmering and vague under the moon. The wind blew soft but insistent sand into my eyes and mouth. I began to shout in the hope that the others were just the far side of the ridge. My yells echoed back to me and faded away. So I gave up and went back to the car. Being outside in the moonlit desert made feel terribly exposed and isolated. The place is too vast and indifferent to be bearable at night. I stretched out in the back of the car, drank some whisky and settled down to sleep. A huge grasshopper which had settled on the ledge of the rear window creaked heavily from time to time, like a pair of ancient corsets. The moon shone in on me and all around was the vast, rustling silence of the desert. Oddly enough, I slept very well.

[10]   At dawn, I climbed the ridge, one of three thin, curving tentacles spreading out from Shiprock. The path I should have taken ran, quite distinct, along the other side. At the end of it, tiny against the desert, was the other car and my friends lying around it in their sleeping-bags.

[11]   The rest of that day was like a bad dream. We had three things to do: find the start of the route; get some more food and liquid from the town; wait for the fifth member of the party to arrive. We were to be in all four Englishmen and an American, all from Princeton. One Englishman was still missing. Simple enough. But what happened in fact was that we were systematically demoralized. First, there was the rock itself: the bulk of the mountain is sheer sandstone, whilst the back is shattered basalt. All of it is utterly rotten. It came away as you touched it, hardly waiting to be pulled. Most of the ordinary holds were useless; the only safe ones were cracks to jam your toes and fingers into. Second, there was the thirst. All day the wind blew steadily; our mouths

and eyes and ears were full of sand; we were parched whenever we were not actually drinking. It was a permanent condition, like the beating of your blood, or the pain of someone with cancer. It seemed impossible that we should ever have enough to drink again. Third, was the heat. Shiprock had never been climbed later than May. This was the end of June. To move into the sun was like swinging open some great furnace door. The whole landscape shimmered and swayed and faded in the heat. The rocks became almost too hot to touch. In the village the temperature was about 110 °F. in the shade. Heaven alone knows what it was out in the desert. Fourth, was the Accident. On the last ascent a man had been killed. When we went to get our stores in the village, we heard of nothing else. ''He was a young guy, just like you-all. Say,'' one would turn to the other, ''he looked just like this guy, didn't he?'' ''Sure. And he bought the same candies. You should have seen him when they brought him in. Gee.'' and so on. We fled from the place as soon as we could. But by the time we drove back across the desert we were sick to death of the whole miserable business: the rotten rock, the thirst, the heat, the shopkeepers' gloating over that poor wretch's death, and the mountain looming there impassively against another unbelievable sunset. It seemed a silly pointless way of getting oneself killed.

[12]   Dick Sykes, the missing Englishman, had still not arrived, so we decided to go up without him. We had our excuses, of course: I had to get back to my family; the others were expected in the Tetons in two days; and so on. But the truth was none of us could bear the thought of another day of tension, heat and waiting like this one. If we didn't climb the mountain the next day, we wouldn't climb it at all. So we loaded ourselves up, like so many mules, with climbing equipment, food, drink and sleeping-bags, and groped in the fading light painfully up to the start of the climb.

[13]   The west wall of Shiprock is basalt. It drops down to a huge, curving overhang. The climb begins on the left side of this, where the lip of the rock sticks out less angrily. Underneath the overhang is a shallow, level, sandy cave shaped like a scimitar. We built a fire, heated some of the precious water for tea and lay down to sleep in the cave. Again I slept surprisingly well, but I was woken a couple of times by faint rustlings. For such a dead lunar landscape, the place seemed strangely unquiet.

[14]   I suppose it goes without saying that the climb, after all the horrors of thinking about it, was perfectly straightforward. We were up before the sun, had a miserable breakfast of cornflakes and tepid baked beans, and were off. It is a violent beginning. You go straight from the ground on to the stirrups[2] on the overhang. But this is mercifully short; four heaves, a little awkward straddling with the feet and we were up. And most important, once we began to climb all the worries and fears and tensions left us. Fear is always a matter of the future tense; the present is too blessedly factual.

[15]   You come over the overhang into a vast amphitheatre of shattered basalt. At the back of it the head-wall goes up a thousand feet in four giant steps. At the bottom, facing you as you pull over the lip, is a plaque to mark the spot where the poor devil had landed last year. He had fallen on the way back from the

_____
[2]stirrups: short rope ladders.

second ascent of the north tower. Still, we had our own work to do. We started to climb the head-wall.

[16]   It was surprisingly easy, just another rock climb, most of it not more than about Grade IV.[3] And provided you jammed in the cracks instead of pulling on the crumbling face, it was quite safe. Towards the top of the head-wall the climbing was harder for a little; but climbing, doing something, was such a blessed relief from thinking about it, that we were going well and quickly. John Wharton, the young leader of the climb, and I were at the top of the head-wall in a couple of hours.

[17]   The others were still two hundred feet down when there was a shout from below. It was Dick Sykes. He had arrived late in the night, and like me, had got stuck in the desert. Now he was angry, roaring at us from far below because we hadn't waited for him. Urged by his annoyance, he climbed the overhang and the first eight hundred feet of the head-wall on his own and unroped. But he had said his say and tied on to a rope before the real difficulties began.

[18]   Once we got to the top of the head-wall we lost the route. There were two ways on: the ordinary route and the north tower which went up vertically in front of us. The latter had been climbed only twice before and was technically harder than the ordinary route, but also much shorter. As for the ordinary: according to the description we had unearthed, we were supposed to rope down a smooth, vertical hundred-and-twenty-foot wall to a ledge, leaving the rope in position for the return. From the ledge the crux of the climb began: a hundred-and-twenty-foot friction traverse.[4] Wharton had seen some horrifying photographs of it at the American Alpine Club. Mercifully, he had not shown the rest of us. After the traverse, there were only two small overhangs between you and the summit of the south tower. From where we perched we could see plenty of smooth vertical walls, but no ledges at the bottom of them. It took a long time to find the right one. It was far below and strewn with cans, as though too many people had waited there far too long a time. But there was no way of fixing a rope to get down there. The walls were quite smooth, without the smallest crack for a piton.[5] Finally, we found two little holes drilled in the rock, where the bolts, of which the Americans are so fond, had been screwed. But being four Englishmen to one American, it had never occurred to us to bring bolts. Only Wharton, in fact, had ever used them. So there we were. It was the north tower or nothing.

[19]   It was, of course, the north tower. The route goes straight up from the platform at the top of the head-wall in two pitches of VI. It is not strenuous, but very thin and very rotten. It took a great deal of juggling with stirrups and pitons. But Wharton and Sykes led it beautifully between them. There was never any question but that we would get up. Only in the last fifty feet did the rottenness of the rock reach a point of lunacy. You could stick your fingers into the stuff, almost like mud. But the Colorado guide who had first climbed it

---

[3]grade IV: in the classification system for assessing the technical standard of individual rock pitches, grade IV is "severe"; VI is the most difficult grade.

[4]friction traverse: way of moving across a smooth rock face that has no foot or hand holds.

[5]piton: a peg for sticking into a rock face.

must have known a great deal about rock structure; there was a string of pitons going straight up this putty, and they were as solid as the rock should have been. We had to climb from one to the other, ignoring the face itself contemptuously.

[20]   We sat on the summit and took the usual photographs. We opened the little steel canister bolted to the top and added our names to the list; we were the third party to get there. Then, since we knew we wouldn't be spending the night on the mountain after all, we passed our water-bottles round with wanton generosity. But the sun was high and the wind still blew parchingly. We could see trees and the San Juan River glinting twenty miles away in the town of Shiprock. Way to the north the Mesa Verde rose cool and blue. So we didn't stay long on the summit. We began to rope down the rotten vertical face at four p.m. By six-thirty we were back at our camp under the overhang, thirteen hours after we left it.

[21]   And that was that. The climb had been hard and was a brilliant lead by Wharton, who was, incidentally, only eighteen. But it was just a climb. It was not, oddly enough, the climbing that made the ascent of Shiprock so difficult. It was the place itself; the eerie, untouched lunar desert, the almost unbearable thirst and heat, the strange sense of threat in its continual rustling sounds. I understood better now why to the Navajos the mountain is sacred. You are often scared climbing, but scare is local: a move out of balance, a loose hold, too much exposure. You climb better when you are scared. But fear is generalized, like superstition. It clings to a place like its shadow. It is when you have to sit still under the shadow, wait and do nothing, that fear goes over you.

[22]   But it could have been worse. The following day I was in one of the trading posts buying a Navajo rug. The shopkeeper had asked me about the climb. Then, just as I was leaving, he added casually: "Say, how many rattlers did you see?" "Rattlers?" I asked. "Sure, rattlers. Rattlesnakes. The place is full of them." And I thought of that rustling, empty cave where we had slept and the deep cracks in the rocks we had so carefully climbed in. Full of rattlesnakes. But, mercifully, we had never known.

VOCABULARY

Use the context of the essay and your dictionary to define the following words.

1. desolate (par. 3)	6. impassively (par. 11)
2. cosmology (par. 4)	7. scimitar (par. 13)
3. saturnine (par. 5)	8. traverse (par. 18)
4. impertinent (par. 8)	9. glinting (par. 20)
5. demoralized (par. 11)	10. lunar (par. 21)

RHETORIC AND IDEA

1. The narrative can be said to be organized into three parts: paragraphs 1 through 12, 13 through 20, and 21 through 22. What is contributed by each part?

2. Paragraph 3 describes the general area of the climb. What is its chief quality?
3. What is the chief quality of the mountain itself, in paragraph 4?
4. What is contributed to the feeling of the pre-climb period by the details of driving in the night (pars. 7, 8, 9)?
5. What, in paragraph 9, is the relation between his feelings and the quality of the area seen in paragraph 3?
6. What is the point of the contrast made in paragraph 14? What is the difference established here between parts one and two of the narrative?
7. How does paragraph 21 continue the point that was discussed in question 6? What is the difference between being ''scared'' and having ''fear''?
8. What is contributed by the anecdote of the last paragraph? How is it related to the essay's continuing idea about doing and thinking?

WRITING ASSIGNMENTS

1. Tell about some action or course of action you undertook, which in the doing turned out to be different from what you had anticipated. Make the point of the difference clear.
2. Tell of a moment or action of crisis or danger in which you learned something new about yourself or others.
3. Narrate a tale about a situation in which you were frightened, stressing the reasons for the fright, the effect on your actions, the final justification or not of your fears.

Margaret Mead and
Rhoda Metraux

On Friendship

[1]   Few Americans stay put for a lifetime. We move from town to city to suburb, from high school to college in a different state, from a job in one region to a better job elsewhere, from the home where we raise our children to the home where we plan to live in retirement. With each move we are forever making new friends, who become part of our new life at that time.

[2]   For many of us the summer is a special time for forming new friendships. Today millions of Americans vacation abroad, and they go not only to see new sights but also—in those places where they do not feel too strange—with the hope of meeting new people. No one really expects a vacation trip to produce a close friend. But surely the beginning of a friendship is possible? Surely in every country people value friendship?

[3]   They do. The difficulty when strangers from two countries meet is not a lack of appreciation of friendship, but different expectations about what constitutes friendship and how it comes into being. In those European countries that Americans are most likely to visit, friendship is quite sharply distinguished from other, more casual relations, and is differently related to family life. For a Frenchman, a German or an Englishman friendship is usually more particularized and carries a heavier burden of commitment.

[4]   But as we use the word, "friend" can be applied to a wide range of relationships—to someone one has known for a few weeks in a new place, to a close business associate, to a childhood playmate, to a man or woman, to a trusted

confidant. There are real differences among these relations for Americans—a friendship may be superficial, casual, situational or deep and enduring. But to a European, who sees only our surface behavior, the differences are not clear.

[5]   As they see it, people known and accepted temporarily, casually, flow in and out of Americans' homes with little ceremony and often with little personal commitment. They may be parents of the children's friends, house guests of neighbors, members of a committee, business associates from another town or even another country. Coming as a guest into an American home, the European visitor finds no visible landmarks. The atmosphere is relaxed. Most people, old and young, are called by first names.

[6]   Who, then, is a friend?

[7]   Even simple translation from one language to another is difficult. "You see," a Frenchman explains, "if I were to say to you in France, 'This is my good friend,' that person would not be as close to me as someone about whom I said only, 'This is my friend.' Anyone about whom I have to say *more* is really less."

[8]   In France, as in many European countries, friends generally are of the same sex, and friendship is seen as basically a relationship between men. Frenchwomen laugh at the idea that "women can't be friends," but they also admit sometimes that for women "it's a different thing." And many French people doubt the possibilty of a friendship between a man and a woman. There is also the kind of relationship within a group—men and women who have worked together for a long time, who may be very close, sharing great loyalty and warmth of feeling. They may call one another *copains*—a word that in English becomes "friends" but has more the feeling of "pals" or "buddies." In French eyes this is not friendship, although two members of such a group may well be friends.

[9]   For the French, friendship is a one-to-one relationship that demands a keen awareness of the other person's intellect, temperament and particular interests. A friend is someone who draws out your own best qualitites, with whom you sparkle and become more of whatever the friendship draws upon. Your political philosophy assumes more depth, appreciation of a play becomes sharper, taste in food or wine is accentuated, enjoyment of a sport is intensified.

[10]   And French friendships are compartmentalized. A man may play chess with a friend for thirty years without knowing his political opinions, or he may talk politics with him for as long a time without knowing about his personal life. Different friends fill different niches in each person's life. These friendships are not made part of family life. A friend is not expected to spend evenings being nice to children or courteous to a deaf grandmother. These duties, also serious and enjoined, are primarily for relatives. Men who are friends may meet in a cafe. Intellectual friends may meet in larger groups for evenings or conversation. Working people may meet at the little *bistro* where they drink and talk, far from the family. Marriage does not affect such friendships; wives do not have to be taken into account.

[11]   In the past in France, friendships of this kind seldom were open to any but intellectual women. Since most women's lives centered on their homes, their warmest relations with other women often went back to their girlhood. The

special relationship of friendship is based on what the French value most—on the mind, on compatibility of outlook, on vivid awareness of some chosen area of life.

[12] Friendship heightens the sense of each person's individuality. Other relationships commanding as great loyalty and devotion have a different meaning. In World War II the first resistance groups formed in Paris were built on the foundation of *les copains.* But significantly, as time went on these little groups, whose lives rested in one another's hands, called themselves "families." Where each had a total responsibility for all, it was kinship ties that provided the model. And even today such ties, crossing every line of class and personal interest, remain binding on the survivors of these small, secret bands.

[13] In Germany, in contrast with France, friendship is much more articulately a matter of feeling. Adolescents, boys and girls, form deeply sentimental attachments, walk and talk together—not so much to polish their wits as to share their hopes and fears and dreams, to form a common front against the world of school and family and to join in a kind of mutual discovery of each other's and their own inner life. Within the family, the closest relationship over a lifetime is between brothers and sisters. Outside the family, men and women find in their closest friends of the same sex the devotion of a sister, the loyalty of a brother. Appropriately, in Germany friends usually are brought into the family. Children call their father's and their mother's friends "uncle" and "aunt". Between French friends who have chosen each other for the congeniality of their point of view, lively disagreement and sharpness of argument are the breath of life. But for Germans, whose friendships are based on mutuality of feeling, deep disagreement on any subject that matters to both is regarded as a tragedy. Like ties of kinship, ties of friendship are meant to be irrevocably binding. Young Germans who come to the United States have great difficulty in establishing such friendships with Americans. We view friendship more tentatively, subject to changes in intensity as people move, change their jobs, marry, or discover new interests.

[14] English friendships follow still a different pattern. Their basis is shared activity. Activities at different stages of life may be of very different kinds—discovering a common interest in school, serving together in the armed forces, taking part in a foreign mission, staying in the same country house during a crisis. In the midst of the activity, whatever it may be, people fall into step—sometimes two men or two women, sometimes two couples, sometimes three people—and find that they walk or play a game or tell stories or serve on a tiresome and exacting committee with the same easy anticipation of what each will do day by day or in some critical situation. Americans who have made English friends comment that, even years later, "you can take up just where you left off." Meeting after a long interval, friends are like a couple who begin to dance again when the orchestra strikes up after a pause. English friendships are formed outside the family circle, but they are not, as in Germany, contrapuntal to the family nor are they, as in France, separated from the family. And a break in an English friendship comes not necessarily as a result of some irreconcilable difference of viewpoint or feeling but instead as a result of misjudgment, where one friend seriously misjudges how the other will think or feel or act, so that suddenly they are out of step.

[15]   What, then, is friendship? Looking at these different styles, including our own, each of which is related to a whole way of life, are there common elements? There is the recognition that friendship, in contrast with kinship, invokes freedom of choice. A friend is someone who chooses and is chosen. Related to this is the sense each friend gives the other of being a special individual, on whatever grounds this recognition is based. And between friends there is inevitably a kind of equality of give-and-take. These similarities make the bridge between societies possible, and the American's characteristic openness to different styles of relationship makes it possible for him to find new friends abroad with whom he feels at home.

VOCABULARY

Use the context of the essay and your dictionary to define the words listed below.

1. commitment (par. 3)   6. compatibility (par. 11)
2. confidant (par. 4)   7. sentimental (par. 13)
3. superficial (par. 4)   8. congeniality (par. 13)
4. situational (par. 4)   9. tentatively (par. 13)
5. enjoined (par. 10)   10. contrapuntal (par. 14)

RHETORIC AND IDEA

1. At least one of the purposes of the Mead and Metraux essay is to define the word *friendship,* to say what a friend is. At what point in the essay are you sure that is their purpose? At what point in the essay do they define *friendship?* What key sentence tells you they are ready to give you a solid definition?
2. Which paragraphs of the essay make up the introduction? Which the body? Which the conclusion?
3. In the staircase diagram below, write the thesis statement and the topic sentences for the three supporting major points. Which paragraphs make up the first major supporting point? Which the second? Which the third?

thesis statement

topic sentence

topic sentence

topic sentence

4. To develop their ideas, Mead and Metraux use comparison and contrast. Which type of structure do they prefer: *ABABAB* or *AAABBB?* Explain.
5. Frequently writers establish coherence between paragraphs by supplying strong links in last and first sentences. Consider, for instance, the links established by Mead and Metraux in the last sentence of paragraph 1 and the first sentence of paragraph 2.

With each move we are forever making new friends, who become part of our life at that time.
For many of us the summer is a special time for forming new friendships.

Find at least five more examples of paragraphs linked through these key sentences and explain how the linking is accomplished.

6. Point out the continuity devices (pp. 145–49) Mead and Metraux use in paragraph 10 to strengthen the coherence of the paragraph.

7. The first sentence of the first paragraph needs support quickly. It gets that support in the second sentence. What rhetorical device do Mead and Metraux use to provide both the evidence and the economy necessary? Explain. Find in the essay at least one other example of the same device.

WRITING ASSIGNMENTS

1. The last sentence of paragraph 9 is a parallel list of four qualities a friend in France draws out of a friend: "Your political philosophy assumes more depth, appreciation of a play becomes sharper, taste in food and wine is accentuated, enjoyment of a sport is intensified." Considering what *you* think a friend draws out in a friend, rewrite the last sentence using the same parallel pattern but supplying your own evidence.

2. In a paragraph or more to be added as paragraphs 15, 16, etc. of the essay "On Friendship," explain American friendship, pointing out its differences and/or similarities in French, German, and English friendship.

3. Write an essay in which you define *friendship* by telling what *friendship* or *friend* means to you and then using examples to illustrate what, to you, people must do to be friends or to show friendship. Take your examples from common knowledge, personal experience, and/or research experience.

4. Write an essay on one of the following topics:

Friendship Demands Sacrifice

Why Friendships Fail

Are Friends Really Necessary?

The Disadvantages of Friendships

(Must, Can, Should) Husbands and Wives Be Friends?

The Differences Between Friends and Acquaintances

George Orwell

Marrakech

[1]   As the corpse went past the flies left the restaurant table in a cloud and rushed after it, but they came back a few minutes later.

[2]   The little crowd of mourners—all men and boys, no women—threaded their way across the market-place between the piles of pomegranates and the taxis and the camels, wailing a short chant over and over again. What really appeals to the flies is that the corpses here are never put into coffins, they are merely wrapped in a piece of rag and carried on a rough wooden bier on the shoulders of four friends. When the friends get to the burying-ground they hack an oblong hole a foot or two deep, dump the body in it and fling over it a little of the dried-up, lumpy earth, which is like broken brick. No gravestone, no name, no identifying mark of any kind. The burying-ground is merely a huge waste of hummocky earth, like a derelict building-lot. After a month or two no one can even be certain where his own relatives are buried.

[3]   When you walk through a town like this—two hundred thousand inhabitants, of whom at least twenty thousand own literally nothing except the rags they stand up in—when you see how the people live, and still more how easily they die, it is always difficult to believe that you are walking among human beings. All colonial empires are in reality founded upon that fact. The people have brown faces—besides, there are so many of them! Are they really the same flesh as yourself? Do they even have names? Or are they merely a

kind of undifferentiated brown stuff, about as individual as bees or coral insects? They rise out of the earth, they sweat and starve for a few years, and then they sink back into the nameless mounds of the graveyard and nobody notices that they are gone. And even the graves themselves soon fade back into the soil. Sometimes, out for a walk, as you break your way through the prickly pear, you notice that it is rather bumpy underfoot, and only a certain regularity in the bumps tells you that you are walking over skeletons.

[4]   I was feeding one of the gazelles in the public gardens.

[5]   Gazelles are almost the only animals that look good to eat when they are still alive, in fact, one can hardly look at their hindquarters without thinking of mint sauce. The gazelle I was feeding seemed to know that this thought was in my mind, for though it took the piece of bread I was holding out it obviously did not like me. It nibbled rapidly at the bread, then lowered its head and tried to butt me, then took another nibble and then butted again. Probably its idea was that if it could drive me away the bread would somehow remain hanging in mid-air.

[6]   An Arab navvy working on the path nearby lowered his heavy hoe and sidled slowly towards us. He looked from the gazelle to the bread and from the bread to the gazelle, with a sort of quiet amazement, as though he had never seen anything quite like this before. Finally he said shyly in French:

[7]   "*I* could eat some of that bread."

[8]   I tore off a piece and he stowed it gratefully in some secret place under his rags. This man is an employee of the Municipality.

[9]   When you go through the Jewish quarters you gather some idea of what the medieval ghettoes were probably like. Under their Moorish rulers the Jews were only allowed to own land in certain restricted areas, and after centuries of this kind of treatment they have ceased to bother about overcrowding. Many of the streets are a good deal less than six feet wide, the houses are completely windowless, and sore-eyed children cluster everywhere in unbelievable numbers, like clouds of flies. Down the centre of the street there is generally running a little river of urine.

[10]   In the bazaar huge families of Jews, all dressed in the long black robe and little black skull-cap, are working in dark fly-infested booths that look like caves. A carpenter sits crosslegged at a prehistoric lathe, turning chair-legs at lightning speed. He works the lathe with a bow in his right hand and guides the chisel with his left foot, and thanks to a lifetime of sitting in this position his left leg is warped out of shape. At his side his grandson, aged six, is already starting on the simpler parts of the job.

[11]   I was just passing the coppersmiths' booths when somebody noticed that I was lighting a cigarette. Instantly, from the dark holes all round, there was a frenzied rush of Jews, many of them old grandfathers with flowing grey beards, all clamouring for a cigarette. Even a blind man somewhere at the back of one of the booths heard a rumour of cigarettes and came crawling out, groping in the air with his hand. In about a minute I had used up the whole packet. None of these people, I suppose, works less than twelve hours a day and every one of them looks on a cigarette as a more or less impossible luxury.

[12]   As the Jews live in self-contained communities they follow the same trades as the Arabs, except for agriculture. Fruit-sellers, potters, silversmiths,

blacksmiths, butchers, leatherworkers, tailors, water-carriers, beggars, porters—whichever way you look you see nothing but Jews. As a matter of fact there are thirteen thousand of them, all living in the space of a few acres. A good job Hitler wasn't here. Perhaps he was on his way, however. You hear the usual dark rumours about the Jews, not only from the Arabs but from the poorer Europeans.

[13]   "Yes, mon vieux, they took my job away from me and gave it to a Jew. The Jews! They're the real rulers of this country, you know. They've got all the money. They control the banks, finance—everything."

[14]   "But," I said, "isn't it a fact that the average Jew is a labourer working for about a penny an hour?"

[15]   "Ah, that's only for show! They're all moneylenders really. They're cunning, the Jews."

[16]   In just the same way, a couple of hundred years ago, poor old women used to be burned for witchcraft when they could not even work enough magic to get themselves a square meal.

[17]   All people who work with their hands are partly invisible, and the more important the work they do, the less visible they are. Still, a white skin is always fairly conspicuous. In northern Europe, when you see a labourer ploughing a field, you probably give him a second glance. In a hot country, anywhere south of Gilbraltar or east of Suez, the chances are that you don't even see him. I have noticed this again and again. In a tropical landscape one's eye takes in everything except the human beings. It takes in the dried-up soil, the prickly pear, the palm tree and the distant mountain, but it always misses the peasant hoeing at his patch. He is the same colour as the earth, and a great deal less interesting to look at.

[18]   It is only because of this that the starved countries of Asia and Africa are accepted as tourist resorts. No one would think of running cheap trips to the Distressed Areas. But where the human beings have brown skins their poverty is simply not noticed. What does Morocco mean to a Frenchman? An orange-grove or a job in Government service. Or to an Englishman? Camels, castles, palm trees, Foreign Legionnaires, brass trays, and bandits. One could probably live there for years without noticing that for nine-tenths of the people the reality of life is an endless, back-breaking struggle to wring a little food out of an eroded soil.

[19]   Most of Morocco is so desolate that no wild animal bigger than a hare can live on it. Huge areas which were once covered with forest have turned into a treeless waste where the soil is exactly like broken-up brick. Nevertheless a good deal of it is cultivated, with frightful labour. Everything is done by hand. Long lines of women, bent double like inverted capital L's, work their way slowly across the fields, tearing up the prickly weeds with their hands, and the peasant gathering lucerne for fodder pulls it up stalk by stalk instead of reaping it, thus saving an inch or two on each stalk. The plough is a wretched wooden thing, so frail that one can easily carry it on one's shoulder, and fitted underneath with a rough iron spike which stirs the soil to a depth of about four inches. This is as much as the strength of the animals is equal to. It is usual to plough with a cow and a donkey yoked together. Two donkeys would not be quite strong enough, but on the other hand two cows would cost a little more

to feed. The peasants possess no harrows, they merely plough the soil several times over in different directions, finally leaving it in rough furrows, after which the whole field has to be shaped with hoes into small oblong patches to conserve water. Except for a day or two after the rare rainstorms there is never enough water. Along the edges of the fields channels are hacked out to a depth of thirty or forty feet to get at the tiny trickles which run through the subsoil.

[20]   Every afternoon a file of very old women passes down the road outside my house, each carrying a load of firewood. All of them are mummified with age and the sun, and all of them are tiny. It seems to be generally the case in primitive communities that the women, when they get beyond a certain age, shrink to the size of children. One day a poor old creature who could not have been more than four feet tall crept past me under a vast load of wood. I stopped her and put a five-sou piece (a little more than a farthing) into her hand. She answered with a shrill wail, almost a scream, which was partly gratitude but mainly surprise. I suppose that from her point of view, by taking any notice of her, I seemed almost to be violating a law of nature. She accepted her status as an old woman, that is to say as a beast of burden. When a family is travelling it is quite usual to see a father and a grown-up son riding ahead on donkeys, and an old woman following on foot, carrying the baggage.

[21]   But what is strange about these people is their invisibility. For several weeks, always at about the same time of day, the file of old woman had hobbled past the house with their firewood, and though they had registered themselves on my eyeballs I cannot truly say that I had seen them. Firewood was passing—that was how I saw it. It was only that one day I happened to be walking behind them, and the curious up-and-down motion of a load of wood drew my attention to the human being beneath it. Then for the first time I noticed the poor old earth-coloured bodies, bodies reduced to bones and leathery skin, bent double under the crushing weight. Yet I suppose I had not been five minutes on Moroccan soil before I noticed the overloading of the donkeys and was infuriated by it. There is no question that the donkeys are damnably treated. The Moroccan donkey is hardly bigger than a St. Bernard dog, it carries a load which in the British Army would be considered too much for a fifteen-hands mule, and very often its pack-saddle is not taken off its back for weeks together. But what is peculiarly pitiful is that it is the most willing creature on earth, it follows its master like a dog and does not need either bridle or halter. After a dozen years of devoted work it suddenly drops dead, whereupon its master tips it into the ditch and the village dogs have torn its guts out before it is cold.

[22]   This kind of thing makes one's blood boil, whereas—on the whole—the plight of the human beings does not. I am not commenting, merely pointing to a fact. People with brown skins are next door to invisible. Anyone can be sorry for the donkey with its galled back, but it is generally owing to some kind of accident if one even notices the old woman under her load of sticks.

[23]   As the storks flew northward the Negroes were marching southward—a long, dusty column, infantry, screw-gun batteries, and then more infantry, four or five thousand men in all, winding up the road with a clumping of boots and a clatter of iron wheels.

[24]   They were Senegalese, the blackest Negroes in Africa, so black that sometimes it is difficult to see whereabouts on their necks the hair begins. Their splendid bodies were hidden in reach-me-down khaki uniforms, their feet squashed into boots that looked like blocks of wood, and every tin hat seemed to be a couple of sizes too small. It was very hot and the men had marched a long way. They slumped under the weight of their packs and the curiously sensitive black faces were glistening with sweat.

[25]   As they went past a tall, very young Negro turned and caught my eye. But the look he gave me was not in the least the kind of look you might expect. Not hostile, not contemptuous, not sullen, not even inquisitive. It was the shy, wide-eyed Negro look, which actually is a look of profound respect. I saw how it was. This wretched boy, who is a French citizen and has therefore been dragged from the forest to scrub floors and catch syphilis in garrison towns, actually has feelings of reverence before a white skin. He has been taught that the white race are his masters, and he still believes it.

[26]   But there is one thought which every white man (and in this connection it doesn't matter twopence if he calls himself a socialist) thinks when he sees a black army marching past. "How much longer can we go on kidding these people? How long before they turn their guns in the other direction?"

[27]   It was curious, really. Every white man there had this thought stowed somewhere or other in his mind. I had it, so had the other onlookers, so had the officers on their sweating chargers and the white N.C.O.'s marching in the ranks. It was a kind of secret which we all knew and were too clever to tell; only the Negroes didn't know it. And really it was like watching a flock of cattle to see the long column, a mile or two miles of armed men, flowing peacefully up the road, while the great white birds drifted over them in the opposite direction, glittering like scraps of paper.

VOCABULARY

Use the context of the essay and your dictionary to define the words listed below.

1. derelict (par. 2)
2. warped (par. 10)
3. wring (par. 18)
4. desolate (par. 19)
5. waste (par. 19)

6. wretched (par. 19)
7. yoked (par. 19)
8. mummified (par. 20)
9. plight (par. 22)
10. galled (par. 22)

RHETORIC AND IDEA

1. Orwell wrote "Marrakech" in 1939. In its conclusion, he makes a prediction. What is that prediction? How sound a prediction was it in 1939? Has the prediction come true in the late seventies and early eighties?

2. Where in the introduction does Orwell make clear the central point of his essay? In which paragraphs later in the essay does he return to the idea and restate it emphatically?

3. "Marrakech" is organized into five distinct parts: paragraphs 1 through 3, 4 through 8, 9 through 16, 17 through 22, and 23 through 27. What is the purpose of each of these parts? Explain.

4. Why does Orwell make his opening sentence a complete paragraph?

5. Orwell depends on organic coherence rather than on supplying the more conventional rhetorical hooking devices used by most of the essayists in this collection. As a result, the readers are a bit surprised as they move from paragraphs 3 to 4, 8 to 9, 16 to 17, and 22 to 23. What holds these parts together? Do you think this style is effective or ineffective? Why?

6. The sentences in "Marrakech" tend to be short, at times even choppy. Is this sentence structure effective? Why or why not? Be as specific as possible.

7. The first sentence of paragraph 3 is a periodic sentence (p. 162). What makes it a periodic sentence? Find at least one other periodic sentence in "Marrakech."

8. Muscular verbs give Orwell's "Marrakech" a vigorous quality. Take this sentence, for instance (verbs italicized):

> When the friends get to the burying-ground they
> *hack* an oblong hole a foot or two deep,
> *dump* the body in it
>   and
> *fling* over it a little of the dried-up, lumpy earth ...

Find as many sentences as you can in which Orwell uses such verbs.

9. In the first sentence of "Marrakech," Orwell says, "... the flies left the restaurant table *in a cloud.*" To make his writing vivid, he uses a metaphor (p 222). In the second paragraph he says, "The burying-ground is ... *like a derelict building-lot.*" He uses a simile (p. 222). Read the essay carefully and make a list of as many metaphors and similes as you can find. How do these "figures of speech" affect the reader?

10. Paragraphs 9 through 16 end on an ironic note. What is that irony? How does it relate to Orwell's overall thesis?

WRITING ASSIGNMENTS

1. Paragraphs 4 through 8 make up a short narrative that develops a clear point—that brown people and their hunger are invisible to the colonialist. Although the idea is clear, Orwell does not state it in this short unit. In a short narrative of your own make a clear point about human unawareness of suffering. Do not make it up; recall an experience you actually had.

2. Write an essay on one of the following topics:
   Do You Have to Be Brown to Be Invisible?
   Invisible People Are Starting to Become Visible
   Some People Are Still Invisible
   Invisible No More
   Athletics: A Key To Visibility

Aristides

Boutique America!

[1]   Now that the dust has settled, the counter-culture's chief contribution to American life becomes clear. The most important influence of that assemblage of 1960s youth and its camp followers was not on politics, or philosophy, or art, or social organization, but on retailing. Yes, retailing. The counter-culture came of age simultaneously with the consumer society, and what could be more fitting than that its participants should turn out to be shopkeepers—that the prefix "counter" should actually come to refer to the counter over which business is done? Fitting, too, that the generation whose chief literary work (a National Book Award winner) has been *The Whole Earth Catalog* should end up living not so much off the land as behind the cash register. The vaunted greening of America, it turns out, has come to little more than the cropping up of plant shops around the country. Candle shops, leather-goods shops, organic food shops, macramé shops, needlepoint shops, handcrafted jewelry and dress shops have brought the commune into the home, or, more precisely, the neighborhood. If one lives anywhere in any of the middle- to upper-middle-class neighborhoods in this country nowadays, one lives in Boutique America.

[2]   To live in Boutique America is to live in a state of permanent transitoriness, a tourist in one's own neighborhood. "Tourism," remarked Lincoln Steffens, "is a moral rest." Yet there is little restfulness about Boutique America. Quite the reverse. A feeling of jumpiness pervades, a sense that the shops that are here today will be gone tomorrow. Shops are the landscape of urban life, the

Reprinted from *The American Scholar,* Volume 44, Number 4, Autumn, 1975. Copyright ©1975 by the United Chapters of Phi Beta Kappa. By permission of the publishers.

trees and shrubs and flowers of city living. But a blight is now on the land: the blight of uniformity. Some judge the interest of a city by the number of blocks of entertaining window-shopping it provides. It is not a foolish measure. Today, walking the shopping districts of many American cities, one experiences a feeling of dislocation not unlike that of waking up in any Holiday Inn or Howard Johnson's Motor Lodge. Where am I—in Georgetown, Westport, Greenwich Village, or Ghirardelli Square? Essentially it doesn't matter. You are in Boutique America.

[3]   Boutique America is the new urban renewal. Old Town in Chicago, once a rather shabby working-class neighborhood, was taken up, and eventually over, by the young and the rising middle class during the early 1960s. Old houses were refurbished, new stores moved in, the place became something of a tourist attraction. On weekends, thousands padded up and down its sidewalks, glancing into the windows of head shops, of bars where first folk-singing, and later rock, was featured, of record and clothing and candle and poster shops. A new neighborhood came into bloom, but it was not to be a hardy perennial. Before the 1960s were out, Old Town, or at least its main drag, had become an adolescent Skid Row, populated by scrawny kids with dirty hair and drug-empty eyes and young blacks made belligerent by bad doctrine. Like an island reclaimed by the sea, the neighborhood slowly sank into its former shabbiness. In Chicago, meanwhile, the action moved farther north—more refurbishing, more new shops of the same kind—to a neighborhood rechristened New Town. New Town flourishes at the moment, but it is difficult not to believe that a Newer Town isn't in the offing.

[4]   Ironies aplenty are involved. Chief among them is that Boutique America set out to counter the creep of uniformity in American life. If Boutique America could be said to have an adversary, then that adversary was Franchise America: that horde of locusts represented by such franchised purveyors of goods and services as McDonald's, Howard Johnson's, Korvette's, Shakey's, and other national fast-food, discount, supermarket, and motel operations that have done so much in recent years to chew up the country- and city-side. Next to franchise bigness, the boutiques offered goods and services on a smaller human scale; next to cold impersonality, the warm personal touch; next to the mass-produced, the handcrafted; next to grossness and crassness, subtlety and delicacy. An anticorporate, an antitechnological, an anti-bureaucratic impulse appears to be behind the boutique idea. These little shops so clearly travel under the banner of art, of individuality, of the good life itself. Might William Morris have applauded? Or might he have gagged? More likely, confronted with the works of Franchise America and Boutique America, he would have announced a plague on both their condominiums.

[5]   Much of the art of the shops of Boutique America seems to have gone into their titles. Never before has such furious energy gone into the titlist's job. Where once might have stood the Howard Street Secondhand Clothing Store, the Nor-Shel Delicatessen (owned, of course, by Norman and Sheldon), or Slotkowski's Restaurant, now instead stands the Rag-Time Boutique, The Moveable Feast, and That Little Bohemian Restaurant. ("That" titles are very big in Boutique America—"That Paper Place," "That Plant Shop," "That Britches Joint" are but a few examples.) Heads and Tails is a boutique

in my own neighborhood that sells cosmetics and women's underwear (à la Frederick's of Hollywood). For simple irrelevance of title to goods sold, there is the Copper Carrot, which sells kitchen products. But perhaps the best all-round title—best at pointing up the absurdity of the artistic impulse put to the service of retailing—is a small men's shop that carries the title Ciao Rudy by Eugene Rondheim. A shop with a byline, as if it were not a shop at all but a short story! Can boutiques with lengthy epigraphs upon their windows, dedications on their doors, be far behind?

[6]   Vulgarity, like bad news, travels fast. E. M. Forster, in his biography of Goldsworthy Lowes Dickinson, remarks that "He wanted a democracy where every one will be an aristocrat." In contemporary America, where nearly everyone appears to be—in the preposition of our day—"into" art, are we about to achieve a democracy where everyone will be an artist? To pursue this matter of titling, why should retailers enjoy a monopoly? What of the professions? Can we look forward to dental offices entitled Put Your Money Where Your Mouth Is, law offices entitled That Litigious Place, churches entitled Pascal's Best Bet, funeral homes entitled Oblivion Unlimited? Ours has always been a country of the widest possibilities.

[7]   Whenever Igor Stravinsky, in his later years, was apprised of some new development in modern art—multimedia, perhaps, or pop art—he would ask, "Who needs it?" It is a good question, and a pertinent one to ask about various of our new boutiques. Who needs all these new plant, candle, leather-goods, needlepoint shops? Hard to say. Certainly many of them, judging by the narrowness of their specialties—shops that sell kites, say, or soap, or wooden toys, or coffee beans—seem to defy the law of supply and demand. They are a refinement on our consumer society, the larger part of which spends a great deal more time in consuming products than in producing them. The refinement is that these boutiques seem designed at least as much for their owners as for their customers. They have upon them the imprimatur of the "creative"—they smack of the inventive, they smell of the adorable, they stink of the cute. Who needs them?

[8]   If anyone senses that this column is written out of personal grievance, his instincts are near perfect. My own neighborhood is, alas, currently under-going boutiquification. Such a nice dull neighborhood it is, too. Or rather *was,* till one day large signs were posted on neighborhood shop windows announc-ing, Paul Revere-like, "The Main Is Coming," "The Main Is Coming." The Main turns out to be a Boutique America shopping center on Main Street. I shall provide a tour of it presently, but first I shall attempt to get at what I so like about my neighborhood and what about it seems to me so worth saving.

[9]   What, really, is wanted from a neighborhood? Convenience, certainly; an absence of major aggravation, to be sure. But perhaps most of all, ideally, what is wanted is a comfortable background, a breathing space of intermission between the intensities of private life and the calculations of public life. In the neighborhood, relationships need not become entangled, behavior need not be triggered by motive. In the neighborhood—between the drama of the household and the battlefield of the career—the casual reigns, the quotidian dominates. In the neighborhood, life mercifully flows on.

[10]   Like the tides of the moon, the neighborhood in which I live has its own regular rhythms. In the early morning hours, there are the nattering of squirrels, the twittering of birds, the creaking of the newspaper delivery man's steel-wheeled cart. Things pick up around eight o'clock, as people set off for work. Showered and shined, ready for drama or dullness as the case may be, they step off to offices and shops. Yellow buses pull up to take children to day-care centers or nursery school, and in the summer to day camp. The majority of the kids go off to grade school three blocks away, or to the junior high school six blocks away, or to the high school a few miles distant. The neighborhood settles down. A young mother walks by with her infant in a pram. A truck from United Parcel stops for a delivery. A cat pads across a lawn. An elderly woman, a cane in one hand, a shopping bag in the other, trudges by. Near eleven, the postman is on the block. After three, school out, children take over the block: a boy bangs a tennis ball against a garage wall, two younger children chase a dog, bikes are everywhere. Around five-thirty, adults begin to return from downtown, some having stopped along the way for groceries or for cleaning. Dampened and rumpled after the day downtown and the subway ride home, they have roughly fourteen hours to give over to dinner, television, reading, lovemaking, and sleep, before starting out again. With the dark, a new quiet sets in. Teen-agers gather at the park or down at the lake; they leave behind them a clinging odor of pot or a few empty beer cans. The streets empty out, and only an occasional dog-walker appears after ten. Safe though the neighborhood generally is, this is still 1975, and even here paranoia is the better part of valor. The next day the same rhythm will begin again.

[11]   Weekends the rhythm changes. Saturday morning the street jumps with people on errands: much toting of laundry, drycleaning, groceries. A more fervid energy is given over to the serious business of play. Couples glide by on bicycles. Tennis rackets are unscrewed from presses, unsheathed from covers. Camping equipment is loaded into trunks or onto car carriers. (In winter, skis replace camping equipment.) A slower, more dispersed traffic is on the street Sundays: people lug home their three or four pounds of *New York Times* or *Chicago Tribune*. In warm weather three couples living in an apartment building north of mine used to bring their breakfasts out to their building's small front lawn—in training for the more spacious life of the suburbs to which they have doubtless repaired by now.

[12]   A more than adequate supply of characters are about. A Negro cowboy roams these streets: a man who looks to be late into his sixties, he strolls about in sheepskin coat, a ten-gallon hat broken in at the brim, curly white sideburns, a bandana round his neck. An elderly woman, pale and frail, walks about wrapped up in an overly large blue raincoat, black men's socks covering her thin legs, a babushka over her head tucked in snugly under the chin. Sitting on the small bench outside the neighborhood news kiosk is a man of glistening ebony color, with a slender head upon which are deployed features of an extraordinary delicacy and elegance. So handsome, so photogenic, so much the grist for a certain kind of art photography does he seem that more than once I have watched a stranger with a camera ask permission to photograph him. He invariably complies, smiling exuberantly, revealing several missing teeth. A woman a few buildings down my block feeds squirrels

by hand at her high first-floor window. Five or six squirrels scale the wall to reach her ledge, and the tableau there presented makes it all too easy to imagine them taking over her apartment. A man in a beret, scraggly gray beard, and matching long hair lives around the corner; he wears all black in the winter, all white in the summer, and does I know not what for a living. Central casting is to be congratulated for supplying these characters.

[13]   "Nice day, Mr. Steadman."

[14]   "Not if you've bet on the Cardinals it isn't, Mr. Aristides."

[15]   He is a neighborhood shopkeeper, runs a cleaning establishment, a solitary man with a solitary vice: gambling on ball games. Unmarried, of middle age, neither an addict nor a fanatic, he is a man who, quite simply, enjoys his gambling. Across the street from Steadman's is the shop of Mr. William Richardson, shoe repair. (Will there be men in future generations who will do such jobs, or will shoes be made to be thrown out when the heels wear down or a hole is worn in the sole?) Mr. Richardson is a Negro, a man of perfect diction and high dignity. Adorning the wall of his shop is a commendatory plaque citing his efforts in behalf of the NAACP. Up the street is Wulf's, a Certified Grocery Store, now in its second generation of ownership. Mr. Wulf, Jr., in his middle forties, is quiet, competent, and roughly six feet six. He once played basketball for Michigan State: one imagines him not much of a scorer but very strong off the boards. Next door to Wulf's, at the corner, is Leo's Pharmacy. Leo's specialities are cameras, which sell pretty well, and flattery of his female customers, which doesn't always sell. "A beautiful day, now that you're here," he will say to one of them. Or "Where is that beautiful smile this morning?" A block away, on Main Street, used to be Joe's Laundromat. A furiously hard worker and an unshakably cheerful man, Joe carries a tattooed number on his forearm, memento of years in a Nazi concentration camp. When Boutique America came into the neighborhood, rents went up all round, and Joe chose to move. Into his place has since been inserted Sawdust, Inc., a shop that sells wooden toys and offers classes in woodcarving.

[16]   I do not want any wooden toys, I do not want any lessons in woodcarving, though I did like to have my laundry done at a reasonable price. Nor do I want to attend classes in "mixed media on canvas," which I note are to be offered up the street at The Tapestree, Inc. Nor, again, do I want classes in macramé, which will be held at the Chicago Bead Company, soon to open at The Main, the Boutique America shopping center (they, of course, would not use the word shopping center but prefer "mall").

[17]   As it turns out, The Main is actually the second Boutique America shopping center in the neighborhood, both of which have been developed by the same man. (A boutique developer? Who says there is no longer any place for the enterprising in America!) That the two are only a block away from each other and may cause some problems of mercantile redundancy seems not to bother any one. The first has seven stall-like shops on two floors, with a restaurant above. "Description is revelation," Wallace Stevens says, so allow me merely to give the titles of these shops: Creative Yarns, Mostly Handmade, Sunny Side Up (which turns out to stock items also "mostly handmade"), The Mixed Bag, The Print Mint, All That Good Green Stuff, and Artesanias. The stores surrounding it on the same block are: Off the Hoof

(leather goods), Stonerope (ceramics, macramé, stoneware, et cetera), The Smithern (custom carpentry, handcrafted jewelry), The Tapestree, Inc. (needlework, latchwork, Rya rug supplies), Mark Levin Woodworks (custom furniture, interiors, and woodenware), and Ye Rams (women's clothing).

[18]   The Main, a block away, very nearly duplicates these various (ah) services, with a few of what the mail order business calls ''add-ons.'' It contains Circe (classical allusions do not care who use them), a women's dress shop also selling handcrafted jewelry; the Green Grocer, another plant shop; Wood 'N' Things, more wooden toys; The Brown Bean, coffee, tea, herbs, and spices; Slipped Disc, records at no discount; My Favorite Soap Opera, soap, stuffed animals, and other debris; House of Teak, second-rate Scandinavian furniture; Neville Sargent Gallery, original paintings, prints, sculpture, and jewelry; Amazingrace, a coffeehouse and folk-singing and rock emporium; and—a brief bow in the direction of utility—The Main Currency Exchange. Still to come are Windy City Kite Works, kites and accessories; The Main Stitchery, one gathers more needlepoint, et cetera; The Chicago Bead Company, mentioned above; and Revenir, a pastry cafe where continental coffee is to be sold. A short way down the block is It's Natural, which carries organic food and such; and down the block in the other direction still another leather shop and I.D., The Idea Store, furniture and knickknackery. In short, the works; as Zorba the Greek might say, the full catastrophe.

[19]   But what is the point of all this ranting? One might argue, simply, that it all comes down to a matter of ''life style.'' Boutique America is the going life style, and it is too bad if it does not happen to be my life style. To which I would rejoin: What if one isn't interested in life style, but just in life, in the flow and weave of it and in its need for order and tranquility? Does Boutique America promise a better life, a new and more intelligent order of things? One wonders. The Main, interestingly enough, for all its ecological look, is currently undergoing zoning difficulties. Its developer, it seems, has failed to provide sufficient parking spaces, and some people in the neighborhood have lodged complaints. Interestingly, too, it has been brought out that the developer, an architect, is part of a development group. Another member of this group turns out to be president of the insurance company for which one of the sons of the mayor of the City of Chicago works. Much talk is in the air about underassessed property taxes and deals of different kinds. It may be Boutique America, but it still sounds pretty much like business as usual.

[20]   Yet it is not quite business as usual. It figures to be jumpier. How long can, say, The Brown Bean last? Will the Windy City Kite Works weather the winter? How much handcrafted jewelry, wooden toys, plants, and needlepoint are needed? One looks for many failures and much turnover of owners—a state, in effect, of permanent transience. In the credits for the movies of the thirties and forties, a man used to be listed as responsible for ''continuity.'' We could use the services of such a man in our lives. In daily life it is precisely continuity that seems in short supply, the sense that things fit together and flow smoothly. Boutique America does not promise to provide it; quite the reverse.

[21]   There is an old story about a man who goes back to his old neighborhood after an absence of thirty-one years. He had left when drafted into the army in World War II, and afterward had settled on the West Coast. Predictably, upon

returning to his neighborhood, he finds everything changed. Where once a family-owned grocery store stood, there now stands a supermarket. Where once a small Greek restaurant stood, now stands a McDonald's. Where once stood Kogan Bros., Jewelers, now stands a Just Pants. But he does note one remnant from the old days, Koussitsky's Shoe Repair, and as he walks by the shop it flashes upon him that thirty-one years ago he left a pair of shoes with Koussitsky and never bothered to pick them up. Could they still be there? Why not, for the hell of it, find out?

[22]   Koussitsky still runs the shop. A bent old man thirty-one years ago, he is even more bent now. Our man says: "Excuse me, Mr. Koussitsky. I don't expect you to remember me, but I used to live in this neighborhood, and thirty-one years ago I left a pair of shoes with you for repair that I never picked up. I'm almost embarrassed to ask, but I wonder, do you still by any chance have them?"

[23]   Koussitsky looks up at him, squints, then says, "Tell me, vas dey black shoes?"

[24]   "Amazing," the man says, "I hadn't even thought about it till you mentioned it, but they were black."

[25]   "Tell me," says Koussitsky, "vere dey ving-tips?"

[26]   "Astonishing," the man says, "they were wing-tips indeed."

[27]   "If I'm not mistaken" says Koussitsky, "you vanted a half sole mid a rubber heel?"

[28]   "That is exactly what I wanted."

[29]   "And von ting more," says Koussitsky. "I believe you vanted taps on the toes. Is zat right?"

[30]   "Right on the button," says the man. "This is wonderful. Do you still have the shoes?"

[31]   Koussitsky looks up at him, squinting, and says, "Dey'll be ready Vendsday."

[32]   Sad to think that before too much longer in America that joke will be utterly incomprehensible.

VOCABULARY

Use the context of the essay and your dictionary to define the words listed below.

1. counter-culture (par. 1)
2. transitoriness (par. 2)
3. blight (par. 2)
4. refurbished (par. 3)
5. purveyors (par. 4)

6. crassness (par. 4)
7. epigraphs (par. 5)
8. vulgarity (par. 6)
9. imprimatur (par. 7)
10. quotidian (par. 9)

RHETORIC AND IDEA

1. .What does Aristides mean by "Boutique America" and by "Franchise America"? Define the two terms. Tell how they are different. Tell how they are alike.

2. Is "Boutique America!" description, narration, exposition, or argument? Explain.

3. Read paragraphs 5 and 10 carefully. Write the topic sentence of each paragraph on the top step of a staircase and arrange the evidence under the topic sentence in logical staircase form. Explain your arrangement to the class, making clear where you have evidence/idea steps.

4. Aristides uses parallel structure frequently. Consider, for example, this sentence from paragraph 1: "Candle shops, leather-goods shops, organic food shops, macramé shops, needlepoint shops, handcrafted jewelry and dress shops have brought the commune into the home ..." The parallel list emphasizes what the writer means by "cropping up." Find an example of parallelism in each of these paragraphs and explain what makes it effective: 2, 4, 7, 10, 11, 18, and 21.

5. What is Aristides' tone in paragraph 6? Is he humorous, angry, happy, sarcastic, what? Contrast the tone of paragraph 6 and paragraphs 10 through 15.

6. What does the last sentence of paragraph 8 do?

7. What idea controls paragraphs 12 through 15? At what point does Aristides begin discussing the boutiquification of his neighborhood?

8. Why does Aristides list in paragraphs 17 and 18 the titles of so many shops? Would a smaller number of representative titles not have done the job more effectively?

9. Why is Aristides bothered by what he calls the "permanent transience" of Boutique America?

10. Explain the relevance of "the old story" Aristides uses to conclude the essay.

WRITING ASSIGNMENTS

1. Paragraphs 8 through 18 of "Boutique America!" are an essay within an essay. Prepare a three-level topic outline of that internal essay.

2. Walk or ride around your neighborhood and take notes on the shopping area(s). Then from your notes form a topic sentence, organize the notes under the topic sentence, and write a fully developed paragraph in which you explain whether or not you live in Boutique America.

3. In a well-developed paragraph (see paragraph 10 of "Boutique America!") answer the following question: What do I really want from my neighborhood? or What does my neighborhood give me?

4. Write an essay on some recent development in your commmunity that promises to change it in some vital way. In the essay make clear what kind of community it is—or was—and how the development will affect it or has affected it. (To prepare, reread paragraphs 8 through 18 of "Boutique America!")

section two

Of Values
and Actions

Bruce Catton

Grant and Lee:
A Study in Contrasts

[1]   When Ulysses S. Grant and Robert E. Lee met in the parlor of a modest house at Appomattox Court House, Virginia, on April 9, 1865, to work out the terms for the surrender of Lee's Army of Northern Virginia, a great chapter in American life came to a close, and a great new chapter began.

[2]   These men were bringing the Civil War to its virtual finish. To be sure, other armies had yet to surrender, and for a few days the fugitive Confederate government would struggle desperately and vainly, trying to find some way to go on living now that its chief support was gone. But in effect it was all over when Grant and Lee signed the papers. And the little room where they wrote out the terms was the scene of one of the poignant, dramatic contrasts in American history.

[3]   They were two strong men, these oddly different generals, and they represented the strengths of two conflicting currents that, through them, had come into final collision.

[4]   Back of Robert E. Lee was the notion that the old aristocratic concept might somehow survive and be dominant in American life.

[5]   Lee was tidewater Virginia, and in his background were family, culture, and tradition ... the age of chivalry transplanted to a New World which was making its own legends and its own myths. He embodied a way of life that had come down through the age of knighthood and the English country squire. America was a land that was beginning all over again, dedicated to nothing

Bruce Catton, "Grant and Lee: A Study in Contrasts," from *The American Story,* ed. Earl Schenck Miers, © 1956 by Broadcast Music, Inc. Used by permission of the copyright holder.

much more complicated than the rather hazy belief that all men had equal rights and should have an equal chance in the world. In such a land Lee stood for the feeling that it was somehow of advantage to human society to have a pronounced inequality in the social structure. There should be a leisure class, backed by ownership of land; in turn, society itself should be keyed to the land as the chief source of wealth and influence. It would bring forth (according to this ideal) a class of men with a strong sense of obligation to the community; men who lived not to gain advantage for themselves, but to meet the solemn obligations which had been laid on them by the very fact that they were privileged. From them the country would get its leadership; to them it could look for the higher values—of thought, of conduct, of personal deport- ment—to give it strength and virtue.

[6]   Lee embodied the noblest elements of this aristocratic ideal. Through him the landed nobility justified itself. For four years, the Southern states had fought a desperate war to uphold the ideals for which Lee stood. In the end, it almost seemed as if the Confederacy fought for Lee; as if he himself was the Confederacy ... the best thing that the way of life for which the Confederacy stood could ever have to offer. He had passed into legend before Appomattox. Thousands of tired, underfed, poorly clothed Confederate soldiers, long since past the simple enthusiasm of the early days of the struggle, somehow con- sidered Lee the symbol of everything for which they had been willing to die. But they could not quite put this feeling into words. If the Lost Cause, sanc- tified by so much heroism and so many deaths, had a living justification, its justification was General Lee.

[7]   Grant, the son of a tanner on the Western frontier, was everthing Lee was not. He had come up the hard way, and embodied nothing in particular ex- cept the eternal toughness and sinewy fiber of the men who grew up beyond the mountains. He was one of a body of men who owed reverence and obeisance to no one, who were self-reliant to a fault, who cared hardly anything for the past but who had a sharp eye for the future.

[8]   These frontier men were the precise opposites of the tidewater aristocrats. Back of them, in the great surge that had taken people over the Alleghenies and into the opening Western country, there was a deep, implicit dissatisfac- tion with a past that had settled into grooves. They stood for democracy, not from any reasoned conclusion about the proper ordering of human society, but simply because they had grown up in the middle of democracy and knew how it worked. Their society might have privileges, but they would be privileges each man had won for himself. Forms and patterns meant nothing. No man was born to anything, except perhaps to a chance to show how far he could rise. Life was competition.

[9]   Yet along with this feeling had come a deep sense of belonging to a national community. The Westerner who developed a farm, opened a shop or set up in business as a trader, could hope to prosper only as his own community pros- pered—and his community ran from the Atlantic to the Pacific and from Canada down to Mexico. If the land was settled, with towns and highways and accessible markets, he could better himself. He saw his fate in terms of the na- tion's own destiny. As its horizons expanded, so did his. He had, in other

words, an acute dollars-and-cents stake in the continued growth and development of his country.

[10]   And that, perhaps, is where the contrast between Grant and Lee becomes most striking. The Virginia aristocrat, inevitably, saw himself in relation to his own region. He lived in a static society which could endure almost anything except change. Instinctively, his first loyalty would go to the locality in which that society existed. He would fight to the limit of endurance to defend it, because in defending it he was defending everything that gave his own life its deepest meaning.

[11]   The Westerner, on the other hand, would fight with an equal tenacity for the broader concept of society. He fought so because everything he lived by was tied to growth, expansion, and a constantly widening horizon. What he lived by would survive or fall with the nation itself. He could not possibly stand by unmoved in the face of an attempt to destroy the Union. He would combat it with eveything he had, because he could only see it as an effort to cut the ground out from under his feet.

[12]   So Grant and Lee were in complete contrast, representing two diametrically opposed elements in American life. Grant was the modern man emerging; beyond him, ready to come on the stage, was the great age of steel and machinery, of crowded cities and a restless, burgeoning vitality. Lee might have ridden down from the old age of chivalry, lance in hand, silken banner fluttering over his head. Each man was the perfect champion of his cause, drawing both his strengths and his weaknesses from the people he led.

[13]   Yet it was not all contrast, after all. Different as they were—in background, in personality, in underlying aspiration—these two great soldiers had much in common. Under everything else, they were marvelous fighters. Furthermore, their fighting qualities were really very much alike.

[14]   Each man had, to begin with, the great virtue of utter tenacity and fidelity. Grant fought his way down the Mississippi Valley in spite of acute personal discouragement and profound military handicaps. Lee hung on in the trenches at Petersburg after hope itself had died. In each man there was an indomitable quality ... the born fighter's refusal to give up as long as he can still remain on his feet and lift his two fists.

[15]   Daring and resourcefulness they had, too; the ability to think faster and move faster than the enemy. These were the qualities which gave Lee the dazzling campaigns of Second Manassas and Chancellorsville and won Vicksburg for Grant.

[16]   Lastly, and perhaps greatest of all, there was the ability, at the end, to turn quickly from war to peace once the fighting was over. Out of the way these two men behaved at Appomattox came the possibility of a peace of reconciliation. It was a possibility not wholly realized, in the years to come, but which did, in the end, help the two sections to become one nation again ... after a war whose bitterness might have seemed to make such a reunion wholly impossible. No part of either man's life became him more than the part he played in their brief meeting in the McLean house at Appomattox. Their behavior there put all succeeding generations of Americans in their debt. Two great Americans, Grant and Lee—very different, yet under everything very much alike. Their encounter at Appomattox was one of the great moments of American history.

VOCABULARY

Use the context of the essay and your dictionary to define the following words.

1. poignant (par. 2)
2. concept (par. 4)
3. obligation (par. 5)
4. deportment (par. 5)
5. justified (par. 6)

6. obeisance (par. 7)
7. implicit (par 8)
8. acute (par. 9)
9. static (par. 10)
10. reconciliation (par. 16)

RHETORIC AND IDEA

1. Bruce Catton sees Grant and Lee as representing two contrasting values, areas, and times in American society. How many paragraphs does he use to set up this general overall pattern before discussing the men one at a time?
2. In this pattern, which man represented the "new chapter"?
3. The way of life represented by Lee is based on what values?
4. Which set of three paragraphs first sets up Lee's values?
5. The way of life represented by Grant is based on which values?
6. Which set of three paragraphs first sets up Grant's values?
7. What is the function of paragraph 12?
8. What key function word of paragraph 13 indicates Catton is now moving into a new stage of his development? What will be the relationship of this stage to the preceding one?
9. What qualities are the basis of the similarities of the two men? Of these, which was the most important for the nation?
10. One key content word is continually used in reference to Lee and his way of life; another is continually used in reference to Grant. What are these two words.

WRITING ASSIGNMENTS

1. Compare and contrast (that is, show the similarities and differences between) two people.
2. Compare and contrast two types, groups, or classes of people.
3. Compare and contrast two types of some general form of entertainment or art.

Stephen Leacock

Americans Are Queer

[1]   Americans are queer people: they can't rest. They have more time, more leisure, shorter hours, more holidays, and more vacations than any other people in the world. But they can't rest. They rush up and down across their continent as tourists; they move about in great herds to conventions; they invade the wilderness, they flood the mountains, they keep the hotels full. But they can't rest. The scenery rushes past them. They learn it, but they don't see it. Battles and monuments are announced to them in a rubberneck bus. They hear them, but they don't get them. They never stop moving; they rush up and down as Shriners, Masons, Old Graduates, Bankers—they are a new thing each day, always rushing to a reunion or something.

[2]   So they go on rushing about till eventually the undertaker gathers them to a last convention.

[3]   Americans are queer people: they can't read. They have more schools, and better schools, and spend more money on schools and colleges than all Europe. But they can't read. They print more books in a year than the French print in ten. But they can't read. They cover their country with one hundred thousand tons of Sunday newspapers every week. But they don't read them. They're too busy. They use them for fires and to make more paper with. They buy eagerly

Stephen Leacock, "Americans Are Queer," *Forum,* April, 1931.

thousands of new novels at two dollars each. But they read only page one. Their streets are full of huge signs. They won't look at them. Their street cars are filled with advertising; they turn their eyes away. Transparent colors, cart wheels and mechanical flares whirl and flicker in the crowded streets at night. No one sees them. Tons of circulars pour through the mails, through the houses, and down the garbage chute. The last American who sat down to read died in the days of Henry Clay.

[4]   Americans are queer people: they can't drink. All of the American nation is haunted. They have a fierce wish to be sober; and they can't. They pass fierce laws against themselves, shut themselves up, chase themselves, shoot themselves; and they can't stay sober and they can't drink. They have a furious idea that if they can ever get sober, they can do big things. But they can't hold it. They got this mentality straight out of home life in Ohio, copied from the wild spree and the furious repentance of the pioneer farmer. The nation keeps it yet. It lives among red specters, rum devils, broken bottles, weeping children, penitentiary cells, barrooms, poison hooch and broken oaths.

[5]   Americans are queer people: they can't play. Americans rush to work as soon as they grow up. They want their work as soon as they wake. It is a stimulant—the only one they're not afraid of. They used to open their offices at ten o'clock; then at nine; then at eight; then at seven. Now they never shut them. Every business in America is turning into an open-all-day-and-night business. They eat all night, dance all night, build buildings all night, make a noise all night. They can't play. They try to, but they can't. They turn football into a fight, baseball into a lawsuit, and yachting into machinery. They can't play. The little children can't play; they use mechanical toys instead—toy cranes, hoisting toy loads, toy machinery spreading a toy industrial-depression of infantile dullness. The grownup people can't play; they use a mechanical gymnasium and a clockwork horse. They can't swim: they use a float. They can't run: they use a car. They can't laugh: they hire a comedian and watch him laugh.

[6]   Americans are queer people: they don't give a damn. All the world criticizes them and they don't give a damn. All the world writes squibs like this about them and they don't give a damn. Foreign visitors come and write them up; they don't give a damn. Lecturers lecture at them; they don't care. They are told they have no art, no literature, and no soul. They never budge. Moralists cry over them, criminologists dissect them, writers shoot epigrams at them, prophets foretell the end of them; and they never move. Seventeen brilliant books analyze them every month; they don't read them. The Europeans threaten to unite againt them; they don't mind. Equatorial Africa is dead sour on them; they don't even know it. The Chinese look on them as full of Orien-tal cunning; the English accuse them of British stupidity; the Scotch call them closefisted; the Italians say they are liars; the French think their morals loose; the Bolsheviks accuse them of Communism.

[7]   But that's all right. The Americans don't give a damn; don't need to—never did need to. That is their salvation.

VOCABULARY

Use the context of the essay and your dictionary to define the following words:

1. rubberneck (par. 1)
2. transparent (par. 3)
3. mentality (par. 4)
4. repentance (par. 4)
5. specters (par. 4)

6. hooch (par. 4)
7. infantile (par. 5)
8. moralists (par. 6)
9. epigrams (par. 6)
10. closefisted (par. 6)

RHETORIC AND IDEA

1. From which of the sources of evidence does Leacock get most of his material? Explain.
2. How many categories does Leacock consider Americans "queer" in? List the categories.
3. Leacock uses a choppy sentence style in "Americans Are Queer." Is this style suited to his purpose? Why or why not?
4. Leacock says Americans are "queer" people. What does he mean by "queer"? Can you think of a better word to describe the Americans he is writing about?
5. "Americans Are Queer" was published in 1931 (ten years before the United States entered World War II). Do you think Americans are still "queer" in the categories Leacock lists? Explain. Would he have to eliminate any of his categories if he were writing the essay today? Would he have to add any categories? Would he have to change his thesis completely?
6. Does Leacock admire Americans, hate them, envy them, what? What tone does he use in "Americans Are Queer"?
7. What common fallacy of logic does Leacock most frequently commit in "Americans Are Queer"? Explain.

WRITING ASSIGNMENTS

1. Imitating the style of "Americans are Queer," take one of the "queer" categories (or supply a "queer" category of your own) and rewrite one of the paragraphs as Leacock would have to write it today.
2. Write an essay that proves or disproves one of the following assertions from "Americans Are Queer."

   Americans can't rest.

   Americans can't read.

   Americans can't drink.

   Americans can't play.

   Americans don't give a damn.

Support your choice with specific examples from American life today as you know it. Feel free to take a stance opposite to Leacock's (Americans *can* rest or *can* read or *can* drink, etc.).

3. Considering America today, write a new "Americans Are Queer" essay.
4. Analyze your region, your state, your county, your city, your town, your neighborhood, or your family, and write your own Leacock essay about the peculiarities of the people of a certain group (state, county, city, town, neighborhood, family).

Eric Sevareid

The Juggernaut of Time

[1] One way to go quietly insane is to think hard about the concept of eternity. Another way, for anyone living in a megalopolis like New York, is to think hard about "progress."

[2] The eerie sensation comes over one that true progress reached the end of its cable some years ago and is now recoiling upon us, an unstoppable juggernaut smashing masses of human beings back toward medieval conditions of life.

[3] The streets are littered with cigarette and cigar butts, paper wrappings, particles of food and dog droppings. How long before they become indistinguishable from the gutters of medieval towns when slop pails were emptied from the second-story windows?

[4] Thousands of New York women no longer attend evening services in their churches. They fear assault as they walk the few steps from bus or subway station to their apartment houses. The era of the medieval footpad has returned, and, as in the dark ages, the cry for help brings no assistance, for even grown men know they would be cut down before the police could arrive.

[5] A thousand years ago in Europe acres of houses and shops were demolished and their inhabitants forced elsewhere so that great cathedrals could be built. For decades the building process soaked up all available skilled labor; for decades the townspeople stepped around pits in the streets, clambered over ropes and piles of timber, breathed mortar dust and slept and woke to the

crashing noise of construction. The cathedrals, when finished, stood half-empty six days a week, but most of them at least had beauty. Today the ugly office skyscrapers go up, shops and graceful homes are obliterated, their inhabitants forced away and year after year New Yorkers step around the pits, stumble through the wooden catwalks, breathe the fine mist of dust, absorb the hammering noise night and day and telephone in vain for carpenter or plumber. And the skyscrapers stand empty two days and seven nights a week. This is progress.

[6]   At the rush hour men outrun old women for the available cab; the strong bodily crush back the weak for a place to stand in suffocating bus or subway car, no less destructive of human dignity than a cattle wagon in the time of Peter the Great. When the buses and subway cars began they represented progress.

[7]   Great parking garages are built, immediately filled with cars; the traffic remains as before, and that is progress. The renowned New York constructionist, Robert Moses, builds hundreds of miles of access highways, and they are at once crammed bumper to bumper with automobiles as long as locomotives carrying an average of about two human beings apiece. Parkinson's general law applies here too, for vehicles will always increase in direct proportion to the increase in spaces to hold them. So skyscrapers and boxlike apartment houses will increase as the money to build them increases. So footpads will increase as the number of possible victims increases. But it's progress.

[8]   I am not surprised that the English writer, Mervyn Jones, concludes after traveling throughout Russia and the United States that ordinary Americans and ordinary Russians are remarkably alike in at least two respects—in the sheer physical misery they are forced to endure in their cities and in the sheer ugliness of jumbled signs and billboards being spread across their once fair countryside.

[9]   They are alike in a third respect. As Jones writes in *Horizon* magazine, both peoples complain remarkably little. Russians don't complain because they don't expect government authorities to listen. American dwellers in our megalopolises don't complain because they have long since abandoned hope. Their authorities may listen, but they know their authorities are helpless. A city like New York is ungovernable.

[10]   The secret, terrible fact is that progress, in all measurable terms of human effort, grace and self-respect ended some years ago in the great ant-hill cities. The juggernaut of time and effort has turned around and is now destroying the recent progressive past.

VOCABULARY

Use the context of the essay and your dictionary to define the following words:

1. megalopolis (par. 1)
2. recoiling (par. 2)
3. juggernaut (par. 2)
4. footpad (par. 4)
5. demolished (par. 5)

6. obliterated (par. 5)
7. suffocating (par. 6)
8. crammed (par. 7)
9. abandoned (par. 9)
10. ungovernable (par. 9)

RHETORIC AND IDEA

1. At what point in the essay does Sevareid most nearly state his thesis? In which sentence does this statement appear?
2. List the points of comparison Sevareid makes between life in New York City and life in medieval cities.
3. List the points of comparison English writer Mervyn Jones makes between the United States and Russia.
4. In paragraph 10, Sevareid refers to "the recent progressive past." Does he make clear what he means by this phrase? Where? If he does not make clear what he means, what do you think he means?
5. What is Sevareid's general tone? In answering the question, take into consideration his use of comparison, his selection of details, his repetition of the word "progress."
6. "The Juggernaut of Time" was originally published in 1964. Is it still an accurate description of progress in the United States? Be specific. Is it still an accurate description of progress in New York City? Be specific.
7. In paragraph 7, Sevareid alludes to Parkinson's general law. What is this law?

WRITING ASSIGNMENTS

1. Write an essay in which you evaluate the progress (or lack of progress) your town has made in the past ten years or so.
2. In an essay use comparison and/or contrast to evaluate the progress that has been made in one of the following areas over a period of time you establish.

television	cars	motorcycles
morals	education	entertainment
your house	your parents	your wife
your children	your husband	religion
music	dancing	vacations
roads and highways	movies	law enforcement

Art Seidenbaum

Plea for Plastics

[1] I was over at the KPFK country fair this month, deep in the wilds of Santa Monica Civic Auditorium, complete with bales of imported hay and bandanas worn over breasts.

[2] The crafts exhibits were competent enough but as I strolled around among the potters and pillow-makers and pouch-stitchers, I realized how much I missed plastic.

[3] Yea, verily, plastic. The same stuff that became the bogeyword for the counter-culture. The same hard, manufactured material that turned into a code for crass taste. The same shiny product that even serves as a metaphor for a superficial person. Amidst the funk frenzies of the '60s, poor plastic got a bad name.

[4] Formica, for instance. Formica may be uniform and unyielding but it does present a durable simple surface. A relief from gross glazes and fake flowers and rock star stencils. The world is drenched in decoration these days. A solid-color plastic achieves purity by contrast.

[5] Something born of machines in a factory is nearly a novelty nowadays. The good KPFK show convinced me California now has a supply of mugs, planters, bowls and nut dishes to last from now to eternity. The hand-turned object has reached obsessive proportions. No amount of accidental breakage will ever bring us back to balance.

[6] What began as a revulsion against mass-made things has achieved a sameness all its own. The fair crafts people at Santa Monica showed essential-

ly the same wares as the spring Renaissance impersonators at Agoura, as the sidewalk merchants at Westwood, as the shopping center streetfolk at Century City, as the weekend exhibitors along the beachfront at Santa Barbara.

[7]   The potters field is out of proportion and we are all being buried in it. There are more feet of clay in Southern California than we have shelf space.

[8]   Clay, I know is organic. And plastic isn't yet biodegradable. And we have a mammoth solid waste problem. And the plastic industry can pollute if it isn't policed. And isn't it wonderful that so many people have gone back to shaping their utensils with their own two hands?

[9]   Not so wonderful anymore. Dull. Unimaginative, uncreative, unoriginal. All the cups runneth over. All the mugs look alike.

[10]   Plastic, properly made, is clean, inexpensive and properly unassertive. It need not come in earth colors, which is certainly a bright switch from the dun and dung shades of contemporary ceramists. Item for item, plastic is lighter in weight and takes up less space—matters of some matter in a dense universe.

[11]   I prefer a plain polyester blouse to a stenciled cotton billboard T-shirt. I like a plastic drinking cup better than a personalized mug with a massive handle. I appreciate machines that make replicas more than people who make copies.

[12]   The time for zero pottery growth is surely here; we suffer from a case of overkiln. I would remind the earth people there's no need to have a weed pot for every weed in the universe. There's no sane reason to make each green thing hang in a bowl like Babylon.

[13]   Let some growing things remain in the soil from which they originally came. Let some soil remain in the soil without firing it into various vessel shapes.

[14]   At least Formica follows function. And no minstrel has yet made a long-playing record on anything but pure plastic.

[15]   People in glass houses should stop throwing pots.

VOCABULARY

Use the context of the essay and your dictionary to define the following words:

1. superficial (par. 3)
2. funk (par. 3)
3. durable (par. 4)
4. gross (par. 4)
5. revulsion (par. 6)

6. impersonators (par. 6)
7. unassertive (par. 10)
8. dun (par. 10)
9. dense (par. 10)
10. replicas (par. 11)

RHETORIC AND IDEA

1. In paragraph 2 Seidenbaum says that as he "strolled around among the potters and pillow-makers and pouch-stitchers" he realized how much he missed plastic. What reason or reasons does he give for missing plastic?

2. What does Seidenbaum mean when he refers to the "funk frenzies of the '60s"?

3. In "Plea for Plastics," Seidenbaum writes several sentence fragments in paragraphs 3, 4, and 9. Find these fragments and then rewrite them in more conventional sentence patterns. Your revisions should maintain the style of Seidenbaum.
4. In paragraph 8, Seidenbaum begins four of the five sentences with "and." Why does he use this repetitious pattern?
5. Find the pun in paragraph 12.
6. Why does Seidenbaum say in paragraph 14 that "no minstrel has yet made a long-playing record on anything but pure plastic"?
7. Point out the similarities and differences you see between the ideas, development, and style of "Plea for Plastics" and "Boutique America!" (pp. 331–37)

WRITING ASSIGNMENTS

1. Visit a local art show and take notes on the pottery, water colors, oils, sculptures, leatherwork, etc. From your notes write an evaluation of the part of the show that was especially appealing or unappealing to you. Your essay should contain a sufficient amount of descriptive detail to let your reader see or feel or smell what you are evaluating.
2. Write an essay in which you show the role plastic plays in your life. Consider such things as cooking, preserving, transportation, clothing, exercise, athletics, entertainment.
3. Using the information you gathered to answer Question 7 above, write a comparison and/or contrast paper on "Plea for Plastics" and "Boutique America!"

Anne Taylor Fleming

The Fear of Being Alone

[1]   At the end of this past summer I had plans to go away for a week, simply a week, without my husband. It was the first time in three years that I was making such a solo pilgrimage, and I was frightened. As I walked down the long corridor to the plane, I looked straight ahead, turning a bottle of tranquilizers over and over in my pocket. I felt like a child lost in a department store; my palms were sweaty and my face was flushed. I tried to remember other solitary departures when I had been similarly discomfited: the walk to the first day of school; the bus ride to Girl Scout camp when I was 9 and my sister, who was also on the bus, was 10 and suddenly wanted nothing to do with me; the first midnight jet to college.

[2]   Of what was I so afraid? I was afraid of being by myself, of being wholly quiet, of being with people who did not know my name and did not care. I was afraid of being liked by strangers and of not being liked by strangers. Mostly I was afraid of being alone again, even for so short a time. After four and a half years of marriage I had simply lost the habit.

[3]   Marriage is not the culprit, though it is an obvious protective mantle against aloneness. The fear of being alone is not reserved for the married just as it is not reserved for women. I have heard stories like mine from young boys and have seen the same childlike fear in the faces of middle-aged men. Nor is this fear the special property of Americans. But we seem, in this country, to fan the fear of being alone. We are raised and in turn raise our children in

357

clumps, in groups, in auditoriums and car pools and locker rooms and scout dens. Great emphasis is placed on how sociable we are as children, on how popular we are with our peers. Great emphasis is also placed on how well children mix in their own families. Despite the alleged falling apart of the American family, the dialogue about familial relations is constant, binding. If only in talk, parents and children do not leave each other much alone. Great nostalgic emphasis is still placed on the ritual togetherness of the family meal. A solitary eater, anytime, anywhere, conjures up one of those sad, empty, too well-lighted diners of an Edward Hopper painting.

[4]   And when for children there is no meal to attend, no group activity, no distraction planned by a weekend father, there is the constant company of the people on TV. A child need never be alone, need never know silence except when asleep. Even then, for urban and suburban children, there are the nonceasing nighttime noises of cars, of neighbors, of arguing or partying parents. To be away from the noise, away from the group—parents or peers— becomes a scary thing and aloneness becomes confused and synonymous with loneliness.

[5]   I used to think that the worst thing I could say to my husband when lying next to him was, "I'm lonely." That, I thought, was very wounding, a reflection on his inability to be company to me. I think now that it's a reflection on me, on my inability to be gracefully alone even in the presence of someone I love. We all marry, in part, to avoid being alone; many of us divorce when we find we can be just as alone in marriage as before, and sometimes more so. Often, women in crumbling marriages conceive babies not to try to hold a man, as the cliche goes, but to guarantee themselves some company—even that of an infant—when that man is gone. After the divorce, for a man or woman, comes the frantic search for a replacement, a new lover, a dog, a singles club, a stronger drink or drug. Waking next to strangers in strange beds—surely, the loneliest habit—is considered preferable to being alone.

[6]   Of this random bedding there has been much written lately, especially by a handful of philosopher-journalists who blame such "promiscuity" on what they call the New Narcissism, the inward-turning, selfish, self-absorption of the American people. Each one of us, their lament goes, is "into" his or her own jollies—the pursuit of happiness having become the pursuit of hedonism—our faces resolutely turned away from the world and its problems. But this is the oddest of narcissisms then, the insecure narcissism of people who do not like to be alone. The anti-narcissists point to the prodigious number and variety of soul searchers—est devotees, Aricans, Moonies, meditators and Rolfers—as proof of the neurotic self-celebration of Americans. But even these soul searchings go on in huge groups; they are orgies of mass psyche scratching. Hundreds of people writhe together on auditorium floors in an attempt to soothe their individual wounds. They jog together and ride bicycles together and walk the most beautiful country roads together in an effort to slim their individual thighs.

[7]   So even if Americans are involved in a manic and somewhat selfish pursuit of psychic and physical fitness, it is a collective not a private pursuit. Everyone is holding hands; they're one long daisy chain of self-improvement. This is, at best, a symbiotic narcissism, the narcissism of people very dependent on one

another, of people afraid or bored to be alone, of people homogenizing into one sex—it is less scary and less lonely, perhaps, to bed with a body that looks and feels more like one's own—of people who need to see reflected in the water not only their own faces but countless other faces as well.

[8]   I do not mean to advertise the advantages of being alone. Many have done that with more conviction than I could. I regard aloneness not as a pleasure so much as an accident that, if one is to be at all happy, must be survived. Nor do I mean to put down narcissism. On the contrary, I find no fault with a certain healthy narcissism. Few among us would undertake the saving of other souls until we first have a stab at saving our own.

[9]   The point is simply that narcissism is not the point and that in many ways it's a misnomer. A true narcissist is a true loner and most of us, raised as we are, make lousy loners. We share each other's beds somewhat freely not out of boldness but out of timidity, out of the fear of being alone. We hunt for gurus not out of self-love, or narcissism, but out of self-doubt. If we are to be even mildly happy and therefore generous of spirit—as the antinarcissists would have us be—then what we need is more narcissism, more privatism, not less. What we need instead of soul-searching sessions are classes on how to be alone: Aloneness 1A, Intermediary Aloneness, Advanced Aloneness. The great joy of these new classes is that attendance would not only not be required, it would be forbidden.

VOCABULARY

Use the context of the essay and your dictionary to define the following words:

1. pilgrimage (par. 1)
2. solitary (par. 1)
3. discomfited (par. 1)
4. ritual (par. 3)
5. frantic (par. 5)

6. narcissism (par. 6)
7. hedonism (par. 6)
8. neurotic (par. 6)
9. manic (par. 7)
10. symbiotic (par. 7)

RHETORIC AND IDEA

1. State Fleming's thesis in your own words.
2. In paragraph 3, Fleming says, "we seem, in this country, to fan the fear of being alone." What evidence does she give to support her claim?
3. What does Fleming mean when she alludes to "one of those sad, empty, too well-lighted diners of an Edward Hopper painting"?
4. In paragraph 4, Fleming says that we learn to confuse *aloneness* with *loneliness*. What evidence does she give to support her observation? What is the difference between the two states?
5. In paragraph 5, Fleming says that "Waking next to strangers in strange beds" must surely be "the loneliest habit." She does not support her assertion. Do you agree or disagree with her? Do you think Ms. Fleming knows from experience? Would she need to have had the experience to know?

6. In paragraph 6, Fleming alludes to (1) est devotees, (2) Aricans, (3) Moonies, (4) meditators, and (5) Rolfers. What do these persons do? Why do the "anti-narcissists" criticize these people for their "neurotic self-celebration"?

7. Why does Fleming say in paragraph 9 that what we need is more narcissism, more privatism?

8. Why would it be forbidden to attend Aloneness 1, Intermediary Aloneness, and Advanced Aloneness, the classes on how to be alone?

WRITING ASSIGNMENTS

1. In a paragraph, describe one of the paintings by Edward Hopper that Fleming alludes to in paragraph 3.

2. Write an essay in which you explain how you were affected or not affected by the emphasis we place in the United States on being sociable, on being popular, on being good mixers. Introduce your paper with an illustration from your own life, as Fleming does her essay.

3. Write an essay on one of the following topics:

> How to Be Alone in a Crowd
> The Impossibility of Being Alone
> Who Wants to Be Alone?
> The Dangers of Being Alone
> The Benefits of Being Alone
> How to Be Alone Without Fear

4. Write an essay in which you describe a true loner. In your paper list the characteristics and use examples to illustrate what true loners do.

Joseph Epstein

Obsessed with Sport

[1]   I cannot remember when I was not surrounded by sports, when talk of sports was not in the air, when I did not care passionately about sports. As a boy in Chicago in the late Forties, I lived in the same building as the sister and brother-in-law of Barney Ross, the welterweight champion. Half a block away, down near the lake, the Sullivan High School football team worked out in the spring and autumn. Summers the same field was given over to baseball and men's softball on Sundays. A few blocks to the north was the Touhy Avenue Fieldhouse, where basketball was played, and lifeguards trained, and behind which, in a softball field frozen over in winter, crack-the-whip, hockey, and speed skating took over. To the west, a block or so up Morse Avenue, was the Morse Avenue ''L'' Recreations, a combined pool hall and bowling alley. Life, in short, was games....

[2]   I lived on, off, and in sports. *Sport* magazine had recently begun publication, and I gobbled up its issues cover to cover, soon becoming knowledgeable not only about the major sports—baseball, football, and basketball—but about golf, hockey, tennis, and horse racing, so that I scored reputably on the Sport Quiz, a regular department at the front of the magazine. Another regular department was the Sport Classic, which featured longish profiles of the legendary figures in the history of sports: Ty Cobb, Jim Thorpe, Bobby Jones, Big Bill Tilden, Red Grange, Man o' War. I next moved on to the sports novels of John R. Tunis—*All-American, The Iron Duke, The Kid from*

Tomkinsville, The Kid Comes Back, World Series, the lot—which I read with as much excitement as any books I have read since. . . .

[3]   All learning of craft—which sport, like writing, most assuredly is—involves imitation, especially in the early stages; and I was an excellent mimic. By the time I was ten years old I had mastery over all the big-time moves: the spit in the mitt, the fluid infield chatter, the knocking of dirt from the spikes; the rhythmic barking out of signals, hands high under the center's crotch to take the ball; the three bounces and deep breath before shooting the free throw (on this last, I regretted not being a Catholic, so that I might be able to make the sign of the cross before shooting, as was then the fashion among Catholic high-school and college players). I went in for athletic haberdashery in a big way, often going beyond mimicry to the point of flat-out phoniness—wearing, for example, a knee pad while playing basketball, though my knees were always, exasperatingly, intact.

[4]   I always looked good, which was important, because form is intrinsic to sports; but in my case it was doubly important, because the truth is that I wasn't really very good. Or at any rate not good enough. Two factors accounted for this. The first was that, without being shy about body contact, I lacked a certain indispensable aggressiveness; the second, connected closely to the first, was that, when it came right down to it, I did not care enough about winning. I would rather lose a point attempting a slashing cross-court backhand than play for an easier winner down the side; the long jump shot always had more allure for me than the safer drive to the basket. Given a choice between the two vanities of winning and looking good, I almost always preferred looking good.

[5]   I shall never forget the afternoon, sometime along about my thirteenth year, when, shooting baskets alone, I came upon the technique for shooting the hook. Although today it has nowhere near the consequence of the jump-shot—an innovation that has been to basketball what the jet has been to air travel—the hook is still the single most beautiful shot in the game. The rhythm and grace of it, the sway of the body off the pivot, the release of the ball behind the head and off the fingertips, the touch and instinct involved in its execution, make the hook altogether a balletic thing, and to achieve it is to feel one of the most delectable sensations in sports. That afternoon, on a deserted side street, shooting on a rickety wooden backboard and a black rim without a net, I felt it and grew nearly drunk on the feeling. Rain came down, dirt washed in the gutters, flecks of it spattering my clothes and arms and face, but, soaked and cold though I was, I do not think I would have left that basket on that after-noon for anything. I threw up hook after hook, from every angle, from farther and farther out, off the board, without the board, and hook after hook went in. Only pitch darkness drove me home.

[6]   I do not say that not to have shot the hook is never to have lived, but only that, once having done so, the pleasure it gives is not so easily forgotten. Every sport offers similar pleasures, the pleasures taken differing by temperament: the canter into the end zone to meet a floating touchdown pass, or the clean, crisp feel of a perfect block or tackle; the long straight drive or the precisely played approach shot to the green; the solid overhead; the pickup on the tricky

short hop or the long ball down one of the power alleys. Different sports, different pleasures. But so keen are these pleasures—pleasures of execution, of craft completed—that, along with being unforgettable, they are also worth recapturing in any available way, and the most available way, when reflexes have slowed, when muscle no longer responds so readily to brain, is from the grandstand or, perhaps more often nowadays, from the chair before the television.

[7]   I have put in days on the bench, but years in my chair before the television set. Recently it has occurred to me that over the years I have heard more hours of talk from the announcer Curt Gowdy than from my own father, who is not a reticent man. I have been thoroughly Schenkeled, Mussbergered, Summeralled, Cosselled, DeRogotissed, and Garagiolaed. How many hundreds—thousands?—of hours have I spent watching sports of all sorts, either at parks or stadiums or over television? I am glad I shall never have a precise answer. Yet neither apparently can I get enough. What is the fascination? Why is it that, with the prospect of a game to watch in the evening or on the weekend, the day seems lighter and brighter? What do I get out of it?

[8]   What I get out of it, according to one fairly prominent view, is an outlet for my violent emotions. Knee-wrenching, rib-cracking, head-busting, this view has it, is what sports are really about, with sports fans being essentially sadists, and cowardly sadists at that, for they take their violence not at firsthand but at second remove. Enthusiasm for sports among Americans is little more than a reflection of the national penchant for violence. Military men talk about game plans; the long touchdown pass is called the bomb. The average pro-football fan, seeing a quarterback writhing on the ground at midfield as a result of the ministrations of Joe Green, Carl Eller, or Lyle Alzado, twitters with glee, finds his ultimate reward, and declares a little holiday in the blackest corner of his heart.

[9]   But this is a criticism that comes at sports by way of politics. To believe it one has to believe that the history of the United States is chiefly one of rape, expropriation, and aggressive imperialism. To dismiss it, however, one need only know something about sports. Violence is indubitably a part of some sports; in some—hockey is an example—it sometimes comes close to being featured. But in no sport—not even boxing, that most rudimentary of sports—is it the main item, and in many other sports it plays no part at all. A distinction worth insisting on is that between violence and roughness. Roughness, a willingness to mix it up, to take if need be an elbow in the jaw, is part of rebounding in basketball, yet violence is not. Even in pro football, most maligned of modern American sports, more of roughness than of violence is involved. Roughness raises the stakes, provides the pressure, behind execution. A splendid because true phrase has come about in pro football to cover the situation in which a pass receiver, certain that he will be tackled upon the instant he makes his reception, drops a ball he should otherwise have caught easily—the phrase, best delivered in a Southern accent such as Don Meredith's, is "He heard footsteps on that one, Howard." Although a part of the attraction, it is not so much those footsteps that fill the stands and the den chairs on Sunday afternoons as it is those men who elude them: the

Lynn Swanns, the Fran Tarkentons, the O.J. Simpsons. The American love of violence theory really will not wash. Dick Butkus did not get us into Vietnam.

[10]   Many who would not argue that sports reflect American violence nevertheless claim that they imbue one wth the competitive spirit. In some who are already amply endowed with it, sports doubtless do tend to refine (or possibly brutalize) the desire to win. Yet sports also teach a serious respect for craft. Competition, though it flourishes as always, is in bad odor nowadays; but craft, officially respected, does not flourish greatly outside the boutique.

[11]   If the love of violence or the competitive urge does not put me in my chair for the countless games I watch, is it, then, nostalgia, a yearning to regain the more glowing moments of adolescence? Many argue that this is precisely so, that American men exist in a state of perpetual immaturity, suspended between boy- and manhood. "The difference between men and boys" says Liberace, "is the price of their toys." (I have paid more than $300 for two half-season tickets to the Chicago Bulls games, parking fees not included.) Such unending enthusiasm for games may have something to do with adolescence, but little, I suspect, with regaining anything whatever. Instead, it has more to do with watching men do regularly and surpassingly what, as an adolescent, one did often bumblingly though with an occasional flash of genuis. To have played these games oneself as a boy or a young man helps immeasurably the appreciation that in watching a sport played at professional caliber one is witnessing the extraordinary made to look ordinary. That a game may have no consequence outside itself—no effect on history, on one's own life, on anything really—does not make it trivial but only makes the enjoyment of it all the purer.

[12]   The notion that men watch sports to regain their adolescence pictures them sitting in the stands or at home watching a game and, within their psyches, muttering, "There, but for the lack of grace of God, go I." And it is true that a number of contemporary authors who are taken seriously have indeed written about sports with a strong overlay of yearning. In the men's softball games described in the fiction of Philip Roth, center field is a place akin to Arcady. Arcadian, too, is the outfield in William Morris's memoir of growing up in the South, *North Toward Home.* In the first half of *Rabbit Run* John Updike takes up the life of a man whose days are downhill all the way after hitting the peak as a high-school basketball star—and in the writing Updike himself evinces a nice soft touch of undisguised longing. In *A Fan's Notes,* a book combining yearning and self-disgust in roughly equal measure, Frederick Exley makes plain that he would much prefer to have been born into the skin of Frank Gifford rather than into his own.

[13]   But most men who are enraptured by sports do not think any such thing. I should like to have Kareem Abdul-Jabbar's sky hook, but not, especially for civilian life, the excessive height that is necessary to its execution. I should like to have Jimmy Connors' ground strokes, but no part of his mind. These are men born with certain gifts, gifts honed by practice and determination, that I, and millions along with me, enjoy seeing on display. But the reality principle is too deeply ingrained, at least in a man of my years, for me to even imagine

exchanging places with them. One might as well imagine oneself in the winner's circle at Churchill Downs as the horse.

[14]   Fantasy is an element in sports when they are played in adolescence—an alley basket becomes the glass backboard at Madison Square Garden, a concrete park district tennis court with grass creeping out of the service line becomes center courts at Wimbledon—but fantasy of this kind is hard to come by. Part of this has to do with age; but as large a part has to do with the age in which we live. Sport has always been a business but never more so than currently, and nothing lends itself less to fantasy than business. Reading the sports section has become rather like reading the business section—mergers, trades, salary negotiaitons, contract disputes, options, and strikes fill the columns. Along with the details of business, those of the psychological and social problems of athletes have come to the fore. The old *Sport* magazine concentrated on play on the field, with only an occasional digressive reference to personal life. ("Yogi likes plenty of pizza in the off-season and spends a lot of his time at his teammate Phil Rizzuto's bowling alley," is a rough facsimile of a sentence from its pages that I recall.) But the magazine in its current version, as well as the now more popular *Sports Illustrated,* expends much space on the private lives of athletes—their divorces, hang-ups, race relations, need for approval, concern for security, potted philosophies—with the result that the grand is made to seem small.

[15]   On the other side of the ledger, there is a view that finds a shimmering significance in everything having to do with sports. Literary men in general are notoriously to be distrusted on the subject. They dig around everywhere, and can be depended upon to find much treasure where none is buried. Norman Mailer mining metaphysical ore in every jab of Muhammad Ali's, an existential nugget in each of his various and profuse utterances, is a particularly horrendous example. Even the sensible William Carlos Willams was not above this sort of temptation. In a poem entitled "At the Ball Game," we find the lines "It is the Inquisition, the/Revolution." Dr. Williams could not have been much fun at the ball park.

[16]   If enthusiasm for sports has little to do with providing an outlet for violent emotions, regaining adolescence, discovering metaphysical truths, the Inquisition or the Revolution, then what, I ask myself, am I doing past midnight, when I have to be up at 5:30 the next morning, watching on television what will turn out to be a seventeen-inning game between the New York Mets and the St. Louis Cardinals? The conversation coming out of my television set is of a very low grade, even for sports announcing. But even the dreary talk cannot put me off—the rehash of statistics, the advice to youngsters to keep their gloves low when in the field, the thin jokes. Neither the Mets nor the Cards figure to be contenders this year. The only possible effect that this game can have on my life is to make me dog-tired the next day. Yet I cannot pull myself away. I want to know how it is going to end. True, the score will be available in the morning paper. But that is not the same thing. What is going on here?

[17]   One thing that is going on is the practice of craft of a very high order, which is intrinsically interesting. But something as important is involved, something

rarer in contemporary life, the spectacle of which gives enormous satisfaction. To define this satisfaction negatively, it is the absence of fraudulence and fakery. No small item, this, when one stops to think that in nearly every realm of contemporary life fraud and fakery have an established—some would say a preponderant—place. Advertising, politics, business, and journalism are only the most obvious examples. Fraud seems similarly pervasive in modern art: in painters whose reputations rest on press agentry; in writers who write one way and live quite another; in composers who are taken seriously but whose work cannot be seriously listened to. At a time when *image* is one of the most frequently used words in American speech and writing, one does not too often come upon the real thing.

[18]   Sport may be the toy department of life, but one of its abiding compensations is that, at least on the field, it is the real thing. Much has been done in recent years in the attempt to ruin sport—the ruthlessness of owners, the greed of players, the general exploitation of fans. But even all this cannot destroy it. On the court, down on the field, sport is fraud-free and fakeproof. With a full count, two men on, his team down by one run in the last of the eighth, a batter (as well as a pitcher) is beyond the aid of public relations. At match point at Forest Hills a player's press clippings are of no help. Last year's earnings will not sink a twelve-foot putt on the eighteenth at Augusta. Alan Page, galloping up along a quarterback's blind side, figures to be neglectful of that quarterback's image as a swinger. In all these situations, and hundreds of others, a man either comes through or he doesn't. He is alone out there, naked but for his ability, which counts for everything. Something there is that is elemental about this, and something greatly satisfying.

[19]   Another part of the satisfaction to be got from sports—from playing them, but also from watching them being played—derives from their special clarity. Sports offer clarity of a kind sufficient to engage the most serious minds. That the Cambridge mathematician G. H. Hardy closely followed cricket and avidly read cricket scores is not altogether surprising. Numbers in sports are ubiquitous. Scores, standings, averages, times, records—comfort is found in such numbers. ERA, RBIs, FGP, pass completions, turnovers, category upon category of statistics are kept for nearly every aspect of athletic activity. (Why, I recently heard someone ask, are records not kept for catchers throwing out runners attempting to steal? Because, the answer is, often runners steal on pitchers, and so it would be unfair to charge these stolen bases against catchers.) As perhaps in no other sphere, numbers in sports tell one where things stand. No loopholes here, where figures, for once, do not lie. Nowhere else is such specificity of result available.

[20]   Clarity about character is also available in sports. "You Americans hold to the proposition that it is self-evident that all men are created equal," I not long ago heard an Englishman say, adding, "it had better be self-evident, for no other evidence for it exists." Sport coldly demonstrates physical inequalities —there are the larger, the faster, the stronger, the more graceful athletes—but it also throws up human types who have devised ways to redress these inequalities. One such type is the hustler. In every realm but that of sports the word *hustle* is pejorative, whereas in sports it is approbative. Two of the hustler breed, Pete Rose of the Cincinnati Reds and Jerry Sloan of the Chicago Bulls, are men who supplement reasonably high levels of ability with unreasonably

high levels of courage and desire. Other athletes—Joe Morgan and Oscar Robertson come to mind—bring superior athletic intelligence to bear upon their play. And Bill Russell, late of the Boston Celtics, who if the truth be known was not an inherently superior athlete, blended hustle and intelligence with what abilities he did have and through force of character established supremacy.

[21]   Whence do hustle, intelligence, and character in sports derive, especially since they apparently do not necessarily carry over into life? Joe DiMaggio and Sugar Ray Robinson, two of the most instinctively intelligent and physically elegant athletes, brought little of either of these qualities over into their business or personal activities. Some athletes can do all but one important thing well: Wilt Chamberlain at the free-throw line, for those who recall his misery there, leaves a permanent picture of a mental block in action. Other athletes—Connie Hawkins, Ilie Nastase, Dick Allen—have all the physical gifts in superabundance, yet, because of some insufficiency of character, some searing flaw, never come near to fulfilling their promise. Coaches supply yet another gallery of human types, from the fanatical Vince Lombardi to the comical Casey Stengel to the measured and aptly named John Wooden. The cast of characters in sport, the variety of situations, the complexity of behavior it puts on display, the overall human exhibit it offers—together these supply an enjoyment akin to that once provided by reading interminably long but inexhaustibly rich nineteenth-century novels.

[22]   In a wider sense, sport is culture. For many American men it represents a common background, a shared interest. It has a binding power that transcends social class and education. Some years ago I found myself working in the South among men with whom I shared nothing in the way of region, religion, education, politics, or general views; we shared nothing, in fact, but sports, which was enough for us to get along and grow to become friends, in the process showing how superficial all the things that might have kept us apart in fact were. More recently, in Chicago, at a time when race relations were in a particularly jagged state, I recall emerging from an NBA game, in which the Chicago Bulls in overtime beat the Milwaukee Bucks, into a snowy night and an aura of common good feeling that, for a time, submerged the enmity between races; laughing, throwing snowballs, exuberant generally, the crowd leaving the Chicago Stadium that night was not divided by being black and white but unified by being Bull fans. The Boston-Cincinnati World Series [of 1975], one of the most gratifying in memory, coming hard upon a year of extreme political divisiveness, performed, however briefly, something of the same function. How much better it felt to agree about the mastery of Luis Tiant than to argue about the wretchedness of Richard Nixon.

[23]   In sports as in life, character does not much change. I have recently begun to play a game called racquet ball, and I find I would still rather look good than win, which is what I usually do: look good and lose. I beat the rum-dums but go down before quality players. I get compliments in defeat. Men who beat me admire the whip of my strokes, my wrist action, my anticipation, the power I get behind the ball. When this occurs I feel like a woman who is complimented for the shape of her bottom when it is her mind she craves admiration for, though of course she will take what praise she can get.

[24]   R. H. Tawney, the great historian of religion and capitalism, once re-marked that the only progress he could note during the course of his lifetime was in the deportment of dogs. For myself, I would say that the chief progress in the course of my lifetime has been in the quality and variety of athletic gear. Racquets made of metal, aluminum, wood, and fiberglass, balls of different colors, sneakers of all materials and designs, posh warm-up suits, tube socks, sweatbands for the head and wrist in various colors and pipings; only the athletic supporter, the old jockstrap, remains unornamented, but perhaps even now Vera or Peter Max is at the drawing board. In any event, with all this elegant plumage available, it is a nice time to be playing ball again.

[25]   Sports can be impervious to age. My father-in-law, a man of style, seriousness, and great good humor who died a year ago in his late sixties, was born in South Bend, Indiana, and in his early manhood left the Catholic Church—two facts that conjoined to give him an intense interest in the for-tunes of the teams from Notre Dame. He loved to see them lose. The torch has been passed on. I now love to see Notre Dame lose, and when it does I think of him and remember his smile.

[26]   When I was a boy I had a neighbor, a man who, after retirement, had a number of strokes. An old man and a young boy, we had in common a love of sports, which, when we met on the street, was our only topic of conversation. He once inspected a new glove of mine, and instructed me to rub it down with neat's-foot oil, place a ball firmly in the pocket, wrap string tightly around the glove, and leave it like that for the winter. I did, and it worked. After his last stroke but one, he seldom left his house. Afternoons he spent in a chair in his bedroom, a blanket over his lap, listening to Cub games over the radio. It was while listening to a ball game that he quietly died. I cannot imagine a better way.

VOCABULARY

Use the context of the essay and your dictionary to define the following words:

1. legendary (par. 2)
2. balletic (par. 5)
3. reticent (par. 7)
4. nostalgia (par. 11)
5. profuse (par. 15)
6. pervasive (par. 17)
7. ubiquitous (par. 19)
8. inherently (par. 20)
9. aptly (par. 21)
10. impervious (par. 25)

RHETORIC AND IDEA

1. Put the topic sentence, evidence, and concluding sentence of paragraph 1 on a staircase diagram. Label the various steps correctly: Idea, Evidence, Evidence/Idea.
2. In paragraph 2, Epstein lists the following "legendary figures in the history of sports": Ty Cobb, Jim Thorpe, Bobby Jones, Big Bill Tilden, Red Grange, and Man o' War. Identify each by sport and achievement.

3. What key word provides the core around which paragraphs 3 through 6 are developed? State the main idea of this unit.
4. In paragraph 7, Epstein says he has been "Schenkeled, Mussbergered, Summeralled, Cosselled, DeRogotissed, and Garagiolaed." What does he mean?
5. Does Epstein watch sports on television to give an outlet to his violent emotions, to regain the glowing moments of adolescence, or to discover metaphysical truths? Explain.
6. In addition to his appreciation of the craft evident in sport, what two reasons does Epstein give for staying up late to watch a baseball game of no real significance?
7. In the first sentence of paragraph 22 Epstein says that "sport is culture." How many reasons does he give to support his claim? What are they?
8. How many examples does Epstein use to develop the main idea of paragraph 22: "It [sport] has a binding power that transcends social class and education"?
9. Point out the key words and phrases that supply the connection between paragraphs 6 and 7, 7 and 8, 8 and 9, 10 and 11, 12 and 13, 15 and 16, 16 and 17, 18 and 19, and 19 and 20.

WRITING ASSIGNMENTS

1. Write an essay in which you give at least three reasons you enjoy playing or watching some particular sport. Use examples to illustrate each reason.
2. Write an essay on one of the following topics:

> Basketball Is Anything but a Non-contact Sport
> Football Is Not as Rough as We Are Led to Believe
> Golf Can Bring Out the Worst in the Best of Persons
> Racquet Ball Is Both Challenging and Great Exercise
> The Loneliest Man Alive Is the Baseball Player Who Has Just Made an Error
> Even Professional Wrestling Demands Craft

3. Write an essay in which you explore why you admire or do not admire a particular athlete in one of the following sports:

skating (ice or roller)	skiing (water or snow)
baseball	football
automobile racing	boxing
tennis	basketball
swimming and diving	gymnastics
soccer	golf
bowling	weight lifting
body building	hockey

The Editors of *Time*

A Long Day
in the Frightful Life

[1] It may be, through the process of adaptation to environment, that future city dwellers will be born with their heads turned sideways—the better to watch behind them. As residents and businessmen seek ways to protect their property and their lives, the soaring crime rate is perhaps matched only by the rising curve of paranoia. Already, the jungle that is the U.S. city is so crisscrossed with fear and alarm wires that the following account of a day in the life of a fictional citizen of a composite U.S. city, based on security measures that already exist, is entirely within the realm of possibility:

[2] John Bryant fought through the fuzz of last night's sleeping pill as the 7 a.m. newsman, activated by the clock-radio, flicked through the details of yesterday's muggings, liquor-store holdups, and sniper attacks. John groped for the light switch—and inadvertently brushed against the "panic button" on the seven-hundred-dollar Tel-Guard alarm console connected to his telephone. Obediently, the system silently dialed the operator and automatically began repeating a recorded message: "Emergency at 250 Lincoln Street."

[3] Still groggy, John shaved, dressed, and went to feed the attack-trained Doberman pinscher that he had leased for $25 a week. Holding out the meat, he forgot and commanded. "Get it!"; the dog obediently bit his hand. He was

still bandaging the wound when two policemen, answering the Tel-Guard summons, began pounding at his door. Fumbling frantically, John managed to undo the three locks on the door, but in the process he dropped the seven-pound vertical steel bar from the $14.50 Police Fox lock on his foot. After apologizing profusely to the cops, he limped back inside to get his overcoat, checked to make sure that his can of Mace was in the pocket, relocked the door, and headed for the bus stop.

[4]   John was already on the step of the bus when he discovered that he had nothing smaller than a $10 bill. "Off you go, Mac" ordered the driver; alarmed by a rash of bus robberies, the city had decreed that all riders must drop the exact fare into the locked fare box. Drivers were allowed to carry no cash on their person. In desperation, John stepped down and turned to a young woman on the curb to ask for change. "Miss," he began, "could you—" She let him have it with her G-G31 tear-gas device, a $24.95 gun that enfolds its target in a twelve-foot by six-foot cloud of tear gas and dye. Blinded, reeling, John staggered off down the street and hailed a taxi.

[5]   Slumping into the rear seat, he was still wiping his eyes when he heard an ominous click: Up front, behind his bulletproof plastic shield, the driver had flicked a switch that locked both rear doors electrically to prevent passengers from taking off before paying the fare. "Where to, fella?" asked a voice from a loudspeaker overhead. John told him. The trip to the office was uneventful, until John put his ten-dollar bill in a revolving tray in the partition and got back change for five dollars. When he pounded on the plastic and protested, the amplified voice informed him that he had only passed through a fiver—and the driver was an off-duty cop. John decided to write off the five dollars.

[6]   The rest of the morning passed peacefully enough—until shortly before noon, when John ducked out to shop for a present for his girl friend's birthday. He had spotted just the thing a few days earlier in a nearby department store: a $1.49 Protectalarm—a battery-operated siren designed to be carried in a woman's purse.

[7]   As he walked through the store, John was followed every step of the way by closed-circuit TV cameras that transmitted his image to a monitoring room upstairs. He found the Protectalarm, pulled out his checkbook, and waited patiently while a new clerk figured out how to work the still camera that photographed every customer paying by check. In her confusion, the clerk wrapped the package without first removing the tags. One of them was a wafer, specially radiated to set off a Knogo sonic alarm in the doorway of the store. John had barely reached the sidewalk when he was surrounded by detectives who accused him of shoplifting.

[8]   By the time the tearful clerk admitted her mistake and the stony looks turned to embarrassed smiles, John decided to call it a day. Exhausted, nerves frazzled, he walked home—carefully skirting shadows. He took a trifle longer than usual to open his triple-locked door. The delay proved unfortunate. Before John could slither inside his urban fortress, three thugs lurking in the vestibule relieved him of his wallet, his watch, and his girl friend's Protectalarm. Then, for good measure, they gave him a whiff of his own Mace.

VOCABULARY

Use the context of the essay and your dictionary to define the following words:

1. adaptation (par. 1)
2. soaring (par. 1)
3. paranoia (par. 1)
4. composite (par. 1)
5. activated (par. 2)

6. inadvertently (par. 2)
7. vertical (par. 3)
8. profusely (par. 3)
9. decreed (par. 4)
10. ominous (par.5)

RHETORIC AND IDEA

1. To what song made popular several years ago by the Beatles does the title allude? Is the allusion appropriate? Explain. (The words of the song appear complete in *The Beatles Illustrated Lyrics.*)
2. Which of the four types of writing is "A Long Day in the Frightful Life"?
3. Is paragraph 1 necessary? Could it be omitted without damage to the meaning of the essay?
4. "A Long Day in the Frightful Life" is satire. What is being satirized in the article?
5. Much of the humor of the essay is based on ironic situations, occurrences that are the reverse of what the reader can reasonably expect to happen. Find as many of these situations as you can.

WRITING ASSIGNMENTS

Write a brief narrative (satirical or otherwise) on the dangers of one of the following:

driving in the city or on the open highway

living in the city or the suburbs or the country

crossing the street

riding the city bus

eating packaged foods

breathing the air

drinking the water

flying in an airplane

sleeping

going on vacation

swimming in fresh or salt water

owning an animal—dog, bird, cat, horse

section three

Of Men and Women, Women and Men

The Editors of *Time*

Male and Female:
The Differences Between
Them

[1] ''The Book of Genesis had it wrong. In the beginning God created Eve,'' says Johns Hopkins Medical Psychologist John Money. What he means is that the basic tendency of the human fetus is to develop as a female. If the genes order the gonads to become testicles and put out the male hormone androgen, the embryo will turn into a boy; otherwise it becomes a girl: ''You have to add something to get a male,'' Money notes. ''Nature's first intention is to create a female.''

[2] Nature may prefer women, but virtually every culture has been partial to men. That contradiction raises an increasingly pertinent question (as well as the hackles of militant feminists): Are women immutably different from men? Women's Liberationists believe that any differences—other than anatomical—are a result of conditioning by society. The opposing view is that all of the differences are fixed in the genes. To scientists, however, the nature-nurture controversy is oversimplified. To them, what human beings are results from a complex interaction between both forces. Says Oxford Biologist Christopher Ounsted: ''It is a false dichotomy to say that this difference is acquired and that one genetic. To try and differentiate is like asking a penny whether it is really a heads penny or a tails penny.'' As Berkeley Psychologist Frank Beach suggests, ''Predispositions may be genetic; complex behavior patterns are probably not.''

[3]   The idea that genetic predispositions exist is based on three kinds of evidence. First, there are the "cultural universals" cited by Margaret Mead. Almost everywhere, the mother is the principal caretaker of the child, and male dominance and aggression are the rule. Some anthropologists believe there has been an occasional female-dominated society; others insist that none has existed.

[4]   Then there is the fact that among most ground-dwelling primates, males are dominant and have as a major function the protection of females and off-spring. Some research suggests that this is true even when the young are raised apart from the adults, which seems to mean that they do not learn their roles from their society.

[5]   Finally, behavioral sex differences show up long before any baby could possibly perceive subtle differences between his parents or know which parent he is expected to imitate. "A useful strategy," says Harvard Psychologist Jerome Kagan, "is to assume that the earlier a particular difference appears, the more likely it is to be influenced by biological factors."

[6]   Physical differences appear even before birth. The heart of the female fetus often beats faster, and girls develop more rapidly. "Physiologically," says Sociologist Barbette Blackington, "women are better-made animals." Males do have more strength and endurance—though that hardly matters in a technological society.

[7]   Recent research hints that there may even be sex differences in the brain. According to some experimenters, the presence of the male hormone testosterone in the fetus may "masculinize" the brain, organizing the fetal nerve centers in characteristic ways. This possible "sex typing" of the central nervous system before birth may make men and women respond differently to incoming stimuli, Sociologist John Gagnon believes.

[8]   In fact, newborn girls do show different responses in some situations. They react more strongly to the removal of a blanket and more quickly to touch and pain. Moreover, experiments demonstrate that twelve-week-old girls gaze longer at photographs of faces than at geometric figures. Boys show no preference then, though eventually they pay more attention to figures. Kagan acknowledges the effect of environment, but he has found that it exerts a greater influence on girls than on boys. The female infants who experienced the most "face-to-face interaction" with their mothers were more attentive to faces than girls whose mothers did not exchange looks with them so much. Among boys, there was no consistent relationship.

[9]   As some psychologists see it, this very early female attention to the human face suggests that women may have a greater and even partly innate sensitivity to other human beings. Perhaps this explains why girls seem to get more satisfaction from relationships with people.

[10]   Even after infancy, the sexes show differential interests that do not seem to grow solely out of experience. Psychoanalyst Erik Erikson has found that boys and girls aged ten to twelve use space differently when asked to construct a scene with toys. Girls often build a low wall, sometimes with an elaborate doorway, surrounding a quiet interior scene. Boys are likely to construct

towers, facades with cannons, and lively exterior scenes. Erikson acknowledges that cultural influences are at work, but he is convinced that they do not fully explain the nature of children's play. The differences, he says, "seem to parallel the morphology [shape and form] of genital differentiation itself: in the male, an external organ, erectible and intrusive; internal organs in the female, with vestibular access, leading to statically expectant ova."

[11]   In aptitude as well as in interest, sex differences become apparent early in life. Though girls are generally less adept than boys at mathematical and spatial reasoning, they learn to count sooner and to talk earlier and better. Some scientists think this female verbal superiority may be caused by sex-linked differences in the brain. Others believe it may exist because, as observation proves, mothers talk to infant girls more than to baby boys. But does the mother's talking cause the child to do likewise, or could it be the other way round? Psychologist Michael Lewis suggests the possibility that girls are talked to more because, for biological reasons, they respond more to words and thus stimulate their mothers to keep talking.

[12]   Evidence that parental behavior does affect speech comes from tests made by Kagan among poor Guatemalan children. There, boys are more highly valued than girls, are talked to more and become more verbal. In the U.S., Psychiatrist David Levy had found that boys who are atypically good with words and inept with figures have been overprotected by their mothers. Psychologist Elizabeth Bing has observed that girls who excel at math and spatial problems have often been left to work alone by their mothers, while highly verbal girls have mothers who offer frequent suggestions, praise and criticism.

[13]   While girls outdo boys verbally, they often lag behind in solving analytical problems, those that require attention to detail. Girls seem to think "globally," responding to situations as a whole instead of abstracting single elements. In the "rod and frame test," for instance, a subject sits in a dark room before a luminous rod inside a slightly tilted frame, and is asked to move the rod to an upright position. Boys can separate the rod visibly from the frame and make it stand straight; girls, misled by the tipped frame, usually adjust the rod not to the true vertical but to a position parallel with the sides of the frame.

[14]   In another experiment, children are asked to group related pictures. Boys again pay attention to details, perhaps putting together pictures that show people with an arm raised; girls make functional groups of, for example, a doctor, a nurse and a wheelchair.

[15]   In all such differences, environmental influence is suggested by the fact that children who think analytically most often prove to have mothers who have encouraged initiative and exploration, while youngsters who think globally have generally been tied to their mother's apron strings. In Western society, of course, it is usually boys who are urged toward adventure. Herein, perhaps—there is no proof—lies an explanation for the apparent male capacity to think analytically.

[16]   In IQ tests, males and females score pretty much alike. Since this is true, why do women seem less creative? Many social scientists are convinced that the reasons are cultural. Women, they say, learn early in life that female ac-

complishment brings few rewards. In some cases, women cannot be creative because they are discriminated against. In other instances, a woman's creativity may well be blunted by fear of nonconformity, failure or even success itself. Unlike men, Kagan says, women are trained to have strong anxiety about being wrong.

[17]   To many psychoanalysts, however, the explanation lies in the fact that women possess the greatest creative power of all: bringing new life into being; thus they need not compensate by producing works of art. Men, it is theorized, are driven to make up for what seem to them a deficiency. That they feel keenly, though unconsciously, their inability to bear children is shown in dreams reported on the analyst's couch, in the behavior of small boys who play with dolls and walk around with their stomachs thrust forward in imitation of their pregnant mothers and in primitive rites and ancient myths. According to these myths, presumably conceived by males, Adam delivered Eve from his rib cage, Zeus gave birth to Athena out of his head, and when Semele was burned to death, Zeus seized Dionysus from her womb and sewed him up in his thigh until the infant had developed.

[18]   There are personality differences between the sexes too. Although no trait is confined to one sex—there are women who exceed the male average even in supposedly masculine characteristics—some distinctions turn up remarkably early. At New York University, for example, researchers have found that a female infant stops sucking a bottle and looks up when someone comes into the room; a male pays no attention to the visitor.

[19]   Another Kagan experiment shows that girls of twelve months who become frightened in a strange room drift toward their mothers, while boys look for something interesting to do. At four months, twice as many girls as boys cry when frightened in a strange laboratory. What is more, Kagan says, similar differences can be seen in monkeys and baboons, which "forces us to consider the possibility that some of the psychological differences between men and women may not be the product of experience alone but of subtle biological differences."

[20]   Many researchers have found greater dependence and docility in very young girls, greater autonomy and activity in boys. When a barrier is set up to separate youngsters from their mothers, boys try to knock it down; girls cry helplessly. There is little doubt that maternal encouragement—or discouragement—of such behavior plays a major role in determining adult personality. For example, a mother often stimulates male autonomy by throwing a toy far away from her young son, thus tacitly suggesting to him that he leave her to get it.

[21]   Animal studies suggest that there may be a biological factor in maternal behavior; mothers of rhesus monkeys punish their male babies earlier and more often than their female offspring; they also touch their female babies more often and act more protective toward them.

[22]   As for the controversial question of female "passivity," Psychoanalyst Helene Deutsch believes that the concept has been misunderstood. "There is no contradiction between being feminine and working. The ego can be active in both men and women," she says. It is only in love and in sex that passivity is particularly appropriate for women. As she sees it, passivity is no more than

a kind of openness and warmth; it does not mean "inactivity, emptiness or immobility."

[23]   Another controversy rages over the effect of hormones. Militant women, who discount hormonal influences, disagree violently with scientific researchers, who almost unanimously agree that hormones help determine how people feel and act. So far, there have been few studies of male hormones, but scientists think they may eventually discover hormonal cycles in men that produce cyclic changes in mood and behavior. As for females, studies have indicated that 49% of female medical and surgical hospital admissions, most psychiatric hospital admissions and 62% of violent crimes among women prisoners occur on premenstrual and menstrual days. At Worcester State Hospital in Massachusetts, Psychologists Donald and Inge Broverman have found that estrogen sharpens sensory perception. They believe that this heightened sensitivity may lead more women than men to shy away from situations of stress.

[24]   One trait thought to be affected by hormones is aggressiveness. In all cultures, investigators report, male infants tend to play more aggressively than females. While scientists think a genetic factor may be involved, they also observe that society fosters the difference by permitting male aggression and encouraging female adaptability. Some suggest that females may be as aggressive as men—but with words instead of deeds.

[25]   The definitive research on hormones and aggression is still to be done. However, it has been established that the female hormone estrogen inhibits aggression in both animal and human males. It has also been proved that the male hormone androgen influences aggression in animals. For example, castration produces tractable steers rather than fierce bulls.

[26]   The influence of androgen begins even before birth. Administered to pregnant primates, the hormone makes newborn females play more aggressively than ordinary females. Moreover, such masculinized animals are usually aggressive as long as they live, even if they are never again exposed to androgen.

[27]   According to some experts, this long-lasting effect of hormones administered or secreted before birth may help explain why boys are more aggressive than girls even during their early years when both sexes appear to produce equal amounts of male and female hormones. Other observers have suggested that the spurt in male-hormone production at puberty could be one of the causes of delinquency in adolescent boys, but there is no proof that this is so.

[28]   Will there some day be a "unisex" society with no differences between men and women, except anatomical ones? It seems unlikely. Anatomy, parturition and gender, observes Psychologist Joseph Adelson, cannot be wished away "in a spasm of the distended will, as though the will, in pursuit of total human possibility, can amplify itself to overcome the given." Or, as Psychoanalyst Therese Benedek sees it, "Biology precedes personality."

[29]   "Nature has been the oppressor," observes Michael Lewis. Women's role as caretaker "was the evolutionary result of their biological role in birth and feeding." The baby bottle has freed women from some of the tasks of that role, but, says University of Michigan Psychologist Judith Bardwick, "the major responsibility for child rearing is the woman's, even in the Soviet Union, the Israeli kibbutz, Scandinavia and mainland China." Furthermore,

though mothering skills are mostly learned, it is a fact that if animals are raised in isolation and then put in a room with the young of the species, it is the females who go to the infants and take care of them.

[30]   "Perhaps the known biological differences can be totally overcome, and society can approach a state in which a person's sex is of no consequence for any significant activity except childbearing," admits Jerome Kagan. "But we must ask if such a society will be satisfying to its members." As he sees it, "complementarity" is what makes relationships stable and pleasurable.

[31]   Psychoanalyst Martin Symonds agrees. "The basic reason why unisex must fail is that in the sexual act itself, the man has to be assertive, if tenderly, and the woman has to be receptive. What gives trouble is when men see assertiveness as aggression and women see receptiveness as submission." Unisex, he sums up, would be "a disaster," because children need roles to identify with and rebel against. "You can't identify with a blur. A unisex world would be a frictionless environment in which nobody would be able to grow up."

[32]   The crucial point is that a difference is not a deficiency. As Biologist Ounsted puts it, "We are all human beings and in this sense equal. We are not, however, the same." In the opinion of John Money, "You can play fair only if you recognize and respect authentic differences."

[33]   Though scientists disagree about the precise nature and causes of these differences, there is no argument about two points: society plays a tremendous part in shaping the differences, and most women are capable of doing whatever they want. Only in the top ranges of ability, says Kagan, are innate differences significant; for typical men and women, "the biological differences are totally irrelevant." Psychiatrist Donald Lunde agrees. "There is no evidence," he asserts, "that men are any more or less qualified by biological sex differences alone to perform the tasks generally reserved for them in today's societies."

VOCABULARY

Use the context of the essay and your dictionary to define the following words:

1. fetus (par. 1)
2. dichotomy (par. 2)
3. morphology (par. 10)
4. adept (par. 11)
5. atypically (par. 11)
6. passivity (par. 22)
7. tractable (par. 25)
8. distended (par. 28)
9. amplify (par. 28)
10. authentic (par. 32)

RHETORIC AND IDEA

1. What proof does John Money give in paragraph 1 that "The Book of Genesis had it wrong"?
2. In paragraph 2, the editors of *Time* ask, "Are women immutably different from men?" With what three views do they answer the question? Which of the three views do the editors develop fully?

3. List the three kinds of evidence (paragraphs 3, 4, and 5) that support the idea that genetic predispositions exist between women and men.

4. What evidence is presented in paragraph 8 to suggest that " 'sex typing' of the central nervous system before birth may make men and women respond differently to incoming stimuli"?

5. In paragraph 10 the editors of *Time* say that Erik Erikson has found that when asked to construct a scene boys and girls aged ten to twelve do different things. How do their scenes differ? How does Erikson attempt to explain the difference?

6. What reasons are given in paragraphs 16 and 17 for males' and females' scoring pretty much alike on IQ tests, yet women's "seeming" less creative?

7. What reasons do the editors of *Time* list in paragraphs 28 through 32 that make it unlikely that there will someday be a unisex society with no differences between men and women, except anatomical ones?

8. In paragraph 30, the editors of *Time* quote Jerome Kagan as saying that "complementarity" is what makes relationships stable and pleasurable. What does he mean?

9. Do the editors of *Time* use AAABBB or ABABAB comparison-and-contrast patterns? Explain with examples.

WRITING ASSIGNMENTS

1. In paragraph 2, the editors of *Time* say, "virtually every culture has been partial to men." But they do not support that assertion. Write a comparison/contrast essay in which you show that the culture of the United States (or another country with which you are familiar) is or is not partial to men.

2. In paragraph 6, the editors of *Time* concede that the male's superior strength and endurance "hardly matters in a technological society." Write an essay in which you agree or disagree with the editors. Develop your idea by using examples from business, industry, public service, military service, education.

3. Write a comparison/contrast paper on the similarities and/or differences between one of the following:

   a male child and a female child

   a niece and a nephew

   a husband and a wife

   a mother and a father

   an adolescent girl and an adolescent boy

   a woman in her twenties and a man in his twenties

Elizabeth Van Guilder

Merged or Submerged

[1]   A funny thing happened on the way to our twenty-fifth anniversary. My husband and I stopped fighting the battle of the sexes and began to think of each other as people. Just when this began we can't pinpoint, but we know exactly when we noticed that it had happened.

[2]   It was the morning my husband turned to me and asked if I would possibly have time to make his lunch for him (he brown bags it to work) because he hadn't had time to do it the night before. I looked at him, and a funny kind of smile came over his face as he caught my thought.

[3]   Twenty-five years ago the dialogue would have gone like this:

> "Where the hell is my lunch? Did you forget it again? If I ran my office the way you run this house—"
> "I'm so sorry, dear; I'll get it right away."

[4]   That night we reminisced about the people we were twenty-five years ago and the people we are today. We are so very different, in our attitudes toward ourselves and toward each other, and particularly in our interpretations of our roles as partners in marriage. In the early days of our marriage, I saw myself as the inheritor of a tradition which made the male unquestioned "head of the house," in every possible connotation of the word. This submission involved all aspects of our living together but was particularly apparent in the manage-

ment of money and in the way we divided all the chores involved in the keeping of the house and the rearing of the family. These traditional roles seem to
be almost nonexistent today, so changed are our concepts of the man—woman
relationship in the light of the attitudes now common in American society.

[5]   I did not think twenty-five years ago that I was a particularly submissive
wife. We had solemnly agreed before our wedding day that *our* marriage would
be different—more modern, more "equal." We defined this, percentagewise,
as 51-49, a distinct improvement over the 60-40 marriages we saw around us.
What was not then apparent to me was that, if simple majority vote is taken, 2
percent is as final as 20. If someone always has two points on you, you don't
often get to win! Not that I wasn't consulted—and, because my husband is an
essentially kind and fair person, I was often allowed to prevail. But it was
always clearly understood by each of us that the concession was *his* to make. In
the event of an impasse he was without question the decision maker. I can
remember saying, quite seriously, "Somebody has to be the captain or the
ship sinks."

[6]   Well, the ship isn't sinking, and we long ago forgot to worry about who was
issuing the orders. In fact, there have been times when the only way the boat
floated at all was for both of us to bail, bail, bail. Together. No, today we seem
to function without any clear definition of just who is boss over what. And my
husband finds this, he says, a pleasant relief from the awesome responsibility
of *always* having to decide. Because, brother, if it goes wrong, you've got only
yourself to blame! This decision making by the male may once have been
essential, but for a modern woman to concede this prerogative is almost a cop-
out on her part, an admission that she doesn't really want to bear her share of
the burden or assume her role as a responsible partner.

[7]   Female irresponsibliity and male dominance were nowhere more evident
than in the management of money. He was the breadwinner, the keeper of the
purse, the dispenser of all goodies. I, like my mother-in-law before me, had
my "housekeeping money" which I could dispense as I chose. Everything
else—for clothing, furniture, curtains, an occasional frivolity—had to be requested, teased, cajoled or bargained for, explained. I practically had to sub-
mit a technical brief outlining the recommendation for expenditure. And yet,
I enjoyed and encouraged this; it was pleasant to continue the childish habit of
dependence.

[8]   Today I have my own checking account, my own job, my own money. We
don't think of money as "his" and "hers," but as "ours." Each has the right
to use what he earns as he sees fit; each of us assumes responsibility for the
mutual obligations involved in running a home and raising a family. There is
no question of dominance and submission: a committee of equals determines
priorities, and the money is dispensed or saved in accordance with the decision.

[9]   The second area, housekeeping, twenty-five years ago was a scene you
wouldn't believe. We were the products of a time gone by, of an age when
women regarded themselves as adjuncts to the male, not really functioning except when they functioned as wives, mothers, and companions in ways acceptable to the husband and father. Our prototypes were our own mothers and the
mothers of most of our friends.

[10]   Women, having little outside the home to interest and motivate them, had to channel all their intelligence and ingenuity into making that home. I patterned myself after my mother-in-law. Because Mom was a bright person with a lot of energy, she had to make her role into something important or it would have been intolerable. So she became Superhousewife. Everything was starched, ironed, cleaned, waxed, scrubbed, shined, slipcovered, doilied, and *kept*. Her house was the most *kept* house I had ever seen. It was beautiful. It smelled good; it looked good; it ran like a clock; and everybody in it was miserable. When you sat down on the couch, Mom hovered nearby, ready to plump up the down cushions as soon as you got up.

[11]   I, too, believed that dust bunnies were a no-no, a smudged window a blot on my personal worth. You won't believe this, but I even ironed my husband's socks. Not without protest, at first, but—well, here's the dialog as George and I recall it, from the day I first performed the ritual of doing the laundry:

> "Honey, my socks aren't ironed."
> A peal of laughter. "You funny thing—who irons socks?'
> Dead silence. Then a growl: "My mother does . . . I like 'em that way."
> "OH."

[12]   Of course, this was before wash-and-wear, and in defense of George and his mother, socks did get a little lumpy. Nor was my Superhousewife mother-in-law by any means unique in this: her friends ironed socks, too. I blush to confess—forgive me, Gloria Steinem—that I dutifully ironed those socks. What's important is not whether I did or didn't—but the simple truth that I never questioned his right to ask (demand) nor mine to comply (obey?).

[13]   Now, with housekeeping removed from the male-dominant/female-submissive syndrome, I am happy to report that the housework still gets done, by whoever is best able (and willing) to do it. If no one can, things wait their turn. Sometimes it's a whole family project, with everybody pitching in to get it done in order to get on to something more interesting. We've streamlined the process in order to achieve the most comfortable home with the least possible effort. Superhousewife, Jr., doesn't live here any more. We're two people living in a reasonably clean and orderly home, with chores divided according to desire and capability—but almost all are interchangeable. He can do dishes or make pancakes without wondering where his masculinity went; I have learned to put away the frivolous pseudo-feminine rites of being a little stupid about money, a little frightened of everything crawly, a little dependent in every situation. I can balance my own checkbook, kill my own spiders, and mix a very fine extra dry martini.

[14]   Looking back to those earlier years, I can remember so clearly how we also divided up the chores of child care. His to love, provide for, play with, teach, or discipline the children; but mine involved all the traditionally female tasks, particularly those connected with the alimentary canal. From feeding to diapering, it was mine. How differently we saw things with the advent of our last child fifteen years after the first! Father was as capable and willing to do any and all of the pleasant or unpleasant tasks, as able to get up at 2:00 A.M., as Mother, and so our third child was in a sense his first; he came to know and enjoy him in a way never open to him before.

[15]   As you can see, it's been a long time since anyone quibbled about which job was whose. We're more analogous now to a well-coordinated team pulling our wagonload of responsibilities. If memory serves me, the best team is the one which together exerts equal effort, at precisely the same time, thus drawing the load with the minimum of friction.

[16]   This change in us is a reflection, I think, of what has been going on in the world in the past few decades. When Betty Friedan wrote *The Feminine Mystique,* it was not so much the call to revolution she supposed it to be as a response to something already in progress. A newer tradition is being born to supplant the old concepts of Man and Woman. These two mythic beings have been recreated as People, who have to decide that the great experience of life is to be shared—not partitioned off into segments labeled ''his'' and ''hers.''

[17]   I think there's a warning in this somewhere for the more militant feminists among us. I suspect they should take a good look at life as we experience it today and compare it with what their mothers and grandmothers knew. Except in a few areas where change necessarily comes slowly, the event has already taken place or is moving inexorably in that direction. To become raucous and demanding, denigrating the male instead of loving him, could be a terrible mistake. It could lead even to a reversal of the beautiful trend, which, all unaware, has come upon us.

VOCABULARY

Use the context of the essay and your dictionary to define the following words:

1. reminisced (par. 4)
2. concession (par. 5)
3. impasse (par. 5)
4. concede (par. 6)
5. dominance (par. 7)

6. alimentary (par. 14)
7. quibbled (par. 15)
8. analogous (par. 15)
9. supplant (par. 16)
10. denigrating (par. 17)

RHETORIC AND IDEA

1. Which paragraphs make up the introduction? Which the body? Which the conclusion?
2. In which sentence in the essay does Van Guilder most clearly state her thesis?
3. Explain how the following sentence from paragraph 4 acts as an organizational base for the body of the essay: ''This submission involved all aspects of our living together but was particularly apparent in the management of money and in the way we divided all the chores involved in the keeping of the house and the rearing of the family.''
4. Explain also how the sentence quoted above in 3 acts as a transitional springboard that makes the entire essay coherent.
5. Which paragraphs does Van Guilder use to develop ''the management of money,'' her first major point? Does she organize her contrast *AAABBB* or *ABABAB?* Explain.

6. Which paragraphs does she use to develop her second major point: housekeeping? Does she organize her contrasts *AAABBB* or *ABABAB?* Which paragraphs of this unit make up the first major subpoint under this second point? Which the second major subpoint?

7. Which paragraphs does she use to develop her third major point: child care? Does she organize these points of contrast AAABBB or ABABAB? Explain.

WRITING ASSIGNMENTS

1. Using as a guide your answers to Rhetoric and Idea questions 5, 6, and 7 above, write a two-level topic outline (pp. 90–91) for "Merged or Submerged." Include the title, the thesis statement, the major (Roman numeral) divisions, and the subdivisions (capital letters).

2. Write an essay on one of the following topics:

   Man's Job; Woman's Job
   Sharing Responsibilities
   A 60-40 Marriage Can (Can't) Be Successful
   The Wife's Job
   The Husband's Job

3. Write an essay in which you describe the operation of the ideal family. Have at least four members in the family.

4. Use one of these suggested titles as an idea for an essay. Feel free to change the title to suit your plan.

   Whose Turn Is It To Do the Dishes?
   Can't You Squeeze the Toothpaste from the Bottom?
   How Much Clout Should Dad Have?
   When Should Mom Be the Breadwinner?
   Who Is the *Real* Captain of the Ship?
   Mom Could Always Get Exactly What She Wanted
   Ironed Socks! What's Wrong with That?

Anne Roiphe

Confessions of a
Female Chauvinist Sow

[1]   I once married a man I thought was totally unlike my father and I imagined a whole new world of freedom emerging. Five years later it was clear even to me—floating face down in a wash of despair—that I had simply chosen a replica of my handsome daddy-true. The updated version spoke English like an angel but—Good God!—underneath he was my father exactly: wonderful, but not the right man for me.

[2]   Most people I know have at one time or another been fouled up by their childhood experiences. Patterns tend to sink into the unconscious only to reappear, disguised, unseen, like marionette strings, pulling us this way or that. Whatever ails people—keeps them up at night, tossing and turning—also ails movements no matter how historically huge or politically important. The women's movement cannot remake consciousness, or reshape the future, without acknowledging and shedding all the unnecessary and ugly baggage of the past. It's easy enough now to see where men have kept us out of clubs, baseball games, graduate schools; it's easy enough to recognize the hidden directions that limit Sis to cake-baking and Junior to bridge-building; it's now possible for even Miss America herself to identify what *they* have done to us, and, of course, *they* have and *they* did and *they* are . . . But along the way we also developed our own hidden prejudices, class assumptions and an anti-male humor and collection of expectations that gave us, like all oppressed groups, a secret sense of superiority (co-existing with a poor self-image—it's not news that people can believe two contradictory things at once.)

Confessions of a Female Chauvinist Sow by Anne Roiphe from *New York Magazine.* Reprinted by permission of Brandt & Brandt.

[3]   Listen to any group that suffers materially and socially. They have a lexicon with which they tease the enemy: ofay, goy, honky, gringo. "Poor pale devils," said Malcolm X loud enough for us to hear, although blacks had joked about that to each other for years. Behind some of the women's liberation thinking lurk the rumors, the prejudices, the defense systems of generations of oppressed women whispering in the kitchen together, presenting one face to their menfolk and another to their card clubs, their mothers and sisters. All this is natural enough but potentially dangerous in a revolutionary situation in which you hope to create a future that does not mirror the past. The hidden anti-male feelings, a result of the old system, will foul us up if they are allowed to persist.

[4]   During my teen years I never left the house on my Saturday night dates without my mother slipping me a few extra dollars—mad money, it was called. I'll explain what it was for the benefit of the new generation in which people just sleep with each other: the fellow was supposed to bring me home, lead me safely through the asphalt jungle, protect me from slithering snakes, rapists and the like. But my mother and I knew men were apt to drink too much, to slosh down so many rye-and-gingers that some hero might well lead me in front of an oncoming bus, smash his daddy's car into Tiffany's window or, less gallantly throw up on my dress. Mad money was for getting home on your own, no matter what form of insanity your date happened to evidence. Mad money was also a wallflower's rope ladder; if the guy you came with suddenly fancied someone else, well, you didn't have to stay there and suffer, you could go home. Boys were fickle and likely to be unkind; my mother and I knew that, as surely as we knew they tried to make you do things in the dark they wouldn't respect you for afterwards, and in fact would spread the word and spoil your rep. Boys like to be flattered; if you made them feel important they would eat out of your hand. So talk to them about their interests, don't alarm them with displays of intelligence—we all knew that, we groups of girls talking into the wee hours of the night in a kind of easy companionship we thought impossible with boys. Boys were prone to have a good time, get you pregnant, and then pretend they didn't know your name when you came knocking on their door for finances or comfort. In short, we believed boys were less moral than we were. They appeared to be hypocritical, self-seeking, exploitative, untrustworthy and very likely to be showing off their precious masculinity. I never had a girl friend I thought would be unkind or embarrass me in public. I never expected a girl to lie to me about her marks or sport skill or how good she was in bed. Altogether without anyone's directly coming out and saying so—I gathered that men were sexy, powerful, very interesting, but not very nice, not very moral, humane and tender, like us. Girls played fairly while men, unfortunately, reserved their honor for the battlefield.

[5]   Why are there laws insisting on alimony and child support? Well, everyone knows that men don't have an instinct to protect their young and, given half a chance, with the moon in the right phase, they will run off and disappear. Everyone assumes a mother will not let her child starve, yet it is necessary to legislate that a father must not do so. We are taught to accept the idea that men are less decent; their charms may be manifold but their characters are riddled with faults. To this day I never blink if I hear that a man has gone to find his

fortune in South America, having left his pregnant wife, his blind mother and taken the family car. I still gasp in horror when I hear of a woman leaving her asthmatic infant for a rock group in Taos because I can't seem to avoid the assumption that men are naturally heels and women the ordained carriers of what little is moral in our dubious civilization.

[6]   My mother never gave me mad money thinking I would ditch a fellow for some other guy or that I would pass out drunk on the floor. She knew I would be considerate of my companion because, after all, I was more mature than the boys that gathered about. Why was I more mature? Women just are people-oriented; they learn to be empathetic at an early age. Most English students (students interested in humanity, not artifacts) are women. Men and boys—so the myth goes—conceal their feelings and lose interest in anybody else's. Everyone knows that even little boys can tell the difference between one kind of car and another—proof that their souls are mechanical, their attention directed to the non-human.

[7]   I remember shivering in the cold vestibule of a famous men's athletic club. Women and girls are not permitted inside the club's door. What are they doing in there, I asked? They're naked, said my mother, they're sweating, jumping up and down a lot, telling each other dirty jokes and bragging about their stock market exploits. Why can't we go in? I asked. Well, my mother told me, they're afraid we'd laugh at them.

[8]   The prejudices of childhood are hard to outgrow. I confess that every time my business takes me past that club, I shudder. Images of large bellies resting on massage tables and flaccid penises rising and falling with the Dow Jones average flash through my head. There it is, chauvinism waving its cancerous tentacles from the depths of my psyche.

[9]   Minorities automatically feel superior to the oppressor because, after all, they are not hurting anybody. In fact, they feel they are morally better. The old canard that women need love, men need sex—believed for too long by both sexes—attributes moral and spiritual superiority to women and makes of men beasts whose urges send them prowling into the night. This false division of good and bad, placing deforming pressures on everyone, doesn't have to contaminate the future. We know that the assumptions we make about each other become a part of the cultural air we breathe and, in fact, become social truths. Women who want equality must be prepared to give it and to believe in it, and in order to do that it is not enough to state that you are as good as any man, but also it must be stated that he is as good as you and both will be humans together. If we want men to share in the care of the family in a new way, we must assume them as capable of consistent loving tenderness as we.

[10]   I rummage about and find in my thinking all kinds of anti-male prejudices. Some are just jokes and others I will have a hard time abandoning. First, I share an emotional conviction with many sisters that women given power would not create wars. Intellectually I know that's ridiculous; great queens have waged war before; the likes of Lurleen Wallace, Pat Nixon and Mrs. General Lavelle can be depended upon in the future to guiltlessly condemn to death other people's children in the name of some ideal of their own. Little girls, of course, don't take toy guns out of their pockets and say ''Pow, pow'' to all their neighbors and friends like the average well-adjusted little boy.

However, if we gave little girls the six-shooters, we would soon have double the pretend body count.

[11]   Aggression is not, as I secretly think, a male-sex-linked characteristic: brutality is masculine only by virtue of opportunity. True, there are 1,000 Jack the Rippers for every Lizzie Borden, but that surely is the result of social forms. Women as a group are indeed more masochistic than men. The practical result of this division is that women seem nicer and kinder, but when the world changes, women will have a fuller opportunity to be just as rotten as men and there will be fewer claims of female moral superiority.

[12]   Now that I am entertaining early middle age, I hear many women complaining of husbands and ex-husbands who are attracted to younger females. This strikes the older women as unfair, of course. But I remember a time when I thought all boys around my age and grade were creeps and bores. I wanted to go out with an older man: a senior or, miraculously, a college man. I had a certain contempt for my coevals, not realizing that the freshman in college I thought so desirable, was some older girl's creep. Some women never lose that contempt for men of their own age. That isn't fair either and may be one reason why some sensible men of middle years find solace in young women.

[13]   I remember coming home from school one day to find my mother's card game dissolved in hysterical laughter. The cards were floating in black rivers of running mascara. What was so funny? A woman named Helen was lying on a couch pretending to be her husband with a cold. She was issuing demands for orange juice, aspirin, suggesting a call to a specialist, complaining of neglect, of fate's cruel finger, of heat, of cold, of sharp pains on the bridge of the nose that might indicate brain involvement. What was so funny? The ladies explained to me that all men behave just like that with colds, they are reduced to temper tantrums by simple nasal congestion, men cannot stand any little physical discomfort—on and on the laughter went.

[14]   The point of this vignette is the nature of the laughter—us laughing at them, us feeling superior to them, us ridiculing them behind their backs. If they were doing it to us we'd call it male chauvinist pigness; if we do it to them it is inescapably female chauvinist sowness and, whatever its roots, it leads to the same isolation. Boys are messy, boys are mean, boys are rough, boys are stupid and have sloppy handwriting. A cacophony of childhood memories rushes through my head, balanced, of course, by all the well-documented feelings of inferiority and envy. But the important thing, the hard thing, is to wipe the slate clean, to start again without the meanness of the past. That's why it's so important that the women's movement not become anti-male and allow its most prejudiced spokesmen total leadership. The much chewed-over abortion issue illustrates this. The women's-liberation position, insisting on a woman's right to determine her own body's destiny, leads in fanatical extreme to a kind of emotional immaculate conception in which the father is not judged even half-responsible—he has no rights, and no consideration is to be given to his concern for either the woman or the fetus.

[15]   Woman, who once was abandoned and disgraced by an unwanted pregnancy, has recently arrived at a new pride of ownership or disposal. She has traveled in a straight line that still excludes her sexual partner from an equal share in the wanted or unwanted pregnancy. A better style of life may develop

from an assumption that men are as human as we are. Why not ask the child's father if he would like to bring up the child? Why not share decisions, when possible, with the male? If we cut them out, assuming an old-style indifference on their part, we perpetuate the ugly divisiveness that has characterized relationships between the sexes so far.

[16]   Hard as it is for many of us to believe, women are not really superior to men in intelligence or humanity—they are only equal.

VOCABULARY

Use the context of the essay and your dictionary to define the following words:

1. replica (par. 1)
2. lexicon (par. 3)
3. prone (par. 4)
4. ordained (par. 5)
5. dubious (par. 5)
6. empathetic (par. 6)
7. chauvinism (par. 8)
8. canard (par. 9)
9. masochistic (par. 11)
10. coevals (par. 12)

RHETORIC AND IDEA

1. Is "Confessions of a Female Chauvinist Sow" argument or exposition? Explain by pointing out what Anne Roiphe's purpose seems to be.
2. In paragraph 1, the writer refers to "my handsome daddy-true" and expresses herself strongly with "good God!" How do these phrases help her establish the tone she wants?
3. In sentence 5 of paragraph 2, Roiphe uses a great deal of parallel structure. Invent a diagram that will illustrate the parallelism in this sentence.
4. In which sentence(s) of paragraph 3 does the writer announce clearly her reason for writing this essay?
5. How many paragraphs does Roiphe devote to the discussion of "mad money"? Which paragraphs are they? Does she stay on the subject the whole time? Define briefly "mad money."
6. In the author's judgment, what is the most dangerous result of both male chauvinist pigness and female chauvinist sowness? In which paragraph does she make this point? Do you agree? Why?
7. In paragraph 11, Roiphe says, "True, there are 1,000 Jack the Rippers for every Lizzie Borden, but that surely is the result of social forms." Who are Jack the Ripper and Lizzie Borden? What point does she use them to illustrate? Explain what she means by the "social forms" which cause this situation.
8. What basic assumption that women have about men does Roiphe attack in her essay?

WRITING ASSIGNMENTS

1. In a narrative essay, show how young women to be popular must learn to flatter young men.

2. Using examples from personal experience, write an essay in which you compare male chauvinist pigness and female chauvinist sowness. Make sure you define your terms carefully.

3. Select one of the following topics as the basis for an essay:

> The Male Stereotype
> The Female Stereotype
> How Parents Indoctrinate Children in Sex Roles
> What Girls (Boys) Have to Fear from Boys (Girls)
> Are Men Less Moral Than Women?
> Woman (Man): The Dangerous Animal
> The Advantages (Disadvantages) of Dating Older Men (Women)

4. In an essay, describe what you consider to be the ideal man, woman, boy, or girl. Make your description as lifelike as possible.

Rhoda Koenig

The Persons
in the Office

[1]   It has been observed, more and more frequently in recent years, that current events are putting the satirists out of business. A newspaper no longer needs an H. L. Mencken, with a deadly wit and an eighteenth-century vocabulary; any teenager can read the press releases and wire copy, and put together a weekly column in which any comment would be superfluous.

[2]   Imagine, for instance, the plight of the would-be satirist of the feminist movement who reads in the *New York Times,* as I did a few months ago, that some of its leaders are speaking out against ''sexual harassment,'' or, as the rest of us would call it, sex in the office.

[3]   Karen DeCrow, president of the National Organization for Women, claims that ''sexual harassment is one of the few sexist issues which has been totally in the closet. It is an issue that has been shrouded in silence because its occurrence is seen as both humiliating and trivial.'' The New York City Commission on Human Rights has also been looking into the problem. One of those who testified before it was the director of the women's section of the Human Affairs Program at Cornell, who has been bringing the issue to the attention of the women of Binghamton. One-third of those responding to her survey said that they tried to ignore on-the-job harassment, in which event it continued or got worse; many of the women complained to a higher authority but found that, more than half the time, nothing was done.

[4]   Now, the feminists are to be congratulated for having rooted out still another area of injustice; however, they have clearly failed to consider some aspects of the case. For a start, a lot of women would feel deprived without a reasonable quota of sexual harassment per week. Indeed, if handed a petition on sex in the office, most women I know would put a check next to "not enough." Furthermore, female employees are not always helpless victims of sexual harassment; some of them are entrepreneurs. Ask any woman whom she'd rather work for: a lecherous man, or her boss's idiot mistress. Those who have been in the latter position know about harassment.

[5]   And, for all its earnestness, the Binghamton study fails to mention the percentage of harassed women who came back with "Not today, thank you," or "Get lost, you toad," or something in between. If the women were struck dumb or ran for help when the men made advances, I can't blame the men for thinking they were acting the part of the coy maiden and giving encouragement for the chase.

[6]   Though the issue of sexual harassment probably won't make its way onto the picket lines or the evening news, it does provide a graphic illustration of what's wrong with much of feminism. The situation is distorted, the questions are over-simplified, and the women involved are told that they are helpless.

[7]   For "women's liberation," ironically, exists on its ability to persuade its adherents that, despite appearances, they are miserable and weak. With jesuitical ingenuity, they go about convincing white, middle-class, college-educated women that society has done them wrong, like the snake-oil salesman whose suggestible listeners began to feel all the symptoms of sciatica, dropsy, and the botts.

[8]   This way of thinking, of course, is not without appeal. Persons whose affluence and civility ensure they will never be beaten as punishment may find flagellation an interesting vice. To those who would make a noble ethos out of failure, contentment with one's lot is equated with ignorance, satisfaction with phlegm. In such circumstances, the discovery of newer and worse irritations assumes the force of a moral quest. For persons who do feel guilt at being dissatisfied, feminism offers absolution. However you have failed, they are told, don't hold yourself accountable. Society is to blame and matters will be set right by feminist fiats and general moral pressure, ensuring that one's wages will be adequate, one's ideas respected, and one's orgasms of the proper quantity and ideological persuasion. In this atmosphere, independent action is unreasonable, and so is independent thought. When confronted with inequities, the believing feminist throws a tantrum, or rises above it all, or awaits the action of the collective avenging conscience.

[9]   These conclusions don't derive solely from contemplating feminist theory. Two women I know purposely make themselves look drab so they won't have to be subjected to male advances, which they wouldn't know how to fend off. Another goes to bed with every man who takes her home, because she hasn't figured out a firm yet tactful way to say no. And a fourth, to whom I showed the article in the *Times,* expressed relief at the thought that the indignities she suffered on the way to the water cooler would soon be over. At the time she said this, she was wearing her usual office costume of—word of honor—off-the-shoulder blouse, short skirt, high heels, and no underwear. All of them,

needless to say, subscribe wholeheartedly to the idea that when they don't get what they want, or have to do something they dislike, some man is responsible, and some other woman ought to do something about it.

[10]   It seems unlikely that the antiharassment forces will ever work up enough steam to roll over the rest of us. Still, I wonder. There are a few disconcerting scents in the wind. Some men I know compliment a woman on her appearance much more hesitantly than they once did; a few even explain that they mean no offense. I have had men assure me of their adherence to all the tenets of woman's liberation, and, when told I could not care less, become intensely suspicious, as if I'm setting some kind of trap.

[11]   For men, much as the feminists would like to build them up in order to support the myth of women as oppressed, are not all that aggressive. They are more like shy woodland creatures, fawns peeping through the thicket of masculine self-protection. A man is someone who, when his boss says something moronic, agrees. A man is someone who eats his burnt steak in silence, rather than offend a waiter he doesn't like. A man is someone who takes you out and, when you want him to put his arms around you and kiss you, sits there carrying on a conversation. In short, all the women I know whose information about men comes from the real world and not from feminist tracts derive enormous merriment from the portrait of man as brutal enslaver. Men aggressive! they say. Ha Ha, that's good. Tell us another one.

[12]   This being so, an all-out war on harassment may not be such a good idea; it could too easily succeed, at least among the more sensitive and, therefore, potentially more interesting type of male. For work, as anyone who has read Studs Terkel knows, can often use all the harassment it can get. Harassment —or as some of us would call it, flirting—is a happier assertion of humanness than sabotage or shoplifting. It gives a woman a reason to be careful with her lipstick in the morning and a topic of conversation for the ladies' room at 4:30. It greases the wheels of social intercourse and makes the day a little less long.

[13]   H. L. Mencken, in his time, acquired a good many enemies, and, were he alive now, would certainly draw upon himself the wrath of every *Ms.* subscriber. Yet, although Mencken often wrote like a misogynist, he had a kind heart. A feminist would probably find the epitaph he composed for himself patronizing, but it captures the spirit I think is important to encourage and preserve. "If, after I depart this vale," Mencken wrote, "you ever remember me and have thought to please my ghost, forgive some sinner and wink your eye at some homely girl."

VOCABULARY

Use the context of the essay and your dictionary to define the following words.

1. superfluous (par. 1)
2. entrepreneurs (par. 4)
3. leeherous (par. 4)
4. earnestness (par. 5)
5. coy (par. 5)

6. graphic (par. 6)
7. ironically (par. 7)
8. suggestible (par. 7)
9. tenets (par. 10)
10. misogynist (par. 13)

RHETORIC AND IDEA

1. Rhoda Koenig's argument actually has two complaints—a more limited one and a broader issue. What is the more limited evil she introduces in paragraphs 1 through 3? What is her attitude toward it? What are the clues to this position?

2. In which paragraph is the limited subject related to the broader, more important issue? What one word in that paragraph is the key to what she says is the real problem?

3. Why does she say it is "ironic" that "women's liberation" tries to persuade its adherents that they are weak?

4. Sum up her full complaint about this aspect of women's liberation as she discusses it further in paragraphs 8 and 9. What is she advocating? Is she opposed to women's liberation?

5. What aspect of the problem is illustrated by the four women she refers to in paragraph 9?

6. On the limited subject, what two arguments against the women's liberation position does she make in paragraph 4?

7. Explain the working of her parallel sentence structure in paragraph 11. How does that structure fit into her tone of argument?

8. What is her point about men in paragraph 11? How does this point fit into her attack on the women's liberation position?

9. Why does she say that the H. L. Mencken quote at the end of her essay captures the spirit she wants to encourage?

WRITING ASSIGNMENTS

1. Use one position taken by some person, group, or movement to illustrate some broader mistake in their argument.

2. Do you agree that H. L. Mencken's quote is in the right spirit? What is good about it or what is wrong about it? What can it be used to illustrate?

3. What is your position about "flirting" or "harassment" in the office or some other public place?

4. What situation or situations do you find wrong in the interactions between the sexes in business or school circumstances?

Tony Schwartz

Living Together

[1]   It used to be called "living in sin"—and Jimmy Carter and millions of other Americans still think of it that way. Last winter, the President even asked a group of government workers to cut it out and get married. And it used to be done mostly by the very rich, who could afford to flout society's rules, and the very poor, who had nothing to lose by ignoring them. But now it's a way of life that takes in college students, divorcees, pensioners and thousands of young adults in transition from swingledom to suburbia.

[2]   Since 1970, Census Bureau figures show, the number of unmarried people of the opposite sex sharing a household has doubled, from 654,000 to 1.3 million—and that almost surely understates the total. "Of the revolutions that began in the 1960s, this is the only one that took hold among young people," says theologian and social critic Martin Marty. "It is not a momentary phenomenon, but a symbolic shift in attitudes that has great social significance."

[3]   And as social shifts go, this one went with blinding speed. It was only nine years ago that a Barnard College sophomore named Linda LeClair created an instant scandal by admitting that she had been living, unmarried, with a man. The news made the front page of The New York Times and LeClair was nearly booted out of college. Today, few major colleges retain parietal rules and many have coed dormitories. If Doris Day and Rock Hudson were

models of uptight virtue in the movies of their day, modern film protagonists, such as Sylvester Stallone and Talia Shire in "Rocky" and Woody Allen and Diane Keaton in "Annie Hall," casually shack up. And if celebrities themselves see nothing new in having live-in lovers, they haven't always flaunted them so openly. People magazine makes a staple of happily unmarried couples, and one recent cover subject, 18-year-old actress Linda Blair, burbled about the 19-year-old musician she lives with—in her parents' house in Westport, Conn. "Mom says nothing stands in the way of love," Linda explains.

[4]   Linda Blair's parents are still the exception, however. Most surveys show that the great majority of parents think that cohabitation is immoral, emotionally unhealthy and unwise. And for the millions of Americans who retain strong and formal religious ties, what used to be called "living in sin" remains just that. "It is unmitigated adultery, which is clearly forbidden in the Bible, seriously injurious to the well-being of families and a sin against God," says Foy Valentine, executive secretary of the Christian Life Commission of the Southern Baptist Convention.

[5]   Social scientists believe the trend toward living together indicates an alarming loss of faith in institutions. "The real issue is not cohabitation but the meaning of marriage," says sociologist Richard Sennett. "Something about making a lifetime commitment of marriage doesn't work any more—that's what cohabiting shows. The idea of a permanent commitment to another human being has lost its meaning." Psychologist Urie Bronfenbrenner believes that cohabitation is seriously weakening the family and undermining the sense of obligation in all love and work relationships. "Society needs some kind of custom or institution in which people are committed to each other, no matter what," he says. "In sleeping together you don't develop those commitments."

[6]   People choose to live together for many reasons—but wariness about the troubled prospects of modern marriage may be the key one. One out of three marriages of couples between 25 and 35 years old will end in divorce and it is partly because of such bleak statistics that, for better or for worse, many people are moving so cautiously toward making lifelong commitments. The women's movement has encouraged its followers to demand the same rights and privileges as men, and many women argue that cohabitation offers the best of both worlds—intimate relationships on the one hand, and freedom from the traditional roles they might adopt in marriage, including economic dependence, on the other. At the same time, with premarital sex widely tolerated and contraception and abortion readily available, couples can openly enjoy intimate relationships without getting married.

[7]   Some people cohabit because they are philosophically opposed to marriage, and others see cohabitation as a practical short-term option when the lease is up or a roommate moves out. But for most couples, living together is a positive trial period or prelude to marriage. "I discovered a lot I never could in a marriage," says 20-year-old student Pamela Brown, who has been living with her boyfriend for the past year in Portland, Maine. "When we lived apart we ate every meal together. Now we don't eat together all the time. If I had been married I would have felt the pressure of filling the wife-and-cook role. I believe in marriage but I'm not ready for it yet. I want a career first."

Most couples who live together do marry sooner or later, especially when they want to have children.

[8]   Cohabitation may be delaying marriage. Since 1960, the incidence of never-married women 20-24 years old has jumped from 28 per cent to 40 per cent; among men aged 23, the never-marrieds jumped from 42 per cent to 52 per cent just since 1970. But conclusive views on its effects are difficult to come by, partly because research in the area is so spotty. While cohabitation has rapidly become a favorite dissertation subject for Ph.D. students and a Cohabitation Newsletter is published for those in the field, the research has focused almost exclusively on college students, the sampling techniques have been notably unscientific and studies aimed at long-term comparisons of couples are almost nonexistent. Most important, the research is frustratingly inconclusive both as to whether cohabitation is generally more or less satisfying than marriage, and whether it helps set the groundwork for better and more enduring relationships.

[9]   This uncertainty is reflected—sometimes ludicrously—in the difficulty couples have trying to find labels for each other and their arrangements. "That is no accident," says San Francisco psychotherapist Lillian Rubin. "Language and custom tend to interact." The absence of such a terminology here, she says, implies that "there is not yet agreement that this is really a legitimate form of coupling." Elizabeth L. Post, author of "The New Emily Post's Etiquette," suggests "covivant" as the most appropriate way to refer to one's roommate. Others have suggested such exotica as attaché, companera, unlywed, paramour, apartmate, checkmate and swain. Some try coy double entendres such as 'spose ("'spose they'll get married?") and sin-law. Parents, suggests Washington, D.C., writer Jane Otten, may finally have to settle for "my daughter's er and my son's um." Most people talk about their "friends," with or without special stress, or just use unadorned first names.

[10]   Cohabitation creates considerable problems of protocol, especially in Washington, some of which journalist Sally Quinn wryly described in a recent Washington Post article. According to Quinn—who shares a house with her executive editor, Ben Bradlee—social secretaries are "having nervous breakdowns" over addressing invitations, making introductions and seating guests according to the rank of their roommates. For invitations both names can be listed on the envelope, alphabetically and on separate lines. When it comes to inviting one partner and not the other, there are no easy answers. The same is true of introductions, although Elizabeth Post suggests an interesting compromise—use "friend" for elders and "the person I live with" for peers. As for seating arrangements, says Quinn, "for now, the protocol demands that the spouse assume the rank of the spouse and an unranked roommate is simply not counted."

[11]   At the White House, where the President's views on living together are well known, protocol problems have been obviated by a rash of marriages since January. Although staffers insist that Carter does not interfere with their personal lives, the fact is that a number of his aides have belatedly tied the knot—including Jack Watson, Greg Schneiders, Tim Kraft and Rex Granum, Federal Trade Commission head Mike Pertschuk and State Department official Richard Holbrooke. "It does seem to defy the laws of probability," admits one White House insider.

[12]   At most other houses, the stickiest protocol problems arise when children show up for visits with their mates. Many parents remain adamantly opposed to letting them sleep together. "I'd never let any of my children shack up in my house on a weekend," says a Westchester, N.Y., mother of four. "I insist on my standards being respected." Columnist Ann Landers, who unstintingly opposes cohabitation, agrees that parents have the right to set the rules in their own household, but cautions them not to be "judgmental" about their children's arrangements.

[13]   More and more parents, however, are trying to adapt to the new morality—no matter how difficult it may prove. Peggy Scott, a New York City mother of four, first confronted the situation six years ago. "We arrived for a weekend at our Vermont house, only to find that my 19-year-old son had been living there with his girlfriend for about ten days. My husband and I felt very shaken up and incredulous and there was this terrible moment where we didn't know what to do. They were not trying to conceal it, though, so we welcomed the girl and just hoped everything would come out all right." It has, at least to parental eyes: they eventually got married. Today, when the Scotts' other sons come home for weekends, they are permitted to stay in the same room with their mates. "It was a very hard decision," says Mrs. Scott, "but I knew they were living together during the week, so what difference did the weekend make?"

[14]   But if societal sanctions against cohabitation are easing, there are still certain legal barriers that remain. Cohabitation, where two unmarried people share a residence and have sexual relations, is against the law in twenty states, with penalties for conviction ranging as high as a three-year jail sentence in Massachusetts and Arizona. Fornication—sexual intercourse between a man and a woman who are unmarried—is a crime in sixteen states. But such laws are rarely enforced.

[15]   For the most part, childless couples living together face only minor hassles—mostly economic. While cohabitors usually get the same rates as married people for life insurance and face no greater problems in obtaining mortgages than do married couples, disadvantages often include higher auto- and home-insurance rates, exclusion from family medical plans, scattered difficulty in renting apartments and traveling in foreign countries, and perhaps most important, a lack of legal standing for their children. Income-tax rates give the best break to the married couple in which only one member works. For moderate-income couples in which both partners work, the tax bite is worse in many cases for those who are married, since they are entitled to a single standard deduction compared with two for singles living together. For example, a married couple earning a joint income of $20,000 may pay nearly $400 more in taxes than a comparable cohabiting couple.

[16]   Old people complain that, for them, the social-security system invites living in sin. Louis Marathon, 80, and Madeline Clarke, 81, met in a Miami nursing home last year and lived together for several months, between his hospital stays. A former schoolteacher, Madeline received $285 a month from her husband's social-security benefits, Lou gets a World War I veteran's pension of $425 a month (he received no social security since he had been self-employed). Last June, they got married and Madeline may now lose her benefits. "If they

cut her off, I'll go to the VA and get an increase as a married man,'' says Louis, a double amputee. Even if their money is reduced, however, the Marathons are glad they married. ''There's more respect,'' says Madeline, who is almost blind. ''If we live together, it's just common-law, and with that anyone could get disgusted and walk out.''

[17]   Is living together any different from marriage? Research indicates that people who live together are less likely than others to be involved with formal religions, and that they see themselves as more liberated from traditional sex roles but just as monogamous as their married counterparts. But beyond that it is almost impossible to generalize. On the one hand, cohabitation can be a sensible way to explore a loving relationship. On the other, it tends to rule out experiments outside one rigid structure. The one conclusion from all the evidence is that the degree of commitment among people living together is considerably less than that of married couples.

[18]   For Rich, 31, and Ilene, 25, both recently graduated from Boston College, living together was anything but a romantic adventure in young love. ''It is much cheaper,'' says Rich. ''We share the costs on rent and food.'' Both anticipate marriage eventually, though not necessarily to each other, and they don't even agree on how and where they'd like to live. Rich wants to look for work in a rural setting; Ilene would prefer an urban one. ''We're trying to work on it but I'm not sure a compromise can be reached,'' says Ilene. Whatever happens, both Rich and Ilene say that their experience has been a good one.

[19]   According to author Gail Sheehy, whose book ''Passages'' explores the stages of adult life, Rich and Ilene's attitude may be appropriate for them. ''Establishing what you want to do and who you are is necessary before you can truly believe that commitment to another person does not threaten your own individuality,'' she says. ''The whole stage in which one is trying to gain a footing in the adult world requires that one put hope and effort into trials. Like early friendships, they may dissolve, but how are you going to learn without trying?''

[20]   What troubles some social critics about the notion of trial intimacy is that it undermines the concept of enduring loyalty that is integral to marriage. ''Intimate bonding should be based on deep concepts of fidelity,'' says Martin Marty. ''A lot that is convenient and exploratory undercuts that. There is no society when everything is based on ad hoc, and if we can't trust each other, we have no lives.'' Notre Dame campus chaplain William Toohey sees living together as part of the problem of making open-end promises. ''I think it is a weakness in society that we have a feverish desire not to be hurt,'' he says. ''Dammit, life is vulnerability. You've got to give of yourself and it does make you vulnerable.''

[21]   Couples who have married after living together confirm the fact that the institution deepens their sense of commitment. Lenny, 29, and Inger, 33, married last May after living together for four years in Washington, D.C. ''One thing it has done is make me realize I am going to drop dead someday,'' says Lenny, an attorney. ''The job has become more serious. I need to get the career going and I'm feeling more responsible.'' ''Until you get married you aren't aware of being part of something that's bigger than yourself'' says Inger.

[22]   For Katie Charles, who is getting married in August after five years of cohabitation, the very things she once feared might encroach on her independence now are welcome. "It's a real step, standing up before your friends and saying I'm going to make my life with this person," says the 30-year-old Chicago mental-health counselor. "Before it was somewhat temporary. Now I'm turned on to the idea of being a family. I'm becoming more traditional than I thought I was. It's a return to the values I learned as I was growing up."

[23]   But the values many young people bring to marriage these days are changing, too. Married couples are just as likely to pursue separate careers and intermingle roles as those who live together. And the problems of married couples and those living together are remarkably similar. "Most of the problems unmarried couples have—sex, money, power, the need for space—are the same ones married couples mention," says Dr. Frederick G. Humphrey, president of the American Association of Marriage and Family Counselors. "Unmarried couples may want the pseudointellectual belief that they are free to leave, but when they split up, the emotional pain and trauma is often virtually identical to married couples getting a divorce." In fact, so many unmarried couples are seeking counseling these days that AAMFC is seriously considering retitling its members "relationship counselors."

[24]   Unlike cohabitation, however, marriage is reinforced by its traditions and religious associations. "Marriage is a form of intimate coercion," says Sennett. "That's why it is ritualized so strongly. It's a legal way of saying you can trust someone to be there." Los Angeles actress Elizabeth Allensworth, for instance, believes that the relationship she had with her former boyfriend might have survived had they been married. As her career got under way, problems developed over independence and money. "All the hostilities, I think, would have been dealt with in a different way if we'd been married," she says. "That's a much more long-range ball game, not just a here-and-now situation. For a couple that's living together, it's so easy to say the hell with you, I'm leaving."

[25]   Some believe, however, that the very fragility of living together makes cohabitors less likely than married folk to take each other for granted. "Married people are more apt to put up with a problem rather than divorce, but couples living together are more likely to try and work out the differences between them," says New York psychiatrist Avodah Offit. "There is the fear of losing each other." But there is also, for many couples, the unspoken issue of "if you really loved me, you would marry me." During almost a year of living together, Jenny and Mark Bluestein had spats over staying out late and small jealousies. "It was the tensions and feelings of wanting to possess without being possessed," says Mark, 25, who works for a beauty shop in St. Louis. "We were both suffering through different insecurities about each other so we both said, 'OK, I'll show you I do too love you.' We got married to solidify the commitment, to reassure each other."

[26]   Many people—especially mothers—believe that the insecurities of living together harm women more than men. "I'm bitterly opposed to living together," says Mrs. Dorothy Grossman, a Nashville mother of four grown

daughters, some of whom have tried cohabiting. "A woman is more subservient to a man if she enters this type of arrangement. The woman goes and sets up house, gives more than 50 per cent of the effort, and when it breaks up she always gets the bad deal. It's almost always the man who walks out."

[27] Some research indicates that the level of commitment among women who live together with men is indeed consistently higher than than of their partners. Ohio State sociologist Nancy Moore Clatworthy interviewed 100 young couples in Columbus, Ohio, and concluded that most of the women consented to living with men only because they felt their partners wanted to. "The women had feelings of guilt," she says. "Living-together couples often haven't proved what they wanted to prove—that marriage is the same as cohabitation."

[28] But in one way, that may be changing. Last December, the California Supreme Court ruled that singer Michelle Triola had the right to pursue her claim for both support payments and property rights from actor Lee Marvin, the man she had lived with for seven years. The ruling said that in the absence of a legal marriage contract—or even a verbal agreement—the court can infer a contract from the conduct of the parties. As a result, Triola—and others in her situation—may have the right at least to communal property if not support after a relationship breaks up.

[29] Since he represented Triola, Los Angeles lawyer Marvin M. Mitchelson has already taken four more celebrity cases. "A problem with the Marvin-Triola decision," says Mitchelson, "is that it states that the court can examine the relationship of the parties to determine who contributed what. So you get back to a fault system"—just what the no-fault divorce law was designed to eliminate. It also means the courts may have to decide the value of services and the equity of imposing the economic obligations of lawful spouses on people who have rejected matrimony to avoid such obligations. Mitchelson foresees that the California finding may encourage couples to sign what he calls "non-nuptial agreements" spelling out what obligations they are and are not taking on.

[30] Although non-nuptial contracts have been advocated over the years, perhaps no one has taken the concept quite as far as Edmund Van Deusen, a 53-year-old California writer. Himself the product of a failed marriage, Van Deusen advertised in a newspaper for a partner. He offered to pay her $500 a month to live with him, provide companionship but not necessarily sex or love, and perform light household duties. That was five years ago. Since then he has been sharing his Laguna Beach home with the woman he chose—under a contract that includes a 30-day cancellation clause on either side. Neither one has exercised it. "A marriage contract is 24 hours a day," Van Deusen says. "We only commit a bargained amount of our time. It allows people who live together to follow familiar rules that also guarantee independence."

[31] At the moment, the overwhelming majority of Americans still strongly disapprove of living together "without benefit of clergy," and even the people involved in those relationships find them not wholly comfortable. If the divorce rate continues to climb, widespread cohabitation may one day peacefully coexist with marriage, either as an interim option or as a practical

alternative. But if it is to be the trend of the future, couples will discover that it is no magic solution: the problems of living together take as much time and effort to work out as the problems of modern marriage.

VOCABULARY

Use the context of the essay and the dictionary to define the words listed below.

1. transition (par. 1)
2. phenomenon (par. 2)
3. cohabitation (par. 4)
4. unmitigated (par. 4)
5. commitment (par. 5)

6. protocol (par. 8)
7. obviated (par. 11)
8. monogamous (par. 17)
9. encroach (par. 22)
10. coercion (par. 24)

RHETORIC AND IDEA

1. Tony Schwartz's *Newsweek* article is organized into a number of subdivisions concerned with different aspects of the subject. As he closes his introductory section, what major contrast does he make between paragraphs 3 and 4?
2. Throughout the piece, many people are quoted to illustrate various points. Explain what the quote by Pamela Brown in paragraph 7 is used to illustrate. What point is illustrated by the Scott family in paragraph 13?
3. Paragraphs 5 through 6 illustrate causes and effects of living together, but not in equal proportion. Which paragraphs deal with causes? What are the clues in the first paragraph after the causes section that show the transition to effects?
4. What particular aspects of the effects are dealt with in the subsection of paragraphs 14, 15, and 16?
5. What point in the next section about attitudes is illustrated by the quote from Martin Marty? Do paragraph 21 and its quote agree or disagree with Marty's position? Why?
6. What is the basis of the organization relating marriage and living together in paragraph 23? Is that same form of organization continued in paragraph 24? Explain why or why not.
7. Do the two quotes in paragraph 25 take the same side on the point being discussed? If they do, explain how each illustrates the point. If they don't, explain the contrasting position taken by each.
8. Sum up the aspects of the subject dealt with in paragraphs 28 through 30.

WRITING ASSIGNMENTS

1. Select one (or two) of the quotes used in the article and write an essay supporting it or disputing it.
2. Write a paper dealing with the causes and/or effects of living together. That is, deal with one or both of these aspects. Present your own opinions

and/or those presented in the article. In dealing with effects, be sure to stress whether you feel they are valuable results or not.

3. Compare living together and being married in terms of the emotional processes involved. Set up either total differences or total similarities or some combination of both; discuss the emotional demands, attitudes, needs, options, levels of commitment, etc.

4. Focus on either a single couple or two. Use them to represent some of the aspects of living together, such as the causes, the emotional processes, the day-to-day realities, the value or harm.

Michael Novak

The Family
Out of Favor

[1] Recently a friend of mine told me the following anecdote. At lunch in a
restaurant, he had mentioned that he and his wife intended to have a second
child soon. His listener registered the words, stood, and reached out his hand
with unmistakable fervor: ''You are making a political statement. Congratula-
tions!''

[2] We live in lucky times. So many, so varied, and so aggressive are the anti-
family sentiments in our society that brave souls may now have (for the first
time in centuries) the pleasure of discovering for themselves the importance of
the family. Choosing to have a family used to be uninteresting. It is, today, an
act of intelligence and courage. To love family life, to see in family life the
most potent moral, intellectual, and political cell in the body politic is to be
marked today as a heretic.

[3] Orthodoxy is usually enforced by an economic system. Our own system,
postindustrial capitalism, plays an ambivalent role with respect to the family.
On the other hand, capitalism demands hard work, competition, sacrifice,
saving, and rational decision-making. On the other, it stresses liberty and en-
courages hedonism.

[4] Now the great corporations (as well as the universities, the political professions, the foundations, the great newspapers and publishing empires, and the
film industry) diminish the moral and economic importance of the family.
They demand travel and frequent change of residence. Teasing the heart with

glittering entertainment and gratifying the demands of ambition, they dissolve attachments and loyalties. Husbands and wives live in isolation from each other. Children of the upwardly mobile are almost as abandoned, emotionally, as the children of the ghetto. The lives of husbands, wives, and children do not mesh, are not engaged, seem merely thrown together. There is enough money. There is too much emotional space. It is easier to leave town than to pretend that one's lives truly matter to each other. (I remember the tenth anniversay party of a foreign office of a major newsmagazine; none of its members was married to his spouse of ten years before.) At an advanced stage capitalism imparts enormous centrifugal forces to the souls of those who have most internalized its values; and these forces shear marriages and families apart.

[5]   To insist, in the face of such forces, that marriage and family still express our highest moral ideals, is to awaken hostility and opposition. For many, marriage has been a bitter disappointment. They long to be free of it and also of the guilt they feel, a residual guilt which they have put to sleep and do not want awakened. They loathe marriage. They celebrate its demise. Each sign of weakness in the institution exonerates them of personal failure.

[6]   Urban industrial life is not designed to assist families. Expressways divide neighborhoods and parishes. Small family bakeries, cheese shops, and candy stores are boarded up. Social engineers plan for sewers, power lines, access roads, but not for the cultural ecology which allows families of different histories and structures to flower and prosper. The workplace is not designed with family needs in mind; neither are working hours.

[7]   Yet, clearly, the family is the seedbed of economic skills, money habits, attitudes toward work, and the arts of financial independence. The family is a stronger agency of educational success than the school. The family is a stronger teacher of the religious imagination than the church. Political and social planning in a wise social order begin with the axiom *What strengthens the family strengthens society.* Highly paid, mobile, and restless professionals may disdain the family (having been nurtured by its strengths), but those whom other agencies desert have only one institution in which to find essential nourishment.

[8]   The role of a father, a mother, and of children with respect to them, is the absolutely critical center of social force. Even when poverty and disorientation strike, as over the generations they so often do, it is family strength that most defends individuals against alienation, lassitude, or despair. The world around the family is fundamentally unjust. The state and its agents, and the economic system and its agencies, are never fully to be trusted. One could not trust them in Eastern Europe, in Sicily, or in Ireland—and one cannot trust them here. One unforgettable law has been learned painfully through all the oppressions, disasters, and injustices of the last thousand years: *if things go well with the family, life is worth living; when the family falters, life falls apart.*

[9]   These words, I know, go against the conventional grain. In America, we seem to look to the state for every form of social assistance. Immigrant Jews and Catholics have for fifty years supported progressive legislation in favor of federal social programs: for minimum wage, Social Security, Medicare, civil rights. Yet dignity, for most immigrant peoples, resides first of all in family

strength. Along with Southern blacks, Appalachians, Latins, and Indians, most immigrants to America are family people. Indeed, virtually all Americans, outside our professional classes, are family people.

[10]   There are, perhaps, radical psychological differences between people who center human life in atomic individuals—in "Do your thing," or "Live your own life," et cetera—and people who center human life in their families. There may be in this world two kinds of people: "individual people" and "family people." Our intellectual class, it seems, celebrates the former constantly, denigrates the latter.

[11]   Understandably, to have become a professional means, often enough, to have broken free from the family of one's birth. (How many wounds suffered there!) To have become successful, often enough, leads to the hubris of thinking one can live, now, in paradise, emotionally unfettered, free as the will to power is free.

[12]   There are many different traditions, styles, patterns, and emotional laws in different ethnic and regional cultures in America. The Jewish family is not quite like the Italian family; the families of the Scotch-Irish of Appalachia have emotional ties different from those of families from Eastern Europe. The communal families of the South Slavs are not like those of the Japanese. There is not *one* family pattern in America; there are many. All are alike in this, however: they provide such civilization as exists in these United States with its fundamental infusion of nurture, grace, and hope, and they suffer under the attacks of both the media and the economic system. Half the families of the nation have an annual income under $12,500; 90 percent have an income under $22,000. How can a family earning, say $11,000 a year (too much for scholarship assistance) send three children to college? or care for its elderly?

[13]   As for the media, outrageous myths blow breezily about. Everyone says that divorces are multiplying. They are. But the figures hide as much as they reveal. Some 66 percent of all husbands and wives stick together until death do them part. In addition, the death that "parts" a marriage comes far later now than it did in any previous era. Faithful spouses stay together for a longer span of years than ever. For centuries, the average death was, for a female, say, thirty-two, and, for a male, thirty-eight. That so many modern marriages carry a far longer span of years with a certain grace is an unprecedented tribute to the institution.

[14]   Finally, aggressive sentiments against marriage are usually expressed today in the name of "freedom," "openness," "play," or "serious commitment to a career." Marriage is pictured as a form of imprisonment, oppression, boredom, and chafing hindrance. Not all these accusations are wrong; but the superstition surrounding them is. Marriage *is* an assault upon the lonely, atomic ego. Marriage *is* a threat to the solitary individual. Marriage does impose grueling, humbling, baffling, and frustrating responsibilities. Yet if one supposes that precisely such things are the preconditions for all true liberation, marriage is not the enemy of moral development in adults. Quite the opposite.

[15]   In our society, of course, there is no need to become an adult. One may remain—one is exhorted daily to remain—a child forever. It is difficult to have acquired a good education, a professional job, and a good salary, without meeting within one's circle of associates not a few adult children. In medieval

paintings, children look like miniature adults. In tableaux from life today, adults appear as wrinkled adolescents.

[16]   Before one can speak intelligently of marriage, one must discuss the superstition that blocks our vision. We lack the courage nowadays to live by creeds, or to state our doctrines clearly (even to ourselves). Our highest moral principle is flexibility. Guided by sentiments we are embarrased to put into words, we support them not by argument but by their trendiness.

[17]   The central idea of our foggy way of life, however, seems unambiguous enough. It is that life is solitary and brief, and that its aim is self-fulfillment. Next come beliefs in establishing the imperium of the self. Total mastery over one's surroundings, control over the disposition of one's time—these are necessary conditions for self-fulfillment. ("Stand not in my way.") Autonomy we understand to mean protection of our inner kingdom—protection around the self from intrusions of chance, irrationality, necessity, and other persons. ("My self, my castle.") In such a vision of the self, marriage is merely an alliance. It entails as minimal an abridgement of inner privacy as one partner or the other may allow. Children are not a welcome responsibility, for to have children is, plainly, to cease being a child oneself.

[18]   For the modern temper, great dreads here arise. Sanity, we think, consists in centering upon the only self one has. Surrender self-control, surrender happiness. And so we keep the other out. We then maintain our belief in our unselfishness by laboring for "Humanity"—for women, the oppressed, the Third World, or some other needy group. The solitary self needs distant collectivities to witness to its altruism. It has a passionate need to love humankind. It cannot give itself to a spouse or children.

[19]   There is another secret to this aggressive sentiment, dominated as it is by the image of enlightenment. Ask, "Enlightenment from what?" and the family appears: carrier of tradition, habit, prejudice, confinement, darkness. In this view, the seeds of reaction and repression, implanted by the family of one's birth, are ready to sprout as soon as one sets up a family of one's own.

[20]   Theories of liberation, of course, deserve to be studied in the light of flesh, absurdity, and tragedy. There is a pervasive tendency in Western thought, possibly the most profound cultural undercurrent in 3,000 years (compared to it, C. S. Lewis said, the Reformation was a ripple on the ocean), in which liberation is imagined as a breaking of the bonds of finiteness. Salvation comes as liberty of spirit. "Don't fence me in!" The Fall results from commitments that "tie one down," that are not subject to one's own controlling will. One tries to live as angels once were believed to live—soaring, free, unencumbered.

[21]   The jading of everyday, the routines of weekdays and weekends, the endless round of humble constraints, are, in this view, the enemies of human liberty.

[22]   In democratic and pragmatic societies, the dream of the solitary spirit often transfers itself into a moral assault upon institutions, traditions, loyalties, conventions. The truly moral person is a "free thinker" who treats every stage of life as a cocoon from which a lovely moth struggles to escape the habits of a caterpillar. The fuzzy sentiment names each successive breakaway "growth" and "development." It describes the cumulative process as "Liberation."

[23]   There is, of course, a rival moral tradition. I do not mean the conventional variant, which holds that fidelity to institutions, laws, conventions, and

loyalties is sufficient. The more compelling alternative—call it "realist"—differs from the romantic undercurrent by associating liberation with the concrete toils of involvement with family and/or familial communities. The romantic undercurrent takes as the unit of analysis the atomic individual. The realist alternative takes as the unit of analysis the family. To put it mythologically, "individual people" seek happiness through concentration upon themselves, although perhaps for the sake of service to others. Most television cops, detectives, cowboys, and doctors are of this tribe. The "Family people" define themselves through belonging to others: spouse, children, parents, siblings, nieces, cousins, and the rest. For the family people, to be human is to be, so to speak, molecular. I am not solely I. I am husband, father, son, brother, uncle, cousin; I am a family network. Not solitary. On television, both *All in the Family* and *Good Times* have as a premise the molecular identity of each character. The dramatic unit is the family.

[24]   There is, beyond the simplicities of half-hour television, a gritty realism in family life. Outside the family, we choose our own friends, like-minded folk whose intellectual and cultural passions resemble ours. Inside the family, however, divergent passions, intellections, and frustrations slam and batter us. Families today bring together professions, occupations, social classes, and sometimes regional, ethnic, or religious differences. Family life may remain in the United States the last stronghold of genuine cosmopolitanism and harsh, truthful differences.

[25]   So much of modern life may be conceived as an effort to make ourselves pure spirits. Our meals are as rationalized and unsensual as mind can make them. We write and speak about sexual activity as though its most crucial element were fantasy. We describe sex as though it were a stage performance, in which the rest of life is as little as possible involved. In the modern era, the abstract has grown in power. Flesh, humble and humbling, has come to be despised.

[26]   So it is no surprise that in our age many resistant sentiments should war against marriage and family. Marriage and family are tribute paid to earth, to the tides, cycles, and needs of the body and of bodily persons; to the angularity and difficulties of the individual psyche; to the dirty diapers, dirty dishes, and endless noise and confusion of the household. It is the entire symbolic function of marriage and family to remind us that we come from dust and will return to dust, that we are part of the net of earth and sky, inspirited animals at play for our brief moment on this planet, keeping alive our race. The point of marriage and family is to make us realistic. For it is one of the secrets of the human spirit that we long *not* to be of earth, not to be bound by death, routine, and the drag of our bodies. We long to be other than we are.

[27]   A generation ago, the "escape from freedom" was described in terms almost the reverse of those required today. In those days, as writers like Erich Fromm rightly worried, many persons were afraid of risks and responsibilities; many sought shelter in various fixed arrangements: in collectivism, in religion, in family. But dangers to freedom change with the generations. In our own time, the flight most loved is a flight from flesh. The restraints Fromm worried about have proven, under the pressures of suburbs, automobiles, jet planes, television, and corporate mobility, all too fragile. Today the atomic individual is as free as a bird. The threat to human liberation

today is that the flesh, the embodied psyche, earthy roots, bodily loyalties, will be dismissed with contempt.

[28]   The consequence of this freedom is likely to be self-destruction. Whoever nourishes spirit alone must end by the ultimate denial of the flesh. A flaming burst of destruction and death is the image that fascinates us (as in *The Towering Inferno*), that most expresses our drift of soul. For fear of the flesh is fear of death. A love for the concrete and humble gestures of the flesh meant, even in the concentration camps, spiritual survival.

[29]   A return to the true conditions of our own humanity will entail a return, on the part at least of a dedicated few, to the disciplines and terrors of marriage and family. Many will resist these disciplines mightily. (Not all, of course, are called to marriage. The single life can have its own disciplines, and celibacy its own terrors. What counts is the governing cultural model. The commitment of ''the family people'' to the demands of our humanity provides a context within which singleness and even celibacy have a stabilizing strength; and the freedom and dedication of the single, in turn, nourish the family.)

[30]   People say of marriage that it is boring, when what they mean is that it terrifies them: too many and too deep are its searing revelations, its angers, its rages, its hates, and its loves. They say of marriage that it is deadening, when what they mean is that it drives us beyond adolescent fantasies and romantic dreams. They say of children that they are piranhas, eels, brats, snots, when what they mean is that the importance of parents with respect to the future of their children is now known with greater clarity and exactitude than ever before.

[31]   Marriage, like every other serious use of one's freedom, is an enormous risk, and one's likelihood of failure is rather high. No tame project, marriage. The raising of children, now that so few die in childbirth or infancy, and now that fate takes so little responsibility out of the hands of affluent and well-educated parents, brings each of us breathtaking vistas of our inadequacy. Fear of freedom—more exactly, fear of taking the consequences—adds enormously to the tide of evasion. The armies of the night find eager recruits.

[32]   It is almost impossible to write honestly of marriage and family. Who would like the whole world to know the secret failures known to one's spouse and one's children? We already hate ourselves too much. Given our affluence and our education, we are without excuses. We are obligated by our own vague sentiments of progress and enlightenment to be better spouses, better parents, than our ancestors—than our own parents, or theirs. Suppose we are not? We know we are not. Having contempt for ourselves, we want desperately to blame the institution which places our inadequacy in the brilliant glare of interrogation.

[33]   Still, just as marrying and having children have today the force of public political and moral statements, it is necessary to take one's private stand. Being married and having children has impressed on my mind certain lessons, for whose learning I cannot help being grateful. Most are lessons of difficulty and duress. Most of what I am forced to learn about myself is not pleasant.

[34]   The quantity of sheer impenetrable selfishness in the human breast (in *my* breast) is a never-failing source of wonderment. I do not want to be disturbed, challenged, troubled. Huge regions of myself belong only to me. Getting used

to thinking of life as bicentered, even multicentered, is a struggle of which I had no suspicion when I lived alone. Seeing myself through the unblinking eyes of an intimate, intelligent other, an honest spouse, is humiliating beyond anticipation. Maintaining a familial steadiness whatever the state of my own emotions is a standard by which I stand daily condemned. A rational man, acting as I act? Trying to act fairly to children, each of whom is temperamentally different from myself and from each other, each of whom is at a different stage of perception and aspiration, is far more baffling than anything Harvard prepared me for. (Oh, for the unselfconscious box on the ears used so freely by my ancestors!)

[35]   My dignity as a human being depends perhaps more on what sort of husband and parent I am, than on any professional work I am called upon to do. My bonds to them hold me back (and my wife even more) from many sorts of opportunities. And yet these do not feel like bonds. They are, I know, my liberation. They force me to be a different sort of human being, in a way in which I want and need to be forced.

[36]   Nothing, in any case, is more poignant and private than one's sense of failing as a father. When my own sense of identity was that of a son, I expected great perfection from my father. Now that I am a father, I have undergone a psychic shift. Blame upon institutions, upon authorities, upon those who carry responsibilities, now seems to me so cheap. Those who fail in their responsibilities have a new claim upon my sympathies. I know the taste of uncertainty. To be a father rather than a son is to learn the inevitability of failure.

[37]   It would be a lie, however, to write only of the difficulties of marriage and family, and not of the beauty. The joys are known. The more a man and a woman are in love, the more they imitate the life of husband and wife; long sweet affairs are the tribute romances pay to matrimony. Quiet pleasures and perceptions flow: the movement of new life within a woman's belly; the total dependence of life upon the generosity and wisdom of its parents; the sense that these poor muscles, nerves, and cells of one's own flesh have recreated a message to the future, carried in relays generation after generation, carried since the dim beginnings. There may not be a "great chain of being." But parents do forge a link in the humble chain of human beings, encircling heirs to ancestors. To hold a new child in one's hands, only ounces heavy, and to feel its helplessness, is to know responsibilities sweet and awesome, to walk within a circle of magic as primitive as humans knew in caves.

[38]   But it is not the private pleasures of family life that most need emphasis today. Those who love family life do not begrudge the price paid for their adulthood. What needs elucidation is the political significance of the family. A people whose marriages and families are weak can have no solid institutions.

[39]   In intellectual terms, no theme is so neglected in American life and thought. The definition of issues given both by our conservatives and by our liberals is magnetized by two poles only: "The state" and "The individual." Both leave the family out. Emphasis on the family appears to conservatives a constraint upon the state, and to liberals a constraint upon the individual. Our remarkable humanitarianism holds that attention to family weaknesses will stigmatize those who suffer. No concept in the heavens of theory is as ill-starred. Turning toward the family, our minds freeze in their turning.

[40]   The time to break taboos in our minds must surely come. Every avenue of research today leads to the family. Do we study educational achievement? nutrition? the development of stable and creative personalities? resistance to delinquency and violence? favorable economic attitudes and skills? unemployment? sex-role identification? political affiliation? intellectual and artistic aspiration? religious seriousness? relations to authority and to dissent? In all these instances, family life is fundamental. A nation's social policies, taken as a whole, are most accurately and profoundly to be engaged by their impact upon the families that make up that nation....

VOCABULARY

Use the context of the essay and your dictionary to define the following words.

1. hedonism (par 3)
2. exonerates (par. 5)
3. denigrates (par. 10)
4. myths (par. 13)
5. imperium (par. 17)

6. minimal (par. 17)
7. finiteness (par. 20)
8. molecular (par. 23)
9. evasion (par. 31)
10. stigmatize (par. 39)

RHETORIC AND IDEA

1. Which sequence of the two paragraphs in his opening most fully sums up Michael Novak's position on the subject of the value of marriage? What is his basic position?
2. How do the "great corporations" and the media contribute to and cause the attack on the value of the family?
3. Sum up the two contrasting positions in paragraph 14 on how marriage affects liberation and freedom.
4. What does Novak say is the central idea in the "superstitions" of our age that lead to the attack on marriage? Explain his definition of this idea.
5. Explain the contrast he makes between the romantic and realist alternatives in paragraph 23.
6. In paragraph 25, he makes the surprising statement that we want to make ourselves "pure spirits." In paragraph 27, as he contines this subject, he talks of our "flight from flesh." His use of these terms is rather special. Does he mean, for example, that we disapprove of sex? What is it we seek? In what ways does marriage return us to the flesh, to being body?
7. Explain the technique of parallel sentence structure used in paragraph 30. What does he use this structure to stress in this paragraph?
8. What personal lessons has marriage taught Novak? What personal pleasures? Why does the family have political significance? Sum up each of his last three points briefly.

WRITING ASSIGNMENTS

1. Discuss how the images and values presented by the mass media either support or deny the value of family.

2. What are the benefits and/or dangers of our current emphasis on the value of self-fulfillment and freedom? Do you agree with Novak that such valuable principles can also have misleading and destructive aspects?

3. What are the values of married life? In what ways are the values related to the demands made by marriage?

4. What are your views on the characteristics and qualities of an ideal marriage or an ideal mate, or the two together?

5. "In our society, of course, there is no need to become an adult. One may remain—one is exhorted daily to remain—a child forever." Support or attack this statement.

section four

Of Knowing
and Learning

Leo Rosten

"Dear Miss O'Neill"

[1]   On the hellish hot days (and the only city more hellish than Chicago, where this happened, is Bombay), Miss O'Neill would lift her wig and gently scratch her pate. She did it absently, without interrupting whatever she was saying or doing.

[2]   We always watched this with fascination. Miss O'Neill was our 7th-grade teacher, and it was the consensus of my more sophisticated peers that Miss O'Neill had, until very recently, been a nun. That was the only way they could explain the phenomenal fact of her baldness. Miss O'Neill, they whispered, had left her holy order for heartrending reasons, and the punishment her superiors had decreed was that she become a slave in the George Howland Elementary School on 16th Street.

[3]   We never knew Miss O'Neill's first name (teachers never had a first name), and when my mother once asked me how old she was, I answered, "Oh, she's *old*," All teachers are *old*. And "old" meant at least 30, even 40—which, to an 11-year-old, is as decrepit and remote and meaningless as, say 60 or 70, though not 100.

[4]   Miss O'Neill was dumpy, moonfaced, sallow-skinned, colorless, and we loathed her as only a pack of West Side barbarians could loathe a teacher of arithmetic. She did not teach arithmetic—but that is how much all of us hated her.

[5]   She was our English teacher, a 33rd-degree perfectionist who drilled us, endlessly, mercilessly, in spelling and grammar and diction and syntax. She

420

had a hawk's eye for a dangling participle or an upright non sequitur, a "not *quite* right" word or a fruity solecism. (Did you know that "solecism" comes from the contempt of Greek patricians for the dialect that thrived in Soloi?) Whenever any of us made an error in composition *or* recitation, Miss O'Neill would send the culprit to the blackboard to "diagram" the sentence! That was the torture we most resented.

[6]   We had to designate the function of every word and phrase and clause; we had to describe how each part of every sentence worked; we had to explain how the parts fit together, and how they mesh and move to wheel out meaning. Before our whole runny-nosed congregation, an innocent child had himself or herself to locate an error, identify a malfunction, explain the *reason* for the correction Miss O'Neill impassively awaited. She waited as if she could sit there until Gabriel blew his kazoo, as our devastating humor had it. And if the offered correction was itself wrong, Miss O'Neill compounded her discipline by making the errant urchin diagram *that* on the board, instructing him to persevere.

[7]   Some kids would break into a sweat as they floundered around, failing to hit the bull's-eye, praying that Miss O'Neill would end their agony by the generous gift of the one good and true answer. But that Miss O'Neill rarely proffered. Instead, she would turn her inquisition from the pupil at the blackboard to the helots in the chairs. "Well, class? ... Jacob, do *you* know the answer? ... No? ... Shirley? ... Harold? ... Joseph?" So heartless and unyielding was her method.

[8]   Each day, as we poured out of George Howland like Cheyennes en route to a scalping, we would pause briefly to pool our misery and voice our rage over the fate that had condemned us to such an abecedarian. Had we known Shakespeare, we would have added one word to Hamlet's brutal advice to Ophelia, making it, with feeling, "Get thee back to a nunnery."

[9]   Miss O'Neill never raised her voice, never lost her patience, never got angry. What was even more surprising, she never had to punish or even threaten our most ingenious troublemakers. For some reason we never discovered, the small impertinences and sly infractions and simulated incomprehensions with which we shrewdly persecuted our other teachers never seemed to get anywhere in the tight, shipshape world of Miss O'Neill's classroom.

[10]   I say that my comrades and I hated Miss O'Neill—but that is not entirely true. I only pretended to hate her. In our sidewalk conclaves, when we chortled over the latest tour de force of Douglas Fairbanks, or mourned the defeat of the noble Cubs by the disgusting White Sox, or matched extravagances about what we would do if we found *ten million dollars,* or imagined the possible surrender of one or another maiden to our lascivious fumblings, I, too, would howl about Miss O'Neill's tyranny, cursing her adamantine ways as fervently as any of my companions. So strong is the desire of a boy to "belong," to be no different from even the grubbiest of his fellows.

[11]   But secretly, my respect for Miss O'Neill—nay, my affection—increased week by week. For I was exhilarated by what I can only call the incorruptibility of her instruction. I found stirring within myself a sense of excitement, of

discovery, a curious quickening of the spirit that attends initiation into a new world. Though I could not explain it in these words, and would have scorned the Goody-Two-Shoes overtone, I felt that Miss O'Neill was leading me not through the irksome labyrinth of English but into a sunlit realm of order and meaning. Her iron rules, her crisp strictures, her constant corrections were not, to me, the irritating nit picking they were to my buddies. They were sudden flashes of light, glimpses of the magic hidden within prose, intoxicating visions of that universe that awaits understanding. It was as if a cloak of wonder had been wrapped around the barren bones of grammar. For it was not grammar or diction or syntax that Miss O'Neill, whether she knew it or not, was introducing me to. She was teaching what earlier generations so beautifully called "right reason."

[12] The most astonishing thing about Miss O'Neill was that she proceeded on the sanguine assumption that she could actually teach a pack of potential roller-skate-derby fans how to write, clear, clean, correct sentences, organized in clear, clean, correct paragraphs—in their native tongue.

[13] I do not think Miss O'Neill had the slightest awareness of her hold and influence on me. Nor was she especially interested in me. She never betrayed an inkling of preference or favoritism for any of her captive flock. Nor was she interested in the high, immortal reaches of the language whose terrain she so brisky charted. She was a technician, pure and simple—efficient, conscientious, immune to the malarky some pupils resorted to. Nothing derailed Miss O'Neill from professionalism.

[14] And that is the point. Miss O'Neill did not try to please us. She did not even try to like us. She certainly made no effort to make us like her. She valued results more than affection, and respect more than popularity. Not endowed with loving or lovable qualities, she did not bother regretting it, or denying it, or trying to compensate for it. She went about her task with no concessions to the we're-all-friends or think-of-me-as-your-pal gambits. She used the forthright "I want" or "You go" instead of the repulsive "Shall we?" Alien to humor of affection, she concentrated on nothing more than transmission of her knowledge and her skill.

[15] I think Miss O'Neill knew what the evangelists of "progressive" education are bound to rediscover: that the young prefer competence to "personality" in a teacher, and certainly to camaraderie; that a teacher need be neither an ogre or a confidant; that what is hard to master gives children special rewards (pride, self-respect, the gratifications of succeeding) precisely because difficulties have been conquered; that there may indeed be no easy road to learning some things, and no "fascinating" or "fun" way of learning some things really well.

[16] I do not know whether Miss O'Neill infected anyone else in my 7th grade with passion for, or even an abiding interest in, English. To me, she was a force of enlightenment.

[17] She has long since shucked her travail among the West Side aborigines. Perhaps she has departed this baffling world to don wings—and, I hope, golden locks, to replace her wig under whose gauzy base she scratched relief from itching. If she is still alive, she must be in her dotage. And if she is among us still, I hope she somehow gets word of these long-belated thanks for a job supremely done. I have never forgotten what she taught.

[18]   To this day, whether I am wrestling an intransigent sentence, or stand glazed before a buck-passing phrase whose improvement eludes me, or flagellate myself for some inspiration that might light up the drab texture of tired prose, whether I am winded by a rodomontade clause in Shaw or knocked cold by a tortured sentence in Talcott Parsons, I find myself thinking of Miss (What-oh-what?) O'Neill—and, sighing, take a sheet of paper and diagram the English until I know—and know *why*—it is right or wrong, or how it can be swept clean of that muddleheadedness that plagues us all.

VOCABULARY

Use the context of the essay and your dictionary to define the following words.

1. pate (par. 1)
2. sallow-skinned (par. 4)
3. solecism (par. 5)
4. urchin (par. 6)
5. proffered (par. 7)
6. helots (par. 7)
7. abecedarian (par. 8)
8. simulated (par. 9)
9. incorruptibility (par. 11)
10. sanguine (par. 12)

RHETORIC AND IDEA

1. Leo Rosten's rhetorical strategy is to reverse his field in the middle of the essay. What has been his approach to Miss O'Neill in the first nine paragraphs? Beginning in paragraph 10, what is his approach? Which part develops his chief point about her?
2. What one key function word does he use in the first sentences of both paragraphs 10 and 11 to show his transition? What does the word indicate about the relationship of the two parts of the essay?
3. What does he finally define as Miss O'Neill's chief value to him? How is this related to her most valuable personal traits as a teacher?
4. In which paragraph are Miss O'Neill's values related to wider problems of education?
5. How does the last sentence of Rosten's closing paragraph provide a restatement of his central thesis?
6. In the first section of the essay, which classroom activities are described in most detail? Why? How is this use of detail related to his central thesis?
7. In the very first sentence of the piece, does the major material come at the beginning or end of the sentence? Explain his use of emphasis and subordination.
8. In paragraph 11, Rosten uses the word *not* in an important way. His use of the word here is a part of what pattern of paragraph development?
9. What is Rosten's purpose in referring to Miss O'Neill's wig and physical appearance? How is this a part of his strategy?
10. What does Rosten not like about "progressive" education?

WRITING ASSIGNMENTS

1. Define the significance—favorable, unfavorable, or both—of a notable teacher of yours.
2. Write an interpretation of a person and/or situation that first takes a negative approach and then switches to a positive.
3. What are the most important ingredients for learning in a classroom?

Joyce Maynard

Not So Golden Rule Days

[1]   I watch them every year, the six-year-olds, buying lunch boxes and snap-on bow ties and jeweled barrettes, swinging on their mothers' arms as they approach the school on registration day or walking ahead a little, stiff in new clothes. Putting their feet on the shoe salesman's metal foot measurer, eying the patent leather and ending up with sturdy brown tie oxfords, sitting rigid in the barber's chair, heads balanced on white-sheeted bodies like cherries on cupcakes, as the barber snips away the kindergarten hair for the new grown-up cut, striding past the five-year-olds with looks of knowing pity (ah, youth) they enter elementary school, feigning reluctance—with scuffing heels and dying TV cowboy groans shared in the cloakroom, but filled with hope and anticipation of all the mysteries waiting in the cafeteria and the water fountain and the paper closet, and in the pages of the textbooks on the teachers' desks. With pink erasers and a sheath of sharpened pencils, they file in so really bravely, as if to tame lions, or at least subdue the alphabet. And instead, I long to warn them, watching this green young crop pass by each year, seeing them enter a red-brick, smelly-staircase world of bathroom passes and penmanship drills, gongs and red x's, and an unexpected snap to the teacher's slingshot voice (so slack and giving, when she met the mothers). I want to tell them about the back pages in the teacher's record book, of going to the principal's office or staying behind an extra year. Quickly they learn how little use they'll

have for lion-taming apparatus. They are, themselves, about to meet the tamer.

[2]   I can barely remember it now, but I know that I once felt that first-day eagerness too. Something happened, though, between that one pony-tail-tossing, skirt-flouncing, hand-waving (*"I* know the answer—call on *me"*) day and the first day of all the other years I spent in public school. It wasn't just homework and the struggle to get up at seven every morning, it was the *kind* of homework assignments we were given and the prospect of just what it was that we were rousing ourselves for—the systematic breaking down, workbook page by workbook page, drill after drill, of all the joy we started out with. I don't think I'm exaggerating when I say that, with very few exceptions, what they did to (not *for*) us in elementary school was not unlike what I would sometimes do to my cats: dress them up in doll clothes because they looked cute that way.

[3]   We were forever being organized into activities that, I suspect, looked good on paper and in school board reports. New programs took over and disappeared as approaches to child education changed. One year we would go without marks, on the theory that marks were a "poor motivating factor," "an unnatural pressure," and my laboriously researched science and social studies reports would come back with a check mark or a check plus inside the margin. Another year every activity became a competition, with posters tacked up on the walls showing who was ahead that week, our failures and our glories bared to all the class. Our days were filled with electrical gimmicks, film strips and movies and overhead projectors and tapes and supplementary TV shows, and in junior high, when we went audio-visual, a power failure would have been reason enough to close down the school.

[4]   But though the educational jargon changed, the school's basic attitude remained constant. Anything too different (too bad or too exceptional), anything that meant making another column in the record book, was frowned upon. A lone recorder, in a field of squeaking flutophones, a reader of Dickens, while the class was laboring page by page (out loud, pace set by the slowest oral readers) with the adventures of the Marshall family and their dog Ranger, a ten-page story when the teacher had asked for a two-pager—they all met with suspicion. Getting straight A's was fine with the school as long as one pursued the steady, earnest, unspectacular course. But to complete a piece of work well, without having followed the prescribed steps—that seemed a threat to the school, proof that we could progress without it. Vanity rears its head everywhere, even in the classroom, but surely extra guards against it should be put up there. I remember an English teacher who wouldn't grant me an A until second term, an indication, for whoever cared about that sort of thing, that under her tutelage I had *improved*. Every composition was supposed to have evolved from three progressively refined rough drafts. I moved in just the opposite direction for the school's benefit: I wrote my "final drafts" the first time around, then deliberately aged them a bit with earnest-looking smudges and erasures.

[5]   Kids who have gone through elementary school at the bottom of their class might argue here that it *was* the smart ones who got special attention—independent study groups, free time to spend acting in plays and writing novels (we were always starting autobiographies) and researching

"Special Reports"—all the things that kept our groups self-perpetuating, with the children lucky enough to start out on top forever in the teacher's good graces, and those who didn't start there always drilling on decimals and workbook extra-work pages. But Oyster River was an exemplary democratic school and showed exemplary concern for slow students—the under-achievers—and virtuously left the quick and bright to swim for themselves, or tread water endlessly.

[6]   It always seemed to me as a Group One member, that there was little in-dividual chance to shine. It was as if the school had just discovered the division of labor concept, and oh, how we divided it. Book reports, math problems, maps for history and even art projects—we did them all in committee. Once we were supposed to write a short story that way, pooling our resources of Descriptive Adjectives and Figures of Speech to come up with an adventure that read like one of those typing-book sentences ("A quick brown fox ..."), where every letter of the alphabet is represented. Our group drawings had the look of movie magazine composites that show the ideal star, with Paul Newman's eyes, Brando's lips, Steve McQueen's hair. Most people loved group work—the kids because working together meant not working very hard, tossing your penny in the till and leaving it for someone else to count, the teachers because committee projects prepared us for community work (getting along with the group, leadership abilities ...) and, more important, I think, to some of them, they required a lot less marking time than individual projects did. The finished product didn't matter so much—in fact, anything too unusual seemed only to rock our jointly rowed canoe.

[7]   The school day was for me, and for most of us, I think, a mixture of humiliation and boredom. Teachers would use their students for the entertain-ment of the class. Within the first few days of the new term, someone quickly becomes the class jester, someone is the class genius, the "brain" who, the teacher, with doubtful modesty, reminds us often, probably has a much higher IQ than she. Some student is the trouble-maker black sheep (the one who always makes her sigh), the one who will be singled out as the culprit when the whole class seems like a stock exchange of note passing, while all the others stare at him, looking shocked.

[8]   Although their existence is denied now, in this modern, psychologically enlightened age, teachers' pets are still very much around, sometimes in the form of the girl with super-neat penmanship and Breck-clean hair, sometimes in the person of the dependable Brain, who always gets called on when the superintendent is visiting the class. Teachers, I came to see, could be in-timidated by a class, coerced or conned into liking the students who were popular among the kids, and it was hard not to miss, too, that many teachers were not above using unpopular students to gain acceptance with the major-ity. They had an instinct, teachers did, for who was well-liked and who wasn't; they learned all the right nicknames and turned away, when they could, if one of their favorites was doing the kind of thing that brought a 3 in conduct. We saw it all, like underlings watching the graft operations of am-bitious politicians, powerless to do anything about it.

[9]   That was what made us most vulnerable: our powerlessness. Kids don't generally speak up or argue their case. No one is a child long enough, I sup-

pose, or articulate enough, while he is one, to become a spokesman for his very real, and often oppressed, minority group. And then when we outgrow childhood, we no longer care, and feel, in fact, that if *we* went through it all, so should the next generation. Children are *expected* to be adversaries of school and teachers, so often, in the choosing up of sides, parents will side with the school. Nobody expects children to like school; therefore it's no surprise when they don't. What should be a surprise is that they dislike it for many good reasons.

[10]   It would be inaccurate to say I hated school. I had a good time sometimes, usually when I was liked, and therefore on top. And with all the other clean-haired girls who had neat penmanship and did their homework, I took advantage of my situation. When I was on the other side of the teacher's favor though, I realized that my sun-basking days had always depended on there being someone in the shade. That was the system—climbing up on one another's heads, putting someone down so one's own stature could be elevated. Elementary school was a club that not only reinforced the class system but created it—a system in which the stutterer and the boy who can't hit a baseball start out, and remain, right at the bottom, a system where being in the middle—not too high or low—is best of all.

[11]   I had imagined, innocently, on my first day of school, that once the kids saw how smart I was, they'd all be my friends. I see similar hopes on the faces I watch heading to the front every September—all the loved children, tops in their parents' eyes, off to be ''re-evaluated'' in a world where only one of thirty can be favorite, each child unaware, still, that he is not the only person in the universe, and about to discover that the best means of survival is to blend in (adapting to the group, it's called), to go from being one to being one in a crowd of many, many others.

VOCABULARY

Use the context of the essay and your dictionary to define the following words.

1. feigning (par. 1)
2. flouncing (par. 2)
3. supplementary (par. 3)
4. jargon (par. 4)
5. progressively (par. 4)
6. self-perpetuating (par. 5)
7. exemplary (par. 5)
8. resources (par. 6)
9. enlightened (par. 8)
10. intimidated (par. 8)

RHETORIC AND IDEA

1. Explain the working of the parallel sentence structure and repetitions in paragraph 1 of Joyce Maynard's interpretive reminiscence. What effects does she achieve with it?
2. By the end of the first paragraph she sums up her basic interpretation through the indirect statement of her metaphor about taming lions. What is this broader meaning of her references to lions and lion tamers?
3. What happens by the end of the first year of school?

4. How do her comments about activities continue to develop the idea of paragraph 2?
5. What is the harmful basic attitude of the schools?
6. What is lost in the emphasis on groups? How does this continue to develop the idea of paragraph 4?
7. What is the system described in paragraph 10? How does it also develop the point of paragraph 4? How did Maynard use the system?

WRITING ASSIGNMENTS

1. Describe the people and events in a situation in your schooling in which some joy, interest, or hope was either fulfilled or disappointed; interpret the reasons for the outcome.
2. What is one of your earliest memories of school and the people there? Through your tone and selection of details, give it a positive or negative impression. You may sum up the reasons directly or suggest them indirectly.
3. What changes should be made in the way some particular level of schooling is taught? What are the current problems? What are the alternatives?

William Golding

Thinking As a Hobby

[1]   While I was still a boy, I came to the conclusion that there were three grades of thinking; and since I was later to claim thinking as my hobby, I came to an even stranger conclusion—namely, that I myself could not think at all.

[2]   I must have been an unsatisfactory child for grownups to deal with. I remember how incomprehensible they appeared to me at first, but not, of course, how I appeared to them. It was the headmaster of my grammar school who first brought the subject of thinking before me—though neither in the way, nor with the result he intended. He had some statuettes in his study. They stood on a high cupboard behind his desk. One was a lady wearing nothing but a bath towel. She seemed frozen in an eternal panic lest the bath towel slip down any farther; and since she had no arms, she was in an unfortunate position to pull the towel up again. Next to her, crouched the statuette of a leopard, ready to spring down at the top drawer of a filing cabinet labeled A-AH. My innocence interpreted this as the victim's last despairing cry. Beyond the leopard was a naked, muscular gentleman, who sat, looking down, with his chin on his fist and his elbow on his knee. He seemed utterly miserable.

[3]   Some time later, I learned about these statuettes. The headmaster had placed them where they would face delinquent children, because they symbolized to him the whole of life. The naked lady was the Venus of Milo. She

was Love. She was not worried about the towel. She was just busy being beautiful. The leopard was nature, and he was being natural. The naked, muscular gentleman was not miserable. He was Rodin's Thinker, an image of pure thought. It is easy to buy small plaster models of what you think life is like.

[4]   I had better explain that I was a frequent visitor to the headmaster's study, because of the latest thing I had done or left undone. As we now say, I was not integrated. I was, if anything, disintegrated; and I was puzzled. Grownups never made sense. Whenever I found myself in a penal position before the headmaster's desk, with the statuettes glimmering whitely above him, I would sink my head, clasp my hands behind my back and writhe one shoe over the other.

[5]   The headmaster would look opaquely at me through flashing spectacles.

[6]   "What are we going to do with you?"

[7]   Well, what *were* they going to do with me? I would writhe my shoe some more and stare down at the worn rug.

[8]   "Look up, boy! Can't you look up?"

[9]   Then I would look up at the cupboard, where the naked lady was frozen in her panic and the muscular gentleman contemplated the hindquarters of the leopard in endless gloom. I had nothing to say to the headmaster. His spectacles caught the light so that you could see nothing human behind them. There was no possibility of communication.

[10]   "Don't you ever think at all?"

[11]   No, I didn't think, wasn't thinking, couldn't think—I was simply waiting in anguish for the interview to stop.

[12]   "Then you'd better learn—hadn't you?"

[13]   On one occasion the headmaster leaped to his feet, reached up and plunked Rodin's masterpiece on the desk before me.

[14]   "That's what a man looks like when he's really thinking."

[15]   I surveyed the gentleman without interest or comprehension.

[16]   "Go back to your class."

[17]   Clearly there was something missing in me. Nature had endowed the rest of the human race with a sixth sense and left me out. This must be so, I mused, on my way back to the class, since whether I had broken a window, or failed to remember Boyle's Law, or been late for school, my teachers produced me one, adult answer: "Why can't you think?"

[18]   As I saw the case, I had broken the window because I had tried to hit Jack Arney with a cricket ball and missed him; I could not remember Boyle's Law because I had never bothered to learn it; and I was late for school because I preferred looking over the bridge into the river. In fact, I was wicked. Were my teachers, perhaps, so good that they could not understand the depths of my depravity? Were they clear, untormented people who could direct their every action by this mysterious business of thinking? The whole thing was incomprehensible. In my earlier years, I found even the statuette of the Thinker confusing. I did not believe any of my teachers were naked, ever. Like someone born deaf, but bitterly determined to find out about sound, I watched my teachers to find out about thought.

[19]   There was Mr. Houghton. He was always telling me to think. With a modest satisfaction, he would tell me that he had thought a bit himself. Then

why did he spend so much time drinking? Or was there more sense in drinking than there appeared to be? But if not, and if drinking were in fact ruinous to health—and Mr. Houghton was ruined, there was no doubt about that—why was he always talking about the clean life and the virtues of fresh air? He would spread his arms wide with the action of a man who habitually spent his time striding along mountain ridges.

[20]   "Open air does me good, boys—I know it!"

[21]   Sometimes, exalted by his own oratory, he would leap from his desk and hustle us outside into a hideous wind.

[22]   "Now, boys! Deep breaths! Feel it right down inside you—huge draughts of God's good air!"

[23]   He would stand before us, rejoicing in his perfect health, an open-air man. He would put his hands on his waist and take a tremendous breath. You could hear the wind, trapped in the cavern of his chest and struggling with all the unnatural impediments. His body would reel with shock and his ruined face go white at the unaccustomed visitation. He would stagger back to his desk and collapse there, useless for the rest of the morning.

[24]   Mr. Houghton was given to high-minded monologues about the good life, sexless and full of duty. Yet in the middle of one of these monologues, if a girl passed the window, tapping along on her neat little feet, he would interrupt his discourse, his neck would turn of itself and he would watch her out of sight. In this instance, he seemed to me ruled not by thought but by an invisible and irresistible spring in his nape.

[25]   His neck was an object of great interest to me. Normally it bulged a bit over his collar. But Mr. Houghton had fought in the First World War alongside both Americans and French, and had come—by who knows what illogic?—to a settled detestation of both countries. If either country happened to be prominent in current affairs, no argument could make Mr. Houghton think well of it. He would bang the desk, his neck would bulge still further and go red. "You can say what you like," he would cry, "but I've thought about this—and I know what I think!"

[26]   Mr. Houghton thought with his neck.

[27]   There was Miss Parsons. She assured us that her dearest wish was our welfare, but I knew even then, with the mysterious clairvoyance of childhood, that what she wanted most was the husband she never got. There was Mr. Hands—and so on.

[28]   I have dealt at length with my teachers because this was my introduction to the nature of what is commonly called thought. Through them I discovered that thought is often full of unconscious prejudice, ignorance and hypocrisy. It will lecture on disinterested purity while its neck is being remorselessly twisted toward a skirt. Technically, it is about as proficient as most businessmen's golf, as honest as most politician's intentions, or—to come near my own preoccupation—as coherent as most books that get written. It is what I came to call grade-three thinking, though more properly, it is feeling, rather than thought.

[29]   True, often there is a kind of innocence in prejudices, but in those days I viewed grade-three thinking with an intolerant contempt and an incautious mockery. I delighted to confront a pious lady who hated the Germans with the proposition that we should love our enemies. She taught me a great truth in

dealing with grade-three thinkers; because of her, I no longer dismiss lightly a mental process which for nine-tenths of the population is the nearest they will ever get to thought. They have immense solidarity. We had better respect them, for we are outnumbered and surrounded. A crowd of grade-three thinkers, all shouting the same thing, all warming their hands at the fire of their own prejudices, will not thank you for pointing out the contradictions in their beliefs. Man is a gregarious animal, and enjoys agreement as cows will graze all the same way on the side of a hill.

[30]   Grade-two thinking is the detection of contradictions. I reached grade two when I trapped the poor, pious lady. Grade-two thinkers do not stampede easily, though often they fall into the other fault and lag behind. Grade-two thinking is a withdrawal, with eyes and ears open. It became my hobby and brought satisfaction and loneliness in either hand. For grade-two thinking destroys without having the power to create. It set me watching the crowds cheering His Majesty the King and asking myself what all the fuss was about, without giving me anything positive to put in the place of that heady patriotism. But there were compensations. To hear people justify their habit of hunting foxes and tearing them to pieces by claiming that the foxes liked it. To hear our Prime Minister talk about the great benefit we conferred on India by jailing people like Pandit Nehru and Gandhi. To hear American politicians talk about peace in one sentence and refuse to join the League of Nations in the next. Yes, there were moments of delight.

[31]   But I was growing toward adolescence and had to admit that Mr. Houghton was not the only one with an irresistible spring in his neck. I, too, felt the compulsive hand of nature and began to find that pointing out contradiction could be costly as well as fun. There was Ruth, for example, a serious and attractive girl. I was an atheist at the time. Grade-two thinking is a menace to religion and knocks down sects like skittles. I put myself in a position to be converted by her with an hypocrisy worthy of grade three. She was a Methodist—or at least, her parents were, and Ruth had to follow suit. But, alas, instead of relying on the Holy Spirit to convert me, Ruth was foolish enough to open her pretty mouth in argument. She claimed that the Bible (King James Version) was literally inspired. I countered by saying that the Catholics believed in the literal inspiration of Saint Jerome's *Vulgate*, and the two books were different. Argument flagged.

[32]   At last she remarked there were an awful lot of Methodists, and they couldn't be wrong, could they—not all those millions? That was too easy, said I restively (for the nearer you were to Ruth, the nicer she was to be near to) since there were more Roman Catholics that Methodists anyway; and they couldn't be wrong, could they—not all those hundreds of millions? An awful flicker of doubt appeared in her eyes. I slid my arm round her waist and murmured breathlessly that if we were counting heads, the Buddhists were the boys for my money. But Ruth had *really* wanted to do me good, because I was so nice. She fled. The combination of my arm and those countless Buddhists was too much for her.

[33]   That night her father visited my father and left, red-cheeked and indignant. I was given the third degree to find out what had happened. It was lucky we were both of us only fourteen. I lost Ruth and gained an undeserved reputation as a potential libertine.

[34]   So grade-two thinking could be dangerous. It was in this knowledge, at the age of fifteen, that I remember making a comment from the heights of grade two, on the limitations of grade three. One evening I found myself alone in the school hall, preparing it for a party. The door of the headmaster's study was open. I went in. The headmaster had ceased to thump Rodin's Thinker down on the desk as an example to the young. Perhaps he had not found any more candidates, but the statuettes were still there, glimmering and gathering dust on top of the cupboard. I stood on a chair and rearranged them. I stood Venus in her bath towel on the filing cabinet, so that now the top drawer caught its breath in a gasp of sexy excitement. "A-ah!" The portentous Thinker I placed on the edge of the cupboard so that he looked down at the bath towel and waited for it to slip.

[35]   Grade-two thinking, though it filled life with fun and excitement, did not make for content. To find out the deficiencies of our elders bolsters the young ego but does not make for personal security. I found that grade two was not only the power to point out contradictions. It took the swimmer some distance from the shore and left him there, out of his depth. I decided that Pontius Pilate was a typical grade-two thinker. "What is truth?" he said, a very common grade-two thought, but one that is used always as the end of an argument instead of the beginning. There is a still higher grade of thought which says, "What is truth?" and sets out to find it.

[36]   But these grade-one thinkers were few and far between. They did not visit my grammar school in the flesh though they were there in books. I aspired to them, partly because I was ambitious and partly because I now saw my hobby as an unsatisfactory thing if it went no further. If you set out to climb a mountain, however high you climb, you have failed if you cannot reach the top.

[37]   I *did* meet an undeniably grade-one thinker in my first year at Oxford. I was looking over a small bridge in Magdalen Deer Park, and a tiny mustached and hatted figure came and stood by my side. He was a German who had just fled from the Nazis to Oxford as a temporary refuge. His name was Einstein.

[38]   But Professor Einstein knew no English at that time and I knew only two words of German. I beamed at him, trying wordlessly to convey by my bearing all the affection and respect that the English felt for him. It is possible—and I have to make the admission—that I felt here were two grade-one thinkers standing side by side; yet I doubt if my face conveyed more than a formless awe. I would have given my Greek and Latin and French and a good slice of my English for enough German to communicate. But we were divided; he was as inscrutable as my headmaster. For perhaps five minutes we stood together on the bridge, undeniable grade-one thinker and breathless aspirant. With true greatness, Professor Einstein realized that any contact was better than none. He pointed to a trout wavering in midstream.

[39]   He spoke *"Fisch."*

[40]   My brain reeled. Here I was, mingling with the great, and yet helpless as the veriest grade-three thinker. Desperately I sought for some sign by which I might convey that I, too, revered pure reason. I nodded vehemently. In a brilliant flash I used up half of my German vocabulary. *"Fisch. Ja. Ja."*

[41]   For perhaps another five minutes we stood side by side. Then Professor Einstein, his whole figure still conveying good will and amiability, drifted away out of sight.

[42]   I, too, would be a grade-one thinker. I was irreverent at the best of times. Political and religious systems, social customs, loyalties and traditions, they all came tumbling down like so many rotten apples off a tree. This was a fine hobby and a sensible substitute for cricket, since you could play it all the year round. I came up in the end with what must always remain the justification for grade-one thinking, its sign, seal and charter. I devised a coherent system for living. It was a moral system, which was wholly logical. Of course, as I readily admitted, conversion of the world to my way of thinking might be difficult, since my system did away with a number of trifles, such as big business, centralized government, armies, marriage. ...

[43]   It was Ruth all over again. I had some very good friends who stood by me, and still do. But my acquaintances vanished, taking the girls with them. Young women seemed oddly contented with the world as it was. They valued the meaningless ceremony with a ring. Young men, while willing to concede the chaining sordidness of marriage, were hesitant about abandoning the organizations which they hoped would give them a career. A young man on the first rung of the Royal Navy, while perfectly agreeable to doing away with big business and marriage, got as red-necked as Mr. Houghton when I proposed a world without any battleships in it.

[44]   Had the game gone too far? Was it a game any longer? In those prewar days, I stood to lose a great deal, for the sake of a hobby.

[45]   Now you are expecting me to describe how I saw the folly of my ways and came back to the warm nest, where prejudices are so often called loyalties, where pointless actions are hallowed into custom by repetition, where we are content to say we think when all we do is feel.

[46]   But you would be wrong. I dropped my hobby and turned professional.

[47]   If I were to go back to the headmaster's study and find the dusty statuettes still there, I would arrange them differently. I would dust Venus and put her aside, for I have come to love her and know her for the fair things she is. But I would put the Thinker, sunk in his desperate thought, where there were shadows before him—and at his back, I would put the leopard, crouched and ready to spring.

VOCABULARY

Use the context of the essay and your dictionary to define the following words.

1. incomprehensible (par. 2)   6. impediments (par. 23)
2. penal (par. 4)   7. clairvoyance (par. 27)
3. opaquely (par. 5)   8. pious (par. 29)
4. depravity (par. 18)   9. gregarious (par. 29)
5. oratory (par. 21)   10. libertine (par. 33)

RHETORIC AND IDEA

1. William Golding's biographical narrative focuses on three grades, or stages, of thinking. In paragraphs 1 through 18 he describes a situation

that set him thinking about thinking. In 19 through 27 he describes teachers. What do the teachers illustrate? To put it another way, they are lower on the staircase of abstractions than the definition of grade-three thinking finally made in paragraph 28. What is their logical relationship to that definition? What is the definition?

2. Define grade-two thinking. Is it an advance on grade-three?

3. What does the anecdote about Ruth illustrate about the problem of grade-two thinking? Here again, an example on a lower level of abstraction illustrates something about a higher generality. What does it illustrate?

4. Where is grade-one thought introduced? How does it differ from grade two?

5. What grade of thinking does Einstein illustrate?

6. In paragraph 42, what further important characteristic of grade-one thinking is added?

7. Notice how the description of the three statues and their position is used throughout, in paragraphs 2, 3, 9, and then in paragraph 34. In paragraphs 2 and 3 how does his interpretation differ from the headmaster's?

8. In paragraph 34 he changes the positions of two of the statues. Why does he say that the new position is a comment on "the limitations of grade three"?

9. What is the significance of the position proposed for the statues in paragraph 47? Why does he place the leopard ready to spring behind the thinker?

10. Has his reaching grade one solved all of his problems?

WRITING ASSIGNMENTS

1. Do you agree that most people confuse their feelings and prejudices with thinking, or do you feel they are aware of their thought processes and logical in their arguments? What examples can you provide?

2. Describe how your thinking about a particular subject changed. Did you move from prejudice to objectivity, belief to cynicism or vice versa, confusion to certainty? What caused the change?

3. What are the values and limitations of having a grade-one "coherent system for living"?

Bob Greene

Are Books an
Endangered Species?

[1]   In the house where I grew up, we had a room we called the library. It wasn't a real library, of course, it was just a small den dominated by a television set. But there were bookshelves built into all four walls, and hundreds of books—hardback books with spines of many colors—surrounded us in that room. The books, collected by my parents and grandparents throughout their lifetimes, were a part of my childhood.

[2]   My generation—the generation that came of age in the 1950s and 1960s—may be the last one to know that feeling, the feeling of being surrounded by millions of words; those words the products of years of work by authors famous and obscure. For now, in the midst of the 1970s, we are seeing a subtle but unmistakable turning away from such things. The houses of America, I fear, may soon include no room for libraries. The hardcover book—that symbol of the permanence of thought, the handing down of wisdom from one age to the next—may be a new addition to our list of endangered species.

[3]   I have a friend who runs a bookstore in a Midwestern college town. He has found that he cannot sell hardback books; paperbacks are his stock in trade, and even those are a disappointment to him. "You know how we used to see people carrying around book bags?" he tells me. "Well, now I look out the window of my shop, and all I see are students carrying packages from the record stores. The students aren't reading any more. They're listening to albums."

439

[4]   And indeed he may be right. Stories of problems young people have with reading are not new, but the trend seems to be worsening. Recently the chancellor of the University of Illinois's branch campus in Chicago said that 10 percent of the freshman at his university could read no better than the average eighth grader. As dismal a commentary as this is, there is an even more chilling aspect to it: of those college freshmen whose reading skills were equivalent to the sixth- to eighth-grade level, the chancellor reported that many had ranked in the *top* half of their high-school classes.

[5]   A professor at the same university said that even after four years on campus, some of the college graduates could hardly read or write. And the ramifications this situation brings to the nation are obvious, and will become even more so in the years to come. Those ramifications are already being felt in the cultural marketplace. A first work of fiction, if it has any luck at all, will sell perhaps 3,000 copies in its hardback edition. Publishers and authors know not to expect much better than that. And a record album? Well, a new group called Boston recently released an album of the same name. It is their first record. So far it has sold 3.5 million copies.

[6]   Much of the problem is that we live in a passive age. To listen to a record album, to sit through a movie, to watch a television show—all require nothing of the cultural consumer, save his mere presence. To read a book, though, takes an act of will on the part of the consumer. He must genuinely want to find out what is inside. He cannot just sit there; he must *do* something, even though the something is as simple an action as opening the book, closing the door and beginning to read.

[7]   In generations before my own, this was taken for granted as an important part of life. But now, in the day of the "information retrieval system," such a reverence is not being placed on the reading, and then saving, of books. If a young American reads at all, he is far more likely to purchase a paperback that may be flipped through and then thrown away. In a disposable age, the book for keeping and rereading is an anachronism, a ponderous dinosaur in a high-speed society.

[8]   The example of books, of course, may be carried too far. A few hardback books—the much-publicized best sellers—are moving well, and the paperback business is one of the nation's true growth industries. But it seems to me that the readers are older, as a group, than they ever were before; this only illustrates the point that a new generation is choosing the passive over the active, the expendable over the lasting.

[9]   My mother writes letters. On special occasions—important birthdays, noteworthy accomplishments—she sits down and puts her thoughts and emotions, the things that are going through her heart, down on paper; and she sends the letters to me, or to my brother or sister. The letters are beautiful and clearly intended for keeping. My mother is of a generation when doing such a thing was expected. Hers is a generation of steamer trunks in the cellar, filled with the important letters of a lifetime, the expressions of love and pride committed to paper.

[10]   I don't write letters. I telephone. Most of the people I know do the same thing. On one level, we are products of phone companies' commercials, telling us how good it is to make our voices heard across the miles. But the real reason

we call instead of write is the same reason we are more likely to turn on television than pick up a book. It is easier. It gets the job done—something happens, a thought is expressed or a story is absorbed—and if it is fleeting, gone in an instant ... well, welcome once again to the 70s.

[11]   This is especially ironic in a season during which such an emphasis has been placed on finding our individual "roots." For while many Americans are toiling to trace the origins of their culture and their beings, a new generation is making sure that future roots will be almost impossible to uncover. It is almost as though we were willing it: we save no written record of who we have been and what we have learned; we "relocate" from place to place at such a dizzying pace that the logical question is whether we are really just moving or running away; we change jobs so easily, that "life-style" has become a more meaningful term than "career"; we standardize and franchise our places of lodging and eating to such an extent that it is almost impossible to distinguish one part of the country from another.

[12]   And what does this mean? What does this preference for the transitory over the lasting bode? Nothing, perhaps. Only what we used to call "civilization" is, in so many small ways, managing to slip away from us, perhaps forever.

VOCABULARY

Use the context of the essay and your dictionary to define the following words.

1. dominated (par 1.)
2. obscure (par. 2)
3. subtle (par. 2)
4. dismal (par. 4)
5. ramifications (par. 5)
6. passive (par. 6)
7. anachronism (par. 7)
8. expendable (par. 8)
9. ironic (par. 11)
10. transitory (par. 12)

RHETORIC AND IDEA

1. Bob Greene uses a room to symbolize a basic contrast that he sets up in paragraphs 1 and 2. What is the room and what does he say has happened to it? What more general contrast does he use this difference to symbolize?
2. Which side of the contrast does paragraph 3 illustrate? How does it point up Greene's basic point in the essay?
3. What do paragraphs 4 and 5 contribute to his argument?
4. In paragraph 6, he gets to a basic reason for the situation that he claims exists. What is that reason? How does he use contrast in this paragraph to explain that reason?
5. Beyond reading, what other troubling aspect of our relationship to books is stressed in paragraph 7?
6. These two problems (as discussed in paragraphs 6 and 7) are summed up in what sentence of paragraph 8? What is that summation?
7. What contrast does he make about letters in paragraph 9 and 10? Which major point does this contrast illustrate?
8. What does he foresee as the long-range results, the consequences, of the situation?

WRITING ASSIGNMENTS

1. Set up a contrast in which two differing rooms illustrate some basic difference between people or their times and cultures. Describe the rooms in some detail and then define what qualities and characteristics of the people are revealed.

2. In what ways (possibly including books but not necessarily limited to books) does our society seem to stress the transitory over the lasting? What are some examples of this stress? What are some of the results?

3. In what ways do people today seem more passive than people of some former period? Or, to take the opposing view, more active?

4. Are you satisfied with your own reading habits? What are your usual reading habits, pleasures, limitations, rewards?

Woody Allen

Examining Psychic Phenomena

[1]   There is no question that there is an unseen world. The problem is, how far is it from midtown and how late is it open? Unexplainable events occur constantly. One man will see spirits. Another will hear voices. A third will wake up and find himself running in the Preakness. How many of us have not at one time or another felt an ice-cold hand on the back of our neck while we were home alone? (Not me, thank God, but some have.) What is behind these experiences? Or in front of them, for that matter? Is it true that some men can foresee the future or communicate with ghosts? And after death is it still possible to take showers?

[2]   Fortunately, these questions about psychic phenomena are answered in a soon to be published book, ''Boo!,'' by Dr. Osgood Mulford Twelge, the noted parapsychologist and professor of ectoplasm at Columbia University. Dr. Twelge has assembled a remarkable history of supernatural incidents that covers the whole range of psychic phenomena, from thought transference to the bizarre experience of two brothers on opposite parts of the globe, one of whom took a bath while the other suddenly got clean. What follows is but a sampling of Dr. Twelge's most celebrated cases, with his comments.

Apparitions

[3]   On March 16, 1882, Mr. J. C. Dubbs awoke in the middle of the night and saw his brother Amos, who had been dead for fourteen years, sitting at the foot of his bed flicking chickens. Dubbs asked his brother what he was doing

there, and his brother said not to worry, he was dead and was only in town for the weekend. Dubbs asked his brother what it was like in "the other world," and his brother said it was not unlike Cleveland. He said he had returned to give Dubbs a message, which was that a dark-blue suit and Argyle socks are a big mistake.

[4]   At that point, Dubbs' servant girl entered and saw Dubbs talking to "a shapeless, milky haze," which she said reminded her of Amos Dubbs but was a little better-looking. Finally, the ghost asked Dubbs to join him in an aria from "Faust," which the two sang with great fervor. As dawn rose, the ghost walked through the wall, and Dubbs, trying to follow, broke his nose.

[5]   This appears to be a classic case of the apparition phenomenon and if Dubbs is to be believed, the ghost returned again and caused Mrs. Dubbs to rise out of a chair and hover over the dinner table for twenty minutes until she dropped into some gravy. It is interesting to note that spirits have a tendency to be mischievous, which A. F. Childe, the British mystic, attributes to a marked feeling of inferiority they have over being dead. "Apparitions" are often associated with individuals who have suffered an unusual demise. Amos Dubbs, for instance, had died under mysterious circumstances when a farmer accidentally planted him along with some turnips.

Spirit Departure

[6]   Mr. Albert Sykes reports the following experience: "I was sitting having biscuits with some friends when I felt my spirit leave my body and go make a telephone call. For some reason, it called the Moscowitz Fiber Glass Company. My spirit then returned to my body and sat for another twenty minutes or so, hoping nobody would suggest charades. When the conversation turned to mutual funds, it left again and began wandering around the city. I am convinced that it visited the Statue of Liberty and then saw the stage show at Radio City Music Hall. Following that, it went to Benny's Steak House and ran up a tab of sixty-eight dollars. My spirit then decided to return to my body, but it was impossible to get a cab. Finally, it walked up Fifth Avenue and rejoined me just in time to catch the late news. I could tell that it was reentering my body, because I felt a sudden chill, and a voice said, 'I'm back. You want to pass me those raisins?'

[7]   "This phenomenon has happened to me several times since. Once, my spirit went to Miami for a weekend, and once it was arrested trying to leave Macy's without paying for a tie. The fourth time, it was actually my body that left my spirit, although all it did was get a rubdown and come right back."

[8]   Spirit departure was very common around 1910, when many "spirits" were reported wandering aimlessly around India searching for the American Consulate. The phenomenon is quite similar to transubstantiation, the process whereby a person will suddenly dematerialize and rematerialize somewhere else in the world. This is not a bad way to travel, although there is usually a half-hour wait for luggage. The most astonishing case of transubstantiation was that of Sir Arthur Nurney, who vanished with an audible *pop* while he was taking a bath and suddenly appeared in the string section of the Vienna Symphony Orchestra. He stayed on as the first violinist for

twenty-seven years, atlhough he could only play "Three Blind Mice," and vanished abruptly one day during Mozart's Jupiter Symphony, turning up in bed with Winston Churchill.

Precognition

[9]   Mr. Fenton Allentuck describes the following precognitive dream: "I went to sleep at midnight and dreamed that I was playing whist with a plate of chives. Suddenly the dream shifted, and I saw my grandfather about to be run over by a truck in the middle of the street, where he was waltzing with a clothing dummy. I tried to scream, but when I opened my mouth the only sound that came out was chimes, and my grandfather was run over.

[10]   "I awoke in a sweat and ran to my grandfather's house and asked him if he had plans to go waltzing with a clothing dummy. He said of course not, although he had contemplated posing as a shepherd to fool his enemies. Relieved, I walked home, but learned later that the old man had slipped on a chicken-salad sandwich and fallen off the Chrysler Building."

[11]   Precognitive dreams are too common to be dismissed as pure coincidence. Here a man dreams of a relative's death, and it occurs. Not everyone is so lucky. J. Martinez, of Kennebunkport, Maine, dreamed he won the Irish Sweepstakes. When he awoke, his bed had floated out to sea.

Trances

[12]   Sir Hugh Swiggles, the skeptic, reports an interesting séance experience:

[13]   We attended the home of Madame Reynaud, the noted medium, where we were all told to sit around the table and join hands. Mr. Weeks couldn't stop giggling, and Madame Reynaud smashed him on the head with a Ouija board. The lights were turned out, and Madame Reynaud attempted to contact Mrs. Marple's husband, who had died at the opera when his beard caught fire. The following is an exact transcript:

MRS. MARPLE: What do you see?

MEDIUM: I see a man with blue eyes and a pinwheel hat.

MRS. MARPLE: That's my husband!

MEDIUM: His name is ... Robert. No ... Richard ....

MRS. MARPLE: Quincy.

MEDIUM: Quincy! Yes, that's it!

MRS. MARPLE: What else about him?

MEDIUM: He is bald but usually keeps some leaves on his head so nobody will notice.

MRS. MARPLE: Yes! Exactly!

MEDIUM: For some reason, he has an object . . . a loin of pork.

MRS. MARPLE: My anniversary present to him! Can you make him speak?

MEDIUM: Speak, spirit, Speak.

QUINCY: Claire, this is Quincy.

MRS. MARPLE: Oh, Quincy! Quincy!

QUINCY: How long do you keep the chicken in when you're trying to broil it?

MRS. MARPLE: That voice! It's him!

MEDIUM: Everybody concentrate.

MRS. MARPLE: Quincy, are they treating you O.K.?
QUINCY: Not bad, except it takes four days to get your cleaning back.
MRS. MARPLE: Quincy, do you miss me?
QUINCY: Huh? Oh, er, sure. Sure, kid. I got to be going . . . .
MEDIUM: I'm losing it. He's fading. . . .

[14]   I found this seance to pass the most stringent tests of credulity, with the minor exception of a phonograph, which was found under Madame Reynaud's dress.

[15]   There is no doubt that certain events recorded at séances are genuine. Who does not recall the famous incident at Sybil Seretsky's, when her goldfish sang "I Got Rhythm"—a favorite tune of her recently deceased nephew? But contacting the dead is at best difficult, since most deceased are reluctant to speak up, and those that do seem to hem and haw before getting to the point. The author has actually seen a table rise, and Dr. Joshua Fleagle, of Harvard, attended a séance in which a table not only rose but excused itself and went upstairs to sleep.

Clairvoyance

[16]   One of the most astounding cases of clairvoyance is that of the noted Greek psychic, Achille Londos. Londos realized he had "unusual powers" by the age of ten, when he could lie in bed and, by concentrating, make his father's false teeth jump out of his mouth. After a neighbor's husband had been missing for three weeks, Londos told them to look in the stove, where the man was found knitting. Londos could concentrate on a person's face and force the image to come out on a roll of ordinary Kodak film, although he could never seem to get anybody to smile.

[17]   In 1964, he was called in to aid police in capturing the Düsseldorf Strangler, a fiend who always left a Baked Alaska on the chests of his victims. Merely by sniffing a handkerchief, Londos led police to Siegfried Lenz, handyman at a school for deaf turkeys, who said he was the strangler and could he please have his handkerchief back.

[18]   Londos is just one of many people with psychic powers. C. N. Jerome the psychic, of Newport, Rhode Island, claims he can guess any card being thought of by a squirrel.

Prognostication

[19]   Finally, we come to Aristonidis, the sixteenth-century count whose predictions continue to dazzle and perplex even the most skeptical. Typical examples are:

[20]   "Two nations will go to war, but only one will win."

[21]   (Experts feel this probably refers to the Russo-Japanese War of 1904-05-an astounding feat of prognostication, considering the fact that it was made in 1540.)

[22]   "A man in Istanbul will have his hat blocked, and it will be ruined."

[23]   (In 1860, Abu Hamid, Ottoman warrior, sent his cap out to be cleaned, and it came back with spots.)

[24]   ''I see a great person, who one day will invent for mankind a garment to be worn over his trousers for protection while cooking. It will be called an 'abron' or 'aprone.'''

[25]   (Aristonidis meant the apron, of course.)

[26]   ''A leader will emerge in France. He will be very short and will cause great calamity.''

[27]   (This is a reference either to Napoleon or to Marcel Lumet, an eighteenth-century midget who instigated a plot to rub béarnaise sauce on Voltaire.)

[28]   ''In the New World, there will be a place named California, and a man named Joseph Cotten will become famous.''

[29]   (No explanation necessary.)

VOCABULARY

Use the context of the essay and your dictionary to define the following words.

1. phenomena (par 2.)
2. ectoplasm (par. 2)
3. bizarre (par. 2)
4. dematerialize (par. 8)
5. precognitive (par. 9)

6. stringent (par. 14)
7. credulity (par. 14)
8. skeptical (par. 19)
9. prognostication (par. 21)
10. instigated (par. 27)

RHETORIC AND IDEA

1. Woody Allen's piece is obviously a satire, more specifically a parody, on the subject of extrasensory perception. What is Allen satirizing? What is his purpose?

2. While he mainly mocks examples of six different types of psychic phenomena, his examples do provide a basis for understanding what the usual claims about those are. In serious terms briefly explain the supposed workings of the processes he spoofs.

3. Particular comic illustrations used indicate the kind of flaw or absurdity being ridiculed. What is it about prognostications, for example, that his list at the end of the essay seems to be mocking.?

4. What do the short sentences at the beginning of paragraph 1 do in setting the mood for the article?

5. Why is the second sentence of paragraph 2 much longer? What comic effect is furthered by this length?

6. One of Allen's regular comic devices is to have a surprising word or phrase in the last half or at the end of a sentence. The humor is caused by Allen's going lower on the staircase of abstractions than the reader expects. For example, in paragraph 6: ''My spirit then decided to return to my body, but it was impossible to get a cab.'' Show three other sentences in which he uses this surprising descent at the end of a sentence.

7. Another device is to have similar surprises, or non sequiturs, in a spirit's responses to questions. Show two examples.

WRITING ASSIGNMENTS

1. Describe in serious terms a psychic experience that you have had or that somebody has reported to you. Or, as Allen has done, write an exaggerated version of a typical story about an extrasensory experience.

2. Apply Allen's approach to the writing of a TV commercial. That is, exaggerate a typical commercial (either a real or invented product) so as to expose its silliness. Describe the visual images and the words.

3. Write a satire of an interview, an investigation, or a trial, in which the usual question-and-answer pattern is carried into non sequiturs and satirical exaggerations.

Arlen J. Hansen

The Imagination Gap

[1]   "Impoverished imagination," I repeated as the Field pollster stared at me in disbelief. Undoubtedly, she had been prepared to check "Taxes," "Crime," "Inflation," or even "Housing." To relieve her of temporary paralysis, I reiterated our conversation: "You asked me what I thought was the biggest problem facing the American people today and I said, 'We suffer from an impoverished imagination.' It's not a new idea with me, you know." Resigned to my persistence, she began to print my answer in the box marked "Other." "Oh," she said. "How do you spell it?"

[2]   As a professor of English who comes in contact with hundreds of young minds each year, I have grown increasingly aware of the absence these days of what the Renaissance man called "fancy." There are fewer and fewer students, I find, who have playful imaginations. Please understand that I am not asking for profound creativity. Or resourceful inventiveness. Rather, I should like to see more students whose minds sparkle. The effervescent champagne of wit, rather than the stale beer of cliché.

[3]   In the '60s, the college student—excluding the yippie, of course, who stayed away from academia—was a sober revolutionary. In class he demanded relevance, and he committed himself to social causes. His imagination was subordinated to his moral sense. Outrage, not playfulness, was the cast of mind of most of the best students. If they skipped class, it was to "work on Gene's or Bobby's campaign," and they said so—teachers' rules be damned.

A lively lot they were, though one sighed for the fear that seemed to line the determination in their eyes. Seeking nothing imaginative themselves, these students showed little gift for play. Reason, relevance and revolution were their three R's.

[4]   But the '60s have passed, if the problems of the '60s have not. And students have become decorous once again. They take notes, No-Doz, and no-nonsense, career-related courses. Solemn industry may have replaced moral commitment, but there is still no imagination.

[5]   Last spring at exam time, one of my best students told me that she would have to miss a few days of class because her grandmother had died. Now, students have been killing off their grandmothers at exam time for decades. I've had students do away with as many as four grandmothers in one year. So, I asked this student how her grandmother had died. "Well, uh, she was in a car accident," the young woman answered. "Where?" She looked blankly at me—"On 101. Near Bakersfield." Since Bakersfield is not on U.S. Highway 101, I tried to help out: "You mean Highway 99?" "Yes," came the answer, followed quickly by "and my brother was with her." The plot was thickening. "How did it happen? I mean, did your brother get hurt, too?" The student brushed some lint off her shoulder. "He's in the hospital." I waited, and eventually she continued. "My father had a heart attack last week." Morbidly capitalizing on the opportunity, I pressed on. "How's he doing?" "OK." "I'll bet the accident gave him a relapse." "I suppose," she said.

[6]   I ended the interrogation. The plot had not thickened at all. It had simply been compounded. She worked by adding on; more is better. The student had killed her grandmother, seriously injured her brother and inflicted a heart attack upon her father. It was ruthless. Cold-blooded. I was reluctant to ask for more, out of fear that she might do damage to her mother and sister as well.

[7]   The poor student simply did not know how to storify. She had no sense for detail. There was no gore, no broken bones, lacerations, shattered glass, screams of terror and pain and no complications. No imagination. It was, in sum, a pitiable attempt, unworthy of a bright college student. I did not excuse her, and she scored high marks on the exam.

[8]   I remember my first dead-grandmother story. I was teaching in a small college in Illinois in 1961, and a student wove me a captivating tale. He knew I was a new teacher; nevertheless, he had sufficient pride in his gift of story-making to spin a fine yarn anyway. His grandmother rode a motorcycle into a bridge abutment just west of Galesburg. The silverhaired old woman had borrowed a Harley from my student's cousin to try out, for a lark. She died three hours later from a cerebral hemorrhage.

[9]   And there was more. The student's father had to be called home from Indianapolis where he had driven to a national hardware convention. The gold-plated class ring that the student was wearing had been a high-school graduation gift from his grandmother, who had not had an opportunity to go to high school. He had been looking forward to spending the summer with her in Galesburg, but now he didn't know what he was going to do. Maybe go to summer school. He took his education so very seriously, or so he protested.

He told this story far better than my summary suggests; he earned his reprieve. Eventually, he earned a Ph.D.

[10]   The day before the Field woman came to my door, two students had made appointments to see me. They both had missed my final exam on the previous day. The first told me that his girlfriend had been raped, which upset him so much that he could not take the final. When I pointed out that his girlfriend herself had not missed the exam, he assured me that he was speaking of a different girlfriend. The second student, who ambled into my office in tennis shorts, told me that he'd been to his grandmother's funeral on the day of the final. She had been wiped out in an auto accident near Bakersfield. "On U.S. 101?" I asked. "No," he said looking quizzically at me, "on 99. I don't think 101 goes through Bakersfield."

[11]   So, naturally, I was ready with my answer when the pollster asked me her question. As I observed when she was leaving, our greatest problem today is either our impoverished imagination or that damned deathtrap near Bakersfield on 99.

VOCABULARY

Use the context of the essay and your dictionary to define the following words.

1. impoverished (par 7.)   6. compounded (par. 6)
2. persistence (par. 1)   7. pitiable (par. 7)
3. relevance (par. 3)   8. sufficient (par. 8)
4. decorous (par. 4)   9. reprieve (par. 9)
5. morbidly (par. 5)   10. ambled (par. 10)

RHETORIC AND IDEA

1. Explain what Arlen J. Hansen means by his first two words—"impoverished imagination"—taking into account what he says in the rest of the essay.
2. What contrast does he draw between the students of the sixties and those of the seventies? On what point, however, does he find them similar?
3. Hansen's analysis of the student's story told in paragraph 5 is made in paragraphs 6 and 7. What does he say her technique is? What flaw of imagination is revealed?
4. Discuss the variety of sentence lengths in paragraph 6 and the effect achieved.
5. What techniques of parallel sentence structure—within a sentence and between sentences—are used in paragraph 7?
6. What are the differences of story-telling technique revealed by the grandmother story in paragraph 8? Which story does he like better and why?
7. Two more stories are used for illustration in paragraph 10. Which kind of story telling and imagination does he use each to illustrate? Why?

WRITING ASSIGNMENTS

1. What are the influences today that tend to make people unimaginative in
   their lives (not just in telling stories) or that tend to make them
   imaginative? Do you feel that people tend to be getting less or more imaginative in the ways they live, think, and tell stories?

2. Invent an elaborate (and maybe even imaginative) but defensible excuse
   for missing some major event—such as an important date, game, party,
   wedding, funeral. Define the situation and then explain why you missed
   it.

3. Narrate an experience in which telling a story (true or not) was necessary
   and important to you. Describe the situation, the story, and the outcome.

section five

Of Media and Audiences

Jerzy Kosinski

Children of TV[1]

[1]   During the last four years, I have taught at Wesleyan, Princeton, and at Yale University. I have often lectured at many schools throughout the country. I am appalled by what I think emerges as the dominant trait of the students of today—their short span of attention, their inability to know or believe anything for more than half an hour. I feel it was television which turned them into spectators, since by comparison with the world of television, their own lives are slow and uneventful. When they first believed that what they saw on TV was real, they overreacted, only to feel cheated when the next program demanded a new emotion. Later, they felt simply manipulated by whatever drama they witnessed. By now, they have become hostile, and so they either refuse to watch the TV altogether or they dissect the medium and throw out all that upsets them.

[2]   It was from the daily log of TV that they accepted the world as single-faceted and never complex. After all, if it was accessible to TV cameras, it couldn't possibly be otherwise. It was digestible and motionlessly marching in front of them. From TV's comic cartoons they first deducted that death is not final, since their hero, no matter how dead, would rise. It was TV that taught them that they need not be experienced but avoid it. Hence, they remain at the mercy of the pain reliever commercials.

[1]Editor's title

[3]   It was TV that first convinced them that drugs were to be trusted and that with their help there was no suffering, no need to be tensed—indeed, unhappy. As a professor of prose I am constantly reminded of television's legacy. The students don't describe. They announce, as if an ever-present screen orchestrated their meaning for everyone. In hundreds of essays, none of them approached killing, illness, passion. All this was dismissed by shorthand, mutilated, suffered, feeling bad. A lover throbs innocence. The recipient sweats sweetness.

[4]   During their scholarly and leisure pursuits, they switch with exactly the same intensity and staying power from subject to subject, as if changing TV channels. Fifteen minutes is all a teacher can hope for, assuming the classroom is freezing and the students' chairs are very uncomfortable. Whether discussing world economics and politics or what's for lunch or a film, they seem incapable of reflecting. Even though their stomachs are full like exotic fishes of the Amazon, they swallow indescriminately, quickly ejecting all as waste.

[5]   Reading, however, is solitary, requiring effort and imagination to translate a symbol into reality. Hence, the youngsters don't venture beyond required reading texts or worse, limit themselves to condensed aids. And so, at the campuses, the novel is not dead. Its readers are dying fast. The students never seem to be alone for more than a few hours. To them, solitude means feeling lonely. When awake, if they ever are, they join the group. Others provide a stage for being turned on, but no more than a TV set can they turn themselves on. This requires assistance and moviemakers, music pushers, encounter group merchants, fashion promoters, and television are there to keep the young plugged in.

[6]   Another myth of this greening of America is the young are using drugs to create mystic experience and self-discovery. A drug, whether soft or hard, is the crudest do-it-yourself identity kit remedy. Using it, many young miss their identity in the same way so many of their elders who are engaged in the so-called sexual revolution miss the meaning of love in the guise of being free.

[7]   Rock is another safely collective rite. At best, they can claim it a shared situation. They listen to music in a group. Deafening sound effectively rules out every exchange and permits each of them to escape direct contact with the others. They barely retain the memory of the lyrics and the beat. The students' political revolution [was] no more than another football trip. There [were] the momentary heroes, the cheer-leaders, the spectators, a bit of virility and of machismo. In ten years, the white young rebels of this country [did not sustain] any ideology, one effective group or party. Politics, after all, [was] for them another channel to turn to and be turned by.

[8]   Those of you who feel that what I have just said is valid, make no mistake. To the young who watch me now, it is nothing but a billboard, temporarily occupied by a public-health message of sorts. They are ready for the next program. Why, therefore, you ask, do I still teach at universities? Because, as with television, there's always a chance for a better program, a different generation, or at least, for a few profound specials.

VOCABULARY

Use the context of the essay and your dictionary to define the words below.

1. appalled (par. 1)
2. spectators (par. 1)
3. manipulated (par. 1)
4. accessible (par. 2)
5. legacy (par. 3)

6. exotic (par. 4)
7. ejecting (par. 4)
8. guise (par. 6)
9. rite (par. 7)
10. machismo (par. 7)

RHETORIC AND IDEA

1. What characteristics does Kosinski consider the dominant trait of today's students?
2. The last three sentences of paragraph 1 are arranged in chronological order. Underline the chronological transitional devices in the three sentences.
3. In sentence 2 of paragraph 2, Kosinski uses a form of paradox called *oxymoron*. Identify the phrase that illustrates the device.
4. What is the central idea of paragraph 3?
5. What is the overall tone of Kosinski's essay? What is his attitude toward television? Toward students?
6. What does Kosinski feel is the most severe result of the young's use of drugs?
7. Why, according to Kosinski, do students not read? Do you feel he is correct in his observations?
8. In what way are the brevity and style of Kosinski's essay relevant to the point he makes? Explain.

WRITING ASSIGNMENTS

1. Write a letter to Jerzy Kosinski in which you take issue with his ideas. Support your position with evidence from your own experience.
2. Watch television commercials for a week with the following question in mind: Do television commercials try to convince viewers to trust dangerous things? Take notes on your findings and use the notes as a basis for an essay.
3. Is the world as presented on television "single-faceted and never complex" as Kosinski insists in paragraph 2? Write an essay in which you use examples from television to illustrate your answer.
4. Kosinski accuses television of producing the short attention span of students. Watch television for an hour a day for the next week and take notes on what you see. When you analyze your findings, comment in a well-developed paragraph on how television does or does not cater to those with short attention spans.

Will Stanton

Real Girls Ask for
Mint Frappés

[1]   The girl on TV has just learned that her lover has found another woman. She sits at the supper table staring dumbly ahead.

[2]   "Ruthie," her mother says, "you haven't touched your supper. What's the matter?"

[3]   "Nothing, Mamma," she says tonelessly, "I guess I'm just not hungry."

[4]   This is probably the most unshakable conviction to be found on TV: A girl who is suffering from unrequited love just isn't hungry.

[5]   This is balderdash. In my younger days I frequently went out with girls who had just been jilted by somebody or other, and they ate like wolves.

[6]   I guess that's what bothers me most about TV dramas—not the major improbabilities, but the fact that they're so out of touch with reality in small matters. I have no trouble accepting a hero who stows away on a rocket or escapes a burning sampan, but how can you identify with a man who can always find a place to park his car?

[7]   There is no respiratory problem on TV. Go to a concert, and at any given moment one person out of three will be coughing. On TV the only person who coughs is the young composer. "Light the candle, Maria," he says, "it's growing dark." Between coughs you can hear the sound of violins. I guess it's sort of like a concert at that.

[8]   Americans use up seven and a half million boxes of tissues a day, but nobody on TV blows his nose. The only time you see a handkerchief is at a

funeral. The old lady has it clutched in her withered hand. "My bambino," she sobs.

[9]   The scene where the hero fixes the girl a drink always annoys me. All she ever wants is a little brandy and not a crème-de-menthe frappé or a Singapore Sling, which is what women usually want me to mix for them. The man sloshes brandy into a couple of glasses, and he and the girl are getting cozy on the couch, while I would still be looking for the bottle opener. He doesn't have to pry ice cubes out of the tray, find a lemon, find a knife, find something to wipe his hands on, try to remember what he did with the jigger, and try to remember which glass is which. I remind myself that it isn't real brandy they're drinking, but it doesn't help.

[10]   Young lovers have plenty of problems on TV, but they also get their share of the breaks. Hand in hand they romp through the woodland in a kind of Swan Lake canter, and when the mood for dalliance strikes them they flop down wherever they happen to be. There are no rocks, burrs, roots or thorns. As far as they're concerned, the whole forest was put out by Beautyrest. They don't even get bitten by mosquitoes.

[11]   The hero of the crime shows gets some breaks too. When he tells the cab driver to follow that car, for instance, he never has any trouble finding a cab. Like the parking place, it's always there when he needs it. The driver never gives him an argument. He never says, "Which car?" or, "You outa your mind?" Nothing like that. He steps on the gas, and off they go. Along the avenue, down an alley, through a tunnel, onto a ferryboat, and there they are, still on the felon's tail. I was at the shopping center the other day trying to find out how to get to a certain place. A fellow told me he was driving right by it, so I should follow him. He was driving a red station wagon with a toboggan on the luggage rack. I lost him before I got out of the parking lot.

[12]   Then there's the girl agent. She's sitting across from her partner in a restaurant booth. Looking around to make sure she's unobserved, she dips her hand in her purse and passes him the microfilm. It makes you wonder if anyone in television has ever watched a real woman try to find something in a real purse. It takes an average of 40 seconds to find her sunglasses, 2 minutes for the car keys, and 3½ for a lipstick. A piece of microfilm would be lost forever.

[13]   People on TV never forget anything. Or hardly ever. Sometimes they can't remember who they are, but they don't forget anything else. The man picks up the phone and a voice says, "Go out to 17094 West 186th Street Apartment 27C and ask for Luther R. Tarasovek. Tell him to find out where Harley Ostendorf was January 18, 1953 between eight-thirty and nine-forty-five."

[14]   "Right," he says and hangs up.

[15]   And they always have the right change. The man goes into the phone booth, reaches in his pocket and comes up with a dime between his thumb and finger. Try it. The first time you'll get a penny, then a nickel, then another penny. The only way you can do it is to bring out all the change in your pocket. Paw through it with your left hand and pick out the dime. Put the rest back. Take the dime in your right hand, pick up the receiver with your left and deposit the dime. Dial your number if you can remember it.

[16]   With telephones, TV has a technique all its own. When somebody makes a call, there are two rings, and the other party answers. If they want to show

there's nobody home, it rings four times, and the caller hangs up. At the other end of the line it works the other way. The fellow is just leaving the girl's apartment as the phone rings.

[17]   "I hate to leave you like this," he says.

[18]   "We've been through all this before," she says. "There's no point in dragging it up again." The phone is still ringing.

[19]   "Well," he says, "———"

[20]   "It's better this way," she says. "What's done is done."

[21]   Everybody in the audience is on the edge of his chair—the phone, for God's sake—answer the phone!

[22]   He says good-bye. She says good-bye. she closes the door, turns around and leans back against it. The phone rings. She starts toward it, stops to adjust a picture, stops at the fruit bowl, eats a couple of grapes, picks up the phone. "Yes?" she says, "Oh, hello, Ford. I was wondering if you'd call."

[23]   People complain that there's nothing new on TV, but I keep having this dream: I turn on the set, and there's this couple—the husband is reading the paper. He has a popcorn hull caught between his teeth. He can't get it out. The wife swats a fly on the front of the TV. She asks if there's anything interesting in the paper. He says no. A light bulb burns out. He goes to the medicine cabinet for some dental floss. The bathroom has all the standard fixtures. He asks her where the light bulbs are. She says there aren't any. She has a mosquito bite. She gets up to scratch it. The phone rings, and he goes over to answer it. A woman asks him if he'd like to buy any awnings. He says no.

[24]   That's about it. Not very exciting, maybe, but I want to know what happens to them, because they're real people. Their problems are my problems. They're my people, and I care.

VOCABULARY

Use the context of the essay and your dictionary to define each of the following words.

1. unrequited (par. 4)
2. balderdash (par. 4)
3. respiratory (par. 7)
4. frappé (par. 9)
5. canter (par. 10)

6. dalliance (par. 10)
7. burrs (par. 10)
8. felon's (par. 11)
9. hull (par. 23)
10. floss (par. 23)

RHETORIC AND IDEA

1. What is Will Stanton's basic complaint? In making this complaint, which kind of situation on television does he stress?
2. In which paragraph does he state his thesis?
3. As he develops his complaint, what is his basic method of organization?
4. As a regular device, Stanton uses which sentence of a paragraph to introduce each new topic?
5. Explain how Stanton uses contrast in developing at least three of his specific topics.

6. The dramatized illustration in paragraphs 17-22 is used to develop which aspect of the telephone problem?
7. What is the function and contribution of paragraph 23?
8. Explain how Stanton develops the topic sentence of paragraph 11.
9. Analyze Stanton's method and strategy in the opening five paragraphs of his article. What has he done first here?
10. What is the most striking aspect of the sentence structure of the last three paragraphs? Are these sentences typical of the whole essay? Why does Stanton use this type of sentence?

WRITING ASSIGNMENTS

1. What is your pet peeve about television? Provide illustrations.
2. What is your opinion of, and response to, the kind of realism, or lack of it, on television?
3. Does television in general show its audience enough of the realities of the world they live in? If so, how? If not, what might be added?

Meg Greenfield

Uncle Tom's Roots

[1]   The last publishing event in this country that was in any way comparable to the phenomenon of "Roots" occurred in 1851. It was the publication, first as a serial and then as a book, of "Uncle Tom's Cabin" by Harriet Beecher Stowe. In fact, there are so many parallels between the two books—as well as between their receptions—that we could do worse than to give Mrs. Stowe a chance to answer the question about "Roots" that seems to be on everybody's mind: What does it all *mean?* I think she can tell us.

[2]   Before we go further, I should say that I share the view of the late critic Edmund Wilson that "Uncle Tom's Cabin" does not deserve the general contempt in which it is nowadays held. Yes, it has stunning lapses into inaccuracy, sentimentality and tub-thumping propaganda. But it also has a grandeur of conception and what Wilson called a "certain eruptive force" that overwhelm these deficiencies. I would say precisely the same thing about "Roots." For the most part, Alex Haley's blacks strike me as being every bit as sentimentalized as Mrs. Stowe's in their unrelieved virtue down through the generations. But all that only heightens—as it is meant to—our rage at their treatment.

[3]   Mrs. Stowe's book was originally going to be called "Uncle Tom's Cabin; or, The Man That Was a Thing." Her subtitle was changed (to "Life Among the Lowly"), but the original expressed her real intention: to make vivid the individual, personal cruelties of the slave system, especially as it tore families

apart, and to expose the monumental insensitivity of those who countenanced it. And, as a deeply religious woman, she would also demonstrate, in what she regarded as Uncle Tom's near-perfect Christianity, the superiority of the oppressed to the oppressor—an amazing capacity on the part of the enslaved blacks to preserve their souls.

[4]   That is not very different from the thrust of "Roots," and there are actually some very similar episodes in the two books. Kunta Kinte's devastation by the sale of his daughter—it is the end of him—put me forcibly in mind of the awful silent reaction of the slave Lucy, in "Uncle Tom's Cabin," when she learns that her child has been sold. Of Lucy, who would that night take her life by drowning, Mrs. Stowe wrote: "The shot had passed too straight and direct through the heart for a cry or a tear."

[5]   There is an emotional truth in these moments that seems to me to transcend the *untruths* of characterization of both Lucy and Kunta Kinte, their implausible, idealized aspects. And in the current controversy over the fidelity of "Roots" to history and nature, I think the book's defenders ought to stipulate as much. "Roots" is romantic and melodramatic, its characters are in many ways unconvincing and unreal. But none of that disturbs its larger human truth.

[6]   The same can be said of the argument over the factual accuracy of "Roots," an argument also reminiscent of that generated by "Uncle Tom's Cabin." As a feat of research and imagination, Mrs. Stowe's enterprise was not unlike Haley's, although one was seeking his historical identity, while the other was seeking to arouse the sensibilities of her countrymen. Mrs. Stowe had had a few encounters with the system she wrote about. But like Haley she undertook prodigious study with a view to re-creating reality. Her biographer, Forrest Wilson, cites, for instance, a letter she wrote to the abolitionist, Frederick Douglass, asking for help in portraying the reality of life on a cotton plantation: "I have before me an able paper written by a Southern planter, in which the details and modus operandi are given from his point of sight. I am anxious to have something from another standpoint."

[7]   Her scrupulous efforts remind me of Haley's. Both sought to achieve verisimilitude. But both, inevitably, made errors of fact. And both also bent reality for the sake of their message, painting things sharper and simpler than they really were. Mrs. Stowe was so disturbed by the charges of inaccuracy that she eventually gathered up supporting research material and published it for her critics to inspect. But that, like the insistence of the defenders of "Roots" that Haley has portrayed life as it was actually lived, seems to me to have missed the point. On the larger historical truth, both win hands down. The detail and background are there to enhance this truth—but they are not the issue. Haley's book, like Mrs. Stowe's, is a work of historical imagination and re-creation. It is fiction, though people tend to forget that.

[8]   You could say that this forgetfulness is a tribute to the emotional power of Haley's re-creation of events, to his skill as a melodramatist—a skill he shares with Mrs. Stowe. The public response to "Uncle Tom's Cabin"—pretelevision, pre-abolition and all—was like the response to "Roots." It was an unexpected and unaccountable wildfire thing.

[9]   Contemporary observers tell us how families read aloud (and wept over) each installment of Mrs. Stowe's saga, how copies of the magazine in which it

appeared were passed from household to household, how printing presses were going 24 hours a day to keep the book available. Uncle Tom and Liza and Simon Legree, et al., joined the national vocabulary overnight, just as Kizzy and Chicken George and Massa Waller have done. Mrs. Stowe did for the audience of the magazine that serialized her more or less what Alex Haley did for ABC's. She was commended by Dickens and Tolstoy and George Sand. She was translated into Finnish.

[10]   And, of course, as is also the case with Haley, her work was oversimplified, exploited and cheapened in the enthusiasm that ensued. One reason people have so low an opinion of her book is that they know it only from the vulgarized dramas that were made from it. In fact, Forrest Wilson tells us, within months of the first magazine installment people were singing Uncle Tom songs and a manufacturer had put out a card game called "Uncle Tom and Little Eva," whose action was "the continual separation and reunion of families."

[11]   "Roots," one likes to think, won't come to that. We are more sophisticated and more somber. Blacks and whites alike are earnestly trying to sort out the meaning and message of "Roots," noting its incorporation of black history into the American experience in a novel way, wondering why it has had the impact it has on themselves and other people.

[12]   Overnight, it has become part of the national folklore, this saga with its enormous power to move, and we all seem mystified by that. Mrs. Stowe would not have been. She knew what she was about, and she anticipated Haley. She wished, she wrote to her editor on the eve of publication, to present slavery "in the most lifelike and graphic manner possible. There is no arguing with *pictures,* and everybody is impressed by them, whether they mean to be or not."

VOCABULARY

Use the context of the essay and your dictionary to define the following words.

1. sentimentality (par. 2)
2. grandeur (par. 2)
3. countenanced (par. 3)
4. transcend (par. 5)
5. implausible (par. 5)
6. fidelity (par. 5)
7. sensibilities (par. 6)
8. scrupulous (par. 7)
9. verisimilitude (par. 7)
10. vulgarized (par. 10)

RHETORIC AND IDEA

1. While Meg Greenfield's main concern is *Roots,* she proceeds by making a series of comparisons to *Uncle Tom's Cabin,* the famous and important pre-Civil War attack on slavery. In paragraph 2, what contrast within *Uncle Tom's Cabin* does she say is also true of *Roots?* Explain.
2. Paragraph 3 sums up the central point of which of the two? What is that central point and purpose?
3. How does the parallel between Kunta Kinte and Lucy, described in paragraph 4, illustrate the point made in paragraph 3?

4. In paragraph 5, Greenfield admits a flaw in both. What is that flaw? What does she say is more important than that flaw?
5. Explain Greenfield's position on the degree of historical accuracy in both books.
6. Explain how the word *both* works in the parallel sentences that set up the comparison in paragraph 7.
7. In what ways were the public responses to both books (and TV series) similar?
8. How does she believe public response to *Roots* will differ from that to *Uncle Tom's Cabin?*

WRITING ASSIGNMENTS

1. Do you agree with Greenfield that a book may have the two kinds of flaws she refers to and still have a ''larger''truth and value? Defend your agreement or disagreement.
2. Describe either of these two books (if you have read either) or any other book, film, or program that you feel makes an attack on a social evil. Define what the nature of the attack is and show how aspects of the work— events, plot, characters, tone—help to dramatize that protest.
3. Draw a comparison between two works (again, books, films, or programs). Find some common denominator that ties them together, and then show similarities and differences in carrying out that common theme or purpose.
4. Sum up the central character traits and personality of a person that you know. In doing so, compare that person's traits to those of one or more historical or fictional people that your audience may know of.

VOCABULARY

Use the context of the essay and your dictionary to define the following words.

1. technological (par. 1)
2. liberation (par. 2)
3. impeded (par. 3)
4. consolation (par. 4)
5. imagery (par. 5)
6. technocrats (par. 5)
7. paraphernalia (par. 6)
8. havoc (par. 6)
9. unprecedentedly (par. 7)
10. preclude (par. 8)

RHETORIC AND IDEA

1. In drawing his interpretation, Carll Tucker compares *Star Wars* and *Close Encounters*. What similarity does he find in the pattern of their plots, and what basic differences?
2. In both films, the world has been corrupted by what? How is this shown in the films? Who are the villains?
3. What are the solutions as seen in the two films? Define the differences in the solutions, as well as the similarities that may exist.
4. In which paragraph does Tucker make a further comparison of Americans today with the characters in the two films? Which of these paragraphs sets the problems and which discusses the options for solution?
5. In what way does technology fail us? What do we dream of as an alternative? Explain.
6. What summary is made about Skywalker's and Neary's relations with the technocrats in paragraph 8?
7. Read the last paragraph carefully. Does Tucker say we are left exactly as Skywalker and Neary are? Are our options the same as theirs only? Is he saying we do live in this "perfect" technocracy? Does he want us to? What final contrast does he make between living in a perfect technocracy and living in a democracy?

WRITING ASSIGNMENTS

1. Interpret the plot of some work of fiction, television, or film, whether science fiction or not. Show how its major events and characters compare with situations, people, options, and values in our own lives. Sum up the statement the work is making about its situations and characters and thus about our lives as well.
2. In a similiar manner, compare two works. Find some common denominator of theme between them, and then show their similarities and differences in carrying out that theme.
3. Evaluate the effects of technology on us today. Take either a strongly argumentative stance, praising advances or attacking harm and dangers, or an expository point of view, balancing both positive and negative aspects. Limit your subject enough so that you can deal with it concretely and define a sharp central thesis to carry a particular claim about technology's positive, negative, or mixed effects.

Karl E. Meyer

On TV: The Barbie Doll
as Sex Symbol

[1]   The most popular series on television last season was *Charlie's Angels*. Its remarkable ratings were due in part to the fact that Farrah Fawcett-Majors, one of its three starlet-heroines, has become America's reigning sex symbol. For a while, it was impossible to pass a newsstand without seeing Miss Fawcett-Majors's face and hairdo on the cover of a half-dozen magazines. But as all the world knows, Miss Fawcett-Majors is now an ex-Angel, having defected from her network, and ABC is nervously awaiting the popular response to her successor, Cheryl Ladd.

[2]   I have nothing against Miss Fawcett-Majors, and I prefer to believe that she quit the show because she could no longer endure its unremitting imbecility. Not even the *Six Million Dollar Man*, starring her husband Lee Majors, is so implausibly plotted and so quintessentially witless. Last season's *Charlie's Angels* was an extended car chase held together by two-way pocket radios, skateboards, and Angel's hair. Charlie, the private eye who employs the three Angels, was never seen on camera; I am sure it was because he was ashamed to show his face.

[3]   What accounted for the show's extraordinary popularity and Miss Fawcett-Majors's startling impact? These are interesting questions that cannot be answered simply. My own hypothesis is that the show represents a triumph of product engineering that enables the pre-teen consumer to move from the playroom to the living room; the kids respond because the cars are like Hot

"On TV: The Barbie Doll as Sex Symbol," by Karl E. Meyer, from *Saturday Review*, October 1, 1977, p. 45.

Wheels and the Angels are like Barbie dolls—with a whiff of sanitized sex thrown in to ensnare the grown-ups. Miss Fawcett-Majors, if I am correct, illustrates a new phenomenon: the trans-generational sex goddess.

[4]   Like automobiles, sex goddesses come in new models, the trend now being to longer bodies, styling for all the family, and teeth that gleam like chrome grillwork. During the 1920s and 1930s, the vamp was an established Hollywood sex symbol. She was usually a European import (Marlene Dietrich, Garbo, Hedy Lamarr), and even on the screen she seemed to exude a dark perfume.

[5]   Later came a distinctly American invention: the good-bad girl. The species was classically defined in 1950 by two psychologists, Martha Wolfenstein and Nathan Leites, in an article titled ''The Good-Bad Girl'':

> She is a good girl who appears to be bad. She does not conceal her apparent badness, and uncertainty about her character may persist through the greater part of the film. The hero suspects she is bad, but finally discovers this was a mistaken impression. Thus he has a girl who has attracted him by an appearance of wickedness, and whom in the end he can take home and introduce to Mother.

[6]   Among the good-bad girls were Rita Hayworth (*Gilda*), Ava Gardner (*The Barefoot Contessa*), and Marilyn Monroe (*The Seven-Year Itch*). Like the vamps, all possessed and even glorified in an overt sexuality; but in the end each usually turned out to be like the girl next door. Thus Lauren Bacall, a very good-bad girl, always got Humphrey Bogart when it became apparent, just before the finale, that she would not sleep with any man who merely whistled.

[7]   The earlier models of sex goddesses were designed to appeal only to post-teens; the Barbie doll is the product of television's quest for a larger audience. I must credit this insight to James Monaco, who has elaborated on the subject in a cogent article in the excellent British film quarterly *Sight and Sound*. Monaco's examples of Barbie doll sex symbols include Miss Fawcett-Majors, Lindsay Wagner (the Bionic Woman), Mary Tyler Moore, and Cher. In Cher's case, there is in fact a Cher doll on the market, complete with navel and an endlessly expensive wardrobe. Farrah is not far behind. There are already two toy items: a doll and a Farrah ''head,'' the latter prompted by the popularity of the Fawcett-Majors coiffure.

[8]   But there is a more arresting point. These sex symbols are not only tall, skinny, toothy, and hirsute; they each display a certain wry wit about orthodox sex roles. Though they are ''good'' girls, they are also saucy girls. (Indeed, their private lives, as exhaustively reported in supermarket gazettes, can be unconventional, as is certainly the case with Cher.) Monaco perceptively remarks:

> Like the structure of *Charlie's Angels* itself, Farrah's notoriety is an ironic and paradoxical mix of old and new values. She's sexy, cute, girlish, obedient, and knows her place, but she's also (mildly) comic and manages to communicate a hint of irony about this traditional role.

[9]   In short, she's safe and transgenerational, but not solemn. She's the sex goddess of the 1970s—a Barbie doll brought to life, with prerecorded repartee. I hope, however, that Miss Fawcett-Majors may find time to meditate on a

poignant comment made by Marilyn Monroe a week before her death: "A sex symbol becomes a thing. I just hate being a thing." Far better to be a fallen Angel.

VOCABULARY

Use the context of the essay and your dictionary to define the following words.

1. unremitting (par. 2)
2. hypothesis (par. 3)
3. sanitized (par. 3)
4. transgenerational (par. 3)
5. overt (par. 6)
6. post-teens (par. 7)
7. hirsute (par. 8)
8. wry (par. 8)
9. orthodox (par. 8)
10. saucy (par. 8)

RHETORIC AND IDEA

1. In which paragraph does Karl E. Meyer first sum up his thesis? In this paragraph he actually expresses two thesis points—about two different, but related topics. What two subjects does he make a claim about in the paragraph, and which of the two does he actually go on to discuss in the rest of the essay?
2. In paragraph 4, when he compares the new trend in sex goddesses to automobiles, does his simile produce a positive or negative impression? Explain.
3. In paragraphs 4 through 7 he sets up a comparison among three kinds of sex goddesses. What basic difference does he set up between the second type and the earliest? Sum up what each of these two types was and what their similarity and basic differences were.
4. He first sums up the new type in paragraph 4. In which paragraph does he return to her? What is the difference in the kind of appeal she is intended to have?
5. Using metaphor, he compares the new type of sex goddess to a Barbie doll. What qualities of the new sex goddesses does he wish to suggest by this comparison? How do these doll-like qualities help to produce the new appeal that is sought?
6. In paragraph 8, he introduces a new aspect of the new type. What is it?
7. Twice in his essay Meyer cites authorities. How does he use each?

WRITING ASSIGNMENTS

1. Pick a popular star or performer (or group) in any area of the entertainment world. Sum up the essential qualities, the essential appeal of the star or group for the particular audience that is attracted, whether limited or general.
2. Pick either a single television show—like "Happy Days"—or a type of television show—like family comedies, nostalgic shows, detective shows,

girl detective shows. Analyze the appeal of the show for its audience. Tell what it offers and supplies them, whether these things are valuable or not.

3. Analyze the kind of image about women presented by a certain character (and the star playing the character) in a film or on television or by a certain type of character found in several shows or films. If you like, you can instead do the same for a man, or develop a comparison between male and female images presented.

Lucy Komisar

The Image of Woman
in Advertising

[1]   Look in a mirror. If you are a woman, what do you see? A woman waxing the
floor? Feeding children? Spraying her hair? Scribbling on a steno pad? Gazing
at a man with mixed reverence and awe? The simple mirrors that hang over
bureaus and on the backs of closet doors only tell us superficial physical things
about ourselves. The real-life mirrors are the media, and for women the most
invidious mirror of all is advertising.

[2]   There once was some concern over the danger of subliminal advertising that
would force people to make subconscious decisions about products or politics.
Advertising today is not subliminal, but its subtle psychological effect is as
devastating as any secret message flashed at high speeds to unsuspecting
viewers. Advertising exploits and reinforces the myths of woman's place with
messages of such infinite variety and number that one might as easily deny
that the earth revolves around the sun as entirely reject their influence. Advertising is an insidious propaganda machine for a male supremacist society. It
spews out images of women as sex mates, housekeepers, mothers and menial
workers—images that perhaps reflect the true status of most women in society,
but which also make it increasingly difficult for women to break out of the sexist stereotypes that imprison them.

[3]   Ironically, one hope remains: that the constant humiliating image of the
role women are expected to play will draw their degradation in lines too bold

Excerpted from Chapter 13, "The Image of Woman in Advertising," by Lucy Komisar, in
Women in Sexist Society: Studies in Power and Powerlessness, Edited by Vivian Gornick and Barbara K.
Moran, ©1971 by Basic Books, Inc., Publishers, New York.

and clear to ignore, and that women finally will arise in disgust and outrage to destroy the distortions reflected by that real-life mirror and to challenge the existence of sexism itself.

[4]   In December 1969, outside Macy's department store in New York City, a group of women staged what may have been the first protest demonstration against the image of women presented by advertising. Mattel Toys, the target of the protest, had run an ad in *Life* magazine to promote its line for the Christmas trade.

> Because girls dream about being a ballerina, Mattel makes Dancerina . . . a pink confection in a silken blouse and ruffled tutu . . . Wishing you were older is part of growing up . . . Barbie, a young fashion model, and her friends do the "in" things girls should do—talk about new places to visit, new clothes to wear, and new friends to meet,

said one part of the ad. The other half declared:

> Because boys were born to build and learn, Mattell makes Tog'l [a set of building blocks for creative play].

The illustration showed a boy playing with

> . . . imaginative and fantastic creatures that challenge young minds to think as they build . . . Because boys are curious about things big and small, Mattell makes Super-Eyes, a telescope that boys can have in one ingenious set of optically engineered lenses and scopes . . . that . . . create dozens of viewing devices—all for science or all for fun.

[5]   "Mattell Limits Little Girls' Dreams" and "Girls Were Also Born to Build and Learn" charged the signs strung out in front of Macy's that day. Passersby were curious. Some stopped to read the leaflets; some nodded their agreement as the sidewalk traffic nudged them on. Media Women, sponsor of the demonstration, wrote a letter to Mattel, but there was no reply.

[6]   Advertising begins stereotyping male and female very early in life: the little girl who was taught to want to be a model or a ballerina and imbued with the importance of how she looks and what she wears grows up to be a thirty-year-old Barbie Doll with advertising still providing the cues.

[7]   Madison Avenue Woman is a combination sex object and wife and mother who achieves fulfillment by looking beautiful and alluring for boy friends and lovers and cooking, cleaning, washing, or polishing for her husband and family. She is not very bright; she is submissive and subservient to men; if she has a job, it is probably that of a secretary or an airline hostess. What she does is not very important anyway since the chief interest in her life is the "male reward" advertisers dangle enticingly in front of her ("Male reward" is, in fact, the argot used in the trade.)

[8]   Behold the compleat woman constructed by American advertising. In adolescence she has passed the stage of playing with dolls, but her life goals and interests have not advanced appreciably, as witnessed by this ad from Parker Pens:

> You might as well give her a gorgeous pen to keep her checkbook unbalanced with. A sleek and shining pen will make her feel prettier. Which is more important to any girl than solving mathematical mysteries.

Later, the Quest for the Holy Male becomes more serious business, with toothpaste, hair color, brassiere, cosmetic, and mouthwash companies all competing to help land the man who is, after all, the prize a young woman has striven for since prepubescence. Ultra Brite toothpaste "gives your mouth sex appeal"; Colgate mouthwash is "the mouthwash for lovers." An ad for bath oil shows a man embracing a woman while the copy blazes away: "Sardo. When you live with a man."

[9]   Nearly half the women in the country work, but you wouldn't think so to look at American advertising. A woman's place is not only in the home, according to most copywriters and art directors, it is in the kitchen or the laundryroom. An ad for IBM declares, "Your wife's office is probably better equipped than yours" and pictures a youthful housewife surrounded by the shining implements of her trade: wall oven, electric stove with grease hood, blender, rotisserie, four-slice toaster, and electric coffee pot.

[10]   If television commercials are to be believed, most American women go into uncontrollable ecstasies at the sight and smell of tables and cabinets that have been lovingly caressed with long-lasting, satin-finish, lemon-scented, spray-on furniture polish. Or they glow with rapture at the blinding whiteness of their wash—and the green-eyed envy of their neighbors. The housewife in the Johnson's Wax commercial hugs the dining room table because the shine is so wonderful; then she polishes herself into a corner and has to jump over the furniture to get out. Bold detergent shows one woman in deep depression because her wash is not as bright as her neighbor's.

[11]   In a country where the low status of maids probably cannot be matched, where the more than one and a half million household workers (98 percent female, nearly two-thirds black) have median year-round, full-time wages of $1,523—they are excluded from the federal minimum wage laws—it is an amazing feat of hocus pocus worthy of Tom Sawyer and Phineas T. Barnum to lovingly declare that domestic labor is the true vocation of women wearing wedding bands.

[12]   There is a special irony in the fact that women, who presumably spend most of their waking hours in the kitchen or laundryroom, receive instructions about how to do their housework from men: Arthur Godfrey, who probably never put his hands into soapsuds, tells women across the country why they ought to add still another step to their washing routine with Axion Pre-Soak. Joseph Daley, president of Grey Advertising, says that men are used because the male voice is the voice of authority. Others add that while the execution of housework is only menial, thus female, the development of detergents and polishes is scientific, therefore male.

[13]   One of some half-dozen female advertising agency presidents, Franchellie Cadwell (Cadwell-Davis), adds another wrinkle to the interpretation of the strategy behind household cleaning product commercials. She thinks the White Knight and Giant-in-the-Washing-Machine images are sex symbols that help housewives assuage their own guilts and imagined inadequacies by acting out a cleanliness neurosis (or fetish!). In any event there is an obvious attempt to promote sexual fantasies with soap advertising. One Lever Brothers commercial tried to project a virtual love affair between housewife and soapsuds. The product, called "Hero," was to be terribly male; women were to be able to have a liaison with the detergent while their husbands were

at the office. ''Hero'' was an animated Greek God, and hundreds of women bearing baskets of laundry were shown worshippng at his feet. The commercial was run in test markets but was withdrawn because of objections from the public—not from women, but from people who protested on religious grounds, saying it was blasphemous! In a commercial for Chiffon dishwashing liquid, a woman is dreamingly doing the dishes when a handsome stranger a la Marcello Mastroianni slips in through the back door, kisses her hand, and gets soap on his lips. End of fantasy.

[14]   The mother role is expressed more by cooking than cleaning. ''Nothin' says lovin' like something from the oven....'' Pillsbury did a study of the American housewife which came up with the not unexpected conclusion that motherhood is her primary drive,—and obviously she loves to stay home and cook. In fact, advertisers appear to believe that women feel *guilty* when they don't spend enough time preparing meals for their families. One marketing consultant declared the Kellogg's corn flakes with freeze-dried bananas failed, because Kellogg ''violated woman's sacred prerogative, that of participating in the preparation of at least a portion of a meal for her family. She wants convenience foods, but she doesn't want to feel guilty or foolish because everything has been done for her.'' The consultant did not consider the possibility that dried-up bananas might be unappetizing.

[15]   Like the ''soaps,'' ads that involve cooking or child care assume that only women can do these jobs—or ought to—except for backyard barbecuing, which was somehow certified as ''male.'' Even advertisers for other products seem to think that women have a cooking fixation. Buick ran an ad with a picture and recipe for seafood mousse on the apparent assumption that there wasn't anything it could say about cars to interest women readers.

[16]   It is recognized that women do work outside the home, but the only work they appear to do in advertising is the kind that allows them to assist, or make life more pleasant for, men. Some of the ads seem to be selling flesh on the hoof. Like this one for Iberia Airlines: ''This nice little blonde from Barcelona will romance you all the way to Spain. And England. And France. And Germany. And ...'' Iberia leaves the rest to your imagination. New York Chemical Bank's ad about its new ''hostesses'' boasts that ''We have a pretty girl who won't let you get in the wrong line.''

[17]   IBM talks about the business man, obviously male, and his secretary: ''If she makes a mistake, she types right over it. If her boss makes a revision, she types just the revision.'' Somehow, secretaries, who are always women, make mistakes; bosses, who are always men, make ''revisions.''

[18]   Dictaphone Corporation adds a new insult to the men-are-bosses-women-are-secretaries routine. A pretty blonde woman in a micro-mini skirt sits at her desk polishing her nails as four worried men try to arouse her interest in some calculating machines. Says the copy: ''Our new line of calculators goes through its final ordeal. The dumb blonde test.''

[19]   Often the image of women as sex object is not cluttered up with the extraneous idea that women hold jobs, even if they are jobs as helpers to men. In the ''pure sex object'' category, women are exploited outrightly for the titillation and amusement, sometimes even the sadistic fascination, of men.

[20]   Myra Janco Daniels, president of Draper Daniels, Inc., in Chicago, sees a "feudal concept of women as property" in some cigarette commercials: "One gets the impression that the girls are given away as premiums athough these brands aren't featuring coupons at present." Silva Thins is the epitome of the genre. The handsome, unsmiling man in dark glasses punishes any woman who presumes to take his cigarettes. With cool deliberation, he deserts them on highways, ocean liners, cable cars, and mountain tops. Another variation in the campaign proclaims: "Cigarettes are like women—the best ones are rich and thin."

[21]   A male columnist in the trade publication *Ad Age* admits that the commercials have "silent masochistic overtones," meaning that the ad relies on the culturally submissive female response. Women, the columnist says, "seem to feel right at home with the situations. They quite willingly put themselves in the place of the suffering heroine." He concludes, "The makers of this campaign demonstrate a shrewd insight into the emotional make-up of today's woman." The hero "summarily puts his girlfriend in her place, exactly where so many women would unconsciously like to be."

[22]   Like the Silva Thins commercial, woman-as-sex-object ads generally seek to fulfill male fantasies about seducing or wielding power over women. For example, "Tonight offer her a daiquiri made with Ronrico, Puerto Rico's tasteful rum. Then watch her slip into something light and comfortable." A promotion for *Newsweek* magazine, featuring scantily dressed harem girls lounging voluptuously around a grinning, rotund Arab sheik, reads: "Compound your interest. Quote *Newsweek....*" An ad for Thane Mills, a company that manufactures cotton, pictures a supercilious-looking man standing over a woman, her eyes cast downward. "The Thane of Scarsdale," trumpets the ad. "In blue-chip suburbs like Scarsdale, or anywhere else, it gives you that special look of authority.... For the man who's in control."

[23]   Automobiles are this country's phallic power symbol, and cars are used to prove a man's masculinity. Obviously, women are the logical props for such symbolism. Myra Janco Daniels calls automobile advertisements "the first fully Americanized fertility rites," wondering wryly whether the final act of love will be between boy and auto, girl and auto, or attain the ultimate in some kind of intercourse among the three.

[24]   The image of women in advertising is as much defined by the ads that omit her as those that exploit her. Business executives and doctors, for example, are always men. Even the language is male-oriented, like General Electric's "Men Helping Man" on an ad that discusses the development of nuclear power plants.

[25]   Advertising did not create these images about women, but it is a powerful force for their reinforcement. It legitimizes the idealized, stereotyped roles of women as temptress, wife, mother, and sex object, and portrays women as less intelligent and more dependent than men. It makes women believe that their chief role is to please men and that their fulfillment will be as wives, mothers, and homemakers. It makes women feel unfeminine if they are not pretty enough and guilty if they do not spend most of their time in desperate attempts to imitate gourmet cooks and eighteenth-century scullery maids. It makes

women believe that their own lives, talents, and interest ought to be secondary to the needs of their husbands and families and that they are almost totally defined by these relationships.

[26]   It creates false, unreal images of women that reflect male fantasies rather than flesh and blood human beings. And the idealization of women is not much healthier than their derogation; goddesses are easily pulled off their pedestals and turned into temptresses and whores.

[27]   Advertising also reinforces men's concepts about women's place and women's role—and about their own roles. It makes masculine dominance legitimate—and conversely questions the manhood of men who do not want to go along with the stereotypes. Why is it masculine for men to wash cars, but a sign of "henpecking" for them to wash dishes? Why is it a man's job to be the breadwinnner and a woman's to be the homemaker? Why do some men feel guilty when their wives work—as if it were a reflection on their own inadequacies? Advertising prolongs the myths of male supremacy, painting pictures of men who are superior to women and etching those images in the eyes of men who use these "eternal verities" as the excuse for forcing women's continued subjugation . . .

VOCABULARY

Use the context of the essay and your dictionary to define the following words:

1. imbued (par. 6)   6. liaison (par. 13)
2. argot (par. 7)   7. extraneous (par. 19)
3. hocus pocus (par. 11)   8. epitome (par. 20)
4. assuage (par. 13)   9. phallic (par. 23)
5. fetish (par. 13)   10. gourmet (par. 25)

RHETORIC AND IDEA

1. If, as Komisar says in paragraph 1, simple mirrors tell us superficial physical things about ourselves, what does she imply real life media mirrors tell us about ourselves?
2. When she calls the media a mirror, what kind of figurative language is Komisar using?
3. Although she does not define what she means in paragraph 2 by "subliminal advertising," Komisar implies strongly what she is getting at. Select two or three phrases that attempt to make her meaning clear.
4. What stereotypes of boys and girls are emphasized by the Mattel Toys advertisement discussed in paragraphs 4 and 5?
5. What characteristics of the woman are implicit in "the compleat woman" described in paragraph 8?
6. To what does Komisar allude when she mentions in paragraph 8 the "Quest for the Holy Male"? Is the allusion appropriate in this essay? Explain.
7. What is the general subject of the unit made up of paragraphs 9–15?

8. In paragraph 15, Komisar makes an inference about why Buick ran an ad for seafood mousse. Is her inference sound? What other inference(s) might one make about Buick's motive?
9. The writer achieves coherence in paragraph 25 by repetition of sentence pattern and use of pronouns. Point out these repeated patterns and underline the pronouns.

WRITING ASSIGNMENTS

1. Study the commercials on television, take careful notes, and write an essay in which you describe the relationship that exists between the women and men in the advertisements. Consider the following types: cosmetics, cleaning agents, kitchen appliances, automobiles, patent medicines, clothing, mouthwash, toothpaste, beer.
2. Write an essay in which you discuss whether advertising always presents men as superior to women. Gather your evidence from radio, television, magazines, newspapers, and/or billboards.
3. In a paragraph developed by examples, show how advertisements present images of women as sex mates, housekeepers, mothers, or menial workers.
4. Using specific examples from advertisements, develop one of the following sentences into an essay:

   Some ads seem to be selling flesh on the hoof.
   Commercials have silent masochistic overtones.
   Automobile advertisements are American fertility rites.
   Advertisements reflect male fantasies about women.
   Advertising prolongs the myth of male supremacy.

5. What changes in the images of women have been made in recent advertising? Define some of these new images and discuss whether they have eliminated old stereotypes or merely modified them.

Ben Marsh

Country Music:
A Rose-Colored Map

[1]   Country music presents two images of life—life as it should be, and life as it should not be. The conflict between these two themes is the force that drives country music; it is this dialectic of right and wrong that makes country music exciting to the millions who listen to it. Perhaps the melodies are formulaic, but it is the lyrics that sell the songs, the descriptions of everyday people facing problems and making right or wrong decisions about them. The right decision is the one that lets people be honest, faithful, moral, and therefore happy.

[2]   Right and wrong in country music are not distributed randomly across the American landscape. Goodness is concentrated in the South and in the countryside, while badness is far more common in cities and in the North. If the lyrics of country songs were all someone knew about America, he would think that everything of value was in the rural South. Country music contains a clear, if incidental, regional geography of the South, describing its terrain, its climate, its agriculture, and its natural resources. Everybody in country songs grew up on a farm in the South, where their parents still live. The normal city in country music is Nashville, the normal river is the Mississippi, the normal beer is Lone Star, the normal crop is cotton, the normal dog is a hound, and the normal food is black-eyed peas. And if the directions given in various songs are treated like a road map, that map says it is "up" to Chicago and Cincinnati, "down" to New Orleans and Georgia, "over" or "across" to the Carolinas, and "out" to Texas or California, while it is "back" to the moun-

tains, and "back" to the farm. The center of country music's map of America is clearly the rural South, especially the mountain states.

[3]   The South, as it is presented in country music, is the best possible place to live, the standard for comparing all other places, especially the Northern city. The North, in general, is a cold, gray, hazy area at the periphery of country music's map, as far from home as one can get. Listen to one song or a hundred, the pattern is the same. If a song is about someone being unfaithful, drunken, jobless, or lonely, it will be in a city, probably in the North. If a song is about family, security, childhood, love, or other pleasant things, it will be in the South, probably on a farm. Texas usually appears as a land of heroic men and romantic women. Canada and Alaska show up as our new frontiers, important places for individualists. And California is an ambiguous place with both Southern and Northern charactersitcs, perhaps a reflection of the conflict between the agricultural and urban parts of that state.

[4]   There are obvious advantages for the writers of allegorical tales like country music's to have a conventionalized geography to reinforce the message. But why does country music use *this* image of America? Why is country music so pleased with the South and so upset with the North? The answer to this question lies not in the actual geography of the United States, but in how country music's audience perceives the geography of the United States. It is not a question of what America is, but of what America means to these people. As a result, the question has to do with far more than just a style of singing, it has to do with the attitudes of the millions of Americans who listen to country music—attitudes about regional differences in American society, about the role of the media as part of the American power structure, and about the value of progress in general.

[5]   One attractive explanation of the geography *in* country music is that it is a reflection of the geography *of* country music. This argument holds that country music views the world from the South because most of the performers, or most of the audience, live in the South. However, this is untrue. Country music is not exclusively Southern in any sense but its history and its perspective. True, most of the older performers came from the South, but many were from Northern states like Illinois and Pennsylvania, or even from Canada. And modern country music stars are from all over the English-speaking world.

[6]   Country music's audience is even less Southern than its performers. The music is indisputably popular in the South, but the evidence—from the distribution of country music radio stations, from performers' itineraries, and from the regional circulation of fan magazines—indicates that country music has more listeners outside the South than in it. Some suggest that this is because a large part of country music's audience is homesick expatriate Southerners living in Northern cities, but the data does not support this. For example, country music is not, as one would expect, especially popular in industrial cities such as Detroit, which traditionally has been a pole of South-North migration.

[7]   Country music's Southern perspective on the world must be treated as symbolism, not reporting. Perhaps country music once glorified the South because it was parochial music about local places, but it is now popular nearly everywhere. In the United States country music is the typical music on stage at small-town high schools and country fairs all across America, and on the

radio in machine shops and beauty parlors, on truckers' tape decks, and on jukeboxes in ten thousand little bars.

[8]   To understand how the vision of America in country music is appropriate to this audience, it is necessary to look carefully at how country music functions in American culture. Country music comes to its audience through the media and must be viewed in that context. Country music's morality plays appear on records, in movies, in magazines, on syndicated television shows, and especially over the radio. The history of early country music is inseparable from the history of early radio, and there are now over 1,700 radio stations in the U.S. that play country music every day. Country music is a radio ministry, and the gospel it preaches—that we should all be moral, righteous, and Southern—makes sense when it is seen in this context.

[9]   Country music's view of America must be compared with another view, as distinctive as country music's but offering a different perspective—the image projected by network television, the wire services, and mass-circulation magazines. In these media virtually all the decisions about content are made in New York, Washington, Chicago, and Los Angeles. Accordingly, the brightest, most exciting, most memorable spots on these, our most frequently reinforced pictures of our land, are the big cities. Compared to them, the South and the rest of the country seem almost featureless, perhaps a little sinister, or maybe just boring.

[10]   Country music's image of America contradicts that of the "mainstream" American media—and that is its appeal. The South is presented as a virtuous place to country music fans all over America not for what it is, but for what it is not. Unlike the North, the seat of the media, the South is not responsible for the shape we are in. According to the media's own reporting, the South has had nothing to do with inflation, taxes, shortages, abuses of federal power, Supreme Court rulings, and so forth. The same innocence of the sins of power that let Jimmy Carter go from ex-governor of Georgia to President in twenty-two months lets country music paint the South as a haven from the sins of the nation.

[11]   The South has escaped bad press mostly because it is underreported, and this is why country music has been free to impose whatever meaning it chooses on the South. When the South has appeared in the national media, it has been portrayed as backward, ignorant, and reactionary. But country music can transform these attributes into virtues: backward easily becomes rustic, ignorant becomes simple and uncomplicated, and reactionary becomes old-fashioned.

[12]   The ability to see a region which is nearly ignored in the media as the best part of America, and to see the centers of media power as the worst part, reflects deep displeasure by millions of Americans with the content of those media. Country music's gloomy image of the North is a reflection of what the audience feels about what is happening to America in general. The South, in contrast, is a picture of how the nation would be if it had not gone astray.

[13]   What country music's audience seeks to escape by vicarious life in the rural South is, in a word, progress. Country music's South is above all old-fashioned. Life in the South means old-fashioned family, old-fashioned religion, old-fashioned values. Life in the South is life in the past, a laundered past without smallpox and without lynchings. This is what country music's

rural Southern perspective is all about—the South has none of the problems of the North, and the country has none of the problems of the city, because the past has none of the problems of the present. Country music's South provides escape from modern America.

[14]   It seems extreme to suggest that millions of Americans feel the need to escape from the land they live in, yet that is the clear message of country music's picture of the world. Escape is certainly a common enough theme in the rest of country music. Drinking, divorce, traveling, prison, and death can all be considered kinds of escape, and all are quite common in country music. To Freud the countryside itself symbolized escape. The rural South is just another kind of escape; it is a place where one avoids the problems of the modern world and lives the simple, friendly, old-fashioned country life.

[15]   Who are the people who feel they need country music's exit and haven from the world we all live in? It is possible to construct a picture of an average country music listener from various kinds of television, radio, and magazine marketing data. The picture of this average person is entirely consonant with his expressed desire to avoid the wrongs of modern American life. Quite simply, the person who needs to escape into the mythically old-fashioned South is the one who is losing something as America progresses. It is not the rural-urban migrant, it is not the second- or third-generation European-American, it is not the Black. All these people have gained as American industrializes, urbanizes, progresses. None of them fear the future and cherish the past. None of them could be as nostalgic as the country music fan for a South that never was.

[16]   Country music is for the small-town American. Country music and its image of America pleases those millions of quiet people in traditional, socially conservative communities who daily face erosion of the values that make their lives meaningful. America is moving from the nineteenth century into mass society not in a smooth glide, but in a series of painful little shocks, and the person most likely to appreciate country music is the person for whom those shocks hurt most. Country music's function is to replenish the system of values that we seem to be losing.

[17]   The image of America in country music may seem extreme and one-sided, but it is in answer to what its audience perceives as an extreme and one-sided world. It is important to these threatened Americans everywhere to know that there is still a region in this land where life is lived as they know it should be, and where there is relief from the changes they fear. The fiction of the rural South in country music is that place.

[18]   By glorifying the south, country music departs radically from nearly every other popular geography of the United States. But country music's message that America is taking drastically wrong directions is radical, too. Country music seems to have almost Marxian overtones in its treatment of the injuries of class. Poverty is ennobling, for example, while wealth imprisons its owners. And some recent songs have been surprisingly militant in their calls for greater social justice through rejection of illegitimate authority and through greater economic equity. Johnny Cash has produced several successful songs in the past few years about men's attempts to get more control on their jobs. In one an auto worker steals a Cadillac "one piece at a time" in his lunchbox; in

another a hungry farmworker steals a strawberry cake from a fancy hotel, after spending weeks picking strawberries; and in a third song a machinist plots that on the day he retires he will punch out his boss as he leaves. The songs are meant to be ironic, yet they are portrayals of what would be acts of revolution if they occurred en masse. In content and even in style, these songs are reminiscent of Woody Guthrie's songs during the Depression.

[19]   Partly because of this radicalness, an odd convergence has taken place between country music and the music descended from the folk/protest tradition of the Sixties, sometimes called ''folk-rock.'' Both are displeased with modern urban America and each uses instrumentation and arrangements derived from their common Appalachian folk origins. The result is that the themes and the performances in the two genres are similar enough that performers like Kris Kristofferson or Commander Cody, who are virtually antithetical in politics, religion, and life-style to the average country fan, can compete in the same market with some performers so puritanical that they will not appear in clubs where liquor is served.

[20]   Country music shares its radically positive image of the South with two other recent national movements. Neither the election of Jimmy Carter to the Presidency, nor those southward migrations of population, industry, and political power to the so-called Sun Belt, would have been possible in the face of strong anti-Southern sentiment. There are obvious differences between the motivations that determine how people vote, where they move to, and what kind of music they listen to, but perhaps all these events are best thought of as manifestations of a single change in attitude. In years to come we can only expect to see more reaction to the old alignment of power in America, power expressed through the government and the major media.

[21]   America was settled by immigrants, and we have never stopped moving. From Plymouth Rock to the Cumberland Gap to the Oregon Trail, if a man did not like life where he was, he could move down the road and it would be different. But we have run out of frontiers. Today, if a new place is needed, an old place must be redefined. Country music is showing us this process in action, as a major American region acquires a new image. However, allegiance to this new South takes place at the expense of allegiance to the country as a whole. The irony of country music's audience considering itself to be an especially patriotic group is that it is loyal to a mythical earlier America as symbolized by the sunny, old-fashioned South of country music, not to America as it now exists.

VOCABULARY

Use the context of the essay and your dictionary to define the following words:

1. dialectic (par. 1)
2. periphery (par. 3)
3. ambiguous (par. 3)
4. perspective (par. 5)
5. expatriate (par. 6)
6. rustic (par. 11)
7. vicarious (par. 13)
8. mythically (par. 15)
9. replenish (par. 16)
10. antithetical (par. 19)

RHETORIC AND IDEA

1. The first stage (paragraphs 1–4) of Ben Marsh's analysis and interpretation of country music stresses what as the general basis of the appeal of country music?
2. How does geography—especially the North and the South—fit into this basic pattern of the music?
3. Marsh's next stage is to analyze why these parts of the country play the roles they do in country music. Paragraph 5 introduces what he calls "one attractive explanation." What is this explanation? Does Marsh agree with it? Why or why not?
4. Explain the relationship of the point of paragraph 7 to that of paragraphs 5 and 6.
5. In relating country music to the media world, which particular medium does he stress as being central to country music's appeal? What media does he contrast this to? What is the viewpoint of these other media?
6. In paragraph 10, he says that in country music the South appeals for what it is not. He develops this further in paragraphs 11 and 12. What does he mean by this?
7. Paragraphs 13 and 14 state this appeal in a more positive manner. What is it that country music offers its audience?
8. What people and what values are reinforced by country music?

WRITING ASSIGNMENTS

1. What is your view of the reasons for the appeal of country music? What aspects of Marsh's explanation do you agree or disagree with? Does he, for example, take into enough account the love songs that are so central in country music?
2. Analyze another form of popular or classical music. Approach it from the standpoint of either your personal taste or your interpretation of public taste. Give the reasons for the appeal of the music, taking into account all aspects of its performance.
3. What does a particular performer or group represent for their fans (or you) and provide them with as the basis of their appeal?

X. J. Kennedy

Who Killed King Kong?

[1]   The ordeal and spectacular death of King Kong, the giant ape, undoubtedly have been witnessed by more Americans than have ever seen a performance of *Hamlet, Iphigenia at Aulis,* or even *Tobacco Road.* Since RKO-Radio Pictures first released *King Kong,* a quarter-century has gone by; yet year after year, from prints that grow more rain-beaten, from sound tracks that grow more tinny, ticket-buyers by thousands still pursue Kong's luckless fight against the forces of technology, tabloid journalism, and the DAR. They see him chloro-formed to sleep, see him whisked from his jungle isle to New York and placed on show, see him burst his chains to roam the city (lugging a frightened blonde), at last to plunge from the spire of the Empire State Building, machine-gunned by model airplanes.

[2]   Though Kong may die, one begins to think his legend unkillable. No clearer proof of his hold upon the popular imagination may be seen than what emerged one catastrophic week in March 1955, when New York WOR-TV programmed *Kong* for seven evenings in a row (a total of sixteen showings). Many a rival network vice-president must have scowled when surveys showed that *Kong*—the 1933 B-picture—had lured away fat segments of the viewing populace from such powerful competitors as Ed Sullivan, Groucho Marx, and Bishop Sheen.

[3]   But even television has failed to run *King Kong* into oblivion. Coffee-in-the-lobby cinemas still show the old hunk of hokum, with the apology that in its use of composite shots and animated models the film remains technically in-

"Who Killed King Kong?" by X.J. Kennedy, from *Dissent*, Spring, 1960. Reprinted by permission of *Dissent*.

teresting. And no other monster in movie history has won so devoted a popular audience. None of the plodding mummies, the stultified draculas, the white-coated Lugosis[1] with their shiny pinball-machine laboratories, none of the invisible stranglers, berserk robots, or menaces from Mars has ever enjoyed so many resurrections.

[4]   Why does the American public refuse to let King Kong rest in peace? It is true, I'll admit, that *Kong* outdid every monster movie before or since in sheer carnage. Producers Cooper and Schoedsack crammed into it dinosaurs, headhunters, riots, aerial battles, bullets, bombs, bloodletting. Heroine Fay Wray, whose function is mainly to scream, shuts her mouth for hardly one uninterrupted minute from first reel to last. It is also true that *Kong* is larded with good healthy sadism, for those whose joy it is to see the frantic girl dangled from cliffs and harried by pterodactyls. But it seems to me that the abiding appeal of the giant ape rests on other foundations.

[5]   Kong has, first of all, the attraction of being manlike. His simian nature gives him one huge advantage over giant ants and walking vegetables in that an audience may conceivably identify with him. Kong's appeal has the quality that established the Tarzan series as American myth—for what man doesn't secretly image himself a huge hairy howler against whom no other monster has a chance? If Tarzan recalls the ape in us, then Kong may well appeal to that great-granddaddy primordial brute from whose tribe we have all deteriorated.

[6]   Intentionally or not, the producers of *King Kong* encourage this identification by etching the character of Kong with keen sympathy. For the ape is a figure in a tradition familiar to moviegoers; the tradition of the pitiable monster. We think of Lon Chaney in the role of Quasimodo, of Karloff in the original *Frankenstein*. As we watch the Frankenstein monster's fumbling and disastrous attempts to befriend a flower-picking child, our sympathies are enlisted with the monster in his impenetrable loneliness. And so with Kong. As he roars in his chains, while barkers sell tickets to boobs who gape at him, we perhaps feel something more deep than pathos. We begin to sense something of the problem that engaged Eugene O'Neill in *The Hairy Ape:* the dilemma of a displaced animal spirit forced to live in a jungle built by machines.

[7]   *King Kong,* it is true, had special relevance in 1933. Landscapes of the depression are glimpsed early in the film when an impresario, seeking some desperate pretty girl to play the lead in a jungle movie, visits souplines and a Woman's Home Mission. In Fay Wray—who's been caught snitching an apple from a fruitstand—his search is ended. When he gives her a big feed and a movie contract, the girl is magic-carpeted out of the world of the National Recovery Act. And when, in the film's climax, Kong smashes that very Third Avenue landscape in which Fay had wandered hungry, audiences of 1933 may well have felt a personal satisfaction.

[8]   What is curious is that audiences remain hooked. For in the heart of urban man, one suspects, lurks the impulse to fling a bomb. Though machines speed him to the scene of daily grind, though IBM comptometers ("freeing the human mind from drudgery") enable him to drudge more efficiently once he

---

[1]Bela Lugosi, an actor in many horror movies.

arrives, there comes a moment when he wishes to turn upon his machines and kick hell out of them. He wants to hurl his combination radio-alarmclock out the bedroom window and listen to its smash. What subway commuter wouldn't love—just for once—to see the downtown express smack head-on into the uptown local? Such a wish is gratified in that memorable scene in *Kong* that opens with a wide-angle shot: interior of a railway car on the Third Avenue El. Straphangers are nodding, the literate refold their newspapers. Unknown to them, Kong has torn away a section of trestle toward which the train now speeds. The motorman spies Kong up ahead, jams on the brakes. Passengers hurtle together like so many peas in a pail. In a window of the car appear Kong's bloodshot eyes. Women shriek. Kong picks up the railway car as if it were a rat, flips it to the street and ties knots in it, or something. To any commuter the scene must appear one of the most satisfactory pieces of celluloid ever exposed.

[9]   Yet however violent his acts, Kong remains a gentleman. Remarkable is his sense of chivalry. Whenever a fresh boa constrictor threatens Fay, Kong first sees that the lady is safely parked, then manfully thrashes her attacker. (And she, the ingrate, runs away every time his back is turned.) Atop the Empire State building, ignoring his pursuers, Kong places Fay on a ledge as tenderly as if she were a dozen eggs. He fondles her, than turns to face the Army Air Force. And Kong is perhaps the most disinterested lover since Cyrano: his attentions to the lady are utterly without hope of reward. After all, between a five-foot blonde and a fifty-foot ape, love can hardly be more than an intellectual flirtation. In his simian way King Kong is the hopelessly yearning lover of Petrarchan convention. His forced exit from his jungle, in chains, results directly from his single-minded pursuit of Fay. He smashes a Broadway theater when the notion enters his dull brain that the flashbulbs of photographers somehow endanger the lady. His perilous shinnying up a skyscraper to pluck Fay from her boudoir is an act of the kindliest of hearts. He's impossible to discourage even though the love of his life can't lay eyes on him without shrieking murder.

[10]   The tragedy of King Kong then, is to be the beast who at the end of the fable fails to turn into the handsome prince. This is the conviction that the scriptwriters would leave with us in the film's closing line. As Kong's corpse lies blocking traffic in the street, the entrepreneur who brought Kong to New York turns to the assembled reporters and proclaims: ''That's your story, boys—it was Beauty killed the Beast!'' But greater forces than those of the screaming Lady have combined to lay Kong low, if you ask me. Kong lives for a time as one of those persecuted near-animal souls bewildered in the middle of an industrial order, whose simple desires are thwarted at every turn. He climbs the Empire State Building because in all New York it's the closest thing he can find to the clifftop of his jungle isle. He dies, a pitiful dolt, and the army brass and publicity-men cackle over him. His death is the only possible outcome to as neat a tragic dilemma as you can ask for. The machine-guns do him in, while the manicured human hero (a nice clean Dartmouth boy) carries away Kong's sweetheart to the altar. O, the misery of it all. There's far more truth about upper-middle-class American life in *King Kong* than in the last seven dozen novels of John P. Marquand.

[11]   A Negro friend from Atlanta tells me that in movie houses in colored
neighborhoods throughout the South, *Kong* does a constant business. They
show the thing in Atlanta at least every year, presumably to the same audiences. Perhaps this popularity may simply be due to the fact that *Kong* is one
of the most watchable movies ever constructed, but I wonder whether Negro
audiences may not find some archetypical appeal in this serio-comic tale of a
huge black powerful free spirit whom all the hardworking white policemen are
out to kill.

[12]   Every day in the week on a screen somewhere in the world, King Kong
relives his agony. Again and agin he expires on the Empire State Building, as
audiences of the devout assist his sacrifice. We watch him die, and by exten-
sion kill the ape within our bones, but these little deaths of ours occur in prosaic surroundings. We do not die on a tower, New York before our feet, nor do
we give our lives to smash a few flying machines. It is not for us to bring to a
momentary standstill the civilization in which we move. King Kong does this
for us. And so we kill him again and again, in much-spliced celluloid, while
the ape in us expires from day to day, obscure, in desperation.

VOCABULARY

Use the context of the essay and your dictionary to define the words below.

1. catastrophic (par. 2)   6. harried (par. 4)
2. oblivion (par. 3)   7. simian (par. 5)
3. hokum (par. 3)   8. ingrate (par. 9)
4. carnage (par. 4)   9. entrepreneur (par. 10)
5. sadism (par. 4)   10. prosaic (par. 12)

RHETORIC AND IDEA

Answer each of the following questions. Wherever possible, support your
answer by referring directly to the text of the essay.

1. What is the function of sentence 1 of paragraph 4? Of the last sentence of
   paragraph 4?
2. What two reasons does Kennedy give in paragraph 4 for the continuing
   popularity of *King Kong?*
3. Point out the irony in the last sentence of paragraph 5.
4. In paragraph 7 what special relevance does Kennedy say *King Kong* had
   for the audience of 1933?
5. Does paragraph 8 have a topic sentence? If it does, which sentence is it?
   If it doesn't, construct one for that paragraph.
6. Point out the topic sentence of paragraph 9. Does Kennedy develop his
   topic sufficiently? What method of development has he used?
7. According to Kennedy (paragraph 10), what forces *really* "combined to
   lay Kong low"?
8. In paragraph 1, point out an obvious example of the author's use of
   parallel nouns and of parallel phrases.
9. In sentence 4 of paragraph 3 Kennedy introduces with the word *none* two
   sets of three parallel nouns. What are the nouns?

10. Which sentence is the topic sentence for paragraphs 2 and 3? Is the topic sentence supported convincingly? Explain.
11. Kennedy mixes seriousness with humor in paragraph 9, perhaps being more humorous than serious. Point out words Kennedy has used to promote humor.

WRITING ASSIGNMENTS

1. Horror and monster movies appear to be very popular means of entertainment. In an essay, account for the popularity of such movies. Make sure your thesis statement is clear. Have at least three divisions—reasons—in your paper, and use examples to support these reasons.
2. Have horror movies changed over the years or are they still much the same as the old-timers? Write an essay in which you compare or contrast some of the early horror films—*Dracula, Frankenstein, King Kong, Mighty Joe Young*—with some of the more recent ones. You may want to compare the old and the more recent versions of *King Kong*.
3. Write an essay on one of the following topics:

   Horror Movies: Fun or Terror?
   Horror Movies: Fright for the Immature
   What Horror Films Reveal About Us
   Sophisticated Horror: Alfred Hitchcock
   Science Fiction Horror
   The New Violence—Realistic Horror

4. Using examples from your own experiences or from what you have read, write a paragraph in which you agree or disagree with Kennedy's explanation for the appeal *King Kong* has in the 1970s for both black and white audiences.
5. As a brief research project, study several reviews of the more recent version of *King Kong*. Analyze the comparisons made between the two versions, and compare some of their statements to points made by Kennedy in this essay.

Index of
Rhetorical
Elements

This index will help you find some of the major rhetorical devices used by the professional writers in Part II of *Staircase*. We have organized the devices under nine major headings: (1) evidence, (2) type, (3) thesis, (4) organization, (5) development, (6) coherence, (7) sentences, (8) diction, and (9) logic. These divisions are roughly equivalent to the major points of Part I.

To prepare the index, we counted the sentences in each paragraph of each essay. But we did not include those numbers in the text itself, feeling that they would clutter the page. Therefore, to use the guide correctly, you will have to count the sentences to find the item you want.

We have not listed all of the rhetorical devices illustrated by each essay. Neither have we identified all of the examples of any of the nine headings. But we feel we have identified those that are most likely to help you understand how to use these writing tools effectively. We are also aware that there may be some disagreement about which device is featured in any given example, knowing that writers do not use one device exclusively in any one sentence or paragraph. A sentence, for instance, may be periodic and parallel at the same time; a writer may use enumeration in a paragraph of comparison or contrast.

Our major objective in this index is to relate the rhetoric of Part I to the writing of Part II.

The following abbreviations are used throughout the index:

conclusion	=	con.	pages	=	pp.
especially	=	esp.	paragraph(s)	=	par(s).
introduction	=	intro.	parallelism	=	/ /
page	=	p.	sentence(s)	=	sent(s).